Autism

by John Marble
Khushboo Chabria
Ranga Jayaraman

FOREWORD BY Dr. Temple Grandin
and Hari Srinivasan

for dummies®
A Wiley Brand

Autism For Dummies®

Published by: **John Wiley & Sons, Inc.,** 111 River Street, Hoboken, NJ 07030-5774, www.wiley.com

For general information on our other products and services, please contact our Customer Care Department within the U.S. at 877-762-2974, outside the U.S. at 317-572-3993, or fax 317-572-4002. For technical support, please visit https://hub.wiley.com/community/support/dummies.

Wiley publishes in a variety of print and electronic formats and by print-on-demand. Some material included with standard print versions of this book may not be included in e-books or in print-on-demand. If this book refers to media that is not included in the version you purchased, you may download this material at http://booksupport.wiley.com. For more information about Wiley products, visit www.wiley.com.

Library of Congress Control Number: 2025932918

ISBN 978-1-394-30100-3 (pbk); ISBN 978-1-394-30102-7 (ebk); ISBN 978-1-394-30101-0 (ebk)

SKY10100831_032525

Table of Contents

Foreword: Unique Journeys, Common Ground

Autism isn't a single experience. While a common thread connects each autistic journey, it shapes each person differently. We are both autistic, but our lives have been very different.

One of us grew up at a time when almost no one understood autism. There were no books, no online communities, and few resources for families. Figuring things out meant trial and error — learning firsthand what worked and what didn't. The other grew up in a world shaped by those who came before — where autism was better understood, families had more information, and autistic voices were finally being heard, thanks to those who pushed for awareness, acceptance, and support.

Our experiences may differ, but we both know what it's like to navigate a world that isn't always built for us. We've both faced challenges, found strengths, and learned the importance of support. It's why we share the same goal: a world that values and includes autistic people.

Dr. Temple Grandin

Today, I am a distinguished professor at Colorado State University, but as a child, I had no speech until the age of four. Loud sounds — like school bells — felt like a dentist's drill hitting a nerve. Fortunately, I had an excellent early education program that started at two and a half, focusing on speech, patience, and daily living skills like brushing teeth and using utensils. No one forced eye contact — that would have been overwhelming. Therapy should help a child progress, not cause distress. There are plenty of debates about the best approaches, but starting early makes a difference.

Autism specialists agree that early support is important for all autistic children. For those like me who don't speak at the typical age, it can be an early sign that leads to support. But it's just as important to pay attention to the needs of kids who do speak on time because early understanding and accommodations help all autistic kids grow and succeed.

When I grew up in the 1950s, my family had structured routines, with three sit-down meals a day. If I forgot to say thank you, my mother reminded me. After lunch, I was allowed to stim, twirling objects in my room for an hour. My mother also encouraged my artistic ability, which later shaped my career. I spent hours drawing, tinkering, and building kites, figuring out through trial and error how to make them fly better. Being allowed to experiment — and make mistakes — helped me learn.

Adolescence was much harder. I was bullied, called names, and had no motivation to study. Eventually, I was expelled for throwing a book at a girl who bullied me. That turned out to be a pivotal moment: I was sent to a special school where I cleaned horse stalls and cared for horses. The work gave me structure and purpose, but I was still an unmotivated student until a science teacher finally got through to me. A good teacher makes all the difference. The best ones are gently insistent and know how to engage a child, and he did exactly that. He made learning exciting, showing me that studying was the key to becoming a scientist. That gave me a reason to care, and my motivation changed overnight.

By the time I graduated college, I had strong work experience. I interned in a research lab, worked as an aide for an autistic child, and spent summers on my aunt's ranch, building gates and leading trail rides. Hands-on learning shaped the skills that defined my career. In designing cattle handling facilities, I've collaborated with talented metalworkers — two almost certainly autistic. Their inventions are still in use today.

Having an interesting career has made my life fulfilling. I am what I do. I've replaced emotional complexity with intellectual complexity — I find it fascinating to figure out how to build things. I've always been more drawn to solving mechanical problems than navigating social ones. I've also seen how much autistic people vary in their social priorities. Some focus on relationships, while others, like me, are more invested in their work.

The most successful careers come from building on an autistic person's natural strengths. The autistic brain is often great at one type of skill while struggling with another, and that's okay. The key is to focus on strengths.

As I point out in my book *Visual Thinking*, some autistic people, like me, think in photo-realistic images, which makes them great at art, design, and mechanical problem-solving but not so much at abstract math. Others think in patterns and excel in math and music. Meanwhile, other autistic thinkers are great at memorizing facts about their favorite subjects and can thrive in jobs that require deep knowledge, like specialized retail.

I emphasize these differences because developing strengths made my life fulfilling, and I want other autistics to have the same chance to build meaningful, satisfying lives.

Hari Srinivasan

I'm awestruck to coauthor this foreword with Dr. Temple Grandin, a trailblazer who shattered expectations and paved the way for many, including myself. Now, on my PhD journey in neuroscience, I'm walking a path that once felt unimaginable. It still feels surreal.

I am autistic with limited spoken communication (though improving — proof that learning isn't just for childhood), ADHD, sensorimotor processing issues, OCD, social anxiety, and co-occurring health challenges. Navigating my body feels like driving with a loose steering wheel — a constant battle between intention and execution. This unease fuels anxiety, avoidance, and social isolation.

Autism brings unique ways of thinking, perceiving, and innovating but also real obstacles. That's why I believe in a dual *opportunities-solutions* approach: creating opportunities that build on strengths while also addressing challenges. This means providing individualized support (therapy, education, and addressing needs) alongside external changes (accommodations, environmental modifications, and shifts in attitudes).

Education became my door to opportunity. UC Berkeley and Vanderbilt gave me structure, meaning, and growth, allowing me to stay curious and engaged. Now, as an autistic neuroscientist researching sensorimotor systems, I get to contribute to both knowledge and solutions.

The solutions side of the approach is just as critical. Much of my childhood was spent in grueling 40-hour therapy weeks with little meaningful return for the effort involved. Instead of forcing autistics into standardized programs, support must fit the individual. A wider range of approaches is needed to address communication barriers, sensory distress, and health challenges. Without real solutions, many autistics with higher support needs will remain stuck at the threshold of opportunity.

Dr. Grandin and I were shaped by different worlds: She grew up when autism was little known, while I grew up in a time when it became an everyday word. Yet despite growing awareness, our understanding is still incomplete. When I was diagnosed at three, only six children were identified as autistic in my school district; within a few years, that number grew to hundreds.

Just as Dr. Grandin highlights the power of early support and structured opportunities in unlocking autistic potential, it's equally important to recognize that not every autistic person benefits from the same approach. Too often, systems assume early struggles mean lifelong limitations, reducing the future to basic care instead of meaningful development. But people learn in different ways, and growth is possible at any age — which is why support must be flexible, informed by the full range of autistic experiences, and available throughout life.

I don't have to love every part of my autism to appreciate how it shapes me — and that's okay. Autism is both an ability and a disability, a strength and a challenge. This book understands that autism isn't a singular experience and offers practical tools to support people in ways that truly meet their individual needs. Because within the vast range of autistic experiences, there lies endless possibility.

Why This Book Matters

As our own lives demonstrate, there's no single way to be autistic, just as there is no single way to support autistic people. But one thing is clear: With understanding, acceptance, and the right support, autistic people can thrive. That's why this book is an essential resource for anyone looking to better understand autism. It offers tools, insights, and practical advice — whether you're autistic, a parent, a teacher, or an ally.

This book isn't about labels or fitting autism into a box. It's about real understanding and strategies that make a difference in daily life. Whether you're supporting an autistic person or simply trying to learn, you'll find useful tools, new perspectives, and maybe even some surprises. Keep reading, stay curious, and get ready to see autism in a broader light.

Introduction

I f you're here, you likely have big questions. Maybe you're wondering what autism really is or whether it applies to you or someone you know. If you're a parent, you might be searching for ways to best support your autistic child. If you're a friend, spouse, teacher, or coworker of an autistic person, you may be hoping to understand their perspective more deeply.

Curiosity, uncertainty, and even apprehension are natural when trying to understand something as vast as the human mind. After all, we're explorers of our own consciousness, yet no one hands us a map at birth. That's why this book exists.

This is your guide to autism — its wonders, its challenges, and the vast spectrum of human thought. In this book, we cut through jargon and outdated ideas, offering clear explanations, practical insights, and perspectives from autistic people, experts, and families.

Autistic people have always been part of the human story. But for much of history, the assumption has been that every mind worked in the same way. Only recently have we begun to grasp the complexity of the human brain — and with it, the many ways people think, feel, and engage with the universe.

So, let's begin. Find a comfortable place, take a deep breath, and get ready to explore the vast and fascinating landscape of the autistic experience.

About This Book

You are here because you are curious — because you want to understand autism — for yourself or someone you love or simply to see the world more clearly. That curiosity is a remarkable thing. It is the foundation of discovery, empathy, and connection. And that is exactly what this book is about.

Autism is not a distant concept. It's woven into the human experience. It shapes how people think, communicate, and interact with the world. It's not something to fix or fear but something to understand. And when we understand, we see more. We see the brilliance in different ways of thinking, the challenges imposed by a world not built for every mind, and the importance of acceptance.

This isn't a textbook. It's not a lecture. It's a conversation. We will cut through unnecessary complexity, set aside outdated ideas, and focus on what really matters: the experiences of autistic people, the science that explains them, and the practical insights that make a difference in daily life.

Whether you're autistic, a parent, a friend, or someone simply seeking knowledge, you're not alone. The search for clarity, for understanding, for connection — it has brought you here. And that's a wonderful place to begin.

Foolish Assumptions

None of us are dummies. You're here because you want a clear, honest understanding of autism — free from stereotypes and misconceptions. We won't talk down to you, and we ask you to approach this book with curiosity and an open mind. Be ready to rethink what you've been told, question long-held beliefs, and consider how you can help build a world that better includes and supports autistic people and their families.

That brings us to assumptions. We all make them, often without realizing it. Some are harmless, but others get in the way of real understanding. Maybe you've heard that autism is only about social struggles or that autistic people don't feel emotions deeply. Perhaps you've been told that all autistic people are either brilliant or incapable, or that autism is something to "overcome." These ideas are common, but they do not reflect reality.

If you're autistic, your brain isn't broken. It's not *less than*, and it's not *more than*. It simply *is*. The same is true for every brain. Autism is not a flaw to fix, nor is it a mysterious superpower. It's a natural way of experiencing the world. Different doesn't mean better or worse; it just means different.

Autistic people exist in every walk of life — thinking, creating, and contributing in ways that shape the world. Their experiences are as vast and varied as the universe itself. They're not puzzles to solve. They're human — fully, wonderfully human.

In this book, we help you understand the beautiful complexity of the autistic experience, recognize the strengths that come with autism, and see autistic people and their families as ordinary, valued, and deserving of support — just like everyone else. But it would be foolish to assume that this means dismissing the difficulties that often come with navigating a world that isn't built for autistic people.

REMEMBER

At the same time, no single book can capture every autistic experience. Autism is different and unique for each person, and the information here won't apply to everyone in the same way. What works well for one autistic person or family may not work for another. Keep that in mind as you read and remember that the best way to understand autism is to listen to autistic people themselves.

Being autistic in our world today presents many challenges. For many, this can be incredibly tough. But if you're not autistic, ask yourself what makes life difficult for you? Whatever it is, those struggles don't make you any less worthy of respect.

Being alive means facing difficulties, but also having strengths, perspectives, and experiences that matter. We are more than our challenges; we are our ideas, passions, and the connections we build. We are *human*. And so are autistic people.

Autism does not make a person less capable, less worthy, or less human. Just as your challenges don't define your worth, neither do theirs. By understanding autism — not as something to fix, but as a natural and meaningful part of life — we move closer to seeing one another with the clarity and respect we all deserve.

Icons Used in This Book

Throughout the book, we have used a set of icons in the margins to highlight the most critical things we want you to take away.

REMEMBER

When you see this icon, you know that the information that follows is important enough to read twice! Information in these paragraphs is often conceptual.

TIP

This icon indicates practical information that often translates key concepts into actionable advice.

WARNING

This icon highlights information that could be detrimental to your understanding and actions if you ignore it. We don't use this one much, so pay attention when we do.

Beyond the Book

One of the biggest things we hear from autistic people and their families is the need for more resources. That's exactly why this book exists — it's your foundation for understanding autism, supporting autistic people, and finding the tools that work best for you. It gives you the core knowledge and strategies you need, but there's always more to explore.

For quick tips and key takeaways, check out the Cheat Sheet, which you can find by searching for **Autism For Dummies Cheat Sheet at** www.dummies.com. To help you go even further, we've put together Neurodiversity Resources, a carefully curated collection of resources, tools, information, and community connections designed to help you navigate challenges, access support, and find what works best for you. You can find it online at www.pivotdiversity.com/resources.

Where to Go from Here

You don't have to read this book cover to cover like a novel. Think of it as a buffet: pick and choose what interests you most. Start by skimming the table of contents and jumping to the chapters that catch your eye.

Short on time? Head to any chapter that interests you — or to Part 7, where we've rounded up key takeaways and tips for quick reference. New to the topic of autism? Start at the beginning for a solid foundation before diving into the rest.

However you choose to read, we hope this book helps you see that the world — and the people in it — is even more varied, complex, and fascinating than you might have imagined.

1

Understanding Autism

Understand autism as a lifelong journey and embrace the diversity of autistic experiences through a neurodiversity-affirming lens.

Reflect on autism as a neurotype and consider how cultural and social contexts shape perceptions of disability.

Familiarize yourself with the autism diagnosis process, including criteria, regional differences, and how to navigate barriers to access.

Explore the unique ways autistic individuals think, communicate, and experience the world to deepen your understanding and empathy.

Chapter **1**

What Is Autism?

Autism is a natural way of thinking, experiencing the world, and connecting with others. It's not a disease or a flaw — it's just one of the many ways brains work. Autistic people often think, communicate, socialize, and respond to their surroundings in unique and meaningful ways.

Autism lasts a lifetime — you're born with it and live with it through every stage of life. While an autistic person may face challenges, they also have amazing strengths, fresh ideas, and talents. No two autistic people are the same — just like no two other people are — but there are common experiences many autistic people share. Understanding what makes autistic people unique and what connects their experiences helps us support them better.

Science has taught us that autism isn't something to "fix" or "cure." It's part of who a person is — and that's a good thing! We've moved away from harmful approaches that tried to change autistic people into someone they're not. Now, the focus is on understanding, accepting, and supporting autistic people with tools and resources that help them live happy, meaningful lives.

In this chapter, we explore the modern understanding of autism, the science behind it, and how autism shapes an individual. To fully understand autism, you need to know about neurodiversity — how variations in the human brain like autism, ADHD, and dyslexia are natural parts of human life.

Understanding Neurodiversity

For much of history, people assumed all brains worked the same way, and differences were seen as defects. This mindset led to harmful practices like forced institutionalization, discrimination, and attempts to "fix" those who didn't conform. Entire groups were misunderstood and excluded, causing significant harm.

Thankfully, we've come a long way. We now understand that every brain is unique, like fingerprints, and that diverse ways of thinking are essential for a thriving society (see Chapter 2). These differences help us innovate and find solutions for problems — solutions not possible if everyone thought the same way.

"The world needs a neurodiverse workforce to help solve some of the big problems of our time," wrote Virgin Group founder Richard Branson in a 2024 LinkedIn post. Branson, an advocate for neurodiversity, highlights how his dyslexic brain processes information uniquely, benefiting his ventures and society. He makes it clear: "neurodiversity should be embraced."

Branson's insight underscores that recognizing neurodiversity doesn't just help individuals who think differently. It helps all of us.

REMEMBER

Neurodiversity acknowledges both the challenges and strengths of different brain types. Both are normal parts of being human.

Organizing brains into neurotypes

Each of our brains is unique; we all process information and interact with the world differently. To make sense of this diversity, we categorize brains into groups, known as *neurotypes*.

Neurotypes are labels for clusters of brains that typically process information or respond to stimuli in similar ways. Examples include autism, ADHD, and dyslexia. These categories help us better understand the incredible variety of human brains.

Everyone has a neurotype — including you! People with brains that function like most others have a neurotypical neurotype, whereas those with different thinking styles — such as autism, ADHD, or dyslexia — have neurodivergent neurotypes. At least 20 percent of people are neurodivergent, which means these differences aren't uncommon.

REMEMBER

Neither neurotypical nor neurodivergent neurotypes are "broken"; they simply reflect different ways of experiencing and understanding the world.

Understanding autism as a neurotype

Autism is one of many neurotypes. Although every autistic person is different, they share many commonalities in their ways of thinking and experiencing the world, which shapes many aspects of their lives, including sensory processing, communication, socialization, and problem-solving. (See Chapter 4 for more.)

REMEMBER

Autistic people have a neurotype that can't — and shouldn't — be "fixed." Embracing this fact shifts the focus from trying to change autistic people to understanding what everyone — including autistic people — needs to thrive.

Expanding Our Understanding of Autism

Autism has been recognized for decades, but our understanding has grown significantly in recent years. Let's explore the ways scientific perspectives have shifted, the latest statistics, and the positive sign of progress indicated by the rising number of autism diagnoses.

Our evolving knowledge

Not long ago, autism was deeply misunderstood. It was thought to be rare and defined by rigid, stereotypical behaviors, often described in terms of "deficits" rather than acknowledging strengths and individuality. Early researchers focused on a narrow demographic, recognizing only a limited set of traits, which excluded many autistic people from being identified.

Families faced harmful blame, with myths like the "refrigerator mother" theory accusing parents of causing autism by being cold or unloving. These beliefs fueled stigma, isolation, and prejudice for autistic individuals and their families.

"Autism became a source of shame and stigma," author Steve Silberman said at a 2015 TED conference. "And two generations were shipped off to institutions 'for their own good.'"

Actor Daryl Hannah was nearly one of them. When she was diagnosed with autism as a child, doctors recommended institutionalizing her, but her mother refused and supported her at home. That decision allowed Hannah to grow up and star in iconic films like *Blade Runner*, *Splash*, *Steel Magnolias*, and *Kill Bill*.

Today, we know better. Autism isn't rare and doesn't fit a single mold. (No human does.) Every autistic person's experiences, challenges, and strengths are unique.

Shifts in perspective and diagnosis

The way autism is diagnosed today reflects significant progress. Diagnoses now account for the wide variety of ways autism can present, recognizing a broader spectrum of traits and experiences. This shift allows more individuals to be identified and supported. (To discover more about the diagnostic process, turn to Chapter 3.)

Our current understanding of statistics

Worldwide, studies suggest that at least 1 percent to 2 percent of people are autistic, with U.S. statistics estimating about 1 in 36 individuals. But what truly matters isn't the exact number; it's how we use our understanding of autism to create a world where everyone can thrive.

These figures represent real people: neighbors, coworkers, family members, and friends. Recognizing autism's diversity helps us build a society that supports and values autistic individuals.

Increasing diagnostic rates?

If you've heard that autism diagnoses are rising, you might wonder what that means. Is autism becoming more common? The short answer is no. The rise in diagnoses reflects improved diagnostic tools, expanded criteria, and greater awareness.

In the past, many autistic people — especially women and people of color — were overlooked due to outdated stereotypes. Today's rising diagnostic rates signal progress, helping us recognize and support those who were previously excluded.

"I feel Black autistic women are just now being embraced because more Black women are starting to be diagnosed," said children's author Ayanna Davis in a 2024 interview with *Learn from Autistic People*. "For so long, Black women were being misdiagnosed, late diagnosed, or not diagnosed at all. As diagnoses become more common, I feel society will become more accepting."

REMEMBER

Autism isn't "increasing"; our understanding is simply catching up. Rising diagnostic rates are a sign of progress, showing that more people — especially those once overlooked — are finally getting the recognition and support they need.

Being an Autistic Person

Every autistic person is, first and foremost, an individual. Autism is a part of who they are, but it is not all they are. Like anyone else, autistic people have preferences, talents, and experiences. Recognizing their individuality is crucial for making meaningful connections and providing the right support.

A lifelong experience

Autism isn't something people outgrow — it's a lifelong experience that shapes development, identity, and opportunities. From childhood to older adulthood, autistic individuals face unique challenges and triumphs at every stage of life.

Shortly after John, from our author team, turned 40, he joined a meditation session with a dozen other autistic people. After sitting quietly together, the group shared lunch and discussed life's challenges. John, who was grappling with his milestone birthday, said, "I just turned 40, and I'm having a hard time processing it," and looked to the group — most of whom were in their 60s — for advice.

"How did you deal with turning 40?" he asked. The room went quiet for a moment until one person laughed and said, "That was so long ago, I don't remember!" The others nodded in agreement. It was a funny moment and a powerful reminder: Autistic people navigate challenges throughout their lives — not just in childhood.

"It's no surprise that autistic kids grow up to be autistic adults," says occupational therapist Meg Ferrell. "As professionals, educators, caregivers, and anyone supporting autistic individuals, we need to do a better job ensuring a smooth transition into adulthood — even if you primarily work with autistic kids."

REMEMBER

Autism is a lifelong journey. Supporting autistic individuals means recognizing their evolving needs and celebrating their growth at every stage of life.

Being autistic in a nonautistic world

Picture yourself landing on a planet designed for beings who think, communicate, and process the world in ways completely different from your own. The lights are too bright, the air smells strange, and everyone expects you to just "get it" without any instructions. That's how autistic people often describe living in a society built around nonautistic norms.

Many aspects of daily life — like communication, social expectations, and sensory experiences — are designed around nonautistic people. This leaves autistic individuals navigating systems that often fail to meet their needs, which can lead to frustration, confusion, pain, lost opportunities, isolation, anxiety, and more.

Researchers are starting to catch up, too. Dr. Kyle Jasmin, writing in *Psychology Today*, described it this way: "Imagine living in a world where your natural way of being is constantly at odds with societal norms. This is a daily reality for many autistic individuals."

REMEMBER

Autistic individuals aren't "wrong" for experiencing the world differently. It's the world that wasn't built with them in mind. The real challenge isn't autism; it's creating a society that embraces all ways of thinking and being.

Diversity of the autistic experience

Autism is incredibly diverse, with each autistic person experiencing it in their own way. From communication styles to support needs, no two autistic individuals are exactly alike. However, there is a common thread that connects these experiences — a unique way of seeing and interacting with the world.

Support needs vary (and that's ok)

Some autistic individuals require significant assistance in daily life, whereas others may need very little. Support can take many forms, such as help with daily tasks, navigating social situations, managing sensory processing differences, or simply offering acceptance and understanding. These varying needs don't make someone "less" autistic or less capable — they simply highlight that autism affects everyone differently.

Different ways of communicating

Communication is another key aspect of the autistic experience. Some autistic people communicate with spoken words (often referred to as "speaking"), while others may not use spoken words at all ("nonspeaking").

Around 30 percent to 40 percent of autistic individuals are nonspeaking, but that doesn't mean they have less to say. Many use alternative methods, such as communication devices or written communication, to express themselves. It's also important to remember that an autistic person's ability to speak can fluctuate. Stress, sensory overload, or emotional states can affect their ability to communicate with spoken words.

All forms of communication are valid, and every person's voice — whether spoken or not — deserves to be heard.

The common autistic thread

Though autistic individuals may appear vastly different from each other, there's a common thread running through their experiences. Autistic people perceive and interact with the world in ways uniquely their own, yet instantly recognizable to each other.

It's helpful to think of France when reflecting on the autistic experience. With nearly 70 million French citizens, no two are exactly alike. A rural farmer in the heart of Bordeaux might have a life that seems worlds apart from an avant-garde fashion designer living in central Paris. Their lives, perspectives, and traits could be radically different. Yet, if they met, they'd instantly and unmistakenly understand and recognize each other as "French."

Autistic people connect in remarkable ways to share information, support each other, and celebrate their shared experiences. Through online forums, in-person meetups, or creative expression like art and writing, these connections form the foundation of a vibrant autistic culture.

These connections also benefit families. By engaging with autistic adults, parents and caregivers can gain insights into their children's experiences, find answers to their questions, and learn practical strategies for providing support.

Understanding autism as a disability

Autism is a disability, but it's important to understand what that really means. A disability doesn't make someone broken or less valuable. It means a person faces barriers because of how they experience and interact with the world. For autistic individuals, these barriers often impact their natural differences in communication, sensory processing, and social interactions.

"Prior to this year, I've never identified as autistic, let alone disabled," wrote Rachel Burns in a 2024 piece for the *Australian Broadcasting Corporation*. "I now see that I have always faced and will always face challenges incomprehensible to most."

Disability is about barriers, not limitations

People often misunderstand disability. The issue isn't that a person is less capable. It's that society is set up to exclude people who think or experience the world differently. Those differences become a disability when environments, systems, or attitudes don't accommodate them.

When people think about disability, they often focus on impairments — specific limitations in how someone manages daily tasks, like poor eyesight, difficulty hearing, or a heart condition that limits physical activity. But the truth is, we all experience impairments at some point. If you've ever been sick, had a broken bone, felt too depressed to see friends, or been too grieved to focus on work, you've dealt with impairments that made everyday tasks harder.

What disables someone?

Disability isn't about the impairment itself; it's about how the world responds to it. For example, a person missing a leg who uses a wheelchair isn't disabled unless they face barriers, like buildings without ramps or inaccessible public transportation, that prevent full participation in daily life.

For autistic individuals, differences in communication or sensory processing become disabilities when they aren't accommodated. An autistic person who doesn't communicate with spoken words but who has access to a communication device isn't inherently disabled because they can express themselves fully. Similarly, sensory processing differences can often be accommodated with adjustments like noise-canceling headphones or access to quiet spaces.

When accommodations are in place, impairments and differences don't have to become disabilities. Autism is experienced as a disability when society fails to accommodate its differences.

Fortunately, things are changing. Schools, workplaces, and communities are expanding communication supports, creating sensory-friendly spaces, and offering tools to assist autistic ways of thinking and processing information.

REMEMBER

The most powerful accommodations of all are acceptance and understanding. These aren't just necessary for autistic people — their families need it too. Parents and caregivers often face the same stigma and lack of support and benefit from inclusive changes as much as autistic individuals do.

Understanding autism as a developmental disability

A developmental disability is an experience that begins in childhood and affects how someone grows, learns, or navigates daily life. These differences become disabilities when our world does not accommodate them. Autism, Down syndrome, and intellectual disabilities are examples of developmental disabilities.

Although autism is a developmental disability, it isn't an intellectual disability. Intellectual disabilities affect how a person thinks, reasons, or learns compared to others their age. Autism, on the other hand, primarily shapes communication, social interaction, sensory experiences, and how information is processed.

Many autistic people have average or above-average intelligence and may excel in areas like memory or pattern recognition. However, because autism affects how the brain processes information, tasks like problem-solving, understanding social cues, or organizing thoughts can be challenging. These difficulties are related to how the brain handles information rather than a lack of intelligence.

It's estimated that around 30 percent of autistic individuals also have an intellectual disability. This rate was once thought to be as high as 70 percent, but it has declined over time as more autistic people without intellectual disabilities are diagnosed. This doesn't make them any less deserving of respect or less normal. Autistic people, including those with intellectual disabilities, should be recognized for their full selves — not just their challenges.

REMEMBER

Many autistic individuals with intellectual disabilities find meaningful ways to work, volunteer, socialize, and even take leadership roles in their communities. However, it's equally important to value those who may not work. Every person deserves respect, dignity, and opportunities to live a fulfilling life.

Understanding How Autism Develops

If you were to ask what causes autism, the honest answer would be, "We don't know." The truth is, we may never know — and that's okay! Autism is a natural variation in how the brain develops and functions, shaped by genetics and other factors.

There are many things we don't fully understand but still value and appreciate. For instance, we don't know all the details of how the pyramids were built, the cultural motivations behind why Stonehenge aligns as it does, or why left-handed people exist. Even the sun's full complexities in sustaining life are not fully known. Yet these unknowns don't diminish their significance. Similarly, not fully understanding autism doesn't lessen the value of autistic people.

WARNING

Trying to understand autism solely by studying genes or biology is like experiencing the Eiffel Tower solely through blueprints, admiring a beautiful car only by studying engineering schematics, or appreciating a symphony just by learning about which model of printer and brand of ink is used to produce its sheet music. Fascinating details — but autism and autistic people are so much more than that!

How genes shape autism

Genes play a major role in shaping traits related to autism. These segments of DNA act as the body's instruction manual, guiding how cells grow, develop, and function. While genes don't determine everything about a person, they heavily influence how the brain and body develop, shaping traits and the ways we interact with the world.

Each gene has a specific role. Some influence how we process sensory information, others guide brain development, and some help cells communicate. However, not all genes act the same way — some are always active, whereas others switch on and off depending on the body's needs. Tools within the body control when genes activate, how strongly they act, and how they interact with one another.

No two people have genes that function exactly the same way, creating the genetic diversity among humans that makes each of us unique. Some of these differences shape how the autistic brain develops and functions, contributing to the wide range of traits and experiences seen among autistic individuals. (Read more on that in Chapter 4.)

REMEMBER

Because we inherit half our genetic material from each parent, family members often share traits that may influence autism. Parents discovering their own neurodivergence after their child's diagnosis is not uncommon.

Khushboo, from our author team, shares, "When we train companies on neurodiversity, people often pull me aside afterward and share how their child's autism diagnosis made them realize they might be autistic too. Many seek their own assessment and finally gain the understanding and support they've needed."

Journalist Nina Hossain shared a similar experience in 2024 in an interview with *The Times of London.* Diagnosed with autism at 50, she realized her neurodivergence while her 16-year-old daughter was being assessed. "Sitting there answering questions about her, my husband and I just kept looking at each other," she said. "As soon as we had a break, we both said at the same time that all those things seem to apply to me as well."

Genetic complexity

Autism is an example of genetic complexity, where many genes interact in complex and sometimes unpredictable ways to shape traits. Scientists have identified hundreds of genes associated with autism, each playing a small role in shaping autistic traits.

Dr. Sue Fletcher-Watson explains it this way during an episode of the *Stories of Autism* podcast: "The genetic contribution to autism is much more like the genetic contribution to height. It's not like you have a tall gene or a short gene. You have many interacting genes that combine to make you taller or shorter."

REMEMBER

This complexity is why autism presents differently in each person. While all humans share the same set of genes, tiny variations in DNA sequences account for the wide diversity among people — and the uniqueness of every autistic individual.

These differences arise from genetic variations (inherited differences), genetic mechanisms (how genes work), genetic mutations (random changes), as well as biological influences and other factors. Each plays a role in shaping how autism is expressed in different people.

REMEMBER

The way genes shape traits in autism is an ongoing area of study. It's known that hundreds of genes are associated with autism, though each may contribute a small part to the overall traits and experiences. The complex interactions between these genes lead to the variability seen in autistic traits.

Genetic variations

Autism is also influenced by genetic variations, natural differences in DNA we inherit from our parents that contribute to individual traits — including autistic traits. These variations explain traits like eye color, hair texture, and blood type. They also account for quirks like why some people have dimples, can roll their tongues, tolerate spicy foods easily, think cilantro tastes like soap, and are early birds or night owls.

Because we inherit half of our genetic material from each parent, these variations help explain why family members share certain traits while remaining distinct from one another. Each parent passes down half of their DNA to each child, but those halves are shuffled uniquely. For example, even within the same family, siblings may look or act differently despite sharing many genetic traits. This happens because siblings inherit different combinations of genetic variations from their parents.

To better understand how genetic variations play a role in autism, here are the main types to consider:

>> **Common variants:** These genetic differences are shared by many people and usually have small, subtle effects on traits. However, when many common variations combine and interact (a process called polygenic interaction), they can subtly shape autistic traits.

>> **Rare variants:** These less common variations often have a stronger influence on specific traits. For instance, rare differences in genes like CHD8 or SCN2A may affect neural connections and sensory processing, contributing to autistic traits like sensory sensitivities or social differences.

>> **Copy number variations (CNVs):** These involve sections of DNA being duplicated or missing. Common CNVs are typically not strongly linked to autism, but rare CNVs in genes like NRXN1 and SHANK3 — which are tied to brain development and information processing — are more strongly associated. These rare CNVs can shape autistic traits in communication, sensory experiences, and social interactions.

REMEMBER

Every human inherits genetic variations, which are passed down through generations. Because genetic variations associated with autism are found in populations across the globe, this lets us know that autistic traits have been a naturally occurring part of the human experience for tens of thousands of years.

Genetic mechanisms

To understand the genetic contributions to autism, you need some understanding of genetic mechanisms — the tools that control how, when, and where genes influence human traits. Think of genes as instruction manuals in your cells, with genetic mechanisms acting like editors that modify the code (gene mutations), on/off switches (gene expression), volume dials (gene regulation), and coordinators (gene interactions). These mechanisms shape how people grow, develop, and adapt to change — and they play an important role in autism.

Gene mutation: modifying the code

Unlike genetic variations, which are traits passed down through generations, genetic mutations are new changes in DNA. Some happen randomly in a person, while others can be inherited if they first appear in a parent's reproductive cells. These mutations occur naturally during cell division, DNA replication, or, in some cases, from exposures like radiation or chemicals.

Now, before you imagine yourself joining the X-Men, know this: everyone experiences genetic mutations. Most are minor and harmless, with no noticeable effect on how the body works. These changes are a normal part of genetic diversity.

While some mutations are inherited from parents, de novo mutations occur for the first time in an individual. Certain de novo mutations have been strongly linked to autism, particularly in genes like DYRK1A, CHD8, and SCN2A, which are involved in brain development and communication.

Although de novo mutations are unique to each individual, similar mutations can occur in the same genes across unrelated people, leading to shared autistic traits. This happens because certain genes involved in brain development have higher mutation rates, partly due to their complexity and frequent activity during cell division. These mutations are a natural part of genetic diversity and don't "cause" autism but contribute to how a particular autistic person's autistic traits are expressed.

REMEMBER

These mutations aren't inherently "good" or "bad." They're simply variations in the genetic code that shape each person's unique traits. Autism isn't caused by a single mutation but by a mix of genetic influences that contribute to how each autistic person experiences the world.

Gene expression: switching genes on or off

Genes don't work automatically; they rely on signals to activate. Human DNA contains thousands of genes, but you don't use all of them all the time. Some genes are evolutionary leftovers, like the one for making vitamin C, which you no longer need because you get enough from food. Others lie dormant, ready to activate when needed — for example, to repair damaged DNA, heal injuries, or help the body adapt to extreme conditions.

When a dormant gene is "switched on," it undergoes gene expression and produces the proteins needed for specific tasks. Through a process called alternative splicing, RNA (which carries genetic instructions) is edited and rearranged to create exactly the right protein for the job. This flexibility allows one gene to produce multiple proteins, adapting to the body's needs.

In autistic individuals, researchers have found unique patterns of gene expression. Some genes are overexpressed (more active), whereas others are underexpressed (less active), particularly in brain regions linked to social interaction, communication, and sensory processing. These differences aren't harmful but reflect how the autistic brain works.

Here are a few examples:

>> **NRXN1:** A gene that helps brain cells send signals to each other. Some research suggests it's less active in some autistic people, which may influence brain networks involved in social interaction.

>> **CNTNAP2:** A gene supporting language networks. Reduced activity might shape communication differences.

>> **SHANK3:** A gene supporting synapse function. Overexpression may contribute to sensory sensitivities.

Overexpressed or underexpressed genes aren't inherently bad. It's like when you adjust a faucet and turn it up or down depending on what you need. While science hasn't yet fully determined why these patterns occur, it has uncovered that they play a key role in shaping how the autistic brain develops and functions.

Gene regulation: turning the volume up or down

Once a gene is activated, gene regulation controls how much activity occurs. Think of gene expression as a light switch (on or off) and gene regulation as the dimmer switch that determines brightness. This ensures the right amount of protein is produced, based on what the body needs.

Gene regulation helps explain why seemingly unrelated traits often appear together. This "volume control" keeps things efficient, allowing multiple traits to share the same regulatory pathway. It's like using one remote to control several devices, so the body doesn't need separate systems for every detail. These byproducts happen because shared pathways regulate multiple traits, and the overall adaptability this brings is usually worth it.

For instance, in humans, red hair and freckles frequently co-occur because they are influenced by the same regulatory pathway. When the activity of the MC1R gene, which controls pigment production, is "dialed down," both traits tend to appear — even if there is no reason for them to.

Another example is in dogs. Genetically, all dogs (even pugs and chihuahuas) share a nearly identical set of genes as wolves, but differences in gene regulation cause traits to diverge and appear differently.

As wolves adapted to living near humans, certain genes in some wolves were "dialed" toward traits like tameness. Because unrelated traits like floppy ears and waggy tails shared the same regulatory pathways, they began to appear together. There's no inherent reason for floppy ears and tameness to be linked (just like red hair and freckles), but sharing the same "dial" means they often show up together. Similarly, in autistic people, certain traits may frequently appear together because they are influenced by shared gene regulation.

This "volume control" is powerful. It lets our DNA direct stem cells to become skin or brain cells, depending on the needs of the body. In autism, gene regulation plays a crucial role. For instance, genes like SHANK3 and FOXP2, involved in brain development and communication, may be "dialed" differently in autistic people.

This is still an active area of research, and while gene regulation provides insights, researchers are still uncovering the full picture.

Gene mediation: coordinating it all

If gene expression is a switch and gene regulation a dimmer, gene mediation is like the project manager, coordinating how genes and traits interact. Gene mediation also integrates environmental factors like diet, social experiences, and stress with genetic activity to shape unique traits.

In autism, mediation might explain how traits cluster. Here are some examples:

>> **Pleiotropy:** One gene influences multiple traits, such as a gene that affects both neuron connections and sensory processing.

>> **Epistasis:** One gene's effects are altered by interactions with others, which might amplify, suppress, or modify certain traits.

This could explain why non-autistic family members of autistic individuals sometimes show related traits, like a preference for routines or deep focus. In one family member, genetic pathways might result in autism, whereas in another, the same pathways may express in subtler ways.

By understanding gene mediation, we can better grasp how genetics, the environment, and brain development work together to shape autistic traits.

The role of biological influences

Genes provide the blueprint for who we are, but they don't tell the whole story. Understanding autism means exploring how genes interact with biology and other factors throughout life.

The gut-brain axis: a two-way conversation

Ever heard the phrase "trust your gut"? Turns out, there's some truth to it. Your gut and brain are constantly connected through the gut-brain axis, a system linking your digestive system and brain that influences how your body and brain work together.

Your gut is home to trillions of bacteria, known as the microbiota, which produce chemicals that affect mood, behavior, and brain development. Research suggests differences in the gut microbiota may influence traits like sensory sensitivities or anxiety by affecting how the brain processes information or handles stress.

A key player here is the vagus nerve, which transmits signals between the brain and major organs, including the gut. These signals can impact mood, sensory experiences, and even behavior. For example, stress or sensory overload can disrupt digestion, creating a feedback loop that may contribute to challenges some autistic people face.

WARNING

A growing number of companies market vagus nerve stimulation (VNS) as a therapy for autism, claiming benefits like improved social behavior, reduced anxiety, or better emotional regulation. While VNS can help with conditions like epilepsy or depression, it is not proven to work for autism. Autism is a neurodevelopmental condition, and biological treatments like VNS cannot reshape autistic traits.

REMEMBER

The gut–brain axis doesn't "cause" autism. It's just one aspect of the complex intersection of genetics, biology, and other experiences that contribute to the autistic experience.

The immune system's role: a balancing act

The immune system protects the body from harmful substances, but it may work differently in some autistic individuals. Some research shows higher levels of inflammation or increased activity in microglia — immune cells in the brain. However, scientists are still exploring what these differences mean and how they relate to autistic traits.

Developmental influences: a lifelong process

Our development doesn't stop at birth — it's shaped by a combination of genetics, biology, and experiences over a lifetime. Factors like prenatal development, early nutrition, sensory input, and social interactions influence how we grow and adapt.

These influences don't "cause" autism, but they shape how autistic traits are experienced. For instance, a supportive environment can help autistic individuals thrive by building on their strengths, while stressful or unsupportive environments may create challenges in areas like communication or sensory regulation.

Environmental factors: context matters

Environmental factors also play a role in shaping how we grow and interact with the world. When it comes to autism, environmental factors don't "cause" autism, which is primarily rooted in genetics. However, there's some evidence that environmental factors may influence how autistic traits particularly develop and are expressed in autistic people, but this research is still emerging and not definitive.

WARNING

Anyone claiming that environmental factors "cause" autism is wrong. These are myths and debunked theories that have circulated over the years, often leading to unnecessary fear and confusion. We'll talk about those myths next.

Clarifying What Doesn't Cause Autism

To clear up any misinformation: Autism isn't caused by vaccines, parenting, diet, screen time, toxins, or childhood illnesses. These myths only distract from what truly matters — understanding and supporting autistic people. Furthermore, blaming the following factors unfairly shifts focus from acceptance to blame:

>> **Vaccines:** The idea that vaccines cause autism has been thoroughly debunked by decades of research. This myth originated from a fraudulent study, and its author lost his medical license for unethical behavior. Vaccines save lives and have no connection to autism — period.

>> **Parenting:** Parenting style has no impact on whether a child is autistic. Parents should never feel guilt or blame for their child's neurotype.

>> **Screen time:** Screen time doesn't cause autism. While excessive screen use can affect focus or social skills in any child, screens can also foster learning and communication.

>> **Diet:** There's no evidence linking autism to diet, gluten, dairy, or food additives. Myths about diet "triggering" autism have been debunked. While some autistic people may have dietary sensitivities, these are co-occurring conditions, not causes.

>> **Toxins:** Heavy metals and other toxins, including thimerosal in vaccines, have no proven connection to autism. Thimerosal was removed from most vaccines decades ago, yet autism rates continue to rise, confirming no link.

>> **Illness:** Childhood illnesses or infections don't cause autism.

REMEMBER

It's important to approach people who believe vaccines cause autism (or other myths) with empathy and understanding. Many hold these beliefs out of fear, misinformation, or a heartfelt desire to protect their kids. When we peel back those layers of fear, we often uncover shared needs for support and a mutual desire to do what's best for our loved ones — needs we can work together to address.

At the same time, some have made conspiracy theories their identity, making it incredibly difficult — if not impossible — to change their minds. Efforts are often better spent modeling compassion, love, acceptance, and support for the autistic people in your life. However, we must never excuse those who exploit these harmful myths for personal gain — whether politicians, influencers, or scam artists — who harm families and undermine public health.

Exploring the Autistic Brain

The autistic brain is uniquely structured and functions in ways that shape how autistic individuals think, feel, and interact with the world. While much is still unknown, research highlights differences in brain development, sensory processing, and thinking.

Autistic brain development and structure

Autistic brains develop differently, with some areas growing more rapidly or following unique trajectories, shaping distinct strengths and challenges from infancy. Key differences in development include the following:

>> **Amygdala:** Crucial for processing emotions, this area often grows faster, potentially contributing to heightened emotional responses or sensory awareness.

>> **Prefrontal cortex:** Essential for decision-making, planning, and understanding social behavior, differences in its structure and connectivity may influence how autistic individuals interpret social cues.

>> **Cerebellum:** Responsible for movement and sensory processing, its unique development may contribute to coordination challenges or heightened sensory experiences.

>> **Hippocampus:** Vital for memory and learning, differences in size and function may shape unique memory profiles in autistic individuals.

>> **Glial cells:** Supporting neuron growth and development, differences in glial cell function in autistic brains are an emerging area of research.

Autistic brain development doesn't always follow a typical timeline. Some children may skip milestones like crawling or start speaking later than expected, whereas others might show advanced skills in memory, problem-solving, or spotting patterns and details that others might miss.

Take Haley Moss, for example. She was nonspeaking as a child, and experts doubted she'd finish high school. Yet Haley met milestones in her own time and is now an attorney, author, and neurodiversity advocate. As Haley says, "I might have hit milestones in a different order than my peers, but I still did so."

REMEMBER

Not all nonspeaking children will one day speak, and that's okay. The goal is to help all autistic kids find ways to communicate that work best for them.

Neural connectivity (sensory processing)

Differences in neural connectivity (how brain regions communicate) and pruning (the removal of unused connections) shape how sensory input is processed. These differences can amplify sensory signals, making experiences more vivid. Key areas involved include these:

>> **Sensory cortex and thalamus:** These areas relay sensory information. Differences in connectivity may influence how efficiently sensory experiences are processed.

>> **The insula:** Involved in internal sensations like hunger or heartbeat, differences here may affect how these sensations are perceived.

>> **Neurotransmitters** (for example, GABA, glutamate)**:** These chemicals help amplify or calm sensory signals. Variations in neurotransmitter balance may shape sensory sensitivities.

>> **Glial cells and pruning:** Differences in pruning, supported by glial cells, may lead to heightened sensory sensitivity in autistic brains.

These differences help explain why sensory experiences in autistic individuals are often more intense and unique (see Chapter 4 for more). While these patterns are common, they are not universal, and research is ongoing.

Social cognition networks

The autistic brain processes social interactions differently, leading to unique strengths and challenges. Here are some key areas:

>> **Amygdala:** Heightened activity here can increase emotional awareness but may lead to greater stress in unfamiliar social situations.

>> **Fusiform gyrus:** Differences in this area may impact facial recognition, making it harder to interpret neurotypical expressions or remember faces.

>> **Default mode network (DMN):** This network often functions differently in autistic brains, which influences how social cues are interpreted.

>> **Mirror neurons:** These neurons help process others' actions and experiences and may function differently in autistic individuals, contributing to unique social processing.

These unique patterns help shape how autistic individuals experience and navigate social interactions. Read more on those differences in Chapter 4.

Executive function and attention

Executive function — planning, focusing, and shifting attention — differs in autistic individuals due to variations in brain connectivity and structure. These differences may include these things:

>> **Prefrontal cortex:** Differences in this area affect planning, decision-making, and attention regulation, shaping flexibility and prioritization.

>> **Neural pruning:** Reduced pruning in areas like the prefrontal cortex may create denser but less streamlined neural networks. However, this may not apply universally.

>> **White matter:** Variations in white matter pathways affect how signals are transmitted, influencing executive tasks.

>> **Corpus callosum:** Differences in this structure, which connects the brain's hemispheres, may influence how the two sides work together.

These differences can enhance focus and attention to detail but make multitasking more challenging (see Chapter 4 for more). And while these differences are common, they do not apply to every autistic individual.

Neuroplasticity and adaptation

Autistic brains exhibit unique patterns of neuroplasticity, the brain's ability to adapt and learn. Here are some examples:

>> **Pleiotropy:** A single genetic factor can shape multiple traits, such as sensory sensitivity and intense focus, often seen together in autism.

>> **Localized neuroplasticity:** Heightened neuroplasticity in specific areas may aid adaptation in focus and detail but challenge broader cognitive tasks like multitasking.

>> **Connectivity differences:** Increased local connectivity strengthens specialized skills but may limit integration across brain regions.

Differences in autistic neuroplasticity help explain why autistic traits, such as focused interests and innovative thinking, exist (more on that in Chapter 4).

Understanding Related Conditions

Autism intersects with other conditions in ways that impact diagnosis and support. This includes former diagnostic labels now recognized as part of autism, conditions that may actually represent autism, common co-occurring conditions, and separate conditions with overlapping traits. Understanding these connections helps clarify diagnoses and provide accurate support.

Former diagnoses now included in autism

Autism now includes conditions once thought to be separate. Examples include

>> **Asperger's syndrome:** Previously a separate diagnosis, this referred to individuals with autistic traits but without significant language or intellectual delays.

>> **Childhood disintegrative disorder (CDD):** Once distinct, CDD focused on significant skill regression after age two, now seen as part of autism.

>> **Pervasive developmental disorder-not otherwise specified (PDD-NOS):** This description was used for individuals with autistic traits who didn't meet diagnostic criteria under previous manuals.

Conditions that may actually be autism

Autistic traits are sometimes misdiagnosed under other labels, reflecting misunderstandings of autism's diversity. Experts believe the following may be autism in many cases but are viewed from a different perspective:

>> **Sensory processing disorder (SPD):** SPD describes heightened or reduced sensitivity to sensory input. While not formally recognized in diagnostic manuals, it's often applied to autistic individuals.

>> **Social communication disorder (SCD):** SCD involves communication and social difficulties without repetitive behaviors. It's often diagnosed instead of autism when key traits are misunderstood.

>> **Nonverbal learning disorder (NVLD):** NVLD describes challenges with social skills, communication, and visual-spatial reasoning. While not an official diagnostic label, it's often applied when autistic traits are misinterpreted.

>> **Oppositional defiant disorder (ODD):** ODD involves patterns of anger, argumentativeness, or defiance. Autism is sometimes misdiagnosed as ODD when sensory overload, frustration, or meltdowns are mistaken for defiance.

Research shows that behaviors called "spirited" in white children are often labeled "defiant" in Black children, increasing the risk of ODD misdiagnosis.

If you suspect a misdiagnosis of ODD, request a reevaluation that considers sensory and communication traits, not just behavior. Seek professionals who understand how cultural differences affect diagnoses.

Regardless of the label — whether "autism" or something else — the goal is to help individuals understand and accept their traits.

In a 2020 interview with *The Today Show*, comedian Chris Rock shared his NVLD diagnosis after friends encouraged him to get assessed for autism. "I just always chalked it up to being famous," he said, attributing his social challenges to others acting nervously around celebrities. Rock's story underscores that self-awareness and acceptance, not labels, are the foundation for deeper understanding and support.

Common co-occurring conditions

Autistic individuals often have additional conditions called co-occurring conditions. Common ones include:

>> **ADHD (Attention-Deficit/Hyperactivity Disorder):** Diagnosed in 50 percent to 70 percent of autistic individuals, ADHD and autism share overlapping traits, including how the brain regulates attention, focus, and impulse control.

>> **Anxiety:** About 40 percent to 50 percent of autistic people experience anxiety, often tied to sensory overload, navigating unpredictable social situations, or other barriers.

>> **Allergies, autoimmune, and digestive issues:** Autistic individuals are more likely to experience these conditions, possibly due to genetic or immune factors.

>> **Dyspraxia (developmental coordination disorder):** Many autistic individuals show dyspraxic traits, including challenges with motor coordination and planning.

>> **Epilepsy:** Over 10 percent of autistic individuals experience epilepsy. While the exact cause is unclear, shared genetic or neurological factors may play a role.

>> **Intellectual disability (ID):** Around 30 percent of autistic individuals have ID, though autism occurs across all levels of intellectual ability.

- **Mood disorders:** Many autistic individuals experience mood disorders, such as depression, often linked to factors like social isolation and chronic stress.
- **PTSD (Post-Traumatic Stress Disorder):** Around 30 percent of autistic individuals experience PTSD from trauma caused by external pressures.
- **Sleep differences:** Up to 80 percent of autistic individuals face sleep differences, often due to melatonin differences, sensory sensitivities, anxiety, or circadian rhythm variations. Many are also "night owls" who naturally stay up late.
- **Tourette's:** Tourette's occurs in an estimated 4 percent to 8 percent of autistic people and shares some neurological pathways with autism, particularly those involved in movement control and dopamine regulation.

REMEMBER

Understanding co-occurring conditions results in better support for autistic individuals because you have a fuller profile of their needs and strengths.

Conditions with traits similar to autism

Some neurodivergent conditions share traits with autism but are distinct in their development. They include the following:

- **Fragile X syndrome:** A genetic condition characterized by developmental delays, social and communication challenges, and repetitive behaviors. Unlike autism, Fragile X has a specific genetic cause and can be diagnosed through genetic testing.
- **Rett syndrome:** A genetic condition in which children develop typically but later lose skills, especially motor abilities. It is diagnosable through genetic testing.

REMEMBER

While Fragile X and Rett syndrome share traits with autism, their distinct causes require tailored diagnoses and support. Understanding these differences ensures individuals receive the care they need.

Talking about Autism

The language we use shapes how we think about autism — and how we treat autistic people. Words and labels can either open doors to understanding or create barriers.

Honoring self-identity

Self-identity is personal, and the words autistic people use to describe themselves carry meaning. Some proudly say "autistic," embracing it as part of who they are. Others prefer "person with autism," focusing on their identity beyond the diagnosis. What matters most is respecting each person's choice.

TIP

Research shows most autistic people prefer identity-first language, like "autistic person." If you're unsure, this is a safe default. However, when talking with an autistic person, it's always best to ask how they prefer to be described.

Shannon Des Roches Rosa from *Thinking Person's Guide to Autism* offers this helpful advice: "What matters most is your intent and respect, not the words you use."

Discarding functioning labels

Imagine meeting someone who says they're autistic, and you ask, "Are you high or low functioning?" It's a common question, but it misses the point.

Each person has a unique mix of strengths and challenges that vary by situation. A person labeled "high functioning" might still need significant support, while someone labeled "low functioning" might have remarkable but unseen skills. Moving away from these labels helps us better understand autism and autistic people. Instead of "ranking" individuals, let's meet them where they are, recognize their strengths and challenges, and provide the support they need.

Rethinking "autism levels"

Autism is often described in levels: level 1 - minimal support, level 2 - moderate support, and level 3 - significant support. While these levels provide a quick snapshot, they don't reflect the full complexity of autism or the individual. Support needs can vary greatly by person and situation, as well as over time.

"Autism 'levels of support' are a useful tool in some ways, a sort of shortcut to understand if an autistic person has relatively higher or lower support needs at the time of their diagnosis," write Joy Gehner and Jennifer Mannheim in a blog post for Seattle Children's Hospital. "However, they don't tell us much about what their future will look like, or what specific supports each person needs to thrive."

Moving beyond "classic autism"

In 2013, labels like Asperger's and PDD-NOS were folded into the broader autism diagnosis. While this made sense, some people still use terms like "classic autism" to describe autistic people with more noticeable traits — often assuming they are less capable than they actually are. This language is limiting, as individuals with less visible traits also face significant challenges and often struggle to have their needs recognized and supported.

Stopping the slur of labeling people "severe"

Labeling autistic individuals as "severe," "severely autistic," or "profoundly autistic" is inaccurate and dehumanizing. These labels create stigma, foster low expectations, ignore strengths, and reinforce harmful stereotypes. In turn, they make it harder for individuals and families to get the understanding, acceptance, and support they desperately need.

Some families use this language to seek understanding and support for their autistic loved ones—and they deserve both, along with our empathy and acceptance for the realities they face. But on a broader level, these specific terms are most often deliberately and aggressively promoted by a small but vocal group of organized individuals pushing outdated beliefs and narrow agendas. In doing so, they regularly use these labels to dismiss autistic voices as incapable or unworthy of speaking about autism, including those they describe as "profound" or "severe."

TIP

Instead of using terms like "severe," focus on understanding each autistic person as an individual and providing support tailored to their needs.

Talking about "treatment"

When people talk about "treating" autism, it's important to know why that term is misleading. Autism isn't a disease or illness that can be "fixed." Calling support approaches "treatment" suggests autism can be cured, which simply isn't true.

WARNING

The word *treatment* is also a favorite of scam artists pushing fake remedies to exploit families. Be careful when you hear it.

Putting a stop to "interventions"

The term *intervention* (or *autism intervention*) is often used by professionals to describe programs, therapies, or services designed to help autistic people. While support is important, calling these services "interventions" can be stigmatizing. Many of these services are also provided to nonautistic people, but the term "intervention" is mostly applied to autistic clients. Let's drop the label and simply call it what it is — support or therapy — just as we do for everyone else.

Adding in some joy

Autism is often discussed only in terms of challenges, but that's an incomplete picture. It's just as important to recognize and celebrate the joy, strengths, and unique perspectives that autistic people bring to their own lives and the lives of others. Autistic joy may be expressed through a passion for a hobby, noticing details others miss, or sharing a unique perspective. Autistic adults often share these moments on social media using *#AutisticJoy*. Regardless of the way someone demonstrates it, autistic joy is real and worth celebrating.

Chapter **2**

Someone You Know Is Autistic

Autistic people are everywhere — friends, neighbors, classmates, and family members — contributing in ways that often go unnoticed but make a real difference. They might be the neighbor who organizes a community garden, the student who finds a creative solution for a school fundraiser, or the family member who offers fresh perspectives on household challenges.

These everyday moments remind us that autistic people are — *well*, people. Just as ordinary as anyone else, with jobs, hobbies, relationships, and quirks. Autistic people don't need to be extraordinary to matter, yet the contributions of some have shaped not only the lives of those who know and love them but also the world itself. And through study and research, we're beginning to understand just how profound that impact has been.

Although we can't retroactively diagnose historical figures, many who shaped our world displayed traits often associated with autism. These include scientists like Benjamin Banneker, Marie Curie, Leonardo da Vinci, Isaac Newton, and Nikola Tesla. Historians have also noted autistic traits in artists such as Michelangelo, Mozart, Andy Warhol, and Tom Wiggins, as well as writers like Hans Christian Andersen, Jorge Luis Borges, Lewis Carroll, Emily Dickinson, and Phillis Wheatley.

Today, many openly autistic individuals are shaping the world in remarkable ways. And while it would be fun to rattle off a list of autistic celebrities and public figures, we don't do that here, you'll find them quoted and referenced in various places throughout this book to show just how varied and impactful their contributions are.

In this chapter, we explore autism's presence throughout history, its influence on society today, and how we can build a future that embraces and celebrates autistic people.

Recognizing Autism's History

Picture this: Thousands of years ago, a small group of early humans gathers around the fire. While the others chat, one person sits off to the side, quietly observing the animals, categorizing them, and noting their movements. They've done this countless times before, spotting patterns others miss — when the herds arrive, how they graze, and how small shifts in behavior signal a storm or change in the weather. Over time, the group has learned to rely on these observations for food, safety, and planning, even if they don't fully understand the person's intense focus or social distance.

Then, suddenly, the observer starts to stim — shaking their arms and rocking their body back and forth. The others notice the shift in energy and follow their gaze. A lion lurks near the camp, eyeing an injured member resting a little too far from the safety of the crowd. The group jumps to their feet, shouting and making noise to drive the predator away, grateful for the life-saving warning.

Scientists believe autistic traits like intense focus, pattern recognition, and attention to detail may have played important roles in early human societies. These skills could have contributed to survival tasks such as identifying edible plants, mapping migration patterns, or innovating tools. Gene variations linked to autism (see Chapter 1 for more) are seen in people from every country, indicating that these traits are ancient and have been part of humanity for at least tens of thousands of years. Autism isn't new or localized; it's a natural and enduring part of the human experience.

These ancient gene variations are thought to reflect the value of diverse cognitive strengths in human communities. Traits associated with autism, such as heightened attention to detail or innovative thinking, may have allowed individuals to contribute uniquely to problem-solving and adaptation. While the exact role autism has played in human development is still being studied, neurodivergent traits like those linked to autism have clearly influenced the evolution of human societies in meaningful ways.

But as human societies grew and became more structured, these unique traits most likely became harder to navigate. Rigid roles and social expectations often clashed with autistic ways of doing things. Misunderstandings about socializing or communication created barriers, pushing many autistic individuals to society's margins.

Throughout history, autistic people have faced rejection, mistreatment, and cruelty, even as society benefited from their unique talents. Among them was Alan Turing, whose code-breaking work is credited with shortening World War II by up to two years, potentially saving an estimated 14 million lives. Despite his contributions, he was persecuted for his differences — excluded, misunderstood, and unfairly treated, ultimately leading to his tragic and early death.

"A genius, a savior, but he was also autistic," said British naturalist and TV presenter Chris Packham, announcing Alan Turing as the winner of the title *The Greatest Person of the 20th Century* following a UK-wide public vote. "So, we betrayed him and drove him to suicide."

Even today, society creates major challenges for autistic people by failing to understand, accept, and support them. Rigid schools and workplaces hinder thriving, while pressure to conform leads to exclusion and loneliness. Navigating environments not built for them often causes anxiety, stress, and exhaustion.

This is especially true for nonspeaking autistic individuals and those who need more help, where misconceptions, low expectations, communication barriers, and a lack of available accommodations can deepen isolation. As a result, too often, people fail to recognize that autistic individuals, regardless of their abilities or need for support, are ordinary people, just like everyone else.

Fortunately, things are changing. We're realizing that human brains don't all work the same, and that's okay. (Read more on that in Chapter 1.) This means we're beginning to appreciate autistic people for who they are and recognize the contributions they make to our world — including Alan Turing, whose name and face were added to the UK's £50 banknote in 2021.

And the contributions autistic people make to society aren't just about the big things — the scientific breakthroughs, the breathtaking art, the world-changing ideas. We're also starting to recognize the everyday impact that ordinary autistic people contribute each day in our families, workplaces, communities, and schools.

This shift is also helping us recognize another historically misunderstood and under supported group: the amazing parents, caregivers, and families of autistic people. For too long, their incredible efforts have been overlooked and underappreciated, despite lifetimes of supporting their loved ones through the challenges they face.

We don't know all the details of autism's impact on history, but we're learning more every day — how society shapes the autistic experience and how autistic people shape the world. While learning about the past is fascinating, it's even more exciting to shape a future where all minds can thrive.

Appreciating Autism's Benefits

Autism brings immense value to our world, often in ways we don't immediately recognize. From innovative problem-solving to a strong sense of fairness, passion, and authenticity, autistic people contribute uniquely and powerfully to society. These strengths improve relationships, communities, and even how we understand the world. Let's look at some of the remarkable ways autism makes our world better.

Innovative problem-solving

Autism fuels much-needed innovation — not just through major inventions or scientific breakthroughs (though those are pretty cool) but also in the everyday challenges of life.

Autistic individuals often notice details and connections others miss, leading to fresh ideas and creative solutions. They might organize a space more effectively, improve a process, or adapt a tool for a specific need — at work or at home.

For too long, we've misunderstood many expressions of this type of problem-solving. Take an autistic person who needs a great deal of support with activities of daily living — who might cleverly arrange their environment to make daily tasks easier, like organizing items by sensory preference. A caregiver might misinterpret this as a rigid habit and try to correct it, instead of seeing it as a brilliant and practical adaptation to life.

TIP

When you see an autistic person tackling a task in a way you think is "wrong" or don't understand, pause and ask yourself, "Is this really a problem, or just a different way of solving one?"

Passion fuels progress

Autistic passion drives extraordinary contributions. When someone deeply focuses on a topic — like coding, animals, art, or trains — that passion fuels expertise, creativity, and innovation. Such hyperfocus and dedication help uncover insights and solutions others might miss.

This passion benefits more than industries or academia. It shapes everyday life. An autistic gardener might develop eco-friendly methods embraced by others. Someone fascinated by systems could improve a library's organization. This ability to stay deeply engaged helps autistic people push boundaries, refine ideas, and drive progress.

Supporting autistic people in their passions benefits everyone through the incredible work and discoveries that follow. Encouraging these focused interests, especially in autistic children, nurtures potential and invests in a future shaped by their brilliance.

Some much-needed clarity

Autistic people often value directness, honesty, and clarity, fostering meaningful interactions and reducing misunderstandings. An autistic coworker might flag inconsistencies that prevent mistakes, or a friend might offer honest feedback others are too afraid to give. Their straightforwardness strengthens teamwork, relationships, and problem-solving by highlighting inconsistencies and offering honest feedback.

In her 2019 Netflix comedy special *Growing*, actor and comedian Amy Schumer reflects on how her husband Chris Fischer's autistic honesty adds both humor and value to their relationship. "He says *whatever* is on his mind," Schumer jokes, sharing that if she asks him if a dress looks bad, hoping for a compliment, he'll bluntly reply, "Yeah! You have a lot of other clothes — why don't you wear those?"

This directness can feel jarring if you're not used to it, but it's a beautiful way to connect — rooted in clarity, authenticity, and care. Autistic communication has long been misunderstood or undervalued, but embracing it fosters genuine, straightforward connections.

TIP

The next time someone skips small talk or gives you unfiltered feedback, consider it a gift. It's their way of ensuring things are clear, honest, and moving in the right direction. It's also a reminder that you are valued enough for them to be genuine with you, and that's pretty great.

A fairer world

Autistic people often have a strong sense of fairness and justice, driving positive change. They may advocate for equality, challenge injustice, or promote fairness in group activities. For example, in friendships, this helps make plans more inclusive. At school, they often stand up for mistreated classmates and foster respect. At home, they may encourage a fairer division of responsibilities.

Dedication to fairness may be misunderstood as being "too rigid" or "too serious," but it stems from a deep desire to make things better for everyone. By appreciating this sense of justice, we can build stronger relationships, more inclusive communities, and a society that treats everyone fairly.

Encouraging authenticity

Autistic people have a remarkable ability to be themselves, often challenging social norms and inspiring others to think differently. In a world obsessed with fitting in, autistic authenticity is a refreshing reminder that connection doesn't require conformity.

This authenticity benefits society in countless ways. At school, it encourages classmates to embrace individuality. In friendships, it fosters deeper connections. At home, it sparks meaningful conversations. Sometimes, being true to oneself means breaking unspoken rules or questioning them — and that's often how progress begins.

Chapter **3**

Diagnosing Autism

Understanding the process of diagnosing autism can be a lot to take in, and it's totally okay to feel a bit anxious or uncertain about it. This chapter is here to help make things clearer and less intimidating, giving you a straightforward guide to what's involved.

Whether you're a parent trying to get a diagnosis for your child, an adult wondering about your own neurodivergence, or a professional looking to learn more, we walk you through each step of the journey. We start by talking about the early signs of autism and how to get a professional evaluation. Then, we dive into the different tools and criteria that specialists use, like the DSM-5 and ICD-11, to make a diagnosis.

We also explain the roles of various healthcare providers in this process and how to navigate any potential challenges that may come up. By the end of this chapter, you should have a solid understanding of how autism is diagnosed and feel more confident about moving forward, whether for yourself or someone you care about. This process can feel big and scary, but you've got this — and we're here to help guide you through it.

Understanding the Diagnostic Process

The process of diagnosing autism often starts with an initial screening, usually prompted by observations from parents, caregivers, or teachers who notice unique behaviors or developmental differences in a child. Adults may pursue a screening because of things they've noticed from their own reflections or because they've been nudged by family or friends who care about them. During this stage, a healthcare provider, like a pediatrician or general practitioner, may use a quick assessment tool to see if further evaluation is needed.

If the screening suggests that autism may be a possibility, the next step is a comprehensive evaluation by a specialist — someone like a developmental pediatrician, psychologist, or neurologist. This evaluation digs deep, looking at the person's developmental history and directly observing how they behave and communicate. For children, parents or caregivers are asked about things like early development, social interactions, communication styles, and any repetitive behaviors or sensory sensitivities. Adults may be asked about their current life experiences and what they remember from childhood.

The specialist may also use standardized tools like the Autism Diagnostic Observation Schedule (ADOS) or the Autism Diagnostic Interview-Revised (ADI-R). These assessments are designed to be interactive and engaging to give the evaluator a better understanding of the person's unique strengths and challenges. The information gathered is then compared to the criteria listed in diagnostic manuals used by professionals. Ultimately, the specialist decides whether the individual meets the criteria for an autism diagnosis.

REMEMBER

The goal of an autism evaluation is to understand the person as a whole, not just go through a checklist. After the assessment, the specialist will review the findings directly with the individual — if they are seeking the diagnosis for themselves — or, when appropriate, with parents, caregivers, or other trusted supporters. The diagnosis should be explained in a way that's clear, respectful, and easy to understand, based on what works best for the person being evaluated. This conversation should also include recommendations for resources and support that fit the individual's needs — helping them, and those in their life, move forward with confidence.

Understanding Diagnostic Criteria

Let's break down what healthcare professionals look for when assessing someone for autism. The diagnostic process involves a thorough evaluation that looks at key areas of behavior and development.

First, they look at how the individual typically communicates and socializes. They assess differences in how someone understands and uses verbal and nonverbal communication, which may include things like engaging in conversations, interpreting body language, and using eye contact. The person's preferences for interacting with others may also be considered.

Next, the evaluator examines patterns of behavior that are often seen in autistic individuals. This includes repetitive behaviors like hand-flapping or organizing objects in specific ways, as well as having strong interests in particular topics or activities. Sensory sensitivities are also considered, such as being sensitive to sounds, lights, or textures.

Let's break down the differences and life experiences that medical professionals consider during the autism diagnostic process:

>> **Communication and social differences:** Autistic people communicate and socialize in ways that are often different from neurotypical people. They build connections, express themselves, and navigate social interactions in ways that feel natural to them, even if their approach doesn't always align with neurotypical expectations. This may include differences in how they use and interpret language, gestures, and tone of voice, as well as how they engage in conversations, interpret social cues, or share interests with others.

>> **Behavioral differences:** Autistic individuals may engage in movements like hand-flapping or rocking, or they may repeat words or phrases, which can be self-soothing or expressive. Many develop deep, passionate interests in specific topics, leading to impressive expertise. They may also stick to routines or rituals, which provides a comforting sense of structure and predictability.

>> **Sensory differences:** Autistic individuals often experience the world through unique sensory perspectives, with heightened sensitivity to sounds, lights, textures, or tastes. These sensory differences can lead to a vivid sensory awareness, where certain stimuli are perceived more intensely.

>> **Impact on daily life:** The traits of autism shape daily life, influencing how someone engages in activities and with others. These traits affect how autistic individuals interact with the world and navigate challenges. While anyone may experience a few traits associated with autism, autistic people often experience a combination of many, creating a distinct impact on their daily lives.

>> **Not explained by other conditions:** These differences aren't better explained by intellectual disability or general developmental delay. Autism and intellectual disabilities can co-occur, but an autism diagnosis focuses on how these traits fit within a person's overall development.

> **Traits present from early childhood:** Autistic traits usually appear in early childhood, highlighting a unique developmental path. Even if they become more noticeable over time, they're part of their developmental trajectory from the start.

WARNING

This whole process should be about understanding the individual — not just labeling them. It's about recognizing the unique ways they experience the world and finding the best ways to support them. If the evaluation process feels off or like a "check-the-box" approach at any point, it's absolutely okay to seek a second opinion. Getting a second opinion can ensure that the evaluation truly reflects the individual's unique experiences and needs, leading to more personalized and effective support.

Understanding flaws in current criteria

The criteria that professionals use to diagnose autism have significant flaws. They focus exclusively on perceived deficits rather than understanding autistic traits as natural variations in thinking, communication, and behavior that can be experienced as challenges or strengths depending on context in the modern world. This framing shapes how professionals assess and diagnose autism — often causing them to misinterpret different expressions of autistic traits or overlook a person's strengths.

Because these criteria focus on outward behaviors, they don't always account for cultural and personal differences in communication, social norms, and expression. For example, in some cultures, avoiding eye contact is seen as respectful, while in others, it might be viewed as a social difficulty. This can lead to misunderstandings in how autism is recognized and diagnosed in autistic people from different cultural backgrounds. (For more on this, see Chapter 17.)

REMEMBER

The goal of a diagnosis should be to understand a person's traits, needs, and strengths — not label or limit them. Nor should it be about measuring them against nonautistic norms or viewing them as a flawed version of someone they are not.

Predicting how criteria evolve from here

As the understanding of autism grows, diagnostic criteria will likely change to better capture the full spectrum of autistic experiences. Future updates may shift from focusing on perceived deficits to highlighting individual strengths and unique ways of thinking. This shift could reduce stigma and create a clearer, more accurate understanding of what it means to be autistic.

Criteria may also become more flexible and adaptable across cultures. Since behaviors and traits are interpreted differently around the world, future guidelines could take a more nuanced approach, helping ensure that autistic people from all backgrounds receive accurate and respectful evaluations.

Advances in neuroscience and genetics may also play a role in refining diagnostic tools. As we learn more about the biological aspects of autism, we could develop more precise methods for identifying it — maybe through biomarkers or advanced imaging techniques. But it's important to remember that these methods are most likely a long way off, or they may not happen at all.

Additionally, including direct input from autistic individuals in the development of diagnostic criteria can make them more accurate (we dive into that more in Chapter 22). We expect autistic subject matter experts — like autistic autism researchers and medical professionals — to be involved in future revisions, ensuring that diagnostic standards better reflect lived experiences.

REMEMBER

Diagnostic criteria should move toward a clearer, more accurate understanding of autism. This means shifting away from deficit-based framing and recognizing autism as a natural way of thinking, communicating, and experiencing the world — where traits can be strengths or challenges depending on the context.

Understanding Assessment Methods

Accurately diagnosing autism involves observing an individual and comparing what is observed to various assessment methods. These tools provide criteria that help healthcare professionals identify autism, but they're not perfect. There are also other methods and guidelines used around the world that play an important role in the diagnostic process.

DSM-5

The *Diagnostic and Statistical Manual of Mental Disorders,* Fifth Edition (DSM-5), is commonly used in the United States and many other countries to diagnose autism. The DSM-5 focuses on unique differences in social communication and interaction, along with distinct patterns of behavior, interests, or activities. It requires that these traits be present from early childhood and have a significant impact on daily life. The DSM-5 also recognizes that autism is a spectrum, which means it acknowledges the wide range of experiences and abilities among autistic people, and it celebrates their diverse ways of thinking and being. (For more on what we mean by *spectrum*, turn to Chapter 4.)

Other tools

The *International Classification of Diseases*, Eleventh Revision (ICD–11), is another major diagnostic tool used globally, especially in countries like the United Kingdom, Canada, Australia, and many European nations. Like the DSM-5, the ICD–11 outlines criteria for identifying autism, focusing on unique social communication styles and distinct patterns of behavior. However, it also considers cultural context and individual differences, recognizing that autism can be expressed in many ways.

Other diagnostic tools are used in different parts of the world. For example, in China, the *Chinese Classification of Mental Disorders* (CCMD), which has its own criteria for diagnosing autism, is often used. These tools, along with others, are tailored to specific regions or populations, reflecting the various ways autism is understood and recognized around the world.

DSM and ICD definitions of autism

The *Diagnostic and Statistical Manual of Mental Disorders* (DSM–5–TR) is the main tool doctors and specialists use to diagnose autism in the U.S. and some other countries. It defines autism based on two key areas:

» Persistent deficits in social communication and social interaction across multiple contexts, as manifested by all of the following, currently or by history:

- *Deficits in social-emotional reciprocity* (for example, difficulty with back-and-forth conversation, reduced sharing of interests or emotions, failure to initiate or respond to social interactions)

- *Deficits in nonverbal communicative behaviors* (for example, poorly integrated verbal and nonverbal communication, difficulty with eye contact and body language, trouble understanding gestures, lack of facial expressions)

- *Deficits in developing, maintaining, and understanding relationships* (for example, difficulty adjusting behavior to fit social contexts, trouble making friends, lack of interest in peers)

» Restricted, repetitive patterns of behavior, interests, or activities, as manifested by at least two of the following:

- *Stereotyped or repetitive movements, speech, or object use* (for example, hand-flapping, echolalia, lining up toys, repeating phrases)

- *Insistence on sameness, inflexible routines, or ritualized patterns of behavior* (for example, distress at small changes, rigid thinking, needing the same daily routine)

- *Highly restricted, fixated interests that are intense or focused* (for example, strong attachment to or focus on specific topics, objects, or activities)

- *Hyper- or hyporeactivity to sensory input* (for example, indifference to pain/temperature; extreme reactions to sounds, smells, or textures; fascination with lights or movement)

For an autism diagnosis, these traits must be present in early development, even if they become more noticeable later; significantly impact daily life, social, or work settings; and not be better explained by another condition.

If this description feels a little off compared to how we talk about autism in this book, that's because the DSM frames autism as a set of deficits — things a person lacks compared to the nonautistic majority. This language and framing are outdated, but because major revisions happen only every 10 to 20 years, the DSM's definition of autism lags behind modern scientific understanding. Future editions are expected to adopt more accurate language and an updated perspective that better represents autistic experiences.

That said, knowing the official wording can be useful when seeking a diagnosis for yourself or your child. Doctors, schools, and support services rely on DSM language, so understanding how autism is described in that context can help you advocate more effectively and access the right support.

In many other countries, including the United Kingdom, Canada, and Australia, doctors use the *International Classification of Diseases* (ICD-11) instead, which defines autism similarly but with a broader, more flexible approach to diagnosis.

Benefiting from Early Diagnosis

Early diagnosis of autism offers a range of benefits that can greatly improve the quality of life for autistic individuals and their families. When autism is identified early, children can receive support that helps with their development and learning. Early diagnosis allows for personalized educational plans, therapies, and services that cater to an individual's unique strengths and needs.

REMEMBER

For families, early diagnosis provides valuable information and resources that help them understand and advocate for their child's needs. It can also lead to better social and communication skills, reduce the risk of co-occurring mental health issues, and foster a positive self-identity. By recognizing and supporting autistic individuals from a young age, we can help them thrive and reach their full potential.

"One of the reasons my son is doing as well as he is, is because we got early, appropriate, and individualized interventions," says Shannon Des Roches Rosa, founder of the neurodiversity-affirming online community *The Thinking Person's Guide to Autism* in an interview with *The Kelsey*. "I can't stress enough how important it is to act early and get your child the support they need as soon as possible."

HOW EARLY DIAGNOSIS CAN SOMETIMES HURT (AND HOW TO GET AROUND IT)

While early autism diagnosis has many benefits, it can also bring some unintended challenges. One of the biggest issues is the risk of lowered expectations from parents, educators, and society at large. When a child is diagnosed early, people may start to make assumptions about their abilities and needs, often focusing more on what they can't do rather than what they can. This can lead to the child being treated with less independence and autonomy, which may hold them back from reaching their full potential and damage their self-esteem.

Another challenge is the emotional strain that an early diagnosis can place on parents and caregivers. It's common for families to feel overwhelmed or anxious after a diagnosis, especially if they don't have the right information, resources, and support. This can sometimes lead to parents becoming overprotective or excessively focused on their child's perceived limitations, which may cause isolation from family and friends and further stress.

But here's the good news: There are ways to avoid these pitfalls. A strengths-based approach is key. This means focusing on the individual's unique abilities and setting high expectations for what they can achieve. Encouraging independence, promoting self-advocacy, and fostering a positive, inclusive environment can help ensure that an early diagnosis leads to empowerment and growth.

Parents can play a crucial role in making sure that an early diagnosis becomes a benefit, not a limitation. They can start by educating themselves about autism and embracing a neurodiversity-affirming perspective that values their child's unique ways of thinking and interacting with the world. Connecting with other families, support groups, and autism communities can provide valuable insights and reduce feelings of isolation.

Additionally, parents should advocate for their child's right to independence and opportunities that allow them to explore their strengths. This may involve working closely with educators to develop personalized learning plans that focus on what the child enjoys and excels at, rather than simply addressing areas of difficulty.

Creating an environment that encourages exploration and self-expression is key. By allowing their child to take risks, make choices, and learn from experiences, parents can help build confidence and resilience. It's also important for parents to regularly reassess their own expectations, ensuring they are pushing their child to achieve their best while providing the support they need to succeed.

For parents and caregivers, adopting this positive approach can make a big difference too. It can reduce anxiety by shifting the focus from limitations to strengths and can foster a sense of empowerment as they watch their child progress and succeed. This not only strengthens family bonds but also creates a more supportive and encouraging environment for everyone involved.

So, while early diagnosis can present some challenges, with the right mindset, education, and support, it can be a powerful tool for helping autistic individuals — and their families — thrive.

Addressing Diagnostic Barriers

Understanding and overcoming the barriers to autism diagnosis is crucial for ensuring that individuals receive the support they need. In this section, we explore common obstacles that can make getting a diagnosis challenging, such as lack of understanding, stigma, limited access to specialists, cost and insurance issues, geographic barriers, late recognition, and systemic barriers.

By recognizing these challenges, individuals and their families can better navigate the diagnostic process, find alternative solutions, and advocate for more accessible and inclusive services. Empowering yourself with this knowledge can make a significant difference in getting a timely and accurate diagnosis, ultimately leading to better support and a more positive experience.

Lack of understanding

One of the biggest barriers to obtaining an autism diagnosis is the general lack of understanding about the condition. Many people, including some healthcare professionals, may not fully grasp the diverse ways autism can present itself. This can lead to misdiagnosis or delayed diagnosis, especially in individuals who don't fit the stereotypical image of autism.

TIP

To combat this, individuals and families can seek out educational resources on autism, such as books, online courses, and support groups. Engaging with communities, both online and offline, can provide valuable insights and shared experiences that enhance understanding. For medical professionals, increasing education and awareness about the wide range of autistic experiences is crucial for improving early and accurate diagnosis. For a deeper dive into this, turn to Chapter 18.

Stigma

Stigma surrounding autism can discourage individuals and families from seeking a diagnosis. Misconceptions and negative attitudes about autism are major obstacles, and the fear of being labeled or misunderstood may lead to reluctance in pursuing evaluation and support.

Ranga on our author team shares that, when his son was diagnosed with autism while in college, he and his wife chose to embrace him as a unique creation of the Universe and focus on how to best support his life journey. Stigma about autism is quite prevalent in the Indian community and they decided to be very open about their son's diagnosis to help reduce that stigma.

TIP

Reducing stigma through education and promoting a neurodiversity-affirming perspective is essential. Sharing personal stories and family experiences can also help. By participating in advocacy groups, engaging in community education, and using social media to spread awareness, we can create a more inclusive environment and break down the barriers that stigma creates.

Access to specialists

Access to specialists trained in diagnosing autism is a significant barrier worldwide, with challenges varying by country. Many areas face a shortage of professionals with the expertise for thorough and accurate assessments, leading to long waiting times and limited options for those seeking a diagnosis.

In the United States, this shortage often results in delays for evaluations, especially in rural areas. Variability in insurance coverage further complicates access, as some plans may not fully cover autism evaluations or related services. Telehealth has become a helpful solution, enabling remote consultations with specialists, which is crucial in areas lacking local expertise. In the United Kingdom, the universal healthcare by National Health Service (NHS) is under strain, leading to long wait times exceeding two years for diagnosis, significantly delaying access to necessary support.

These barriers are not unique to the U.K. and U.S. In other countries, especially in regions with less developed healthcare infrastructure, the shortage of trained specialists can be even more pronounced, with fewer solutions available. Expanding the training of general healthcare providers to better recognize and diagnose autism could improve access to diagnostic services across different healthcare systems, ensuring more individuals receive timely diagnoses regardless of their location.

Geographic barriers

Geographic barriers in rural or remote areas often limit access to diagnostic services, causing delays or missed diagnoses. Telehealth has become a crucial solution, enabling remote evaluations and consultations with specialists. This technology allows for assessments without requiring long-distance travel, making it especially valuable where specialists are scarce.

Some regions have introduced mobile clinics or outreach programs to bring diagnostic services to underserved areas. These mobile units, staffed by trained professionals, offer on-site evaluations, consultations, and follow-up care. For example, in the U.K., mobile units visit rural communities to help individuals who may otherwise face long waits or travel challenges.

Efforts to improve access include expanding training for general healthcare providers to perform initial screenings and assessments for autism, easing the burden on specialists and shortening waiting times. Additionally, governments and organizations are increasingly advocating for policy changes and funding to support these initiatives, making diagnostic services more accessible. By combining telehealth, mobile clinics, and expanded training, significant progress is being made in reducing geographic barriers to autism diagnostic services. However, ongoing investment and innovation are essential to fully address these challenges.

Cost and insurance

The cost of diagnosis can be prohibitive, and insurance coverage often varies. To navigate this, individuals can explore community resources, nonprofit organizations, and government programs that offer financial assistance or low-cost diagnostic services. Advocating for better insurance coverage and understanding your insurance policy can also help manage costs.

Many school systems provide no-cost assessments for children. Some colleges and universities provide them to their enrolled students as well.

TIP

Late recognition

Many autistic people grow up without realizing they are autistic. Perhaps their traits are misunderstood, or they've been misinterpreted by medical professionals as indicating another condition. Thus, many may go through life without a diagnosis, missing out on crucial support and understanding.

TIP

Raising awareness about the diverse presentations of autism, improving diagnostic tools, and modernizing diagnostic criteria can help. (See Chapter 18.) Adults seeking their own diagnosis can improve their experience by educating themselves about autism using internet resources and documenting their strengths and challenges to share with providers. (You can find a list of resources at www. pivotdiversity.com/resources.)

Cultural barriers

Cultural differences can affect how autism is recognized and diagnosed. In some cultures, behaviors like avoiding eye contact or small talk may be seen as normal or respectful, causing delays in seeking a diagnosis. In places where there's strong stigma around developmental differences, families may hesitate to pursue evaluation due to fear of social backlash.

Dr. Sandra Waxman, a developmental psychologist at Northwestern University, explains, "In most European-American families, children are encouraged to make eye contact, but this isn't universal. In some cultures, direct eye contact is seen as disrespectful, especially between children and adults."

TIP

To improve the diagnostic process, seek healthcare providers who understand and respect diverse cultural backgrounds. Educating yourself about how autism can present differently across cultures and advocating for assessments that consider these variations can make a big difference.

Gender barriers

A lack of understanding about gender expressions and differences can significantly hinder autism diagnosis. Historically, diagnostic criteria have been based on research mainly involving males, which may explain why autism is diagnosed four times more often in males than in females. Autistic girls and women may display different traits, like a stronger ability to mask or camouflage their differences in social situations, leading to their challenges being overlooked or misunderstood.

"If I had a pound for every time someone said, 'Oh! But you don't look autistic,' I'd be a millionaire by now," British autism advocate Dr. Carly Danesh-Jones,

MBE, told *The Guardian* in 2021. Danesh-Jones, who was awarded a Member of the Order of the British Empire (MBE) in 2016 for her advocacy on behalf of autistic women and girls, emphasizes that gender barriers were a significant reason she didn't receive her autism diagnosis until she was 32. She also shared how her autistic daughters faced similar challenges, recalling how a head teacher once pulled her aside and said, "'Autism only happens in boys, yet you profess to have two autistic girls,' basically calling me a liar — and that was really painful."

Raising awareness about gender differences in autism can lead to more accurate diagnoses. Danesh-Jones's advocacy highlights how challenging misconceptions can push for more inclusive diagnostic practices. Seeking culturally competent healthcare providers and understanding how autism presents across gender presentations help ensure fair and accurate diagnoses for everyone.

Systemic barriers

Diagnosing autism is often made more difficult by biases in healthcare practices, unequal distribution of services, and insufficient support for diverse populations. Marginalized communities, for example, frequently experience delayed or missed diagnoses because the people in those communities don't match the typical autistic profile. Underfunding of autism services also restricts access to crucial diagnostic resources.

Addressing these challenges requires collective efforts — advocating for policy changes, increasing funding, and ensuring healthcare practices are fair and inclusive. These steps are crucial for making the diagnostic process more accessible and equitable for everyone (more on that in Chapter 21).

When a Diagnosis Isn't Possible

If you think you or your child may be autistic but can't get a formal diagnosis right now, don't worry; there are still ways to get support. Start by educating yourself with reliable online resources to better understand autism, recognize traits, and find strategies that work. Connecting with online support groups and forums can provide valuable advice and emotional support from others who've been in similar situations. For starting points, find a list of resources at www.pivotdiversity.com/resources.

Additionally, focus on practical accommodations that can make everyday life easier. Simple adjustments like creating sensory-friendly spaces or using visual schedules can have a big impact. Remember, while a formal diagnosis is helpful, understanding and support are what truly matter for you or your child.

Chapter **4**

Understanding Autistic Traits

Autistic traits are the unique ways autistic people think, feel, and interact with the world. These traits — like sensory sensitivity, intense focus, or a preference for routine — aren't just challenges; they're also strengths that shape how autistic individuals connect with others, solve problems, and express themselves. By understanding these traits, you can appreciate the diversity of autism better and learn how to create environments where autistic people can thrive.

In this chapter, we talk about the reasons to appreciate autistic traits, how the autistic brain thinks and makes sense of its world, and how the autistic brain helps autistic people process their senses in vivid ways, feel emotions deeply, and communicate and connect with others.

WARNING

This chapter provides a general overview of common autistic traits, but it's important to remember there's much more nuance to how autistic traits are expressed or experienced than we have room to cover here. Traits can vary depending on the individual and context, and they may change over time or not show up at all in some autistic people. It's essential to keep this in mind to avoid oversimplifying autism and to ensure each autistic person is seen for who they truly are, with their own unique experiences, strengths, and needs.

A 2023 Drexel University study found that 41 percent of TikTok videos with the hashtag #autism were inaccurate, while 32 percent overgeneralized autism. This shows how easily stereotypes and oversimplifications can emerge, leading to misunderstanding, stigma, and misrepresentation of autistic people.

REMEMBER

That's why it's so important to approach the traits discussed in this chapter with nuance and openness. Each autistic person is unique, so understanding their traits means recognizing them as individuals, not stereotypes. Keep this in mind as you read, and you'll be better equipped to appreciate the full depth and diversity of autistic experiences.

Understanding Spectrum Conditions

When you hear *autism spectrum*, you might imagine a straight line with "a little autistic" on one end and "a lot autistic" on the other. It's a common idea, but it doesn't truly reflect how the spectrum works. Autism isn't a simple line; it's more like a swirling galaxy, full of pinpoints of light, each representing an autistic trait. And each autistic person forms their own unique constellation within this galaxy of stars.

This circular spectrum reflects the wide range of traits and experiences that make up autism. It's not a scale from mild to severe. Instead, think of it as a big, round menu. If you're not autistic, you might recognize a few items. However, autistic people will relate to many of the menu items, but the specific combination familiar to each autistic person will be unique.

It's understandable that people might still find it difficult to not think of the autism spectrum as a straight line. To help, let's look at another spectrum condition: epilepsy.

Epilepsy is a spectrum condition because it includes a wide variety of seizure types, triggers, and intensities. For example, one person with epilepsy might have mild seizures triggered by flashing lights, another might experience severe seizures with no clear trigger, and yet another might only have seizures during sleep. Yet all of these individuals are epileptic, sharing a similar experience despite their individual traits.

Autism works the same way. It's not about being "more" or "less" autistic; it's about the unique combination of traits that makes each autistic person who they are. Autistic people may share traits, but those traits can appear very differently from person to person. They can also shift and change over time and in different situations, creating unique "shimmers" within each person's constellation that reflect their traits at any given moment.

As you move through this chapter, keep in mind that the autistic traits discussed form part of the swirling galaxy we described. Each trait — sensory sensitivity, communication differences, or unique ways of thinking and moving — can appear differently for every autistic person, or may not shine at all.

In this chapter, we talk in generalities, so remember that each individual's combination of traits is unique, like their own constellation in the sky. Yet there's a shared brilliance — a common experience — that gathers autistic people together among the stars. If neurotypical traits and people form a galaxy called Andromeda, then autistic people are the Milky Way.

Appreciating Autistic Traits

Autistic traits are valuable parts of how autistic people connect, solve problems, and experience the world. Recognizing and understanding these traits helps you better support autistic individuals in meaningful and practical ways.

Autistic traits throughout life

Autistic traits last a lifetime, but how an autistic person experiences them can evolve over time. Age, environment, stress levels, and personal growth all play a role in shaping how traits are expressed.

A parent of an autistic child might meet an autistic adult and think, "Wow, you're not anything like my child!" Naturally, a 40-year-old autistic person will express their traits differently than someone who is 4 or 14 years old. As autistic people grow older, their life experiences, learning, growth, and environments shape how their autistic traits show up.

Understanding challenges in context

Challenges often arise when the environment doesn't meet an autistic person's needs, not because of a flaw in the individual. Sensory overload in a crowded room or difficulty with constant change aren't personal failings — they're mismatches between a person's traits, surroundings, and interactions.

Recognizing these challenges shifts the focus to practical solutions and away from "fixing" the person. Small adjustments, like offering flexibility or rethinking expectations, can make a big difference in helping autistic people feel supported and comfortable.

Seeing the whole person

Autistic people have traits beyond their autism — interests, talents, and qualities that make them unique. They might be amazing storytellers, skilled athletes, or deeply passionate about music. While these traits can be influenced by autism, they also stand on their own.

It's important not to assume a person's every challenge or reaction is "because of autism." Like anyone else, autistic people have preferences, quirks, and personalities that are simply part of being human. Oversimplifying their experiences misses the bigger picture.

Appreciating the value of understanding

Understanding autistic traits helps you appreciate how autistic people think, feel, and act. Instead of seeing someone as "overreacting" to loud noises or bright lights, understanding helps you see that their sensory world is often more intense than you and others realize. This same understanding highlights autistic strengths like intense focus, attention to detail, and deep passion, which enrich families, workplaces, and communities.

TIP

Here's a bonus for the nonautistic reader: Understanding autistic traits can help you reflect on yourself. It encourages you to think about how you communicate and connect with others. By learning to "translate" between autistic traits and your own, you can build stronger connections with autistic people and other people, too.

Understanding the impact of identity

Autistic experiences are influenced by many factors beyond autism itself. For instance, an autistic girl might be overlooked because people don't expect autism to "present" like hers, while an autistic person of color may face unique challenges shaped by societal expectations.

Similarly, an autistic person who is highly articulate might have their needs dismissed because they don't fit stereotypes, while someone who is nonspeaking or who needs more support than others might be excluded from opportunities because others underestimate their abilities. Recognizing these overlapping influences helps you support autistic people in ways that respect their whole selves, not just one part of who they are.

How the Autistic Brain Thinks

The autistic brain approaches the world in ways that are both unique and fascinating. It often focuses deeply, notices details others might miss, and connects ideas in creative, unexpected ways. While every autistic person is different, understanding these common thinking styles — like nonlinear thinking, logical problem-solving, and deep focus — can help you appreciate their strengths and navigate challenges with them. Let's explore how the autistic brain processes and organizes thoughts!

Patterns of thinking

The human brain is amazing, and everyone's brain works in all kinds of ways! For example,

>> Critical thinking helps people analyze and evaluate information to figure out what makes sense.

>> Logical thinking follows clear, step-by-step reasoning to solve problems.

>> Emotional thinking taps into feelings or "gut instinct" to guide decisions.

No single way of thinking is the best. Each one has a role, and together they make thought process powerful and flexible.

Linear versus nonlinear thinking

Humans often rely on two primary thinking styles: linear and nonlinear. Linear thinking follows a straight path, moving step-by-step from one point to the next. It's perfect for tasks with clear steps, like following a recipe to measure ingredients, mix them in order, and bake at the right temperature and time.

Nonlinear thinking works more like a web, connecting ideas creatively or unexpectedly. It's ideal for brainstorming or solving problems that need fresh perspectives. Imagine planning a road trip — not just following GPS directions but exploring scenic routes, comparing options, and adapting as you find new stops or shortcuts.

Different neurotypes have favorites

Most people lean on two main thinking styles: linear thinking and emotional thinking. Linear thinking is great for routine tasks, like planning your day, whereas emotional thinking works great for quick decisions or in social situations.

However, autistic brains tend to rely on nonlinear thinking (the "web" we mentioned earlier) for planning and logical thinking to stay on track. While they can use linear and emotional thinking when necessary, these aren't typically their default styles.

Everyone — autistic or not — can use any thinking style, but each person has their favorites. People naturally tend to prefer one style over another, and certain neurotypes, like autism, tend to favor specific styles more often.

Associative thinking

Nonlinear thinking often includes associative thinking — spotting connections between ideas. If nonlinear thinking is the "web," associative thinking is how the pieces in that web link together. A strong associative thinking style helps many autistic individuals notice patterns and connections others might miss — like a detective piecing together seemingly unrelated clues.

For example, they might notice how a "click" in a machine signals maintenance is needed, how a slight change in someone's routine hints at stress, or how certain colors in the sky predict the weather. In daily life, this ability helps autistic people make sense of the world, problem-solve, and explore new ideas.

Many autistic people use daydreaming as a way to tap into their associative thinking. It helps them explore ideas, make unexpected connections, and focus on what brings them joy. This kind of imaginative thinking and inner reflection often leads to creative problem-solving and new perspectives.

This often starts early in life. Autistic children are sometimes described as being lost "in their own little world," but the truth is, they're far from lost. They're busy learning, exploring, and creating in ways that might not always be obvious to others.

Using logical thinking

Autistic people often excel at logical thinking, building clear, organized frameworks to solve problems. Unlike linear thinking, which follows a strict, step-by-step path, logical thinking focuses on structure and reasoning, even if the steps happen out of order.

When tackling problems, autistic thinkers tend to approach them systematically. Think of it like organizing a bookshelf: grouping books by genre, size, or author and then adjusting the arrangement until everything fits perfectly. This methodical, flexible approach brings calm, order, and efficiency to even the busiest thoughts.

REMEMBER

Logical thinking and nonlinear thinking might seem like opposites, but they work beautifully together. Autistic people often rely on logical thinking for structured tasks, like planning their day or solving problems. At the same time, nonlinear thinking fuels creativity and helps uncover fresh ideas, making these two styles a powerful combination.

How the Autistic Brain Uses Focus

Focus can be an incredible strength for autistic people, allowing them to dive deeply into topics, organize thoughts, and generate creative ideas. When something sparks their interest, they often concentrate with remarkable intensity.

Hyperfocus: entering the flow state

Hyperfocus is a deep, immersive state where distractions fade, and a person becomes fully absorbed in their task. For many autistic individuals, this state unlocks exceptional attention to detail, mastery, and creativity. In the right environment, hyperfocus can lead to innovative problem-solving and impressive productivity.

However, hyperfocus has its challenges. Time can slip away, causing other duties to be overlooked or deadlines to be missed. Transitioning out of hyperfocus can also be tricky because it feels like being yanked out of a deep trance.

Abrupt interruptions — like someone calling your name, a loud noise, or an unexpected schedule change — can feel jarring, causing anxiety or disrupted thoughts. This sudden shift can lead to frustration, meltdowns, or shutdowns as the brain processes the change. Gentle transitions and clear warnings can ease this shift, making it more manageable.

TIP

Provide a gentle warning before switching tasks, and allow time for a natural stopping point. This small adjustment makes transitions smoother and less stressful.

Focused interests

Focused interests are a hallmark of the autistic experience. They're deep passions that spark joy, help autistic individuals absorb knowledge quickly, and lead to expertise and valuable skills.

These interests can be about anything — science, history, animals, music, coding, trains, languages, art, or even vintage radios and deep-sea creatures. As an autistic child in Canada, actor Dan Aykroyd was fascinated by the paranormal, pouring his energy into learning all he could. "I became obsessed by Hans Holzer, the greatest ghost hunter ever," Aykroyd told *The Daily Mail* in 2013. "That's when the idea of my film *Ghostbusters* was born."

When autistic people dive into their passions, they often become experts, opening doors to careers, creative projects, or lifelong fulfillment. As a child, Dr. Temple Grandin spent hours observing animals, fascinated by their behavior. She turned this passion into a career, where her deep understanding helped her notice subtle details — like shadows or dangling chains — that startled cattle. This led her to design facilities that reduced animal stress and revolutionized the livestock industry.

Autistic people apply their focused interests in many ways. Professional surfer Clay Marzo's deep connection with the ocean gives him remarkable wave-reading skills, while musician Questlove has turned his passion for music history into a legendary career (more on him in Chapter 6).

Focused interests are as unique as fingerprints. Some people dive deeply into one passion, whereas others explore a variety of interests over time. These interests often evolve, shaped by experiences and environments.

Processing speeds and the autistic brain

Some autistic individuals quickly spot patterns or visual details that others might miss, while processing things like social cues or managing a lot of information at once might take longer. It's not about being "slower" or "faster" — it's about focusing on information differently.

Processing speed can be affected by factors like sensory overload or interruptions. Taking more time to process doesn't mean someone isn't paying attention. It often means they're absorbing more details or carefully thinking through their response.

How the Autistic Brain Organizes Thoughts

The autistic brain processes and organizes thoughts in unique ways, often relying on patterns, logic, and deep focus. While some people think in a more linear, step-by-step way, many autistic individuals approach ideas through webs of connections, intense interests, or a combination of nonlinear and logical thinking.

Understanding these differences helps highlight the strengths and creativity of autistic thinkers. It also offers insight into how they navigate the world, solve problems, and express themselves in ways that are distinctive and meaningful.

Executive functioning and planning

Executive functioning is like the brain's project manager — it helps you stay organized, manage time, and prioritize tasks to tackle what needs to get done. These skills vary widely based on neurotype, culture, and life experience.

Linear thinkers often thrive in cultures that emphasize precise time management and step-by-step planning. On the other hand, nonlinear thinkers — like many autistic individuals — may find these expectations challenging but excel in environments that value flexibility and creative problem-solving. Their approach might not follow a straight line, but it often leads to innovative and effective results.

REMEMBER

While autistic people are sometimes described as having executive functioning challenges, their skill in this area can depend on the environment and perspective. In spaces that support their unique thinking style, autistic individuals often thrive by using determination, intense focus, and logical problem-solving to manage tasks successfully.

Structure and stability: keeping thoughts organized

Many autistic people thrive with structure and stability because predictable systems reduce the stress of shifting expectations, sensory input, and unspoken social rules. Having a clear plan allows the brain to focus on what matters without constantly adapting to surprises — like following a reliable map.

Structure also supports executive functioning by providing clarity and reducing mental strain. Tools like schedules, checklists, or visual aids make tasks feel more manageable. Remember, structure isn't about control; it's about helping someone feel confident and capable.

Routines: a secret weapon for autistic thinkers

Routines are essential for many autistic people. They provide structure, simplify decisions, and reduce the stress of navigating an unpredictable world. Predictability creates a reliable flow, like starting the morning with the same steps or maintaining a consistent meal schedule. This not only reduces decision fatigue but also saves mental energy for unexpected challenges.

Beyond offering stability, routines channel nonlinear thought processes into clear, actionable steps. They address sensory needs, bring security, and empower autistic people to tackle tasks and solve problems effectively.

REMEMBER

Routines are frameworks that empower many autistic people to approach each day with confidence and clarity.

What happens when routines are disrupted

For many autistic people, disruptions to routine can feel destabilizing. Routines provide stability and predictability, so unexpected changes — like a canceled appointment or a delayed bus — can throw off the day.

This can trigger anxiety, make focusing harder, and drain the mental energy routines typically save. Tasks like planning or decision-making become more difficult, and for some, the stress can lead to a meltdown or shutdown when it's too much to process.

TIP

Disruptions don't have to derail the day. Backup plans with alternative activities or comforting tasks can help. Build "flex time" into routines for unexpected changes, and use calming techniques — like deep breathing, sensory tools, or quiet time — to manage emotions and refocus. Just like anyone, an autistic person's capacity to navigate sudden change grows as they do. As children become adults, they can keep building problem-solving skills that help them handle change with more confidence and flexibility.

Multiple tasks and transitions

Managing multiple tasks or transitions can feel overwhelming for many autistic people. The autistic brain often works best when it can focus deeply on one thing at a time, so switching tasks or stopping suddenly requires a lot of mental energy. Unexpected transitions can feel chaotic, disrupting focus and causing frustration.

The issue isn't ability; it's about how the autistic brain organizes information. Transitions can interrupt the autistic brain's natural flow, and so can juggling multiple tasks. These things become even more difficult when sensory input, social interaction, or the pressure for quick decisions are involved.

Proactive strategies can make a big difference. Clear expectations, advance warnings, and visual aids — like schedules or timers — help transitions feel more predictable. Also, breaking tasks into smaller steps and allowing time to adjust reduces stress.

How the Autistic Brain Uses Memory

Autistic people often excel in long-term memory. They can recall details, facts, and experiences that others may forget, making them great storytellers, experts in their interests, or the go-to person for obscure facts. However, short-term memory can feel more limited, especially in fast-paced environments

Think of it like having a vast, organized library for long-term memories but only a small notebook for new ones. Tasks like following spoken instructions or recalling recent conversations can be more challenging when too much is happening at once.

Long-term memory is a clear strength, but it can be coupled with emotional intensity. Past experiences — good or bad — can feel as vivid as if they happened yesterday. While this makes negative moments or broken promises especially painful, it also allows for deep connections to meaningful events and a strong sense of personal history.

The autistic brain and decision-making

Decision-making in the autistic brain often involves a deep dive into details. Autistic people carefully weigh options and consider multiple outcomes, leading to well-thought-out choices. However, this process can become overwhelming when there's too much information or pressure to decide quickly.

Decisions are about more than just picking the best option. For many autistic people, they're also about managing uncertainty, avoiding sensory or emotional overload, and making choices that align with their needs and values. This thoughtful approach makes autistic individuals excellent strategic thinkers, but it can also lead to "decision paralysis" when too many options or fear of mistakes make decisions harder.

Simplifying the process can help. Break decisions into smaller steps, limit options, and provide plenty of time to think. Visual aids like pros-and-cons lists or flowcharts make things clearer. So can borrowing the neurotypical idea of "good enough" — choosing a workable option rather than the perfect one.

Cognitive flexibility and the autistic brain

Cognitive flexibility — shifting between ideas, tasks, or perspectives — can vary greatly in autistic people. Many find it challenging to adapt quickly, particularly when routines or expectations shift unexpectedly. For example, an autistic person might struggle to adjust if a scheduled meeting is suddenly moved or a favorite activity is canceled without warning.

However, this trait is also a strength. The ability to focus intensely on one task allows for high productivity and deep expertise in specific areas. Autistic people often excel in environments that let them explore topics thoroughly without frequent disruptions or the need to constantly shift focus.

How the Autistic Brain Uses Senses

Taste, touch, sight, sound, and smell are fundamental ways we understand the world, often taught to kids early in school. But for many autistic people, these senses can feel turned all the way up — like hypersensitive antennas picking up more signals than most people.

Imagine feeling textures sharply, hearing a whisper across the room, or tasting every subtle flavor in a meal others find plain. These heightened senses can bring incredible joy and a rich appreciation of the world. But they can also become overwhelming, leading to distraction, discomfort, or even physical pain when the sensory input becomes too intense.

Differences in sensory input

The autistic brain processes sensory information differently (see Chapter 1), leading to hypersensitivity (extra sensitivity to certain stimuli) or hyposensitivity (reduced sensitivity or craving more intense input). Hypersensitivity might mean bright lights are overwhelming, certain fabrics are unbearable, or a noisy room feels intense. Hyposensitivity, on the other hand, could mean not noticing pain, craving deep pressure (like tight hugs), or seeking strong smells, flavors, or textures.

The beauty of autistic sensory perception

Autistic sensory experiences can be incredibly vivid and beautiful. Many autistic people notice details others miss, have an exceptional ear for music, or appreciate subtle tastes and smells. These sensory differences often inspire creativity and bring fresh perspectives to fields like art and science.

Photographers and artists train for years to notice light, color, and texture in unique ways. They see how light reflects, changes tone, and creates mood, noticing shades and patterns others might miss. Many autistic people naturally process senses in similar ways, creating moments of beauty and wonder.

An autistic person might stop to admire how light shimmers off leaves, pause to hear the pitch of a bird's song, or savor complex flavors in a dish that others find bland. For many, sensory perception is a vivid and joyful part of their world.

When the world feels too loud: sensory challenges

As amazing as autistic sensory processing can be, it can also be overwhelming. Noisy classrooms, brightly lit offices, or crowded stores may quickly become too much. Sounds like buzzing lights, traffic, or loud conversations can feel unbearably loud, while scratchy textures might make clothes uncomfortable. Strong smells or bright lights can trigger pain and discomfort, making everyday tasks like socializing, working, or running errands stressful.

Stress, fatigue, or chaotic environments can make sensory challenges worse. Stress amplifies sensory input, making sounds, lights, or textures feel more intense. Fatigue reduces the brain's ability to filter sensory input, and chaotic or unpredictable environments can add to the difficulty, turning routine activities into challenges.

You may be wondering whether autistic people always process sensory information with the same intensity. The answer is no. Sensory input isn't always the same in terms of its vividness, beauty, or overwhelming ways. Factors like environment, mood, energy levels, health (for example, an oncoming cold, fluctuating hormone levels), and stress affect sensory responses. Some days, sensory input may feel heightened; other times, it may feel similar to how neurotypical people experience it. This variation reminds us that each autistic person's sensory experience is unique and constantly changing.

REMEMBER

Each autistic person experiences sensory input differently. What soothes one may overwhelm another, and every person's experience can change depending on the situation.

Sensory seeking versus sensory avoiding

Autistic people often have unique preferences for sensory input. Some are sensory seekers, craving sensations like spinning, exploring different textures, or enjoying loud music. Others are sensory avoiders, steering clear of overwhelming inputs like loud noises, bright lights, or crowded spaces. Many people are a mix of both.

Supporting sensory seekers could mean providing outlets for moving like bouncing, jumping, or engaging with sensory friendly tools like weighted blankets. For sensory avoiders, minimizing overstimulation with quiet spaces, reduced noise, or dimmed lights can help.

REMEMBER

Autistic people can be both sensory seekers and avoiders, depending on the situation. Additionally, the kind of sensory support a person needs depends on context. For example, what helps a child in school might look different from what an adult needs at work or in daily life. That's why teaching autistic people to recognize and advocate for their sensory needs is important, so they can build independence and confidently navigate different environments as they grow.

Sensory overload: causes and coping

Sensory overload happens when the brain gets overwhelmed by too much sensory input at once. For autistic people, this can occur in environments with bright lights, loud noises, strong smells, or too many people talking at the same time. It's like having all the sensory channels turned up to full blast, leaving no room to breathe. Overload can lead to panic, frustration, or the need to shut down and escape.

Coping starts with recognizing triggers. Tools like noise-canceling headphones, sunglasses, or fidget items can help reduce sensory input before it becomes overwhelming. Having access to a quiet, secure space for retreat helps. Recovery time is just as important — sensory overload isn't something that passes quickly, and the brain needs time to settle. Patience and support are key to helping someone recover and can go a long way in preventing meltdowns or shutdowns.

Body awareness and internal signals

Some autistic people experience challenges with body awareness (proprioception), which helps us sense where our body is in space — like knowing where your arm is without looking. They may also struggle with internal signals (interoception), such as recognizing hunger, needing the bathroom, feeling too hot or cold, or knowing when to rest.

These challenges can make activities like team sports harder, but they can also lead to success in individual activities that emphasize repetition and focus. Sports like surfing, tennis, or martial arts allow autistic individuals to build muscle memory, refine movements, and develop deeper body control through practice and endurance.

How the Autistic Brain Feels Emotions

We all feel and express emotions and empathy in our own way, and autistic people are no different — though their ways of doing so might look different from others.

How autistic people process emotions

Autistic people experience and process emotions in unique ways. Some feel emotions intensely and quickly, whereas others need more time to recognize and express them. It's not about being less or more emotional; it's about processing feelings in a way that aligns with how their brains work.

Emotional intensity can feel amplified, like the volume is turned all the way up. This can make emotions overwhelming during stress, sensory overload, or unexpected changes, sometimes leading to meltdowns or shutdowns as the brain resets. However, this emotional depth can also bring incredible joy, driving passion, creativity, and meaningful relationships.

Recognizing and expressing emotions can vary, too. Some autistic people take extra time to identify their emotions or may express them in ways others don't immediately understand, such as through actions, facial expressions, or creative outlets like art. When emotions become overwhelming, they may need time alone to process privately before re-engaging.

TIP

If you're supporting an autistic person, give them time and space to process their emotions. Patience and understanding allow them to express their feelings in ways that feel natural and comfortable.

Empathy toward others

Autistic people may express empathy differently than expected, but that doesn't mean they lack it. Many feel emotions and empathy deeply — sometimes so intensely that it becomes overwhelming.

This intensity can make traditional expressions of empathy challenging. For instance, an autistic person might feel deeply moved by someone's sadness but struggle to find the right words or actions, leading to misunderstandings. Instead, their empathy often shows through actions, like offering practical help, sitting quietly with someone who's upset, or sharing personal stories to show they understand. While sharing stories might seem self-centered to neurotypical people, it's often a heartfelt way of connecting.

A strong sense of justice

Many autistic people have a powerful sense of fairness and right and wrong, driving them to stand up for what's just. This passion makes them dedicated advocates, whether they're fighting bullying, promoting issues, or calling out hypocrisy.

However, this strong dedication can bring challenges. Situations requiring compromise or flexibility may feel frustrating, and witnessing injustice can deeply affect their emotional well-being. Even so, their persistence in standing up for what's right frequently has a positive impact on the people around them.

Emotional regulation and co-regulation

Emotional regulation means managing feelings in ways that fit the situation. For many autistic people, this can be challenging because emotions and sensory inputs often feel more intense. Strategies like taking breaks, using calming tools (like sensory toys or deep breathing), or sticking to routines can help. Emotional regulation isn't about suppressing feelings but finding safe, effective ways to manage them.

For some, co-regulation can help. Coregulation is emotional support from a trusted person, offering reassurance or creating a calming space. It's different from codependency. It's a mutual, trust-based process that helps someone regain balance during emotional stress.

REMEMBER

Sensory experiences and emotions are deeply connected for autistic people. Overwhelming inputs, like loud noises or bright lights, can trigger anxiety. Soothing sensations — like calming music or soft textures — can provide comfort and relief.

How the Autistic Brain Communicates

Autistic communication is unique, often emphasizing clarity, honesty, and directness. This straightforward style can sometimes differ from neurotypical expectations, but it's simply another way of expressing thoughts and feelings. Recognizing and understanding these differences is key to improving communication and building stronger connections.

Let's explore some of the ways autistic people prefer to communicate and how embracing these preferences can foster mutual understanding.

A preference for directness

Autistic people often prefer direct, clear communication and may struggle with subtle hints or subtext. They value conversations where things are said plainly to avoid misunderstandings. Direct communication is not meant to be blunt or rude, and what's said is meant exactly as stated, without hidden meanings.

As Jamie A. Heidel of *The Articulate Autistic* explains, "We think it, we feel it, we express it — whether we've known you for 20 seconds or 20 years."

Indirect communication, such as saying "I'm fine" when upset, can be confusing for autistic people because they may interpret language literally and take such statements at face value. For example, if someone says, "We're having a party on Saturday," a neurotypical person might hear it as an invitation, but an autistic person may interpret it as just a fact about the speaker's plans.

TIP

Using clear phrases like "I'm upset," "I need help," or "You're invited to my party" avoids confusion and makes conversations easier to understand. Likewise, if you're not sure what an autistic person is implying by their communication, ask for clarification.

You can't be serious: interpreting sarcasm in speech

Sarcasm relies on tone, context, and exaggeration to convey the opposite of what's meant. It's often used for humor, bonding, or criticism. While it's a myth that autistic people can't understand sarcasm, it can be tricky in certain situations — especially when the tone or context isn't clear.

Many autistic individuals understand sarcasm well, particularly when they're familiar with the speaker's humor style. However, vague or unclear sarcasm can still cause confusion. As John from our author team shares, "I typically get when friends are being sarcastic, but a small part of me still wonders if they're being serious or not."

This uncertainty is common, as sarcasm often depends on subtle cues like voice tone, facial expressions, or context, which can be harder to interpret. Even when sarcasm is understood, it doesn't always feel comfortable for everyone.

TIP

Many autistic people are great at using sarcasm, but they may also appreciate it being clarified when used. When in doubt, be clear and direct.

Get to the point: little need for small talk

Small talk is meant to break the ice and ease social interactions, but for many autistic people, it can feel awkward or even pointless. That's because autistic brains often prefer direct, meaningful conversations. Discussing the weather or asking a general question like "How's it going?" might not spark interest because they don't provide much depth or purpose.

Instead of small talk, many autistic people thrive in conversations about shared interests or meaningful topics. These types of discussions feel more natural and engaging, allowing for deeper connections. That doesn't mean autistic people can't do small talk; they might just need more time to learn the rules or find it draining to keep up with unspoken expectations.

In cultures or countries where small talk isn't common, autistic people may face fewer challenges. For example, cultures that favor directness or value silence in social settings can provide more comfortable environments for autistic individuals to navigate conversations without the pressure of idle chatter.

TIP

If you're chatting with an autistic person, skip the small talk and dive into something real. Ask about their interests or share a meaningful thought. You might be surprised how quickly the conversation takes off!

Alternative communication methods

Not everyone communicates best with spoken words — and that's perfectly fine. Many autistic people use alternative communication methods that suit them better, such as AAC (augmentative and alternative communication) devices, which allow users to type or select symbols to create sentences. Other methods include sign language, written messages, or nonverbal gestures.

These communication styles are valid and valuable. They're not "less than" other methods — they're effective tools for clear expression, especially when spoken communication feels overwhelming or isn't possible. Everyone deserves the ability to communicate in ways that work best for them.

Repetition and scripting

Repetition and scripting are common and resourceful tools for autistic communication. Repeating phrases can help someone process information, find comfort, or express excitement. Scripting — using memorized lines from shows, books, or past conversations — provides structure in unpredictable or overwhelming situations.

Far from being "unoriginal," repetition and scripting are creative ways to simplify communication. For example, an autistic person might use a movie quote to convey a feeling or rehearse a conversation to reduce anxiety, build confidence, and connect with others.

These strategies vary widely among individuals. For some, repetition and scripting are occasional tools. For others, they are frequent and essential for navigating social environments effectively.

Vocal volume and tone

Autistic people may speak in ways that differ from what others expect. Some may speak loudly, whereas others may speak so softly they're hard to hear. They might prefer brief, one-word answers or give detailed, expansive responses. Others may use a "flat" or monotone voice, which can feel unfamiliar to some.

For example, when we asked a former student if he was excited about his new job, he simply replied "yes" in a monotone voice and walked away. While some might interpret this as sarcastic or unemotional, those who knew him recognized his genuine excitement in his brief response.

Body language

Speech varies across cultures, and so does body language: facial expressions, gestures, and posture. A gesture that's friendly in one culture might seem rude in another. Similarly, how we use body language to communicate depends on context and the biases we bring to interactions.

These differences extend to neurotypes, too. Autistic people often understand each other's body language — like facial expressions and gestures — quite well. However, when autistic and nonautistic people interact, misunderstandings can arise. Nonautistic individuals might rely on body positioning, such as leaning forward to show engagement or crossing arms to signal defensiveness. Autistic people, on the other hand, can engage deeply in conversations without relying on these cues.

TIP

Clear communication helps avoid misunderstandings caused by differences in body language. As entertainer Michelle Visage says, "Stop relying on that body," and remember that everyone expresses themselves physically in unique ways.

Eye contact

In some cultures, eye contact signals interest, respect, or connection. For many autistic people, however, maintaining eye contact takes so much effort that it's hard to focus on the conversation. Looking away often helps them process and listen better. For others, direct eye contact can feel intrusive, uncomfortable, or even physically painful.

"Avoiding eye contact is one of the things I find myself automatically doing to minimize the quantity of incoming sensory information," explains Judy Endow, an autistic clinical worker in Wisconsin. "I don't consciously think about avoiding contact. It just happens because that is how my brain works."

REMEMBER

Never force eye contact with an autistic person. Not looking at you isn't a sign of disrespect or disinterest. It's simply a different way of engaging. Look for other signs of interest, like asking questions, nodding, or thoughtful responses. Respecting their comfort with eye contact leads to better, more meaningful communication.

TIP

Autistic individuals often prefer sitting side-by-side during conversations, especially when discussing something important or difficult. Follow their lead and sit next to them instead of facing them. Researchers call this the "side-by-side effect" because it encourages relaxation and openness, but we like to call it "the autistic approach."

How the Autistic Brain Socializes

Autistic people value connection just as much as anyone else, but they may navigate social interactions differently from neurotypical norms. These differences aren't about a lack of interest or ability. They reflect natural variations in how people socialize. Understanding these differences can help build stronger, more meaningful connections.

Interpreting social cues

Autistic and neurotypical people often express and interpret social cues differently, leading to misunderstandings. Neurotypical social norms rely on subtleties like tone, body language, or indirect hints, which might not register for autistic individuals or may be taken literally. Autistic communication, which is often more direct, can sometimes seem blunt or rude to neurotypical people when it's simply meant to be clear.

The double empathy problem — a term coined by researcher Dr. Damian Milton — explains that misunderstandings happen because both groups follow different social "rules." Research supports this, confirming that challenges come from differences on both sides, not a deficit in one group.

Making and maintaining friends

Autistic people's approach to friendships often differs from neurotypical norms. These differences aren't better or worse — they're simply unique. Understanding these approaches helps foster stronger and more meaningful connections.

Bonding through shared Interests

Friendships for autistic people often grow from shared passions. Whereas neurotypical friendships may start with casual conversations or shared environments (like school or work), autistic friendships frequently form around mutual hobbies, topics, or activities. Autistic people often love to dive deeply into conversations about something they genuinely enjoy, which makes socializing feel natural and fun.

For neurotypical people, showing interest in an autistic person's passions is a great way to build trust and form a lasting, meaningful friendship.

Being faithful and loyal friends

Autistic people are often deeply loyal and dedicated friends. When they form connections, they value them highly and offer unwavering support. They may go out of their way to help a friend or keep promises, even when challenging. This loyalty stems from a strong sense of integrity and appreciation for genuine relationships, creating meaningful, lasting bonds.

Barriers to making friends

Despite their strengths — like loyalty, creativity, and empathy — autistic people can face challenges in forming friendships. Social interactions often involve unspoken cultural rules, such as knowing when to join a conversation or recognizing sarcasm, which can lead to misunderstandings or missed opportunities.

Neurotypical people may unintentionally create barriers by relying on subtle cues or assuming silence on the part of the autistic person means disinterest. Autistic ways of showing care — such as sharing facts or offering help — might be dismissed as "different" or misunderstood, even though they are genuine attempts to connect.

Casual social settings can also pose challenges. Sensory sensitivities and a preference for meaningful conversations can make crowded parties or fast-paced group chats overwhelming, even when autistic people want to participate.

Challenges in feeling Included

Feeling included can be difficult in a world built around neurotypical social norms. Unspoken rules, fast-paced conversations, and subtle cues may not come naturally to autistic people, leading to misunderstandings and exclusion. Societal attitudes can compound the problem, leaving autistic people isolated despite their desire to connect.

Clear communication is crucial. Autistic people often rely on direct, explicit invitations to feel welcome. Without one, they may hesitate to join, and therefore miss out on activities. John, from our author team, jokes: "Autistic people are like Dracula on your doorstep; we're unable to step inside without a clear and direct invitation to come in."

TIP

Want an autistic person to feel included? Be specific and direct. For example, instead of saying, "Feel free to join us," say, "We'd love for you to sit with us today at lunch."

Navigating additional challenges

Socializing is challenging for everyone, but autistic people often face unique obstacles. In this section, we share two common examples.

A high level of trust

Autistic people often trust others naturally, taking people at face value and believing they'll follow through on promises. This openness can foster deep and genuine connections when met with honesty. However, it can also leave them vulnerable to manipulation or deception because they may miss red flags or fail to notice inconsistencies between words and actions.

Minor changes to plans or broken promises — things neurotypical people might not see as a big deal — can feel upsetting. For autistic individuals, these moments may feel like a breach of trust, especially if they rely on consistency for a sense of security.

TIP

Neurotypicals: Stick to your word and communicate changes early. Autistic people: Understand that neurotypicals may not see small changes as broken trust. Clear communication helps bridge this gap.

Not remembering faces

While neurotypical people often rely on faces to identify others, autistic individuals may focus on details like hairstyles, clothing, or voices. This can make recognition harder when someone's appearance changes. About 20 percent of autistic people experience face blindness (prosopagnosia), compared to 2 percent of the general population.

Face blindness can vary with context. For example, someone might recognize a barista at a coffee shop but struggle to identify them in a different setting, like a grocery store. This can lead to social anxiety about forgetting faces.

TIP

A simple trick is to greet others with a friendly "Nice to see you!" It works perfectly when you're unsure whether you've met someone before.

How Autistic Bodies Respond

Human bodies react to stress, focus, and comfort in ways that help manage daily life. Autistic people experience these needs, but their bodies may express them in unique ways.

Stimming

Stimming (short for *self-stimulation*) involves repetitive movements or sounds, like tapping a foot, fiddling with a pen, pacing, or humming. Everyone stims to some degree — it helps process emotions, manage stress, or stay focused. For autistic people, stimming can be a frequent and essential part of self-regulation.

The next time you're at a concert, notice how people sway, tap, or raise their hands in rhythm with the music — that's stimming. It's a natural, universal behavior. While it's especially common among autistic people and those with ADHD, it also shows up in cheering sports fans or excited audiences at concerts. Stimming was once thought specific to autism, but it's now recognized as a universal human need to cope and focus.

REMEMBER

Don't stop someone from stimming. It's their way of regulating emotions, managing stress, and staying focused.

TIP

Stimming should be encouraged, but if a stim isn't safe — like spinning with arms out in a tight space — or is too loud for certain settings, try redirecting it instead of stopping it. A quieter movement, a fidget tool, or a designated spot for high-energy stimming can help. The goal isn't to get rid of stimming; it's to make sure it works for both the person and their environment.

WARNING

Stimming is a healthy, normal way to self-regulate, but self-injurious behavior (SIB) involves repetitive actions that result in self-harm, such as hitting, biting, or scratching. Although they may look similar, each serves different purposes. Stimming helps with self-regulation, whereas SIB signals distress or unmet needs. Recognizing this distinction is key to providing the right support.

TIP

Look for patterns to understand what is causing SIB — for example, pain, sensory overload, or emotional distress — rather than focusing only on stopping it. Doing so can help guide support through safer alternatives, environmental changes, or addressing unmet needs.

Needing alone time

For many autistic people, alone time is essential for recharging and processing experiences. This might involve retreating to a quiet space to rest and regain energy. They aren't trying to avoid others as much as they're trying to find balance.

Socializing, even when enjoyable, can be draining, especially in noisy settings or when navigating expected social rules. Alone time allows autistic people to decompress and reset, making future interactions more positive. This need isn't tied to being introverted or extroverted. Even autistic extroverts who thrive in social settings often need time alone to recover and maintain their energy.

Understanding masking and autism

Masking occurs when an autistic person hides or changes their natural behaviors to fit neurotypical expectations. It's like wearing a social disguise. Examples include forcing eye contact, holding back stimming, or mimicking typical conversation patterns to avoid standing out or being misunderstood.

While masking may seem helpful in certain situations, it often comes at a cost. Constantly monitoring yourself is exhausting, and over time, it can lead to stress, anxiety, and burnout. Many autistic people describe masking as feeling like they can't truly be themselves.

Masking also makes it harder for others to recognize an autistic person's true needs. If an autistic person hides their struggles, others might assume everything is fine and withhold the support that's needed. This highlights the importance of creating environments where autistic people feel safe to unmask. When they can be themselves and feel accepted, it benefits everyone by fostering authenticity and understanding.

The autistic body under extreme stress

Stress affects everyone, but for autistic people, it can uniquely amplify sensory sensitivities and physical responses. We'll discuss here briefly three responses to extreme stress: meltdowns, shutdowns, and burnout. For more on stress and behavior, see Chapter 7.

Understanding meltdowns

Autistic meltdowns are intense physiological and neurological responses to being overwhelmed by sensory input, social pressure, or extreme stress. They happen when the brain and body can no longer regulate emotions or sensory input, triggering the fight-or-flight system. This surge in stress response releases adrenaline — increasing heart rate and may cause dizziness or shakiness — and can lead to an energy crash once the meltdown subsides.

Meltdowns aren't tantrums. They're involuntary reactions to overload. Some people cry, shout, or throw things; others withdraw, hide, or have trouble speaking. Many seek comfort through physical pressure, a quiet space, or repetitive movements like stimming.

Meltdowns can last minutes to more than an hour, ending suddenly or gradually. Recovery takes time, often leaving the person physically and mentally drained — many describe it as feeling like they've "been hit by a truck." This exhaustion can also lead to embarrassment, self-isolation, or anxiety about re-engaging socially, sometimes requiring an extended recovery period.

TIP

If someone is having a meltdown, stay calm and provide a quiet, safe space. Speak softly, be patient, and avoid offering advice. Deep pressure, like a weighted blanket or gentle hug, may help, but always ask permission first because unwanted touch can increase anxiety. Parents can reassure children during calm moments that follow a meltdown with phrases like, "I understand and love you," and later work together to create a "meltdown plan" for the future.

Understanding shutdowns

Shutdowns occur when the brain withdraws to cope, like a computer going into sleep mode. It's the brain's way of managing overwhelming stress or information.

During a shutdown, a person may be quiet, withdrawn, or unresponsive, struggling to speak, move, or engage.

It's important to note that shutdowns can vary widely. They may involve partial responsiveness, where someone appears calm but feels overwhelmed inside, or complete withdrawal from their surroundings. These responses are unique to the individual and the situation.

Shutdowns differ from meltdowns in that they are inward reactions. While meltdowns involve crying or yelling, shutdowns leave someone feeling disconnected, drained, or frozen. They might appear calm but feel overwhelmed or worried inside. Shutdowns can happen suddenly or gradually and last from minutes to hours.

TIP

Recovery takes time and space. The best way to help is to stay patient, avoid pressuring them to respond, and offer quiet support. If someone is in a shutdown, they're not ignoring you; their brain is saying, "I need a break."

Understanding burnout

Autistic burnout happens when the demands of daily life — like socializing, sensory overload, masking, or responsibilities — become too overwhelming. It's more intense than typical burnout, draining energy, focus, and the ability to function. Burnout can show up as extreme fatigue, trouble communicating, or difficulty with everyday tasks. Some may need to withdraw from social interactions or take longer to recover after stress. It often builds up over time, especially when someone feels forced to mask or endure unsuitable environments. Recognizing burnout early and allowing time for rest is crucial for recovery and preventing further exhaustion.

2
Raising Autistic Kids

Chapter **5**

Understanding and Being Understood

H ave you ever traveled where no one spoke your language? That struggle to communicate can be frustrating, anxiety inducing, and isolating. For many autistic children, that's how life feels every day, but it doesn't have to stay that way.

Just like you'd find ways to connect in a foreign country, there are strategies to help your child bridge the communication gap. This chapter explores practical ways to support their communication by understanding their unique style, expanding their abilities, and creating environments where they feel safe and confident.

Whether your child communicates with spoken words, through gestures, or with augmentative and alternative communication (AAC) devices, these strategies are about meeting them where they are and helping them grow. Communication isn't just about words; it's about connection. This chapter helps you build that connection with your child.

Exploring Autistic Communication

For a long time, the mistaken consensus was that autistic people had communication deficits — that they were "broken" versions of humans needing to be "fixed" when it came to expressing themselves. But that's far from the truth. Autistic people have always been communicating, just in ways that weren't always understood or recognized.

We now know autistic people often communicate in ways easily understood by each other but less so by nonautistic folks (more on that in Chapter 4). They may use specific body language, facial expressions, or direct, literal speech — things that make sense to other autistic people but can be harder for nonautistic people to grasp.

That doesn't mean there aren't challenges. There definitely are! But those challenges don't come from being "broken"; they come from living in a world not designed for autistic communication styles. For many, communication can be tough and frustrating. Some face barriers not due to a lack of ability but because society isn't built to accommodate their needs or understand the diverse ways they communicate.

This is where the *social model of disability* comes in. It suggests people are disabled not by their differences but by the barriers society creates (more on that in Chapter 1). So, instead of trying to "fix" autistic communication, we need to better understand it, remove the barriers autistic communicators face, and create spaces where different communication styles are understood, accommodated, and supported.

REMEMBER

This doesn't mean there's nothing you can do to help your child strengthen their communication skills. It just means recognizing that communication looks different for everyone, and those differences should be respected and embraced.

If you're an autistic child growing up as the only autistic person in your family, this mismatch in communication styles can be really tough. It can feel like you're speaking a language no one around you understands. And to make things even more challenging, there's no handbook to help autistic kids or their parents decode these communication differences.

We're still learning about the many ways that autistic kids and adults naturally communicate, and there's still a lot we don't know! But here's the thing: We don't have to know everything about autistic traits to help autistic kids communicate and to communicate with them.

TIP

What matters most is an open mind and a willingness to listen, observe, and adapt. By being flexible and supportive, we can create an environment where autistic children feel safe to express themselves, even if their communication looks different from what we're used to. It's about meeting them where they are and valuing their voice, however it comes through.

Recognizing Early Signs of Differences

You may notice early on that your autistic child communicates differently than other children their age. These differences might show up in how they use sounds, gestures, or respond to social cues. Some autistic children may speak later than their peers, some may not speak at all, and others might use sounds or actions in unique ways. These differences are important clues to your child's natural communication style.

Chapter 4 dives deeper into autistic communication differences and in this chapter, we explore some early signs often seen in autistic infants and toddlers.

Communication differences in autistic infants

Here are some communication differences you might notice in your autistic infant:

>> They may not babble as much as other babies.

>> They might repeat certain sounds over and over.

>> They may not smile back or make much eye contact.

>> They could seem less interested in playing social games like "peek-a-boo."

>> They may not reach out or gesture often to show they want something.

>> They might bristle at being touched or held (often due to sensory sensitivities).

Communication differences in autistic toddlers

Let's now look at some communication differences you might notice in your autistic toddler:

>> They might say their first words later than other children.

>> They may use fewer words overall.

>> They might show you what they want by bringing items to you instead of asking.

>> They may use fewer gestures like pointing, waving, or nodding.

>> They could communicate through behaviors, sounds, or body language unfamiliar to you.

>> They may not look at you as much when listening, talking, or interacting.

>> They might focus intensely on certain toys or objects during play.

>> They may not respond when you call their name.

REMEMBER

Around 25 to 30 percent of autistic people are nonspeaking or minimally speaking. While they may not use spoken words as their primary form of communication, many still communicate effectively through other means, such as sign language, assistive technology, or written communication. For more on supporting nonspeaking or minimally speaking autistic children, see Chapter 8.

Communication differences in older autistic children

As your child grows, other communication differences might emerge. Some autistic children may find back-and-forth conversations challenging; struggle with interpreting irony, sarcasm, or idioms; or have difficulty picking up on neurotypical cues like tone of voice or facial expressions. They might speak in short, direct sentences, or, alternatively, talk extensively about a favorite topic without noticing if others aren't as engaged. Some autistic children also experience selective mutism, where anxiety or specific situations make it hard for them to speak, even if they can in more familiar settings. (For more on communication differences in older children and adults, see Chapter 4.)

Supporting Autistic Communication

Supporting your autistic child's communication is one of the most important things you can do for their growth and well-being. Communication is how your child connects with the world, shares their needs, and builds relationships. Whether they communicate through speech, gestures, writing, or assistive technology, it's crucial to honor and nurture the ways they naturally express themselves.

By understanding and validating their unique communication style, you help them feel seen, heard, and valued. This not only boosts their confidence but also builds emotional resilience. When we embrace autistic communication, we empower our children to thrive in a world that often misunderstands them.

Here are some simple ways to support your child's communication:

>> Be patient and give them time to respond or share their thoughts.

>> Avoid forcing them to communicate in ways that feel uncomfortable or unnatural.

>> Create a calm, supportive environment where they feel safe to communicate.

>> Focus on understanding their needs, even if they express them differently than expected.

>> Use tools like pictures, devices, or sign language if they help your child communicate better.

>> Celebrate progress, no matter how small.

By supporting their communication style, you help your child feel confident and empowered in their own voice.

Teaching autistic communication

Your autistic child has a unique way of communicating. Understanding and supporting that is key to helping them feel seen and heard. The goal here is to help them embrace their natural communication style — whether it's through gestures, sounds, pictures, typing, or behaviors.

It's rare that autistic people are taught about their natural ways of communicating. (We explore autistic communication traits more deeply in Chapter 4.) Helping your child understand and accept how they communicate is the first step they'll take in growing their own communication skills.

Here are a few ways you can help your autistic child understand and accept their natural ways of communicating:

>> **Acknowledge their communication style:** Let your child know that the way they communicate is valid and important, whether they use spoken words, gestures, facial expressions, body movements, nonspeech sounds like humming or vocalizations, assistive communication tools, or other methods.

>> **Celebrate their strengths:** Focus on the ways they successfully express themselves and reinforce that their communication style is unique and valuable.

>> **Model acceptance:** Show your child that it's okay to communicate differently by being patient, supportive, and nonjudgmental in all interactions.

>> **Encourage self-advocacy:** Teach them to express their needs and preferences when it comes to communication, empowering them to advocate for themselves in various settings.

>> **Involve them in planning:** Ask them how they feel about different ways of communicating and involve them in decisions about using tools or strategies that work best for them.

REMEMBER

It's never too late to help an autistic individual embrace their communication style. Learning to feel confident in how they communicate is powerful at any age.

Teaching neurotypical communication

Just as it's important for your child to understand their own communication style, it's equally important they learn about neurotypical communication because they'll encounter these styles in everyday life.

WARNING

The goal isn't to simply teach your child to mimic neurotypical communication. Instead, the focus should be on helping them understand their own communication style, understanding how neurotypical people often communicate, and building bridges between these styles. It's about equipping your child with the tools to navigate both worlds while staying true to themselves.

TIP

Here are some common neurotypical communication methods that might be unfamiliar to your autistic child:

>> **Tone of voice:** Neurotypical people often change their tone to express emotions like sarcasm or excitement.

>> **Facial expressions:** Reading facial cues, like smiling or frowning, is a key part of neurotypical communication.

>> **Eye contact:** Neurotypical people often expect consistent eye contact during conversations to show engagement.

>> **Body language:** Certain gestures, posture, and movements, like nodding or crossing arms, convey meaning beyond words.

>> **Small talk:** In many cultures, conversation about things like the weather or daily life is common in neurotypical interactions.

>> **Turn-taking in conversations:** Neurotypical people usually follow a pattern of waiting for their turn to speak.

>> **Personal space:** Neurotypical people may have specific expectations for how much space to give each other during interactions.

>> **Indirect communication:** Some neurotypical people use hints or implied meaning instead of saying things directly.

Understanding these methods can help your child navigate social situations with neurotypical peers while honoring their own communication style.

REMEMBER

Teaching your child about neurotypical communication isn't about changing them. It's about giving them tools to navigate differences. Think of it as learning a second language.

Bridging communication styles

Helping your child bridge the gap between autistic and neurotypical communication styles can be incredibly empowering. It's about teaching them to "translate" between the two, so they can understand both their own way of communicating and how others might communicate without ever losing their sense of self.

TIP

Not all children may be able to "translate" or do it without a lot of energy expenditure. Always encourage self-advocacy: When they don't understand neurotypical communication, it's appropriate to say, "I don't understand. Please say in a different way."

REMEMBER

This skill gives your child the ability to adapt in different situations, knowing when to adjust their approach or explain their communication style to others. The focus is on flexibility and self-advocacy — helping them navigate communication across styles while staying true to who they are. It's a tool for navigating the world, not a demand to conform.

WARNING

Helping your child understand, accept, and use their natural way of communicating comes first — always. Any teaching of neurotypical communication should build on, not replace, how they already express themselves. Think of it like trying to learn a second language without first understanding their own — it would be a total disaster. Nothing would click, frustration would skyrocket, and they'd be left struggling to make sense of it all. Sadly, this has been the traditional approach for autistic children, causing lasting damage — leaving many feeling unheard, disconnected, and forced to mask who they are.

Helping Your Child Communicate

One of the most important things you can do as a parent or caregiver is help your autistic child find ways to express themselves. Expressing ourselves is crucial for sharing our thoughts, feelings, and experiences, and for connecting with others.

For your autistic child, this might involve exploring communication tools like pictures, gestures, or technology, or simply giving them more time to respond. It could also mean helping them find unique ways to showcase their strengths, passions, and emotions. Supporting their natural communication style is key to helping them feel understood and valued.

REMEMBER

When you actively support your child in expressing their thoughts, needs, and feelings, you're not just helping with communication; you're fostering their overall growth. Encouraging self-expression gives them the confidence to navigate the world on their own terms. This improves their communication skills, boosts emotional well-being, and strengthens their connections with others. When your child knows they can express themselves freely, their ability to communicate will continue to grow.

TIP

The following communication tools can help autistic children express their thoughts, needs, and feelings — especially when using spoken words is challenging. Here are some tools that can support your child's communication:

>> **Picture Exchange Communication System (PECS):** A system where children use pictures to express needs, ideas, or feelings by exchanging them with someone.

>> **Speech-generating devices** (SGDs)**:** Devices that let nonspeaking children select words or symbols that are then spoken aloud.

>> **Communication apps:** Apps on tablets or smartphones that help kids build sentences and express thoughts verbally or through text.

>> **Communication boards:** Nonelectronic boards with pictures, letters, or phrases that the child can point to for communicating their needs.

>> **Visual schedules:** Picture-based schedules that help children understand routines by showing what's happening next in their day.

>> **Visual timers:** Tools that show how much time is left in an activity to help with transitions.

>> **Sign language:** A useful tool for both nonspeaking and speaking children to communicate without relying on verbal speech.

» **Social stories:** Personalized stories that explain social situations, helping children learn what to expect and typical responses (for example, meeting someone new).

» **Writing and typing:** A great option for children who feel more comfortable expressing themselves through written words rather than speech.

» **Interest-based communication:** Conversations or activities centered around your child's favorite topics to encourage communication.

These tools provide a variety of ways to support your child's communication, no matter what their preferred method of expression.

Exploring Strategies for Growth

Helping your autistic child develop their communication skills means creating an environment that fosters confidence, patience, and understanding. It's about encouraging their natural communication style while offering the tools and opportunities they need to expand those skills over time. By supporting their unique needs and celebrating each step forward, you lay a strong foundation for growth.

REMEMBER

The goal is to build your child's ability to connect with the world in ways that feel authentic to them. This helps them grow at their own pace while empowering them to navigate different communication situations effectively.

Actively listening

One of the best ways to support your autistic child's communication growth is by practicing active listening. This means giving your full attention to what your child is communicating — whether through words, gestures, or other cues — while trying to understand, respond, and remember what's being shared. Active listening strengthens your connection and encourages your child to communicate more, knowing they're truly being heard.

Here are some examples of parents practicing active listening to help their child grow their communication skills:

» A child builds a tower with blocks and smiles. The parent acknowledges it and asks, "What are you going to do next?" This shows they're paying attention, encouraging the child to share more.

>> A child is pacing and upset but not speaking. The parent calmly says, "I'm here when you're ready." This builds trust, letting the child communicate at their own pace.

>> At breakfast, a child keeps staring at the cereal box. The parent says, "Can you show me what you're thinking?" Recognizing nonverbal cues helps connect the child's thoughts with communication.

In each of these examples, the parent's actions create a supportive environment, making the child feel understood and encouraging more communication.

TIP

A key part of active listening is compassionate curiosity. This means being genuinely interested in what the other person is feeling or thinking without judgment or trying to fix things immediately. It's about listening to truly understand their experience. Read more on compassionate curiosity in Chapter 17.

REMEMBER

Giving your child your full attention, not interrupting, and reflecting back what they've expressed builds their confidence. It shows them that their communication is valued and encourages them to engage more frequently and confidently.

Building trust and rapport

Building trust and rapport with your autistic child is essential for supporting their communication. When they feel safe, understood, and respected, they're more likely to open up and share in ways that feel comfortable for them. Trust creates a solid foundation where your child knows you're there to listen and support them, whether they use words, gestures, or other forms of communication.

Taking the time to understand their unique communication style and respecting their sensory needs shows them that you truly value who they are. By building this strong connection, you're not only helping them communicate more effectively but also fostering a deeper bond of trust that will support them in all areas of life.

Providing consistency and reliability

Consistency and reliability help your child feel secure, which is essential for self-expression. When children know what to expect, it reduces anxiety and sensory overload — both of which can make communication more difficult.

REMEMBER

Creating a stable, reliable environment allows your child to focus less on uncertainty and more on communicating. Consistency in routines, expectations, and interactions helps your child feel safe, making it easier for them to express themselves.

Establishing routines, using visual schedules, and giving clear, consistent cues about what's coming next provides stability. This predictability helps your child feel more secure and encourages better communication. When they feel safe, they're more likely to engage, process information, and respond in ways that work best for them.

>> Use simple, consistent language to help your child process and respond more easily.

>> Be predictable in your responses, so your child feels safe to communicate.

>> Set clear expectations and follow through on promises.

>> Stick to routines and use visual schedules to reduce anxiety and keep them engaged.

>> Give advance notice of changes to help them prepare and stay open to communication.

Creating this environment not only encourages communication but also builds confidence.

Autistic children thrive with consistency and clear expectations. In a world that often feels unpredictable, reliable routines reduce the stress of unpredictability and empower them to communicate their needs and thoughts with confidence.

Communicating clearly

Using clear, direct language with your autistic child can greatly improve how they understand and engage with you. Saying exactly what you mean reduces confusion and frustration, making communication smoother for both of you.

Autistic children tend to process information better when it's straightforward and less vague. Skipping sarcasm, metaphors, or overly complex phrasing gives them a clearer idea of what you're asking. For example, instead of saying, "Can you give me a hand?" consider saying, "Please help me carry this."

As an example, John, from our author team, shares a memory from when he was six: "One hot summer day, I overheard a relative suggest that we brew a pot of tea, chill it, and serve it 'on the rocks.' So, I ran out to a boulder in our front yard and patiently sat on it, quietly waiting 'on the rocks' for the tea for well over two hours."

It's a common misconception that autistic people can't understand sarcasm or metaphors. They can, but these concepts can be tricky because they rely on subtle cues and context.

Striving for continuous learning

Continuous learning means your child is always gaining new skills and building on what they already know. It's about learning a little bit every day — whether through therapy, social interactions, or during regular activities. Communication skills, in particular, grow with practice and repetition. By giving your child regular opportunities to try new things, they can improve at their own pace.

Every experience is a chance to reinforce communication, whether through practicing new words or gestures or learning how to navigate social situations. This steady learning process builds your child's confidence, helping them express themselves more clearly and adapt to new challenges. By encouraging this growth, you're giving them the tools they need to connect and thrive.

REMEMBER

Continuous learning isn't just for your child. It's for you too. As their communication skills develop, you'll figure out how to better support them, understand their needs, and adjust your approach. This might mean adopting new strategies, finding what works best, and staying flexible in how you communicate together.

TIP

Having open conversations about how others may expect your child to communicate is an important part of continuous learning. For example, Khushboo, from our author team, teaches her neurodivergent clients to let interviewers know if they need extra time to process questions. Similarly, you can teach your child to let a teacher know they might need a moment to think before answering. This helps your child advocate for their own needs and helps others provide the right support.

REMEMBER

You play a key role in continuous learning by advocating for your child's communication needs. Sharing these needs with teachers, family, and others helps them provide better support. This ongoing dialogue teaches others how to engage effectively while reinforcing your child's learning in supportive environments.

Adapting to sensory needs

Sensory differences can greatly impact how your autistic child communicates. Loud noises, bright lights, or busy environments may overwhelm them, making it harder to focus or express themselves. Certain textures or sensations might also be distracting or uncomfortable, affecting their interactions. Sensory overload can lead to shutdowns or meltdowns, further complicating communication.

TIP

Creating a calm, sensory-friendly environment can make a huge difference in helping your child communicate. This could include offering noise-canceling headphones, allowing them to fidget with sensory toys, or choosing quieter, less crowded spaces for conversations. Encouraging your child to express their sensory preferences also helps them feel more in control. By understanding and supporting their sensory needs, you create a safe space where they can communicate in ways that work best for them.

Observing differences in nonspeaking children

Sensory differences can be harder to identify in nonspeaking autistic children, but you can observe what works best by noticing how they behave in different settings. For example, they may communicate more easily in quiet, familiar environments or feel more comfortable socializing while wearing certain textures of clothing.

TIP

Observe how your child responds to different sensory inputs, such as noise levels or the texture of food. These observations can offer valuable clues about what might be affecting their communication. Adjusting the environment to reduce discomfort can support your child's ability to express themselves naturally and safely.

Securing support

You don't have to navigate these challenges alone. As your child grows their communication skills, there are professionals who can provide valuable support.

Seeking professional support

Seeking professional support can have a significant impact on helping your autistic child communicate. Specialists who focus on both verbal and nonverbal communication can tailor their approaches to meet your child's specific needs.

TIP

Here are some key specialists who can support your child's communication:

>> **Speech language pathologists (SLPs):** SLPs help children develop speech and language skills, focusing on sound, vocabulary, and comprehension. For nonspeaking children, they can introduce AAC methods like communication boards.

>> **Occupational therapists (OTs):** OTs help with motor skills and sensory processing, which are crucial for communication. They also address sensory sensitivities and fine motor skills needed for tasks like writing or using AAC devices.

>> **Developmental therapists:** These therapists take a holistic approach, helping children build communication and social skills suited to their developmental stage.

>> **Music and art therapists:** Creative therapies offer nonverbal outlets for communication, helping children express emotions and connect in ways that feel more natural.

REMEMBER

Tailoring support to your child's individual needs is key to helping them develop their communication skills and reach their full potential.

Reaching out to family, friends, and community

Family, friends, and your community can be key in supporting your autistic child's communication. When others understand your child's communication style — whether through speech, gestures, or alternative methods — they can offer valuable support in daily interactions. Family gatherings, playdates, and community events become opportunities for your child to practice communicating in supportive environments.

TIP

Encouraging others to use clear, direct language, be patient, and respect your child's pace helps create a supportive network. This makes your child feel more comfortable and confident in expressing themselves. Everyone plays a part in helping them thrive.

Chapter **6**

Understanding Sensory Experiences

magine walking into a crowded park on a warm day and hearing conversations, a dog barking, and the rustling of leaves. You smell fresh-cut grass and food from a nearby stand, and you feel the warmth of the sun on your skin. Sensory input surrounds you, shaping your experience and how you feel. Every sound, smell, and touch adds a layer to the world around you.

But not everyone processes sensations the same way. A light breeze might feel soothing to some but prickly and distracting to others. Autistic people often experience sensory input more intensely, affecting daily life. This chapter explores how sensory differences show up in autistic children and ways to support them.

Understanding Sensory Differences

Understanding your child's sensory differences is key to supporting them (see Chapter 4 for an overview). Knowing what overwhelms or helps them allows you to create safer, more manageable environments, reducing stress and strengthening your bond. This awareness improves daily routines and supports their emotional well-being.

Identifying types of sensory input

Observe how your child reacts to sensory input. Do they avoid bright lights or cover their ears in loud places? Are they drawn to soft textures but dislike certain fabrics? Some seek strong input, like deep pressure, vibrant colors, or loud music. These patterns reveal what makes them feel comfortable or overwhelmed.

TIP

Notice what sensory input your child avoids or seeks. This helps you understand their needs and adjust environments to reduce stress. Every child is different — meet them where they are, support their sensory world, and create a space where they can thrive.

Understanding visual sensory differences

Sight is a primary way we understand the world, from recognizing faces to appreciating nature. But not everyone processes visual information the same way. Here's how visual sensory differences can shape your autistic child's experience of their surroundings:

>> **Sensitivity to bright lights or colors:** Your child might squint, cover their eyes, avoid looking at certain lights or colors, or get easily distracted by them. But they may also find comfort in soft, calming lights, light patterns, or specific colors they enjoy.

>> **Fascination with movement:** While rapid movement, like spinning fans or flashing lights, might overstimulate, they may also find these movements captivating or soothing, focusing intently on how things move in a way that brings them comfort.

>> **Challenges with clutter:** Busy, cluttered spaces can be overwhelming, and a well-organized environment may help your child thrive. However, their own space might still be cluttered. They may have their own system, get absorbed in activities, and not notice the mess or find comfort in familiar surroundings — though too much clutter can still become overwhelming.

Understanding sound sensory differences

Sounds can be soothing, uplifting, annoying, or exhausting, depending on volume, context, and how our brains process them. For autistic people, sounds may seem louder, harder to ignore, or overwhelming. Here are common sound-related sensory experiences in autistic children:

» **Covering ears:** Loud noises like sirens, alarms, or crowds may cause distress. Even quiet sounds — like a distant hum or high-pitched tone — can feel just as overwhelming.

» **Seeking out certain sounds:** While some noises are too much, others bring comfort. Your child may enjoy tapping, humming, white noise, or repeating songs and sounds for predictability. Music, nature sounds, or even loud mechanical noises can help them feel grounded.

» **Background noise:** Busy environments can make focusing, thinking, and communicating harder, sometimes even painful. But heightened sound sensitivity can also be a strength, helping them notice subtle details or distant sounds others miss. In quieter settings, this can create a richer sensory experience.

Understanding touch sensory differences

From the feel of clothes to a simple hug, touch can mean different things to different people. Many people don't realize that autistic individuals often experience the sensation of touch in more intense or unique ways. Let's dive into some common differences you might notice in your autistic child:

» **Sensitivity to textures:** Some textures — like scratchy fabrics, tight clothes, or sticky substances — can feel unbearable, while soft, tagless clothing may be comforting. Your child might avoid wool or synthetic fabrics but love smooth, silky textures or soft blankets. Sensory responses can change depending on the moment and their needs.

» **Dislike of light touch:** A tap on the shoulder, a brush of the hand, or light contact can feel irritating or even startling. But deep pressure — tight hugs, weighted blankets, or firm handshakes — can be calming.

» **Sensitivity to temperature:** Many autistic kids are highly aware of temperature changes, feeling discomfort in spaces that are too hot or cold. They may seek control over their environment — wrapping up in blankets, finding cool spots, or adjusting the thermostat.

Understanding smell sensory differences

Smells can trigger memories or affect our mood, but for some, scents can be more powerful than others realize. This is true for some autistic children, who can often have stronger reactions to certain scents than most:

» **Avoiding certain smells:** Some autistic kids react strongly to odors that others barely notice — like cooking food, cleaning products, or natural scents like dirt or rain. These smells can be distracting or even cause headaches or nausea, making scent-neutral environments important when possible.

>> **Seeking other smells:** Some scents — like fresh bread, pine trees, favorite essential oils, or even odors others might find unpleasant — can be calming and provide comfort in stressful situations.

Understanding taste sensory differences

Taste is one of those senses we don't always think about, but it can have a big impact on daily life. The following list explores how taste preferences and sensitivities can be heightened for some autistic children:

>> **"Picky" eating:** It's not just preference — many autistic kids avoid certain foods due to sensory sensitivities. Textures or flavors may feel overwhelming or unbearable, while familiar foods provide comfort and predictability. What seems like "picky" eating is really about finding foods that align with their sensory needs.

>> **Seeking strong flavors:** Some autistic kids prefer bold, intense tastes — spicy, sour, or salty — because they provide a clearer, more predictable sensory experience than bland foods.

>> **Preferring to eat the same foods over and over:** Familiar foods offer comfort, reducing the unpredictability and anxiety of trying new flavors. Repeating meals isn't just a habit; it makes mealtimes more manageable.

Understanding body awareness

Body awareness helps us understand where we are in space, but that sense can vary from person to person. With autistic children, body awareness may look significantly different than most. Let's take a look at some ways those differences might show up:

>> **Seeking movement:** Your child may crave deep pressure or activities like jumping, pushing, or pulling, which help them feel grounded.

>> **Avoiding movement:** Some kids may be uneasy with swinging, spinning, or uneven surfaces. They might avoid team sports due to unpredictable movements but excel in individual sports like tennis or swimming, where they can move at their own pace.

- **Difficulty with coordination:** Tasks requiring balance or precise movements, like catching a ball or riding a bike, may be frustrating. With time and practice, they can improve in ways that work for them.

- **Body positioning difficulties:** They might bump into things, misjudge distances, or struggle with how much force to use when holding objects. This can lead to unintentional collisions or dropping items.

- **Seeking specific body positions:** Certain body positions, like sitting cross-legged, leaning into something, or lying on the floor, may provide comfort and stability.

Understanding balance and motion

Some autistic children may experience differences in how they process balance and motion. These differences can present both challenges and opportunities. Here are a few things to keep in mind:

- **Seeking spinning or swinging:** Your child might love spinning in circles, swinging, or other activities that provide a sense of motion.

- **Avoiding certain movements:** They may also be fearful of activities that challenge their balance, like climbing or going down slides.

- **Challenges with coordination:** Your child might struggle with activities that require balance and coordination, like riding a bike or climbing. This can be frustrating, but with practice, they can often improve their skills.

- **Repetition as a strength:** Autistic kids who enjoy repetition may excel in individual sports or hobbies like gymnastics or skateboarding, where they can refine movements through practice.

- **Sensitivity to movement:** Fast or unpredictable motion, like swings or car rides, may feel overwhelming. However, this heightened awareness can also enhance their abilities in activities requiring precision.

TIP

Occupational therapists can provide valuable insights and strategies for managing sensory sensitivities.

Understanding autism and dyspraxia

Dyspraxia, also called developmental coordination disorder (DCD), is when someone has trouble coordinating physical movements. This might make tasks like writing, tying shoes, or even running feel extra difficult. When we talk about autistic children, dyspraxia can be part of the picture, as it often overlaps with autism.

In fact, about 50 to 75 percent of autistic people experience some level of motor coordination challenges, compared to around 5 to 6 percent in the general population. This can impact how they learn physical skills or interact with others because things like making hand gestures or using eye contact might feel awkward or tough to manage.

The good news is that understanding these coordination differences can help parents figure out how best to support their kids, whether it's through finding new ways to practice motor skills or just understanding how these challenges might affect their social confidence.

Recognizing negative sensory responses

When your autistic child has a negative sensory response, like covering their ears, melting down in a noisy place, or refusing certain clothes, it can feel frustrating. But it's important to remember that these reactions aren't about "bad behavior" or your child trying to be difficult. (For more on behavior response, check out Chapter 7.)

These responses happen because their brain processes sensory input differently, and things like sound, light, or textures can feel overwhelming or even painful. What seems like a small irritation to you might feel completely overpowering to them. Understanding this can help you respond with more patience and empathy.

TIP

Instead of seeing these moments as discipline issues, approach them with curiosity and compassion. Try to figure out what sensory input might be triggering your child's response and recognize it as their body's way of communicating discomfort or stress. By understanding the cause, you can help your child feel more supported and find ways to manage those overwhelming sensations more effectively.

REMEMBER

Shifting your mindset from *They're acting out* to *They're reacting to something overwhelming* can help you respond in a calmer, more supportive way. By recognizing their sensory triggers and helping them find ways to manage or avoid overwhelming situations, you're setting the stage for them to feel more comfortable and understood and for you to be better equipped to help them navigate their sensory world.

Supporting Sensory Differences

Understanding and supporting your child's sensory differences can make a huge difference in their daily life. In this section, we talk about how to create a sensory-friendly environment that works for your child and how to embrace and celebrate their unique sensory strengths. The goal is to help your child feel more comfortable while also recognizing and encouraging the things that make their sensory experience special.

Creating a sensory-friendly environment

Make your home more comfortable by adjusting lighting, using soft natural light, and reducing noise with headphones or white noise. Offer comforting textures like soft blankets or favorite fabrics. Keep the space flexible to adapt to your child's needs, creating a safe and supportive environment.

Here are some strategies to make everyday environments more predictable and supportive, helping your child feel more secure:

TIP

» **Pay attention to routines:** Consistency can be comforting for sensory regulation. Establish predictable daily routines to help your child know what to expect.

» **Monitor temperature:** Ensure the environment is at a comfortable temperature; some autistic children may be more sensitive to heat or cold. Layering clothes or offering weighted blankets can provide comfort.

» **Visual stimuli:** Calming colors like blues and greens, soft lighting, and minimal clutter can create a soothing environment. If your child craves more stimulation, try colorful art, sensory lights, or textured objects. Gentle motion, like a mobile or lava lamp, can be calming without overwhelming their senses. The goal is to balance their space to meet their needs without overstimulation.

» **Simplify transitions:** Transitions can be tough for autistic kids, especially with added sensory input. Tools like visual schedules, timers, or verbal cues can help them process changes more easily and move between activities with less stress.

» **Introduce calming sensory activities:** Offer sensory-friendly tools, like fidget toys, stress balls, or weighted items that help self-regulation.

» **Mindful tech use:** Screens and video games can be great for many autistic kids, offering calming or stimulating sensory input. But balance is key; adjust brightness and sound and encourage a healthy mix of tech time with other calming activities.

» **Create personalized sensory kits:** Pack a kit with your child's favorite calming items — like noise-canceling headphones, fidget toys, or a comforting fabric — so they have sensory tools when they need them.

These strategies can make everyday environments more predictable and supportive, helping your child feel more secure.

Celebrating your child's sensory strengths

Celebrating your autistic child's sensory strengths is a way to help them embrace what makes them unique. Maybe they have an incredible attention to detail, noticing patterns or textures others overlook, or perhaps they find deep joy in certain sounds, movements, or visuals.

REMEMBER

Sensory differences in autistic individuals aren't just challenges; they can be sources of creativity, focus, and connection. By highlighting what they *love* about their sensory experiences, you're helping them see that their differences aren't something to hide or fix but something to appreciate and even celebrate.

TIP

Encouraging your child to explore and lean into their sensory strengths can also open up new opportunities for them. Whether they use their heightened awareness to develop an intense interest, like music or art, or find comfort in sensory activities that bring them calm, those strengths are valuable.

REMEMBER

It's important to show your child that their sensory world is valid and beautiful, and that their way of experiencing life can be a real advantage. Celebrating these strengths with your child sends a powerful message: Their sensory experiences are an essential part of who they are, and they should feel proud of that.

Practicing Effective Strategies

Supporting your child's sensory needs is key to helping them feel more comfortable and confident.

Teaching sensory regulation skills

Helping your child regulate sensory input starts by building their awareness of how different sensations affect them. You can guide them by gently pointing out patterns, like when loud spaces overwhelm them or certain textures bring comfort. For example:

TIP

>> Help your child understand how their brain and body react to sounds, lights, or touch by explaining that there's nothing wrong with how they process the world — it's just about discovering what works best for them. As they start noticing these patterns, they'll gain more control over how they respond. Together, you can figure out what overwhelms them and what brings comfort, helping them find balance.

> » Try practical strategies like sensory breaks, noise-canceling headphones, or creating quiet spaces at home. Encourage calming methods like deep breathing, practicing movement, or using sensory tools to help them manage their surroundings in a way that feels supportive and empowering.

REMEMBER

Over time, they'll naturally find what works best. It's about giving them the tools and confidence to manage their sensory input comfortably.

Integrating sensory tools

Building agency and self-reliance in your child is key to helping them navigate the world with confidence. When they learn how to recognize their own needs and make decisions about what works best for them, they become more independent and capable of handling different situations. This kind of self-awareness and adaptability is what sets them up for success, both in the short term and as they grow.

REMEMBER

Teaching your child to use sensory tools is a key part of their personal growth. It's not just about finding quick fixes but about helping them learn how to manage their sensory experiences in a way that works for them. When they can identify what tools support their needs, they start building self-regulation skills and gaining the confidence to advocate for themselves in different environments.

Introducing sensory tools — like noise-canceling headphones, fidget toys, or calming apps — gives your child the power to manage their sensory world. Let them experiment with different options to find what helps most. Encourage them to recognize when they're feeling overwhelmed and guide them in choosing the right tool to stay focused and calm.

REMEMBER

The goal here is to build their self-awareness and confidence so they can reach for these tools independently, whether at home, school, or out in the world. This isn't just about managing challenges; it's about empowering your child to take control of their environment and feel more comfortable in everyday situations.

Using sensory strengths to learn

Your child's sensory differences open up exciting opportunities for exploration and discovery. Whether they're drawn to certain textures, sounds, or visuals, these sensory experiences can guide their curiosity and fuel their desire to learn. For instance, a child who is highly attuned to sound might develop a deep interest in music or language, while a child who seeks tactile experiences could thrive in hands-on activities like building or crafting.

By encouraging them to follow what naturally captures their attention, you're helping them explore the world in a way that feels meaningful and engaging. Their sensory differences can become a lens through which they discover new passions and learn more deeply about the things they love.

Helping your child communicate needs

Understanding their sensory needs gives your autistic child a sense of control and helps them feel more at ease, reducing stress and boosting confidence. Teaching them to communicate these needs — through words, gestures, or visual aids — enables self-advocacy and promotes independence, making it easier to manage their day and reducing meltdowns or misunderstandings.

HOW DIFFERENCES CAN SHAPE A CAREER

Questlove, the legendary drummer and frontman for The Roots, has openly shared how his sensory differences as a child helped shape his career in music. Now the bandleader for *The Tonight Show starring Jimmy Fallon*, Questlove's work spans music, film, and culture, making him a beloved and influential figure in entertainment.

"I was always in a trance with things that spun — especially records," Questlove told Terry Gross in a 2013 episode of *Fresh Air*. "My babysitters and my aunts used to always say, 'He is the first child to never give us trouble. Like, he doesn't scream. He doesn't even talk. All you have to do is get a stack of records, put them on the turntable, and he'll literally just sit there and watch them turn.'"

He went on to explain that "after the third or fourth hour of it," his babysitters and aunts would start to worry. He added, "I would take my dad's records and just spin them on my index finger to watch them twirl. I liked the way the logo looked in rotation. They just thought that was kind of strange."

In the 1970s, when autism diagnoses weren't as common, Questlove's parents still noticed his unique behaviors and took him to specialists. At a time when sensory differences were often misunderstood, neurodivergent children like him faced confusion and concern. But instead of suppressing his fascinations, his parents embraced them, encouraging his love of rhythm. This support allowed him to play drums at an adult level by age 8 and make his first appearance at Radio City Music Hall by 12, launching an extraordinary career.

Those early sensory fascinations laid the foundation for his success. Questlove isn't just a Grammy-winning musician; he's also a celebrated producer, DJ, author, and filmmaker. In 2022, he won an Academy Award for *Summer of Soul*, a documentary that revived the forgotten 1969 Harlem Cultural Festival. By embracing his sensory differences, Questlove spun what others saw as "problems" into a career that inspires and connects millions across music, film, and culture.

Building Sensory Awareness

Once you understand your child's sensory needs, share this with others to create a supportive environment. The more people are aware of what helps or overwhelms your child, the more comfortable and confident they will feel at home and in the community.

Educating family and friends

Talk openly with loved ones about your child's sensory differences. Explain how loud gatherings, bright lights, or other factors affect them. Encourage questions and support by offering quiet spaces or self-regulation tools. This builds a network that respects and understands your child's needs.

Adapting school settings

Keep communication open with teachers. Share your child's sensory challenges and strengths, and discuss accommodations like noise-canceling headphones or flexible seating. Regular check-ins ensure a supportive learning environment that prevents sensory overload.

REMEMBER

The goal is to create a space where your child feels comfortable and supported, making learning and growth easier.

Raising awareness in your community

Small changes can make a big impact. Talk to businesses and event organizers about sensory-friendly options like quiet hours, varied seating, clear signage, and soft lighting. Raising awareness creates a more inclusive environment for your child and others in the community.

Chapter **7**

Responding to Behavior and Stress

As a parent or caregiver of an autistic child, navigating behavior and stress can feel overwhelming, but you're not in this alone. Behavior is communication, and when your child is stressed — whether from sensory overload, anxiety, or frustration — they're expressing something deeper through their actions.

The goal isn't to "fix" behaviors but to understand what's driving them. By focusing on underlying causes, you can help your child feel heard and understood. Compassion and collaboration matter. When you respond with empathy and adapt to their needs, you build trust and resilience, empowering them to manage stress in ways that work for them.

Understanding Behavior and Stress

It's normal to feel confused or worried when your child's behavior seems out of control, especially during stressful moments. But behavior is communication. Meltdowns, shutdowns, or what looks like "acting out" are often their body's way of coping with situations that feel too big or fast.

Autistic children experience heightened stress because our world isn't built with their needs in mind. Loud noises, bright lights, and sudden changes can overwhelm their senses, and social interactions can add more pressure. When stress builds, meltdowns or withdrawal help them cope.

REMEMBER

These behaviors aren't defiance; they're stress responses. Recognizing sensory and emotional overload and offering support — like quiet spaces, sensory tools, or extra time to decompress — helps your child feel safe and empowered. In doing so, you're not just managing behavior; you're building trust, resilience, and a stronger relationship.

Understanding self-injurious behavior

Not all autistic children engage in self-injurious behavior (SIB), but for those who do, it can be distressing. SIB — like head-banging, scratching, or biting — is often a response to overwhelming stress, sensory overload, or frustration. It can also be a way for some autistic children to communicate unmet needs or express pain they can't verbalize. While alarming, these behaviors help them cope with something unbearable in the moment.

Distinguishing SIB from stimming

It's important to differentiate SIB from stimming. Stimming, like hand-flapping or rocking, is usually harmless and helps autistic children regulate sensory input or emotions. Unlike SIB, which can cause harm, stimming is a positive self-soothing mechanism that generally doesn't need intervention unless it poses a safety risk. See Chapter 4 for more on stimming.

Coping with self-injurious behavior

To cope with SIB, start by identifying triggers like overstimulation or unexpressed pain. Offer alternatives like sensory tools, quiet spaces, or communication aids. In the moment, create a calm environment and redirect your child's attention to safer sensory input, like squeezing a stress ball. Additionally, occupational therapists can provide further strategies.

REMEMBER

By addressing triggers and offering supportive tools, you help your child feel more in control and provide healthier ways to cope with stress.

Using emotional support strategies

Emotional support is key to helping your autistic child manage stress and behavior. A neurodiversity-affirming approach meets them where they are, accepts how they process emotions, and offers tools that fit their needs rather than trying to "fix" them.

Teach your child to identify emotions using tools like emotion charts and provide safe spaces to decompress. Instead of changing behavior, focus on understanding the why — stress, sensory overload, or anxiety — and help them manage those triggers. Regular check-ins, validation, and structure, like visual schedules, reduce stress and build trust.

REMEMBER

The goal is to empower your child with tools that honor their individuality, not force them into neurotypical standards.

Positive behavior support

Positive behavior support builds your child's strengths and creates an environment for success rather than punishing their behaviors. Understanding why behaviors happen helps them find healthier ways to express their needs. Work with your child to identify triggers like sensory overload or frustration and develop proactive strategies to reduce stress before it escalates. For children with challenging behaviors, trauma-informed approaches like collaborative problem solving teach skills such as flexibility, frustration tolerance, and problem-solving.

Reinforce positive behaviors with encouragement and recognize when your child manages difficult situations well. This helps them develop self-regulation and builds confidence, allowing them to thrive while honoring their neurodivergence.

Considering medication

Before considering medication, determine whether behaviors stem from sensory overload, emotional distress, or other unmet needs, as these can sometimes be misinterpreted as core autistic traits. Remember that no medication exists specifically for autism, though some can help with co-occurring conditions like anxiety or depression.

WARNING

Be wary of ads or online claims promising that medication can "treat" or "cure" autism. These assertions are false and often exploitative. There is no drug, gadget, or treatment that can "cure" or "fix" autism. At best, those making such claims are misguided; at worst, they're preying on families to make money instead of providing real support.

REMEMBER

The goal isn't to suppress behaviors but to help your child feel balanced and empowered. Work with healthcare providers and involve your child when possible to ensure medication respects their autonomy and individuality.

Coping with Meltdowns

Meltdowns can be tough for kids, parents, and caregivers, but understanding why they happen makes a big difference.

Understanding meltdowns

Meltdowns aren't tantrums or defiance; they're full-body reactions to overwhelming situations. When the world feels too big or loud, a meltdown is one way your child processes that overwhelm. It's not something they can control or turn off. Every child experiences meltdowns differently; some cry or scream, while others withdraw. They key is recognizing that a meltdown means, "I can't handle this," even if they can't say it.

Dealing with meltdowns

During a meltdown, your role is to create a safe, calm space. This might mean reducing sensory input — lowering noise, dimming lights, or giving them space. Be a steady presence, letting them know they're safe and understood. Afterward, reflect on what triggered the meltdown to help avoid similar situations or manage them better next time.

REMEMBER

Meltdowns aren't something to fear or punish. They're a chance to understand your child's limits. Responding with patience and compassion helps them feel more secure in an overwhelming world.

Identifying common triggers

Every autistic child is unique, but many share common meltdown triggers. Recognizing your child's triggers is the first step in helping them manage overwhelming situations. Noticing patterns can reveal what tends to set off a meltdown. You may find these common triggers apply to your child:

>> **Sensory overload:** Bright lights, loud noises, strong smells, or crowds can overwhelm a child. Tools like noise-canceling headphones, sunglasses, or fidget toys can help your child cope.

>> **Emotional overload:** Anxiety, frustration, or excitement can build when emotions are hard to process. Teaching regulation strategies like deep breathing or taking sensory breaks helps your child regain calm.

>> **Changes in routine:** Sudden shifts in plans or unexpected visitors can cause distress. Using visual schedules or giving countdowns before transitions can help your child feel more in control.

>> **Communication barriers:** Struggling to express needs or feelings can lead to frustration. Visual aids, gestures, or alternative communication devices can reduce this stress.

The key to coping with triggers is prevention and preparation. Identify what tends to cause meltdowns, then reduce those triggers when possible or equip your child with tools and strategies to handle them.

TIP

Creating a "meltdown toolkit" filled with sensory items, calming techniques, or a quiet space to retreat to can give your child the resources they need when they feel overwhelmed.

REMEMBER

Meltdowns aren't failures. Recognizing triggers and offering support help your child navigate a world that can feel too overwhelming.

Recognizing signs of oncoming meltdowns

One of the most helpful things you can do is recognize the early signs of a meltdown. Meltdowns usually build up over time, and being tuned into your child's signals allows you to step in with support before things escalate.

Common signs include increased agitation, repetitive behaviors (like rocking or pacing), or social withdrawal. Your child may show heightened sensory sensitivity — covering their ears, squinting in bright light, or avoiding touch. Some children become more verbal; others may quiet down. Physical cues like clenched fists or fidgeting can also signal stress.

For example, if noisy environments overwhelm your child, watch for restlessness or ear-covering as cues to offer noise-canceling headphones or move to a quieter space. If changes in routine are stressful, distress or repeated questions may signal a need for extra reassurance or visual cues.

Recognizing early signs helps prevent or reduce the intensity of meltdowns. It's about spotting patterns, responding with empathy, and offering support before things become overwhelming. Over time, your child can learn to identify these signs and use their tools to manage emotions and their environment.

Practicing de-escalation, support, and after-care

When a meltdown starts to build, focus on de-escalation. Step in with calming strategies that work for your child — whether it's removing them from a chaotic environment, offering calming tools like weighted blankets, or giving them space to self-regulate. Stay calm and use simple, reassuring language to let them know they're safe. Aim to create a sense of calm and control without overwhelming them more.

During a meltdown, your child isn't in control of their emotions, and it can be exhausting for them. Offer support without trying to "fix" the situation immediately. Move them to a quiet space and lower sensory input by dimming lights or reducing noise. If they're okay with touch, offering a hand or hug can help, but if not, just being nearby and providing calm reassurance can be enough.

After the meltdown, your child may need time to recover. Offer comfort with a favorite activity or a quiet space. Don't rush them to talk about it. When they're ready, gently reflect on what triggered the meltdown and what might help next time. This helps build emotional awareness and gives them tools to cope in the future. And don't forget to take care of yourself as well. See Chapter 8 for how.

De-escalation, support, and aftercare are about patience and creating a safe space. By staying calm and offering comfort, you help your child regain confidence and feel supported in an often overwhelming world.

Tailoring responses to each child

No two autistic children are alike, so handling each child's meltdowns needs to be individualized. What helps one child may not work — or could even make things worse — for another.

For example, one child may need noise-canceling headphones and a quiet space in chaotic environments, while the other benefits from visual schedules and time to prepare for transitions. Each child requires a unique approach during and after a meltdown based on their specific needs.

By understanding their triggers and coping strategies, you can create personalized responses that help them feel safe and understood. Beyond managing meltdowns, it also empowers your child to handle overwhelming situations in ways that work for them, building confidence and strengthening your relationship.

Coping with Shutdowns

While meltdowns often get the most attention, shutdowns are another common response when autistic children feel overwhelmed. A shutdown looks very different from a meltdown.

Understanding shutdowns

A shutdown occurs when your child's brain and body retreat in response to sensory overload, emotional overload, or exhaustion. Unlike a meltdown, which is more outward, a shutdown is about withdrawal. Your child may stop responding, become quiet, avoid eye contact, or freeze. They may also struggle to move or speak or seem disconnected from what's happening.

Shutdowns are the body's way of protecting itself when things become too overwhelming. Rather than acting outwardly, they retreat inward to avoid further stress. Like meltdowns, shutdowns aren't intentional or defiant; they're a coping mechanism that's often misunderstood because they're quieter and less obvious.

Dealing with shutdowns

Responding to a shutdown requires a different approach than handling a meltdown. During a shutdown, your child often needs space and quiet more than anything. They may not respond to verbal reassurance or comforting gestures right away, so focus on creating a calm environment. Reduce sensory input — dim lights, lower noise levels, and remove any stimuli contributing to their shutdown. Give them the time and space to self-regulate, whether by sitting quietly or engaging in a calming activity.

Shutdowns, like meltdowns, often have triggers such as sensory overload or emotional stress. Recognizing early signs, such as withdrawal, becoming unusually quiet, or unresponsiveness, can help you intervene with de-escalation strategies before the shutdown fully happens. If shutdowns are frequent, prolonged, or difficult to distinguish from other medical issues, consult a doctor to rule out conditions like seizures or other neurological factors.

REMEMBER

Shutdowns aren't intentional. They happen when the brain is overwhelmed, burned out, or exhausted and may sometimes be linked to the body's freeze response. However, they are more often a reaction to ongoing sensory, social, or emotional overload rather than an immediate stress response. This low-energy state helps the brain cope by shutting down non-essential functions and conserving energy. Either way, shutdowns signal that your child is overloaded and needs time and space to recover. With patience and a calm, supportive approach, you can help them feel safe and return to balance when they're ready.

TIP

With patience and a calm, supportive approach, use the following strategies to help them feel safe and guide them back to a place of calm when they're ready.

» **Facilitating a calm environment:** During a shutdown, your child needs a calm, safe space to recover at their own pace. Minimize sensory input — by dimming lights, lowering noise, and keeping the space soothing. Offer familiar calming objects like a weighted blanket or fidget tool, but don't force them if they're not ready.

» **Respecting autonomy:** Honoring your child's autonomy during a shutdown helps them feel safe. Avoid too many questions or pressuring them to respond before they're ready. Simply being nearby provides comfort and a sense of safety as they re-regulate in a low-pressure environment. Pushing them to interact too soon can make them feel trapped. Trust they'll rejoin when ready. Your role is to provide a calm presence. Respecting boundaries strengthens trust and helps them feel supported.

» **Supporting recovery and reengagement:** After a shutdown, your child will need time to fully recover and reengage. Support them gently as they ease back into the world. Offer low-pressure activities like drawing or a favorite game to allow them to come back at their own pace without rushing into social interactions or conversations.

» **Offering acceptance:** As your child reengages, this is an opportunity to discuss the shutdown — if they're ready. Frame it as a way to help them understand their experiences. Ask them what made them feel overwhelmed and how you can help next time. Give them a say in how to handle shutdowns in the future.

» **Building resilience:** Helping your child build resilience over time is a shared learning process. Each shutdown offers insight into what overwhelms them and what helps them recover. Work together to recognize early signs and develop self-regulation techniques, like sensory breaks or deep breathing. Create predictability with visual schedules.

REMEMBER

Empowering your child with understanding and support builds resilience, helping them feel more in control during overwhelming situations. It also reassures them that they're never navigating this alone.

Addressing Wandering

Wandering, or elopement, is something many autistic children engage in. While it can be worrying for parents and caregivers, understanding *why* it happens is the first step toward addressing it effectively.

Wandering as a coping mechanism

Wandering can serve as a coping mechanism for autistic children dealing with sensory overload or anxiety. When their surroundings become too overwhelming, wandering offers them an escape to regain calm. It's a way to self-soothe and manage stress when they feel overstimulated or out of control. By identifying triggers, you can help reduce the need for wandering and create safer, more supportive environments.

Wandering as exploration and learning

Wandering isn't always about escape — it's also a form of exploration. Many autistic children are naturally curious and may wander to seek sensory experiences or spaces that feel calming. By understanding this motivation, you can provide safer opportunities for them to explore while ensuring they're secure. Recognizing the positive side of wandering allows you to support their independence and curiosity in safer ways.

Addressing safety concerns

Balancing safety and independence is key when addressing wandering. Rather than restricting movement entirely, offer safe opportunities to explore, like fenced outdoor spaces or supervised walks.

Tools like GPS trackers, wearable identification, or alarms on doors and gates can offer peace of mind without limiting your child's autonomy.

These tools help with safety but don't address the triggers behind wandering. Pairing safety measures with efforts to identify and address the causes of wandering empowers your child to cope, learn, and explore while keeping them safe and giving you peace of mind.

Promoting alternatives to wandering

Reducing wandering involves providing alternatives that allow your child to cope with stress, sensory overload, or the need for exploration in safer ways. By offering activities and tools that meet their needs, you create outlets that help them manage their environment and curiosity without feeling the need to run. These strategies fall into three categories: coping with stress, sensory regulation, and exploration.

Coping with stress

If your child wanders due to stress or anxiety, offering calming alternatives is key. Teach relaxation techniques like deep breathing or mindfulness to help manage feelings that overwhelm. Encourage the child to practice self-advocacy by recognizing when a space feels overwhelming and confidently requesting to leave, whether due to anxiety or sensory challenges. Find out what works best for you and your child.

Create a home "safe space" with soothing and familiar items. This helps relieve stress and reduces the urge to wander as a stress response.

Sensory regulation

For children who wander because of sensory overload, offer sensory-friendly environments. Set up a quiet space with tools like noise-canceling headphones, fidget toys, or weighted blankets. Sensory breaks with dim lighting or physical activities like swinging can help them self-regulate without needing to escape.

Exploration and learning

If curiosity drives your child's wandering, redirect it into safe activities. Video games, educational apps, and hands-on activities like LEGO or crafting offer structured exploration. Outdoor activities like nature walks or scavenger hunts can also provide safe, supervised adventures.

Hands-on activities like LEGO, crafts, or science experiments are great ways to engage a child's curiosity. For kids who enjoy movement, structured outdoor play, nature walks or scavenger hunts, channels their adventurous spirit while keeping them safe.

These alternatives for stress relief, sensory regulation, and exploration help your child cope and explore safely, reducing the need for wandering.

Dealing with Social Isolation

For an autistic child, social isolation means feeling disconnected from others, despite wanting to connect. It's like standing on the edge of a conversation, unsure how to join. Unspoken social rules — like reading facial expressions or knowing when to speak — can feel overwhelming.

Over time, this struggle leads to feeling disconnected, even in a room full of peers. Socializing, effortless to others, can become exhausting, causing them to withdraw — not from disinterest, but for self-preservation. This creates a painful cycle: wanting to connect but not knowing how, leading to loneliness. For an autistic child, social isolation isn't about choosing to be alone; it's about feeling unable to connect in a world that doesn't always make sense.

REMEMBER

Social isolation can be a tough and often misunderstood. While some autistic kids prefer more alone time than neurotypical peers, it's important to distinguish between choosing solitude and experiencing social isolation.

Supporting alone time

Autistic children often find social environments overwhelming. Sensory overload, difficulty reading social cues, or feeling out of sync with their peers can make engaging with others feel exhausting or even impossible. As a result, they may withdraw, not because they don't want to interact, but because they need a break from the stress those interactions can create.

Many autistic children genuinely need more alone time to recharge. Alone time is a choice and can be restorative: a healthy way to self-regulate, relax, process, and feel comfortable without the demands of social interaction. This is different from social isolation, which is often involuntary and can stem from feeling excluded, misunderstood, or overwhelmed, leading to loneliness and distress.

Coping with social isolation

To reduce social isolation, create safe, comfortable connection opportunities. Start with one-on-one interactions or playdates with understanding peers. Structured activities, like games or mutual interests, can make socializing more predictable. Explore groups or clubs where your child can meet others who share their passions, like coding, art, or animals.

REMEMBER

Respect your child's need for downtime while helping them build meaningful connections. Encourage social interaction but don't force it, and create opportunities for play with other autistic children. Offer tools for navigating social situations, like learning neurotypical cues, role-playing, or using communication aids. Balance is key.

Chapter **8**

Raising Kids with Complex Needs

If you're the parent or caregiver of an autistic child who needs multiple supports for daily living, you're on a journey that's both challenging and deeply meaningful. Every day, you pour love, effort, and energy into supporting your child, and that dedication matters more than you know. We know the quiet victories you celebrate — those small, powerful moments that reflect the incredible bond you share with your child.

It's easy to get caught up in labels like "nonspeaking" or "high support needs." While these terms can be helpful, they don't define a child or capture their individuality, strengths, or potential. In this chapter, we'll keep it simple and just call them children — because every child is more than a label, and what matters most is understanding and supporting them as whole people.

This chapter gives you tools, encouragement, and a reminder that you're not alone. You're doing something extraordinary, and we deeply appreciate everything you do. We see you.

Embracing the Journey

Raising a child with complex needs is a unique and meaningful journey. Your child's way of experiencing and interacting with the world is not something to be fixed. It's something to be understood and supported. That said, the challenges of caregiving are real. Communication can be one of the toughest parts because learning to understand your child's emotions and needs without spoken language requires patience, creativity, and persistence. When their needs aren't understood, meltdowns or frustrations can happen, making patience and understanding essential.

Accessing therapies or resources can also be draining, with long waitlists, high costs, or limited availability. On top of that, social stigma or misunderstandings can leave you feeling judged, adding to the emotional weight. Despite these challenges, your dedication and love make a huge difference in your child's life, helping them feel seen, supported, and valued.

Alongside these challenges are also moments of incredible joy. You develop a deep, unique bond with your child as you learn to connect in ways that go beyond words — through gestures, expressions, or augmentative and alternative communication (AAC) tools. Small victories, like using a device to communicate or achieving a new skill, bring pure joy and pride. These moments foster patience, empathy, and a profound appreciation for your child's strengths and individuality, filling your journey with love and meaning.

You have an opportunity to learn alongside your child, celebrate their unique ways of seeing the world, and find joy in their progress. Embrace the journey with patience, love, and flexibility, knowing that you're building a life where your child feels supported, valued, and understood.

Exercising compassion in your care

Compassion — for both your child and you — is essential. Be patient with progress, even when it's slow, and celebrate small wins. Allow yourself to feel emotions like frustration or sadness without guilt, and remember, self-care is not selfish. It's necessary to recharge.

TIP

Set realistic expectations; you don't need to do everything perfectly. Focus on your child's strengths and embrace their individuality. Surround yourself with supportive people who understand your journey, and use kind, encouraging language with yourself. Forgive yourself when things don't go as planned. Being human means doing your best, not being perfect. Compassion strengthens your bond and helps you navigate challenges with love and resilience.

Being adaptable and open to learning

Parenting an autistic child requires flexibility and a willingness to grow alongside them. Every child is unique, so what works for one may not work for another. Staying open to new strategies and perspectives helps you better support your child and deepen your connection.

TIP

Let go of rigid expectations and embrace your child's pace. Celebrate progress, even if it looks different from typical milestones. Understanding behaviors like stimming helps you see the world through their eyes and appreciate their needs.

REMEMBER

Flexibility means trying different approaches. What works today might not work tomorrow, and that's okay. Explore tools, routines, and resources, and don't hesitate to seek help from professionals or other parents. Be kind to yourself. This journey has challenges, but it's also full of growth. Celebrate your child's successes and your own progress, building love and resilience together.

Building a strong support network

Building a support network is essential. It offers emotional support, practical help, and valuable advice to make caregiving easier. Parenting can feel isolating, but connecting with friends, family, or other parents reminds you that you're not alone.

TIP

A strong network can also provide practical help, like giving you a break, helping with tasks, or attending appointments with you. Other parents and professionals can share advice, recommend tools, or point you to resources that can help.

REMEMBER

Support networks are also great for advocacy. Team up with other families to push for better services and greater understanding for autistic children. Plus, having people who accept and understand your child creates a more supportive environment for them to thrive. A good network not only helps your child; it helps you take care of yourself, too.

Celebrating your child's strengths

Every child has unique qualities, and this is especially true for autistic children. Focusing on your child's strengths — like their passions, memory, or sense of humor — helps them feel valued and boosts confidence (see Chapter 4 for more on strengths). Embracing their individuality strengthens your bond and adds joy to the relationship.

REMEMBER

Acknowledging strengths builds resilience and encourages your child to face challenges confidently. Celebrate small achievements, like trying something new, to reinforce their sense of accomplishment. Embracing their unique talents and interests shifts the focus from struggles to strengths, creating a supportive environment.

Noting achievements and progress

Recognizing your autistic child's achievements is a powerful way to boost their confidence and encourage growth. Each step forward — whether it's using an AAC device, trying a new food, or learning a new skill — is a meaningful victory that deserves acknowledgment.

REMEMBER

Progress might not follow traditional milestones, and that's okay. Success is about your child's unique journey. Simple gestures like praise, a high-five, or a smile can reinforce their pride and motivation. Celebrating these moments not only builds your child's confidence but also reminds you of the growth and strength you've both shown. It's a way to create joy in the present while fostering hope for the future.

Developing Daily Living Skills

Teaching your child daily living skills is essential because it helps them build independence, confidence, and a sense of accomplishment. These skills, like dressing, eating, and personal hygiene, are building blocks for their future that enable them to participate more fully in their own care and routines.

REMEMBER

Even small steps toward independence can make a big difference in how your child feels about themselves and their place in the world. You're not just teaching them tasks; you're empowering them to grow and thrive.

Teaching essential life skills

Helping your child learn life skills like dressing, feeding, and personal hygiene takes patience and understanding. Start with simple tasks, like brushing teeth or putting on clothes, and break them into small, clear steps. Visual tools like pictures or charts can guide them through each part of the task. A consistent daily routine helps make learning these skills easier and less overwhelming.

TIP

Show your child how to do the task first, as many autistic children learn best by watching. Offer process praise and recognitions for each step they complete. The positive reinforcement builds confidence and motivation. Use tools that simplify tasks, like spoons with larger handles or clothes with easy fasteners. Encourage practice, and guide them gently if they get stuck to help them learn problem-solving skills.

Occupational therapy can be a valuable support in this process. An occupational therapist (OT) can assess your child's specific needs and recommend strategies, tools, and adaptations to help build independence. They can also provide sensory-based techniques to make daily tasks more comfortable and manageable.

REMEMBER

Be patient and flexible, remembering that every child learns at their own pace. Celebrate small wins and focus on progress, not perfection. Over time, these skills will help your child build independence and confidence.

Creating routines and visual schedules

Structured routines and visual schedules can help your autistic child feel safe, reduce anxiety, and understand their day. A predictable routine makes transitions easier and helps your child gain a sense of stability and independence.

Create a daily routine with set times for key activities like meals, school, play, and bedtime. Break it into simple steps, and use a visual schedule with pictures, symbols, or words — whatever works best for your child. For example, a morning schedule might include pictures of brushing teeth, getting dressed, and eating breakfast.

TIP

Use tools like laminated cards, a whiteboard, or apps for planning, and keep the schedule in a visible spot. Review it regularly with your child. Over time, visual schedules can help them complete daily tasks more independently and feel more confident about their routine.

Encouraging household participation

Involving your child in household activities isn't just about doing chores. It's about teaching life skills, fostering greater independence, and helping them feel like a valued part of the family. Encouraging children when they make even small contributions can build confidence and a sense of belonging.

TIP

Start with simple tasks like sorting laundry, setting the table, or watering plants. Break tasks into small, manageable steps, and use visual aids or clear instructions to guide them. For example, show pictures of each step for setting the table.

REMEMBER

Focus on effort, not perfection. Offer support when needed but let them take the lead where they can. Incorporating their interests — like organizing or matching items — can make tasks more engaging. With patience, encouragement, process praise, and recognitions, your child will develop valuable skills and feel proud of their contributions.

Skill building for greater independence

Supporting your child means finding the balance between providing care and giving them space to grow. Like a gardener tending a sapling, it's important to offer the right support — tools like AAC devices or accommodations — while also allowing your child to develop more independence at their own pace.

REMEMBER

Too much support can hold back growth, but stepping back when the time is right helps your child discover their strengths and build resilience.

Teaching your child skills for more independence is about more than just learning tasks — it's about building their confidence and showing them they're capable. Starting small and breaking skills into manageable steps makes the process less overwhelming and more successful. Each small step mastered is a big step toward independence.

TIP

Focus on one skill at a time. Take handwashing. Break it into steps. Start by teaching them to turn on the water while you help with the rest. Add more steps as they grow comfortable and provide visual aids or prompts to guide them. Praise their efforts, even when things aren't perfect. Consistency and patience are key, and over time, you can reduce the support you provide, letting them take on more themselves.

REMEMBER

Independence looks different for every child as they grow into adulthood. For some, it might mean managing a job or living with minimal support, whereas for others, it could mean actively participating in their care and daily routines with consistent help. The important thing is fostering their ability to make choices, express preferences, and contribute to their own life in meaningful ways. No matter the level of support they need, these skills help create a life where they feel empowered and valued.

Navigating the School System

Navigating the school system to enable your child to learn can be a daunting task. In this section, we equip you with the information and resources you will need for the task.

Working with schools to create a personalized education plan is key for good educational outcomes. A plan may include visual supports, sensory-friendly spaces, and teaching at a pace that works for your child. Regular communication with teachers helps ensure your child gets the right support.

Advocacy matters. Stand up for your child's needs by asking for services, therapies, and accommodations. Finding advocacy groups by searching phrases like "IEP advocacy help for autistic children" and joining them can offer helpful resources and support. By advocating, you can improve your child's educational experience.

Using individualized education programs

An Individualized Education Program (IEP) is a school plan tailored to your child's needs. It starts with an evaluation to understand their strengths and challenges. Parents, teachers, and specialists provide input. From there, goals and accommodations are established based on the specific needs of the student, such as using an AAC device to improve communication or building social skills. The plan also includes services like speech therapy and supports like visual schedules or sensory breaks. (Read Chapter 10 for more information about IEPs.)

REMEMBER

Collaboration is key. Parents, teachers, and therapists should work together and adjust the plan as your child's needs evolve.

Classroom accommodations

Classroom accommodations can make a big difference by creating an environment where they can learn and feel safe. Some example accommodations include having a teacher's aide for extra support, visual schedules to help with transitions, sensory-friendly spaces for breaks, or tasks tailored to match their learning style. The goal of the accommodations is to make sure your child has the tools and support they need to thrive in the classroom. Talk with the teacher and IEP team to figure out what will work best for your child's unique needs.

REMEMBER

Advocating for accommodations means working with teachers and specialists to create a plan (for example, an IEP), that includes tools your child needs. Stay involved by checking in regularly and making adjustments as needed. Clear communication and persistence ensure your child gets the support they need to succeed.

Assistive technology

Assistive technology can make learning and communication much more accessible for your child. This might include an AAC device to support communication, noise-canceling headphones for sensory needs, or apps and tools to help with organization and focus.

REMEMBER

The best tools depend on your child's needs, so work with the IEP team to find the right fit and ensure the technology becomes part of their daily routine. The objective is to equip your child with tools that help them succeed.

Specialized instruction

Specialized instruction tailors teaching to your child's unique needs, like one-on-one support, small groups, or breaking lessons into manageable steps. The goal is to help them build skills — academic, social, or life — in ways that work best for them. Collaborate with the IEP team to ensure the instruction aligns with your child's strengths and challenges.

Behavior intervention plans

Behavior Intervention Plans (BIPs) are common for autistic students, especially when they express behaviors that interfere with learning, socializing, or safety. Schools often use BIPs as part of an IEP to address behaviors in a structured, supportive way.

TIP

A good BIP looks at why the behavior is happening — like communicating, avoiding overwhelm, or meeting a sensory need — and builds positive supports that respect your child's unique needs. Green flags include plans that teach new skills, provide accommodations including environmental adjustments, and focus on preventing challenges. It should be flexible, collaborative, and centered on helping your child feel safe and understood.

WARNING

Be cautious of plans that push compliance or try to make your child act less autistic because they can lead to masking, stress, long-term mental health challenges, or trauma.

REMEMBER

The best BIPs aren't about changing who your child is. They focus on supporting your child in navigating the world in ways that work for them.

Choosing the right educational setting

Choosing the right educational setting for your child means finding what best supports their needs and strengths. Options like public schools, specialized programs, private schools, or homeschooling each have benefits, so explore what fits your child's learning style and development and your abilities and resources.

TIP

Look for a school that provides the right supports, like speech therapy or sensory breaks, and has teachers trained to work with autistic children. The environment should feel safe, with spaces for sensory needs and chances for social interaction. Communication with the school is key to ensuring your child gets what they need.

Public schools may offer inclusion programs, allowing your child to learn alongside peers with the support of an IEP or 504 plan. Some have specialized classrooms for children who need a more structured setting. Private schools or autism-specific programs can provide focused teaching, while homeschooling offers a fully personalized approach. Visiting schools and meeting with educators can help you decide what's best for your child.

REMEMBER

Inclusive education can be especially valuable because your child has the chance to learn alongside their peers while getting the necessary support. It promotes acceptance and understanding, helping all students grow together. When schools value each child's strengths and celebrate differences, it creates a positive environment where your child can thrive. (Read more in Chapter 10.)

Ensuring Health and Medical Care

Making sure your child gets the right medical care is important. Regular checkups and treating any health problems quickly can go a long way in keeping them healthy and happy. When you have the right medical team on your side, it can make a big difference for your child's well-being and quality of life.

TIP

Seek recommendations for autism friendly providers from autism advocacy groups or local support communities. Prioritize those providers who take a patient-centered approach and are willing to accommodate sensory sensitivities and individual needs.

Coordinating care and support

Aligning your child's care among doctors, therapist, school staff, and more is essential to ensure everyone works toward the same goal: helping your child feel safe, supported, and able to thrive. Coordination isn't just about avoiding confusion; it ensures your child gets care that meets their unique needs.

Share information among your child's doctors, therapists, and caregivers so everyone understands how different interventions connect. For example, if your child is in therapy for motor skills, their doctor should know how that ties to any medications or health conditions. Similarly, a therapist can monitor how medications for anxiety or ADHD affect communication or social engagement.

TIP

Make sure therapies align with your child's strengths and preferences. Treatments that feel overwhelming or mismatched can add stress instead of support. Advocate for approaches that respect your child's individuality and natural way of experiencing the world. You know your child best, and your input is crucial.

REMEMBER

Coordinating care can be overwhelming, so don't hesitate to ask for help. Case managers, school staff, or trusted professionals can keep things organized and ensure good communication. By working together and staying focused on what's best for your child, you can build a support system that feels less chaotic and more empowering for both of you.

Managing co-occurring conditions

Many autistic children experience conditions like anxiety, ADHD, epilepsy, sleep disorders, motor issues, or gastrointestinal problems. (For more on this, turn to Chapter 1.) These co-occurring conditions can add complexity, but with a thoughtful approach, you can help your child feel better and thrive. It's about understanding how everything connects and creating a plan that supports your child as a whole.

TIP

Work with your child's support team to see how these conditions interact with autism. For example, anxiety might increase behavioral difficulties, or gastrointestinal issues could make focusing harder. Understanding these connections helps you plan therapies, medications, or adjustments to routines, like changes in diet or sensory-friendly spaces.

REMEMBER

Emotional support is just as important as physical care. Predictable routines, calming activities, and quiet spaces can help your child feel safe and at ease. Managing co-occurring conditions can feel overwhelming, but with the right support and steady steps, you'll see progress and growth.

Ensuring preventative care

Regular health check-ups are essential for autistic children to monitor their physical, developmental, and mental health. These visits help catch potential issues early, such as epilepsy, sleep problems, or digestive challenges. Preventative care — like vaccinations, dental check-ups, and eye exams — also plays a big role in improving quality of life and long-term health.

REMEMBER

Vaccines are safe and thoroughly tested, and they're an important part of protecting your child from serious illnesses.

TIP

Choose healthcare providers who adapt to your child's needs and discuss sensory sensitivities, communication challenges, or anxiety. Simple adjustments, like quieter appointment times or reducing waiting room stress, can make visits easier. You can make healthcare visits easier by bringing items like noise-canceling headphones, a favorite toy, or a weighted blanket to help your child stay calm. If they have communication differences, let the doctor know their needs ahead of time, like using visuals or allowing extra time to explain things. By staying on top of regular check-ups and preventative care, you're helping your child build a strong foundation for their physical health and overall well-being. With thoughtful planning and open communication, these visits can become a positive part of your child's care routine.

Administering medications if needed

If your child needs medication, understanding why it's being prescribed and how it can help is important. Medications might be used to treat things like anxiety, ADHD, epilepsy, sleep problems, or gastrointestinal issues. Always have a detailed conversation with the doctor about what to expect, possible side effects, and how the medication fits into your child's care plan.

TIP

Stay consistent with the medication schedule. Tools like a pill organizer or setting alarms on your phone can make it easier to remember. Watch how your child responds — whether they're improving or having side effects — and share that information with the doctor during regular check-ins. These updates help make sure the medication is working as intended or signal that adjustments are needed.

Keep a detailed list of all your child's medications and supplements because they can interact with each other. If your child has trouble swallowing pills, talk to the pharmacist about alternatives like liquids or chewables. Staying organized and in close communication with your doctor ensures your child's medication is safe, effective, and meets their unique needs.

Self-Care for Parents and Caregivers

Taking care of yourself — physically, emotionally, and mentally — is essential when you're caring for someone else. The caregiver role can be demanding, and without self-care, it's easy to feel drained or overwhelmed. Prioritizing your own well-being helps you stay present, patient, and better able to support your child.

Taking care of yourself

Taking care of yourself isn't just important. It's essential. With caregiving, appointments, and advocacy filling your days, it's easy to overlook your own needs. But your well-being directly impacts your ability to support your child. Just like a car needs a battery to run, you need to keep your metaphorical battery charged to keep going for your child. Caring for yourself is part of caring for them.

REMEMBER

Self-care doesn't have to be extravagant or time-consuming. It can be as simple as making time to take a walk, watch your favorite show, or call a friend. The key is carving out moments that let you recharge. If you have a partner, family member, or trusted friend who can step in for even a short while, let them. It's okay to ask for help.

Joining a support group or connecting with other parents in similar situations can make a big difference. Talking to someone who truly understands can be a huge relief, and they might share tips or resources to make life easier. If you're feeling overwhelmed, don't hesitate to reach out to a therapist or counselor for tools to navigate challenges.

REMEMBER

Self-care isn't selfish; it's necessary. You're doing an amazing job, but you're human too. Taking care of your physical and emotional health helps you show up for your child and sets an example of resilience for your family. You deserve care just as much as your child does.

Finding respite care and support

Finding respite care and support services for your child is an important step — for both your child and you. Being a caregiver can be physically and emotionally demanding, and taking a break doesn't mean you're failing. It means you're taking care of yourself so you can give your best.

TIP

Respite care provides temporary relief while ensuring your child is well cared for. It comes in different forms: someone coming to your home, your child going to a specialized daycare, or even a situation that involves overnight care. Start by asking your child's doctor, therapists, or local autism organizations for recommendations. They often have networks of trusted providers. Government programs or nonprofits may also offer financial assistance or lists of vetted caregivers. If you're unsure, ask for a trial visit or meeting before committing.

REMEMBER

Support services not only give you a break but they can help your child thrive. Look for programs offering skills training, recreational activities, or therapy that align with your child's strengths and interests. Connecting with other parents through support groups or online communities can help uncover resources you might not have known about.

Take your time to find care that feels right for your family. Ask questions, and don't hesitate to seek support. Both you and your child deserve it. This step can make a meaningful difference for both of you.

Building your caregiving routine

Creating a sustainable caregiving routine is key to supporting both your child and you. Trying to do everything all the time leads to burnout, so focus on a daily rhythm that balances structure and flexibility. Break tasks into manageable steps, prioritize what's essential, and let go of perfection. A routine isn't about strict schedules. It's about finding what works for your family.

TIP

Giving yourself even 10 minutes to rest or take a walk is important. Ask for help from family, friends, or respite care services, and don't hesitate to delegate tasks. When you're recharged, you're better able to care for your child.

Connecting with other caregivers

Connecting with other parents and caregivers of autistic children can make a huge difference. Because they're in a situation similar to yours, they're people who truly understand your joys and challenges and can offer practical advice and emotional support.

TIP

You can connect through local support groups, online communities, or social media. Even a quick conversation with someone who gets it can help you feel less alone. These relationships are about sharing experiences, offering support, and building a network of people who celebrate your wins and lift you up when things get hard. You don't have to do this alone.

Connecting with autistic adults

Connecting with autistic adults can be one of the most valuable things you do as a parent. While their experiences might seem different from your child's, they can offer insights you won't find elsewhere. Autistic adults understand the world in ways that professionals or caregivers may not because they know what challenges exist and what support truly helps.

TIP

Start by exploring autistic-led organizations, social media, or local advocacy groups. Many autistic adults are happy to share their experiences and offer guidance. Listening with an open mind can challenge assumptions and help you better understand your child's needs. Learning from autistic adults gives you a deeper understanding and tools to support your child's growth.

Planning for the Future

Planning your child's future can seem like a big task, but breaking it into steps makes it easier. Start by estimating long-term needs like housing, medical care, and support. Then, explore financial tools like a special needs trust, which allows you to save for their future without affecting access to benefits like disability income or healthcare.

REMEMBER

Another important step is building an emergency fund. Life is unpredictable, and having money set aside for unexpected expenses like sudden medical needs or caregiving changes can save a lot of stress. If you're in a place that offers something like an Achieving a Better Life Experience (ABLE) account, you can look into establishing one. It's a tax-friendly way to save for disability-related expenses like education, technology, or therapies.

Estate planning is also critical. Update your will, consider life insurance to fund care after you're gone, and plan for guardianship or decision-making to ensure your child's needs are managed in the future.

TIP

You don't have to figure this out on your own. Financial planners, attorneys, and disability advocates can help guide you. It's about taking small steps now to create a safety net for your child's future.

REMEMBER

Advocating for your child's rights is crucial to ensuring they have the support they need for a fulfilling life. Start by understanding their legal rights under laws like IDEA in USA, which guarantees access to education, healthcare, and services.

Supported decision-making

As your child grows into adulthood, they deserve the chance to make their own choices about their life, just like anyone else. That doesn't mean they have to figure it all out on their own; sometimes, making decisions takes a bit of support, and that's where you can play an important role.

Supported decision-making is about working together to explore options, understand choices, and make decisions that feel right for them. It's not about stepping in and taking over. It's about being a guide, a sounding board, or a trusted resource when they need it. This approach respects their independence while giving them the tools and confidence to navigate the world. It's a way to empower them while staying connected and supportive as they take the lead in their own life.

Guardianship, where a court appoints someone to make decisions for a person about day-to-day issues, used to be the go-to option for disabled adults. It often limited independence and decision-making rights. Now, there's a shift toward supported decision-making, which helps people stay in control of their own lives while getting support to make informed choices. It's a move toward more empowerment and respect for their autonomy.

WARNING

It's important to approach any discussion of guardianship cautiously. This is because some professionals may automatically recommend guardianship without considering your child's abilities or less restrictive options, which could unnecessarily limit their independence and legal rights.

Ask yourself tough questions: Does your child need full decision-making support, or can they thrive with help in specific areas? Consulting with legal experts, advocates, and disability rights organizations can help you make an informed choice.

TIP

Before pursuing guardianship, explore alternatives like Supported Decision-Making Agreements (SDMAs). These allow your child to retain their legal rights while designating trusted supporters to help them understand options, communicate choices, and ensure their preferences are respected. Other options, like conservatorship or power of attorney, can provide tailored support for financial and legal decisions without taking away all rights. The goal is to balance guidance with autonomy.

SDMAs are officially recognized in many states, but not everywhere. If they aren't legally recognized where you live, you can still create a private agreement that follows the same principles. Disability rights groups can be a great resource. They often provide advice, online templates, and even in-person legal clinics to help you get started.

REMEMBER

The goal is to create a future where your child feels respected, supported, and empowered to live a life that's uniquely theirs. Thoughtful planning ensures they have the tools and care to thrive on their own terms.

Centers for Independent Living

In the United States, Centers for Independent Living (CILs) are incredible community resources designed to help disabled people, including autistic adults with high support needs, live more independently. They offer a range of services, like skills training, advocacy, and help navigating housing or employment.

For families, CILs can provide guidance, connect you to support networks, and help you learn how to empower your loved one while offering the right level of support. They focus on respecting individual goals and helping people build the lives they want regardless of the kind of support they need to get there. To connect with these centers, check out the list of resources at www.pivotdiversity.com/resources.

Additionally, many countries have organizations similar to CILs that support disabled individuals in achieving autonomy and full community participation. These organizations often share the core principles of consumer control, peer support, self-help, self-determination, and advocacy.

Considering housing options

Planning for your child's future means considering housing that helps them live safely and thrive in their community. Inclusive models that integrate them into the broader community are often the best choice, promoting connection, independence, and belonging while providing needed support. Options might include living at home with in-home supports, shared housing, or transitioning to semi-independent living.

A good way to evaluate housing options outside of your own home is to consider the "Burrito Rule": Can your child decide at any time to go to the kitchen and enjoy a burrito in their own space and on their own terms? (Something that every other adult is able to do.) Green flags include housing that fosters this level of independence, allowing your child to live comfortably in their community while receiving support.

Involve your child in decisions as much as possible, respect their preferences, and plan early to ensure they feel safe, supported, and empowered in a home that allows them to truly be part of their community.

Considering employment options

Work can be a great way for your adult child to build skills, gain independence, and connect with their community. Integrated jobs, where autistic people work alongside nondisabled coworkers, are especially valuable. These roles focus on inclusion, pay fair wages, and celebrate strengths and individuality.

Avoid segregated workshops or sheltered programs that isolate autistic people and pay below minimum wage (increasingly illegal in many places). These settings can limit opportunities for skill-building and connection. Instead, look for inclusive workplaces that offer proper training, reasonable accommodations, and respect for your child's abilities and preferences.

TIP

Volunteering is also a great option if paid work isn't the right fit. It lets them explore interests, engage with their community, and gain purpose on their own terms. Volunteering at places like libraries, animal shelters, or food banks can build confidence and provide meaningful experiences.

It's important to recognize that not every autistic adult will be able to or want to work — and that's okay. Work isn't the only way to build a meaningful life. If employment isn't the right fit, there are other ways to create structure and connection.

REMEMBER

It's important to find programs that don't just "babysit" your adult child, but engage them in meaningful ways. Look for programs that offer recreational activities, social opportunities, or skill-building workshops tailored to their interests. The goal is to create a life where your child feels valued, connected, and able to thrive, whether that's through work, volunteering, or other community-based activities.

Establishing a trust for your child

A trust sets aside money or assets for your child, managed by a trustee you choose. It ensures funds are used for your child's needs without affecting their eligibility for benefits, protecting their financial future while preserving access to programs with income or asset limits.

Types of trusts to consider

Trust types and rules vary by country. Common options include:

>> **Discretionary trusts:** These trusts give the trustee full control over how and when funds are used for your child, providing flexibility while protecting access to benefits.

>> **Support trusts:** These provide funds specifically for your child's care and living expenses but may have stricter rules in some countries regarding benefits eligibility.

>> **Pooled trusts:** These are managed by nonprofit groups that combine resources from multiple families while keeping individual accounts separate. They are often cost-effective.

>> **Special needs trust:** These hold money or assets for a disabled person without affecting their eligibility for government support like disability income or healthcare. It's designed to cover expenses that government benefits don't.

Things a trust can cover

A trust supplements, not replaces, government benefits, providing funds for things that enhance your child's quality of life. This can include assistive technology, therapies, education, recreational activities, personal care, housing, transportation, or travel, depending on local laws. However, the specific things a trust can pay for depends on the type of trust and the laws in your region.

How to set-up a trust

To set up a trust that secures your child's future while aligning with your family's goals and local laws, follow these key steps:

1. **Consult a local legal expert.**

   It's essential to work with an attorney specializing in estate planning and disability law in your region because trust laws vary.

2. **Appoint a trustee.**

   The trustee manages the trust's funds and ensures they're used appropriately. Choose someone trustworthy, organized, and knowledgeable about your child's needs or consider a professional trustee service.

3. **Decide how to fund the trust.**

   You can fund the trust with cash, investments, or other assets like life insurance policies. Speak with a financial advisor as you plan.

4. **Document your child's needs.**

   Write a detailed guide outlining your child's preferences, routines, and care needs to help the trustee make informed spending decisions.

5. **Review and update regularly.**

   Circumstances change, so revisit your trust periodically to ensure it still meets your family's needs and complies with local laws.

Nonprofits and community groups are valuable resources for setting up a trust. They offer workshops, guides, and connections to affordable legal experts. Disability-focused organizations and pooled trusts can also provide financial planning support.

Trusts around the world

Trusts vary by location. In the UK, families use Discretionary Trusts for disabled beneficiaries. In Canada, the Registered Disability Savings Plan (RDSP) complements trusts for long-term planning. Australia's Special Disability Trusts protect access to pensions while providing support.

In the United States, Special Needs Trusts (SNTs) preserve eligibility for benefits like SSI and Medicaid, with the ABLE Act offering another savings option. Other regions may rely on pooled or private trusts. It's essential to understand local laws to choose the right trust for securing your child's future.

3

Supporting the Growth of Autistic Kids

Apply strategies to support cognitive development in autistic children, leveraging unique learning patterns, executive functioning, and technology.

Navigate the school system to access special education, implement inclusive strategies, and address unique learning needs.

Foster autistic socialization by embracing unique connection styles, encouraging peer interactions, and building self-advocacy skills.

Empower autistic teens by supporting emotional growth, promoting independence, ensuring mental health, and preparing for adulthood.

Chapter 9

Growing Cognitive Skills

Supporting your child's development is like helping a young plant grow. Just as plants need sunlight, water, and the right soil, children need love, guidance, and opportunities to learn. You provide the "sunlight" through encouragement and warmth, the "water" through consistent care, and the "soil" through a safe and engaging environment. With your patience and attention, they'll grow strong, develop their own unique "branches," and thrive in their own way.

In this chapter, we explore different ways to support your autistic child's development by sparking curiosity, encouraging learning, and creating a space that nurtures their emotional and intellectual growth.

Supporting How Autistic Kids Think

Autistic children think and process the world in unique ways, and there's no one-size-fits-all approach. Their cognition often involves different ways of processing information, solving problems, and interacting. (For more on this, turn to Chapter 4.)

These traits can be strengths but may also come with challenges needing understanding and support. As a parent or caregiver, knowing how your child's mind works helps you connect and support their growth.

Autistic kids might notice details or patterns others miss, discover creative solutions, or have strong memories for topics they love. However, they may find switching tasks hard, struggle with abstract ideas, or need extra time to process things.

TIP

Be patient and give your child the time they need to answer questions or move between tasks. Allowing them to go at their own pace can lower frustration and build their confidence.

REMEMBER

Understanding how your child thinks isn't just about seeing the challenges; it's about celebrating their unique perspective. Focusing on their strengths — whether it's their attention to detail, deep focus, or creativity — helps them feel valued and capable.

Understanding how your child learns

Every child learns differently, and finding what works for your autistic child can boost their confidence and growth. Once you understand their learning style, tailor their environment to fit their needs. For visual learners, use charts and videos. For auditory learners, try educational stories or discussions. For hands-on learners, go for lessons that include movement.

Watch how your child tackles tasks and processes information. Do they prefer hands-on activities, suggesting a kinesthetic learning style? Are they more engaged with pictures and diagrams, showing a visual learning preference? Or do they enjoy listening to stories, hinting at an auditory style? Notice when they're most focused and whether they prefer working alone or with others.

TIP

Tie learning to your child's interests to make it fun and meaningful. If they love nature, try counting rocks, learning about plants, or joining a nature club. This helps them feel understood and valued.

REMEMBER

Learning styles can change over time or with different subjects. Stay flexible and be ready to adapt. By understanding and supporting your child's unique way of learning, you help create a strong foundation for their success at school and beyond.

Taking a strength-based approach

Focusing on your autistic child's strengths helps them thrive. A strength-based approach builds on their unique talents, skills, and interests for learning and development. Instead of just addressing challenges, it highlights what they excel at, like problem-solving, creative art, or special interests. Integrating these strengths into daily activities makes school and home life more enjoyable and engaging.

TIP

Create spaces where your child feels comfortable expressing themselves through drawing, writing, or technology, showing that their voice matters. Assign tasks that match their abilities to build confidence and independence.

Nurturing focused interests

Autistic kids often have strong passions, like trains, animals, or art. These interests aren't just fun — they're powerful tools for learning and boosting confidence. If your child loves space, for instance, use that interest to teach math, reading, or science. Tying learning to what they enjoy keeps it engaging and meaningful.

TIP

Focused interests can also foster social connections and skill-building. Encouraging your child to share their passion or join related clubs helps develop communication and teamwork skills, making social interactions more natural.

These interests can also teach life skills like responsibility and problem-solving. For example, a child who loves animals might take on caring for a pet or work on a project about animal habitats. Supporting their passions builds confidence, strengthens connections, and shows them how to apply their strengths in other areas.

Encouraging play and exploration

Play is a powerful way for autistic kids to learn, grow, and express themselves. It helps build confidence, supports cognitive development, and can look different for each child — and that's perfectly okay. Some kids might prefer structured play, like building with blocks or working on projects, while others may engage in sensory play with sand, water, or tactile toys. These activities can be calming and fun, especially for those with sensory sensitivities.

REMEMBER

Play can also mean different things for autistic children, and they might explore and enjoy it in their own way. This could include parallel play, where they play next to others without direct interaction, or focusing deeply on a specific activity. Both are normal and valuable forms of play.

TIP

Tailoring play to fit your child's interests and strengths makes them feel understood and encourages exploration. For example, if your child loves trains, set up a track-building activity that challenges their creativity and problem-solving skills.

Interactive play can also be an opportunity to build social skills. Activities like turn-taking games or simple role-playing with peers can encourage collaboration and communication in a low-pressure setting. Gradually introduce new types of play at a comfortable pace to help expand their experiences while ensuring they feel safe. Letting them lead playtime and celebrating their successes, no matter how small, supports their confidence and helps them learn in a way that feels natural and fun.

Improving Executive Functioning

Executive functioning refers to a set of mental skills that help with planning, staying organized, managing time, and completing tasks. These skills also play a role in emotional control, problem-solving, and adapting to changes. For autistic children, developing strong executive functioning can make a big difference, helping them become more independent and better able to face challenges in school and beyond.

Building organizational skills

Supporting autistic children in building organizational skills starts with structured routines and simple tools. Picture schedules, checklists, and labeled bins can make everyday tasks like getting dressed or packing a school bag easier to manage. Breaking tasks into smaller, simpler steps and keeping routines consistent helps them feel more in control and understand what's coming next. Activities like sorting toys by color or arranging books by size can teach organizational skills in a fun way. Using timers to set expectations and praising their progress helps keep them motivated.

For teens, practical strategies that meet daily needs are key. To-do lists, calendar apps, and clearly labeled storage help keep track of work tasks, appointments, and household responsibilities. Tackling bigger projects by breaking them down into steps, such as categorizing paperwork or cleaning one section of a room at a time, can make these tasks more manageable. Timers and reminders help with time management, while celebrating small wins can boost confidence.

Establishing and maintaining routines

Routines help autistic kids feel secure, reduce stress, and build independence. Start with simple daily tasks, like morning or bedtime routines, and add more as they become comfortable. Visual aids like picture charts or lists help them follow along. Keeping routines at the same time daily helps make them a habit.

Create visual schedules suited to your child's age and development. Younger children might benefit from picture charts, while older kids could use written lists or apps. Place these schedules in easy-to-see spots, like the bathroom or homework area. Sticking to regular times for meals, homework, and bedtime helps to build routines.

To ease transitions, give reminders like, "Five more minutes," or use a specific toy or song as a signal to switch tasks. Involve them in planning routines, like packing their backpack or cleaning up toys. Including breaks and teaching them to handle changes calmly will make routines a positive, confidence-building part of their day.

Improving task initiation and completion

Starting and finishing tasks can sometimes be a challenge for autistic children, but breaking tasks down into smaller steps can help make it easier. Daily schedules and reminders can also help. A set routine shows them what to expect, and timers or countdowns can signal when it's time to start.

Instead of saying, "Clean your room," guide them with steps like, "Put toys in the box" or "Put clothes in the hamper." Visual aids like checklists or pictures clarify tasks and provide a sense of accomplishment. Letting your child choose the first task gives them a sense of control. With practice and positive feedback, autistic children can gain confidence completing tasks independently.

Navigating task and life changes

Helping autistic people navigate changes in tasks or life events can be smoother with structure, clear communication, and gradual transitions. Start by explaining upcoming changes in simple language, and use visual aids or social stories to make the information clearer. Break down the change into smaller, manageable steps, and provide a clear schedule or timeline so they know what to expect.

To ease anxiety, use calming techniques like deep breathing or having a comfort item nearby. Practice small routine changes regularly to build flexibility. With patience and support, they can gain confidence and handle changes more comfortably.

Supporting memory and learning

Many autistic kids may have a fantastic long-term memory but may struggle with working memory, which helps a person keep things in their mind for short periods and aids in using that information to decide what to do. To support them, break information into smaller, manageable parts, group related ideas, summarize key points, and create written reminders. Regular repetition helps information stick. Visual aids like charts, diagrams, and pictures benefit visual learners, while songs, rhymes, and discussions are great for auditory learners.

TIP

Engage different senses to reinforce learning. Writing things down, acting out ideas, or using movement can aid memory. Connect new material to familiar interests for easier recall. Tricks like rhymes, acronyms, or memory games can help with harder concepts. Keep the learning space distraction-free, follow routines, and allow breaks.

Teaching your child about emotions

To teach your child about emotions, use clear, visual tools like emotion cards or simple drawings to introduce emotions, and connect these to real-life situations in a way that makes sense to them. Keep language straightforward and relatable and show that there's no one "right" way to experience or express emotions.

Storytelling and role-playing are fun ways to explore emotions and reinforce that all feelings are valid. Encourage them to share their feelings in their own way and celebrate their progress to build confidence and emotional awareness.

Encourage your child to talk about their feelings and provide words for expression. Ask, "Are you happy or upset?" and guide them if needed. Praise their efforts to identify or express emotions to build confidence and foster connection.

TIP

To teach perspective-taking, help your child understand that others may have different thoughts or feelings. Try simple activities, like discussing how characters in a story might feel or asking, "How do you think your friend feels when you share your toy?" This helps make the concept clearer and supports empathy.

Enhancing Problem-Solving Skills

Building problem-solving skills is essential for everyone, but it's especially important for autistic children. These skills help them navigate daily life with greater confidence, make decisions, and become more independent.

REMEMBER

Problem-solving promotes critical thinking and adaptability, which are crucial for learning and interacting with others. For autistic kids, having strong problem-solving abilities can make a big difference in handling changes, managing emotions, and feeling more in control of their environment.

Encouraging flexible thinking

Flexible thinking helps autistic kids handle changes and new experiences with less stress, building resilience and adaptability. Developing this skill makes daily life smoother and helps them feel more comfortable with unexpected events. Encourage flexible thinking by showing that new approaches can be positive. Start small, like taking a different route to the park or trying a new snack. Use clear explanations and visual aids to show what's happening and why.

Role-playing and "what if" scenarios make trying new ideas feel safe and fun. Celebrate their effort when they adapt with praise or small rewards to build confidence. These steps help them become more comfortable with change over time.

Problem-solving for real life

Problem-solving skills help autistic children handle daily challenges, make decisions, and gain confidence. These skills are key for managing tasks, resolving conflicts, and adapting to new situations.

TIP

Teach problem-solving in simple steps: Identify the problem, brainstorm solutions, pick the best option, try it, and review what worked or didn't. This makes learning clear and manageable. For example, if your child can't find their favorite toy, guide them to try ideas like checking under the bed or asking a sibling. Practice real-life situations like forgetting homework or sharing toys to make lessons relatable.

Activities like building with blocks, board games, and creative tasks teach problem-solving in a fun way. Show how you solve problems, like having a backup plan. Gradually introduce more complex tasks, such as choosing activities or planning projects. With practice, kids gain confidence and handle challenges independently.

Fostering Creative and Abstract Thinking

Encouraging creative and abstract thinking in autistic children builds flexibility, problem-solving skills, and new ways to understand the world. These abilities help them adapt, communicate clearly, and face challenges confidently. Activities like drawing, storytelling, and imaginative play allow kids to explore ideas and feelings, moving beyond rigid thinking and enhancing problem-solving skills.

Abstract thinking involves imagining possibilities, understanding symbols, and grasping complex ideas. This type of thinking supports everyday skills like understanding jokes, predicting outcomes, and making decisions. By nurturing these abilities, parents can help their children feel more confident, communicate more effectively, and approach challenges with greater independence.

Storytelling and imaginative play

Storytelling and imaginative play are great for teaching and self-expression. They help build language, emotional understanding, and social skills. Reading simple stories with pictures or creating stories together can teach children about emotions and relationships. Using toys or puppets to act out stories makes it more engaging.

TIP

Imaginative play allows kids to take on roles like shopkeeper or doctor, helping them practice talking, sharing, and social skills. If they're unsure how to start, join in to build their confidence and creativity. Combine storytelling and play by acting out a favorite story or creating one with toys or costumes. Praise their efforts and let them take the lead. These activities support learning, confidence, and safe exploration.

REMEMBER

Autistic children may engage in imaginative play in ways that differ from typical expectations. They might appear to be staring off into space, reinforcing the stereotype that they're "lost in their own little world." In reality, they are often deep in thought, exploring ideas, creating stories, or playing out scenarios internally. This quiet, internal play is as valuable as more typical play, helping them process their world and spark creativity.

Engaging with arts and crafts

Arts and crafts are excellent for supporting learning and development in autistic children. Activities like drawing, painting, and crafting not only boost motor skills and creativity but also make learning hands-on and enjoyable. For instance, drawing or painting can teach colors and shapes, while creating bead patterns or building with clay reinforces math and fine motor skills. Using sensory-friendly materials, such as soft clay or textured paper, can enhance comfort and enjoyment, especially for children with sensory differences.

Using Technology and Multimedia

Technology and multimedia can support learning for autistic children in tailored ways. Apps, videos, and interactive games make learning visual and hands-on, aiding understanding and retention. When matched to their strengths, technology engages and builds confidence.

Educational apps use visuals, sounds, and interaction to make lessons enjoyable and motivating. Apps for academics, like math games, and visual schedules build key skills. Augmentative and alternative communication (AAC) apps help nonspeaking children express themselves, reducing frustration and fostering independence, whereas social skills apps offer safe role-play practice.

TIP

Multimedia tools, such as videos and audio recordings, keep lessons engaging and simplify learning. Visual aids like animations explain complex ideas, and interactive games encourage active participation at their own pace. Choose tools that fit your child's needs, interests, and sensory preferences. Keeping content simple and free from distractions makes learning more effective and fun.

Chapter **10**

Navigating the School System

Navigating the school system as an autistic child's parent or caregiver can be overwhelming. Rules and processes aren't always clear, and finding what works takes effort. But with knowledge and support, you can guide your child with confidence.

In this chapter, we explore how to understand your child's learning style and share that with their teachers to help them succeed. We break down mainstreaming and special education services and how each can benefit your child. You find out how to navigate special education processes and collaborate with educators to create a plan that fits your child's needs. Plus, we talk about finding the support you need.

Understanding How Your Child Learns

Every child learns differently, and this is especially true for autistic kids. Understanding their unique strengths and challenges is key to helping them succeed. Pay attention to how they learn best — what they excel at and where they need support — and share this with their teachers to create a better learning experience.

Recognizing learning differences means understanding how your child interacts with the world, not just where they struggle. Some kids excel in memory, pattern recognition, or deep focus, whereas others need support with instructions or transitions — and that's okay.

TIP

Notice how your child engages with tasks. Do they learn best through hands-on activities or visual aids? Are they more focused alone or in groups? Identifying these patterns helps shape their learning environment to match their needs and build confidence.

REMEMBER

Learning styles can change over time or with different subjects. Tailoring education to your child's strengths fosters confidence and excitement about learning. Patience, encouragement, and teamwork make a big difference.

Understanding learning differences

Autistic kids often learn in ways that don't always fit a typical classroom. Understanding how your child learns differently helps you support them at school and beyond.

Learning differences aren't deficits or failures; they're just different ways of thinking, processing, and problem-solving. Some autistic kids have sharp detail recognition, strong memories, or deep focus — sometimes beyond their neurotypical peers. Others may struggle with following instructions, switching tasks, or handling noisy environments.

REMEMBER

All humans face challenges, and for autistic children, learning differences can come with their own challenges. Recognizing them helps you better support your child in a way that works for them.

Appreciating the importance of learning differences

Understanding how your child learns helps you support them better at home and collaborate effectively with their teachers and support team. Learning differences can show up in how your child reads, writes, focuses, or interacts with classmates. When you recognize these differences, you and the school can adjust teaching methods and the classroom setup to fit your child's needs. This sets the stage for them to feel more comfortable, confident, and ready to succeed.

Recognizing common learning differences

Learning differences show up in many ways, and they're different for every child. Here are a few examples you might notice:

>> **Attention:** In some, focus can be intense on topics of interest but hard to sustain on less engaging tasks.

>> **Reading:** Some autistic kids may read early and fluently, while others might struggle with decoding words or understanding what they read.

>> **Writing:** Handwriting can be hard for some due to coordination differences, and organizing thoughts on paper may also be tricky.

>> **Processing speed:** Some kids need more time to understand and respond, while others process very quickly.

>> **Sensory-based learning differences:** Bright lights, loud noises, or certain textures can be distracting or overwhelming in the classroom, while some kids seek sensory input like spinning, touching, or making sounds.

>> **Social learning differences:** Understanding neurotypical body language, unspoken rules, or group work expectations can take more effort, while neurotypical children are seldom taught how autistic kids naturally prefer to socialize.

>> **Memory:** Some may remember details extremely well but struggle with following multi-step instructions.

>> **Executive function:** Planning, organization, and starting or switching tasks may be difficult.

TIP

Learning differences aren't a child's fault — they're just part of how their brain works. And while they come with challenges, they also bring strengths worth celebrating. Your child might have an incredible memory, a knack for spotting patterns, or a creative way of solving problems. These strengths can be powerful learning tools. Work with teachers to build on what your child does well to keep them engaged. For example, if they love animals, weaving that interest into reading or math can make lessons more relatable and enjoyable.

WARNING

Celebrating your child's unique way of learning doesn't mean ignoring their challenges. These difficulties are real and can make school and daily life tough. Acknowledging them is key to getting the right support. By recognizing both strengths and challenges, you can find solutions that build on their abilities while providing the support they need.

Supporting learning differences

As a parent or caregiver, you're an observer, supporter, and advocate. Pay attention to how your child learns best. Do they prefer hands-on activities, listening to stories, or visual aids like charts and pictures?

Once you understand their learning style, tailor their education to fit the style. If they learn well with visual aids, use charts, diagrams, or videos to help them grasp new ideas. If they thrive with hands-on activities, incorporate interactive lessons and projects that let them get involved directly.

REMEMBER

Share your observations with teachers so they can adapt lessons based on needs. Asking questions, suggesting changes, and discussing what works helps create a great learning experience for your child.

TIP

Create a comfortable space at home to study. This might mean fidget toys to aide concentration or creating a familiar routine. Small adjustments can make learning less stressful and more enjoyable.

Identifying strengths and challenges

Autistic kids may face challenges that make school difficult, but understanding these challenges — and how to support them — can help them thrive. It's equally important to recognize and celebrate their strengths to help them grow and succeed.

TIP

Observe how your child learns, interacts, and navigates school. Challenges might include difficulties with reading, writing, math, focus, memory, or social interactions. Some kids struggle with following instructions, staying on task, or completing assignments. Others may have difficulties with fine motor skills, speech, or managing emotions.

REMEMBER

Parents, caregivers, and teachers play a key role in identifying patterns and sharing observations. Combining insights from home and school gives a clearer picture of learning needs. Professionals like school psychologists, speech therapists, and occupational therapists can provide screenings and strategies for support.

Making a difference with early support

Identifying your child's challenges as early as possible is crucial. So is recognizing their strengths. Early recognition allows you to access the right help sooner, whether that's special teaching strategies, sensory tools, or neurodiversity-informed social skills programs. The earlier your child receives support, the more comfortable and successful they will feel in school.

Spotting strengths and using them

Recognizing challenges is important, but so is celebrating strengths. Many autistic kids excel in areas like attention to detail, memory, math, art, or problem-solving. These strengths can make learning more effective and engaging.

TIP

Work with teachers to weave your child's strengths into their learning. If they're passionate about a subject, use that to keep them engaged. Building on what they do well boosts confidence and makes school more enjoyable.

Understanding your child's challenges, building on their strengths, and working closely with the school are key to a positive learning experience. This collaborative approach helps your child feel confident, comfortable, and grow in their own way.

Understanding overlapping conditions

Many autistic children also have other conditions that impact how they learn and interact at school (see Chapter 1). Being aware of these helps you and their school team build a more complete support plan.

Overlapping conditions can impact focus, organization, and information processing. For example, an autistic child with dyslexia may excel in pattern recognition but struggle with reading fluency, needing support with decoding while benefiting from visual or hands-on learning.

Recognizing importance of overlapping conditions

Schools sometimes mistake overlapping conditions for autistic traits. ADHD-related attention differences might be seen as autism, while social anxiety may be assumed to be a natural part of being autistic. If your child struggles with reading, autism may be blamed when dyslexia could be the real issue. Identifying these differences ensures your child gets the right support.

Understanding these conditions is important for providing the best support. An autistic child with dyslexia may need different strategies than an autistic child with ADHD. Recognizing this helps schools create tailored plans to better support individual learning.

Supporting autistic kids with overlapping conditions

When your autistic child has overlapping conditions, it affects how they engage and learn. Here are some key tips to help them succeed:

>> **Adapted materials:** Teachers may need to adjust lessons to match your child's specific needs, such as using audiobooks for reading challenges or providing speech-to-text tools for writing difficulties.

>> **Communication with teachers:** Make sure the school knows all of your child's diagnoses to avoid misunderstandings.

>> **Ask for evaluations:** If your autistic child's challenges seem to go beyond autistic traits, request assessments for other conditions like ADHD, learning differences, or mental health needs.

>> **Collaborate on support:** Work with the school to create plans that include all needed accommodations, like flexible seating or quiet spaces.

>> **Stay observant:** Watch how your child's needs change over time. Some conditions may become more noticeable in different situations.

Understanding and addressing overlapping conditions helps create a learning environment that plays to your child's strengths and manages their challenges with effective strategies. By working closely with teachers and school staff, you can ensure your child receives the understanding and support they need to thrive.

Navigating Educational Approaches

The way schools support autistic children has changed a lot. In the past, many were placed in separate classrooms that aimed to meet their needs but often led to feelings of isolation.

Today, there's more focus on inclusion. Schools now recognize that learning alongside peers benefits all students. This shift has brought about approaches like mainstreaming, where students with disabilities join general education classrooms with additional support as needed. Mainstreaming helps autistic children feel included, build social skills, and develop a sense of belonging. It also fosters growth in non-disabled peers, teaching them to collaborate and socialize with classmates who think and learn in different ways.

Mainstreaming: Bringing kids together

Mainstreaming means autistic students learn in general classrooms for some or all of the day, with extra support when needed. It's not just about kids being in the same classroom — it's about all different types of children working together on projects, playing with each other at recess, and learning side by side. This allows autistic and non-autistic students to learn important skills like communication, collaboration, and understanding different ways of thinking. Teachers also find new ways to support everyone's learning, creating a classroom that works better for all.

Special education: Tailoring support

Special education focuses on adapting teaching and support to fit each child's unique needs. For autistic children, this can include various services like speech therapy, occupational therapy, social skills training, and specialized teaching methods. These supports help them overcome learning challenges and engage with lessons in ways that work for them.

Special education programs are often based on plans like Individualized Education Plans (IEPs) in the United States and Canada; Education, Health, and Care Plans (EHCPs) in the UK; or similar plans in other countries. These plans are made with input from parents, teachers, and specialists, outlining each child's goals, needs, and support services.

Blending both approaches

A mix of mainstream and special education can create a flexible, inclusive, and supportive learning environment. Being in a general classroom helps autistic kids build social connections, practice communication, and engage in shared learning. At the same time, targeted special education services ensure their unique learning needs are met. Here's how it often works:

>> **Coteaching:** In many schools, general education and special education teachers work together in one classroom. This model gives all students access to both teachers' expertise, so autistic kids receive specialized support without being separated.

>> **Classroom aides:** Some students might benefit from having a trained aide in the classroom who can help them stay on track, understand instructions, and manage sensory needs. This way, they get the help they need while staying in the main classroom.

>> **Modified materials:** Teachers might adapt lessons or use specialized tools that match the child's learning style and level.

>> **Therapies and services:** Services like speech or occupational therapy can often be provided in the classroom, making them a natural part of the school day or in a separate setting if needed for focus.

When done well, this approach benefits everyone. Autistic kids feel included and supported, their peers learn empathy and understanding, and teachers create classrooms that value diversity.

As a parent or caregiver, you help shape your child's school experience. Pay attention to how they respond to different settings, and work with teachers and specialists to find the right balance of support. Your insights are essential to building a plan that works.

Collaboration between parents, teachers, and specialists creates a school environment where autistic children feel safe, included, and ready to learn. The goal is a learning experience that builds confidence, fosters friendships, and helps every child thrive in their own way.

Navigating Educational Services

If you believe your child could benefit from special education services, understanding how to navigate the system can make a big difference. While it may seem complicated at first, being prepared and informed can help you approach it with confidence. This section walks you through key steps and offers practical advice.

Recognizing when support might help

The journey often begins when you realize your child might need extra help — whether with focus, communication, social interactions, or staying on track with schoolwork. These observations can come from what you see at home, conversations with teachers, or feedback from other caregivers.

Reach out to your child's teacher or school to discuss what you've noticed. In some places, this means making a formal request for an evaluation.

Engaging the evaluation process

During the evaluation, the school or an educational team will look at your child's strengths and areas where they may need support. This process usually includes tests, observations, and input from you and their teachers to get a complete picture of how your child learns and what specific support will be most helpful.

Give your permission for these evaluations and share what you observe at home. Your insights add valuable context and create a fuller understanding of your child's needs. Also, discuss with your child so they understand what will happen and why, as appropriate.

Determining eligibility

After the evaluation, a team — including teachers, specialists, and you — reviews the results. If appropriate, your child should also be included. The team decides if your child qualifies for special education based on how their learning differences influence their ability to thrive in a typical classroom.

REMEMBER

Ask questions if anything is unclear. It's essential to understand what the results mean and how they affect your child's education.

Creating a plan for support

If your child qualifies for special education services, the next step is developing a plan that meets their unique needs. In the United States and Canada, this is known as an Individualized Education Plan (IEP), while in other countries, there are similar plans, such as EHCPs in the UK. These plans set clear goals, list accommodations, and outline the services your child will receive, like speech therapy or specialized teaching techniques.

REMEMBER

Stay involved in this process and involve your child, as appropriate. Share strategies that work at home and suggest accommodations that could be helpful at school, such as extended test time, quiet testing areas, use of calculators or fidgets, or wobble chairs. Your input ensures the plan reflects your child's needs.

Creating a solid education plan for your child takes teamwork and preparation. Here's how to make it work:

>> **Understand the process:** Learn the purpose and structure of the plan, whether it's an IEP, EHCP, or another type, so you can participate confidently in its development.

>> **Come prepared:** Bring documents like evaluations, medical reports, and past plans. Write down questions or concerns ahead of time to stay focused.

>> **Ask questions:** Make sure you fully understand everything discussed in meetings.

>> **Seek support:** Find a community partner, a knowledgeable friend, or an experienced educational advocate to guide you.

>> **Focus on strengths and challenges:** Identify your child's strengths, challenges, and goals before the meeting. Have a clear list of concerns and suggestions ready.

>> **Build relationships:** Keep open, respectful communication with teachers and therapists.

>> **Set clear goals:** Create specific, realistic, and trackable goals for academic and social needs.

>> **Discuss accommodations:** Include therapies and services, ensuring they're detailed in the plan with frequency and duration.

>> **Address support for self-regulation and emotional well-being:** Include strategies to support emotional regulation and social interaction.

>> **Plan progress checks:** Agree on how progress will be monitored, ask for regular updates and allow flexibility for changing needs.

>> **Keep records:** Document all meetings, communications, and changes.

>> **Know your rights:** Understand education laws and your options for mediation if needed.

>> **Stay flexible:** Be ready to adjust the plan as your child's needs change.

>> **Be patient:** Allow time for trial and error; finding what works best for your child may take time.

By following these tips and collaborating with the school, you can create a plan that supports your child's growth and success.

Using a collaborative approach

Working together with everyone involved in your child's education is key to making sure they get the support they need. A collaborative approach brings together parents, teachers, therapists, and school administrators to create a plan that fits your child's strengths and needs.

As a parent, you play an essential role. Your observations and insights from home help educators build a well-rounded, practical plan.

REMEMBER

Collaboration goes beyond meetings and paperwork. I involves advocacy, strong partnerships, and open communication. Working together creates a team dedicated to your child's growth and success.

Reviewing progress

Once the support plan is in place, it's important to stay connected with your child's teachers and support team. Regular check-ins help monitor how things are going, and most plans are reviewed at least once a year to make adjustments if needed.

TIP

If your child's needs change, don't wait for the next review. You can request a meeting at any time to update the plan and ensure it stays effective.

Advocating for your child

Advocating for your child means knowing your rights and staying involved. Parents can request evaluations, suggest changes to support plans, and challenge school decisions. Knowing the laws that protect your child's education, such as the Individuals with Disabilities Education Act (IDEA) in the United States, can help you feel confident in your role.

TIP

Connect with local or online communities and support groups. Other parents can share advice, resources, and remind you that you're not alone. See section Seeking Support for additional resources.

REMEMBER

Be an active participant in meetings, stay informed about your child's progress, and speak up when changes are needed. You can request evaluations, appeal decisions, and use mediation or due process if there are disagreements. Understanding and using these rights ensures your child's education supports their unique needs.

Seeking Support

Navigating the education system can be challenging, but the right support makes a big difference. It helps you understand your rights, access services, and communicate effectively with teachers and specialists. Support can come from professionals, community resources, and experienced parents.

TIP

An *educational advocate* or *parent advocate* helps families navigate the school system and secure the right support. They can guide you through special education processes, explain your child's rights, and help you prepare for meetings. Advocates can also attend meetings to ensure your concerns are heard and that the school follows through on agreed-upon support. Their help is especially valuable if you feel overwhelmed or aren't sure what to ask for.

With the right guidance, you can create a plan that supports your child's academic, social, and emotional growth. Seeking support helps set them up to thrive in an inclusive school environment.

Tapping into professionals

Educational specialists and tutors can be key in helping your child succeed. They offer personalized instruction and targeted strategies that fit your child's unique learning style and needs. Let's look at some.

>> **Special education teachers and specialists** manage IEPs or similar plans, adapt lessons, and tailor teaching methods to work for your child.

>> **Educational therapists** help with reading, writing, math, and organization, building confidence and improving school skills.

>> **Social skills coaches** use role-playing and social stories to support your child's natural way of socializing, boosting confidence in peer interactions.

>> **Inclusion specialists** adapt learning materials and train staff in inclusive practices, helping autistic children feel valued in mainstream classrooms.

>> **Assistive technology specialists** provide tools like adaptive keyboards and speech-generating devices, working with families to tailor support.

>> **Speech therapists** support communication, spoken language, and social interaction so your child can express themselves confidently.

>> **Occupational therapists** help with skills for daily school life, like fine motor tasks and sensory strategies.

Drawing on community and peer support

Connecting with a supportive community can greatly benefit autistic children by fostering social, emotional, and academic growth. Being around people who understand them can make a big difference.

TIP

Check out local autism organizations and advocacy groups. They often offer workshops, resources, and chances to meet other families. Parent support groups can be great for advice and connection. Social media groups, especially those led by autistic adults, can provide valuable insights into your child's experiences, strengths, and challenges. Autistic adults can share what helped them in school, obstacles to watch for, and advocacy tips that parents and professionals might overlook.

Schools and community centers may have social groups or inclusive activities where kids can safely interact. Look for opportunities tied to their interests. like sports, art, or music.

Seeking financial aid

Financial aid can help families cover the costs of therapies, specialized programs, and services that schools may not fully fund.

Look into government programs, scholarships, and savings plans. Supplemental Security Income (SSI) and Medicaid waivers can help with therapy and education costs. Scholarships from autism advocacy groups can also help cover specialized education expenses. In the United States, 529 ABLE accounts allow families to save tax-free for disability-related costs.

State and local resources are also worth exploring. Schools may offer funding through IEPs or similar plans. Community organizations and nonprofits may provide grants, and vocational rehabilitation (VR) agencies can support job training and higher education. Assistive technology specialists can also help secure funding for adaptive tools.

Chapter **11**

Helping Autistic Children Socialize

For all people, socialization is a huge part of childhood, but for autistic kids, it often unfolds in ways that are a little different — and that's not just okay; it's something to be embraced. Autistic children have their own unique ways of connecting with the world, and when you understand and support these differences, you're setting the stage for them to thrive.

In this chapter, we dig into some practical, real-world advice on helping your autistic child build meaningful relationships. This isn't about making them fit into a neurotypical mold. It's about recognizing and celebrating the way they naturally socialize and helping them navigate the world on their own terms.

Supporting Autistic Socialization

Let's start with a simple truth: The way your autistic child socializes is just as valid as any other form of interaction. They might connect through shared interests, like having an in-depth conversation about dinosaurs, or prefer parallel play, when they sit side by side with a friend while each does their own thing. These are real, meaningful connections that are just as important as more traditional social interactions.

Some autistic kids communicate in unspoken ways — through gestures, facial expressions, or creative outlets like art or music. These forms of expression are powerful and should be celebrated. Your goal is to support and embrace these unique ways of socializing and not to change them.

Understanding autistic socializing

A few years back, John, from our author team, was sitting in the audience at an international autism research conference when a speaker presented research that claimed that autistic children lack interest in socializing or playing with others their age. To support this, the researcher shared photos of autistic children calmly touching or staring at objects while other kids mixed their toys and interacted with one another. The researcher's point was that young autistic children didn't like to play.

"They're playing!" John remembers his row shouting in unison. Unlike most of the audience, his conference row was filled with autism researchers and advocates who were either autistic themselves or the parents or siblings of autistic kids.

John and those around him knew something from experience that the researcher did not: Autistic children may socialize and play in ways that look different to some, but they're still playing and socializing all the same. It's not a lack of play or socialization, just a different way of doing it.

Autistic children often prefer parallel play, where they socialize and play alongside others without direct interaction, whereas neurotypical kids tend to favor cooperative play, where they directly engage with each other. Although both groups sometimes favor one approach over the other, the truth is that neither form of play is exclusive to one group or the other, and both are valid ways to connect and have fun. Autistic children *do* socialize, though their ways of interacting may be unfamiliar and sometimes misunderstood.

There are lots of ways that autistic people, including autistic kids, socialize that may be unfamiliar. Understanding these differences and engaging them helps grow your child's ability to connect with others as they grow (to learn more about differences in autistic socialization, turn to Chapter 4).

Encouraging autistic socialization

Your autistic child has a unique way of socializing that deserves understanding and support. Forcing them to fit into typical social patterns isn't the goal. Instead, your goal is to help them grow into their own social style with confidence.

Start by observing how your child naturally interacts with others. Do they prefer parallel play, where they're happy playing alongside peers rather than directly with them? Do they connect over specific interests, diving deep into topics that excite them? Whichever way your child socializes, they deserve to be supported.

TIP

Here are some ways that you can support the natural ways your autistic child may prefer to socialize:

>> **Provide environments that suit their style.** Create opportunities for social interactions that feel safe and comfortable for them. Smaller group settings, familiar places, and quiet environments can help reduce sensory overload and allow your child to socialize in ways that work for them.

>> **Encourage socializing on their terms.** Instead of trying to make your child fit into typical social expectations, give them the space to connect with others in ways that feel natural to them. This could mean sitting quietly with a friend or engaging in a focused activity together. Both are valid forms of social connection.

>> **Celebrate their unique social wins.** Whether they're bonding over a shared interest or simply enjoying the presence of others nearby, acknowledge these moments as real social successes. Show your child that their way of interacting is valuable and meaningful.

REMEMBER

By supporting your child's natural way of socializing, you help them feel confident in their connections with others. Socializing doesn't have to look a certain way. What matters is that your child feels understood and valued in how they relate to the world.

TIP

Educating others — family members, teachers, peers — about the value of autistic socialization is key. When everyone understands that autistic ways of building relationships are meaningful, it creates an inclusive environment where your child can grow with confidence and a strong sense of self.

Teaching about neurotypical socializing

Helping your child understand how neurotypical kids socialize can make a significant difference in how they navigate social situations. The objective is to build bridges between different social styles, not change who your child is. By explaining that everyone socializes differently and offering clear examples of varying approaches, you can help your child feel more comfortable and confident in social settings.

Teaching autistic kids about neurotypical socializing shouldn't mean teaching them to mask — hiding or changing who they are just to fit in. Masking is exhausting and takes a serious toll on emotional well-being. Before anything else, autistic kids need to understand and value their own way of socializing — how they naturally communicate, connect, and build relationships. As they grow, it can help to explain certain neurotypical norms when situations call for it, but more structured learning is best saved for adolescence, when they can put that information into context without feeling pressured to change.

Autistic kids often experience trauma from being pressured to mask while socializing — whether by schools, therapists, or social expectations. If your child has been through this, take a trauma-informed approach to teaching them about neurotypical socializing. This means recognizing past harm, creating a sense of safety, respecting their boundaries, and making sure they never feel pressured to conform. Learning about neurotypical socializing should feel safe, not like another demand to fit in.

Start by explaining that everyone socializes differently, and that's totally fine. Neurotypical children might use more spoken communication, make frequent eye contact, or enjoy group activities. Use simple examples to show these behaviors, emphasizing that these differences are just other ways people connect.

Role-playing can be helpful for some kids, but it's important to know that some autistic children may find it a bit artificial or uncomfortable. If your child seems resistant, try guiding them through real-life scenarios instead. Encourage them to observe and ask questions about social interactions they notice around them. This approach can make neurotypical socializing more relatable and less intimidating.

Encourage your child to talk about what they see in the world around them. If they notice peers doing something new or different, discussing these observations together can help break down the mystery of neurotypical socializing.

Above all, teach your child to appreciate and accept their own social preferences. This is their foundation for understanding how others socialize. Reinforce that their ways of connecting are just as valid. Helping them understand neurotypical socializing isn't about changing who they are; it's about giving them tools to navigate the world and bridge different social styles.

Bridging social "languages"

Autistic and neurotypical kids tend to socialize in different ways. Neither is right or wrong; they're just different. The goal of teaching social skills should be to help kids understand and respect both their own natural way of socializing and how others interact, so everyone feels more comfortable and can connect more easily.

That starts with teaching autistic and neurotypical kids about each other's social styles. Right now, this rarely happens, but it should. When both groups learn what to expect from each other, they can build stronger friendships without feeling like they have to change who they are.

REMEMBER

Helping your autistic child navigate social interactions starts with understanding how they naturally connect. Instead of forcing them to socialize a certain way, give them support to express themselves, set boundaries, and engage with others in ways that feel right to them. They should also have the option to use neurotypical social behaviors when they want to and have the energy for it. Think of it as learning a second "social language." Make sure your child is comfortable with their own "language" first before introducing neurotypical social norms.

TIP

When introducing neurotypical social norms, focus on giving your child tools, not rules. Explain the purpose behind things like neurotypical eye contact or small talk so they can understand these behaviors rather than feeling pressured to use them.

Think of it like traveling to another country — how much of the language and customs would you expect your child to learn and use while visiting? Probably some basics to get by, but not total fluency overnight. The same idea applies to socializing. Let your child learn at their own pace, and as they grow, they can decide which neurotypical social norms feel useful and comfortable for them.

WARNING

Never force an autistic child to make eye contact. Not making eye contact doesn't mean they aren't listening or engaged (more on this in Chapter 4). For many autistic individuals, focusing on eye contact can make thinking harder, distract from the conversation, and cause stress. For some, it can even cause sensations of physical pain. But that doesn't mean you can't teach them about how others use eye contact when socializing.

TIP

Encourage your child to talk about how they like to socialize. For example, you might teach them how to explain to their friends if they prefer less eye contact, need more time to think before responding, or enjoy playing next to others instead of face to face.

Also, help your child learn strategies for managing social situations. For example, teach them how to politely excuse themselves if they need a break, steer conversations toward topics they're comfortable with, or let others know when they need time alone. These strategies can help them feel more in control and less overwhelmed when socializing.

By learning to understand different social "languages," your child can feel more confident in social situations and build stronger relationships with both neurotypical and autistic friends.

Evaluating resources for your child

Parents often look to social skills programs to support their autistic child, but it's important to choose one that respects your child's individuality and autistic experience. The best programs focus on giving children the tools to communicate and interact in ways that match their personal style and needs, helping them connect with others while honoring their unique perspectives.

TIP

Look for programs that celebrate your child's strengths and communication style rather than pushing them to fit into neurotypical norms. Green flags include approaches that adapt strategies to your child's interests and ways of interacting, while also promoting self-acceptance and building confidence. A good program should help your child understand social cues in ways that resonate with them, not force them into rigid, one-size-fits-all methods.

Choose programs that are neurodiversity-informed and involve both you and your child in setting goals and adjusting strategies. A quality program should also be trauma-informed, meaning it takes into account any negative experiences your child may have had with forced socializing or attempts to make them conform to neurotypical expectations. Such experiences can cause stress and discomfort, so a trauma-informed approach aims to create a safe, supportive space that avoids further harm while promoting authentic and comfortable interactions.

WARNING

Any program that simply teaches your child to mimic neurotypical social behaviors may do more harm than good. It can increase their anxiety, stress, and emotional exhaustion by pushing them to conform to norms that don't come naturally.

On his website *Autistic Not Weird*, writer Chris Bonnello warns that when you force an autistic child to "fit in" with neurotypical expectations, "you're teaching them that who they are is not acceptable. Instead, we need to help them understand that it's okay to be themselves and that social success can happen on their own terms."

REMEMBER

Only teaching your child to socialize like neurotypical peers can make them feel like their natural way of connecting is "wrong." This can crush their self-worth and lead to loneliness, social disconnection, and even depression. Quality programs support autistic socialization and help children build real connections that honor their true selves.

Facilitating Social Interaction

Helping autistic children connect with others starts with creating opportunities that respect how they naturally interact. It's not just about setting up playdates; it's about offering the right support and creating environments where they can build real relationships with peers, family, and the broader community.

Helping your child socialize with peers

Encouraging your child to connect with others is key to building friendships and confidence. In order to help them do that, this section covers some ways to make those connections easier and more comfortable:

TIP

>> **Encourage shared interests:** Find activities or hobbies your child enjoys and arrange playdates or group events around those interests.

>> **Use structured activities:** Games with rules, building projects, or arts and crafts provide clear frameworks for interaction, which reduces anxiety.

>> **Keep group sizes small:** Smaller groups can feel less overwhelming and help your child connect more easily.

>> **Peer mentoring programs:** Consider involving your child in a peer mentoring program where older autistic and neurodiversity-informed nonautistic kids provide support and companionship.

>> **Prepare in advance:** Talk through upcoming social events to help your child feel more comfortable with what to expect.

>> **Model social behaviors:** Demonstrate and talk through social behaviors like turn-taking and sharing during play to build their confidence. Be sure to explain the reasons why people do things in this way as well.

REMEMBER

Make sure your autistic child has opportunities to socialize with other autistic kids. It can let them connect in ways that feel natural and without the pressure to adapt or mask. Around others who think and communicate like they do, they're often more confident, understood, and at ease. In these settings, there's less pressure to conform to neurotypical social norms — so they can interact in ways that make sense to them, whether through shared interests, parallel play, or their own unique communication. These friendships can build confidence, foster emotional resilience, and lead to meaningful connections on their own terms.

Helping your child socialize with family

Strong family relationships are foundational for any child. Create regular opportunities for your autistic child to engage with siblings, parents, and extended family through shared activities. Family game nights, cooking together, or outdoor outings are great ways to strengthen bonds.

REMEMBER

Educating family members about autism and your child's needs helps create a more supportive and understanding home environment.

TIP

When educating family and close friends, start with the basics: Neurodiversity is a normal part of being human. Encourage them to approach your child with compassionate curiosity — focusing on understanding rather than assumptions. Help them see the value in including autistic people for what they bring to the table and accepting them for who they are. When family and friends embrace this mindset, they create the psychological safety that allows your child to be themselves, strengthening relationships and making social interactions more positive for everyone.

Engaging your community

Getting your autistic child involved in community groups can open up incredible avenues for them to explore their interests and passions. Whether it's through your place of worship, volunteer organizations, local clubs, or special interest groups, these environments provide space for your child to engage in activities they genuinely enjoy while also helping them build social connections.

For example, a child with a love for animals might thrive in a volunteer group at an animal shelter, or a child with a fascination for music might find joy in participating in a church choir. These groups not only nurture their interests but also create opportunities for them to socialize in ways that feel comfortable and meaningful.

Creating inclusive social environments

Creating inclusive social environments means ensuring that activities and settings are accessible and welcoming to all children. Advocate for sensory-friendly spaces and events that accommodate various needs, such as quiet areas and visual supports. Work with educators and community leaders to promote inclusion and acceptance, ensuring your child has equal opportunities to participate and thrive in social settings.

REMEMBER

It's not just about physical spaces, though. It's about fostering a culture where differences are not just tolerated but embraced. By educating others on neurodiversity and the unique ways autistic children socialize, you're helping to build an environment where all kids can feel understood, respected, and valued. When we create these spaces, we're not only helping autistic children, but we're showing all kids that there's more than one way to connect and build friendships.

Teaching conflict resolution

Teaching conflict resolution is essential for helping your child navigate social interactions. It's not just about managing disagreements; it's about helping your child understand their own social style and how it intersects with the social styles of others, including neurotypical peers.

Start by reinforcing the foundation you've already laid: helping your child recognize how they naturally socialize and how their neurotypical peers might approach social situations differently. This understanding is a powerful tool for resolving conflicts because it allows your child to see where communication might be breaking down.

TIP

Here are some tips for you to help your child deal with conflicts:

>> **Understand and express feelings:** Help your child identify and express their feelings, whether through words, gestures, or visual aids. The goal is for them to feel confident in expressing themselves in ways that feel natural.

>> **Recognize neurotypical social cues:** Teach your child to interpret social cues like body language and tone of voice, not to conform but to better understand situations. This gives them insight into why a conflict might arise.

>> **Teach self-advocacy:** The most important skill you can teach your child for handling conflict is self-advocacy — asking questions, expressing needs, and letting others know when something isn't working. Conflict can be confusing, and nonverbal cues aren't always reliable. If they're interested, you can help them explore common neurotypical cues like body language and tone of voice to help recognize rising tensions. But even if they learn some cues, they may not always be able to rely on them. Instead of focusing on reading signals, help them build confidence in speaking up, clarifying misunderstandings, and setting boundaries in ways that work for them.

>> **Use clear and calm communication:** Encourage your child to communicate their needs and boundaries calmly. Teaching them phrases or signals to use when they need a break can empower them to manage social stress.

>> **Practice perspective-taking:** Help your child see situations from both their own and their peers' perspectives. Role-playing or talking through real-life scenarios can make this skill easier to learn.

>> **Teach compromise and negotiation:** Show your child how to compromise in ways that feel comfortable for them. If they and a peer have different ideas about play, guide them toward a solution that includes both.

>> **Seek help when needed:** Let your child know it's okay to ask for help from a trusted adult when conflicts become overwhelming. Reinforce that seeking help is a sign of strength.

By grounding conflict resolution in an understanding of both their own social style and their peers', your child can approach disagreements with greater empathy and confidence. This not only helps them resolve conflicts but also strengthens their ability to build meaningful relationships.

Facilitating socializing for children who need varied supports

Autistic children who are nonspeaking or need lots of support have the same desire for connection and socialization as any other kid, and they need to be supported. Typical strategies to facilitate autistic social interactions may need to be adapted to meet their needs.

TIP

Here are some adaptions you may want to consider with your child:

>> **Use communication tools consistently:** Whether your child uses AAC devices, picture exchange systems, or sign language, the key is consistency. Make these tools a part of your everyday routines to help your child become more comfortable and expressive over time.

>> **Encourage parallel play:** For some autistic children, engaging directly with others might feel overwhelming. Parallel play — where children play side by side but not directly with each other — can be a comfortable first step toward social interaction. Over time, this can naturally progress into more direct forms of engagement.

>> **Simplify social interactions:** Break down social activities into very small, manageable steps. For example, instead of expecting full participation in a game, start with something simple like handing a toy to another child or responding to a smile or greeting.

>> **Offer guided group activities:** Organize small, highly structured group activities where each child has a defined role. For instance, in a cooking activity, one child could pour ingredients while another stirs. This structure provides clear expectations and reduces social pressure.

>> **Use communication partners:** Pair your child with a trusted adult or peer who understands their communication methods. This person can help interpret their needs and facilitate interactions with others, acting as a bridge between your child and their social environment.

>> **Incorporate familiar routines into social settings:** Build social activities into your child's existing routines, such as incorporating another child into a morning snack or a simple activity they enjoy doing daily. This provides comfort and predictability while encouraging interaction.

Encouraging Self-Advocacy

Self-advocacy helps autistic children navigate socialization because it empowers them to engage with others on their own terms.

For example, a child who knows they need a quiet space after a certain amount of social activity can express that need and take a break before feeling overwhelmed. Or, if they prefer to communicate using an AAC device, self-advocacy allows them to confidently use it in social settings, ensuring they can participate in conversations without feeling pressured to speak aloud.

"You will not always be around to advocate for your child," write the authors of the website *Learn From Autistic People* in their article "5 Tips for Teaching Autism Self-Advocacy." It's important to help your child build the confidence they need to learn, work, and live comfortably."

REMEMBER

Your child won't always have you by their side. So, teaching them to advocate for themselves among peers and in other social settings is essential to their success. By helping them express their needs and boundaries, you empower them to navigate social situations more and more on their own.

TIP

Building self-advocacy skills helps autistic children handle tricky social situations, like group play or unfamiliar social environments, in ways that fit their sensory and communication needs. It allows them to ask for support when needed, step back from activities that feel uncomfortable, or suggest alternatives that work better for them, making socialization more accessible and enjoyable.

REMEMBER

Encouraging self-advocacy in social settings helps children approach interactions with confidence, knowing that their way of connecting with others is valid. It shifts the focus from simply "fitting in" to creating authentic social experiences that respect their individual needs and strengths.

Teaching your child self-advocacy

Teaching your child self-advocacy for socialization is about helping them understand that they can — and should — be in control of how they connect with others. Start by guiding them to recognize what makes them feel comfortable or uncomfortable in social situations. This could be as simple as using feeling charts to help them pinpoint their emotions or having open conversations about what they like or dislike when interacting with peers.

TIP

One of the best ways to teach self-advocacy is by showing it yourself. When your child sees you ask for help, say no, seek clarification when you don't understand, or explain when you need a break, they learn it's okay to do the same. Role-playing social scenarios, like asking a friend to slow down or needing quiet time, can also help them practice speaking up for their needs.

Another key part of this process is teaching them about their social rights. For instance, they have the right to take a break if they're feeling overwhelmed, to use communication tools if spoken words is hard, or to say "no" if they don't want to participate in an activity. Understanding these rights empowers them to engage in social situations with confidence, knowing they can set boundaries without fear.

Respecting others' self-advocacy

Teaching your child to respect the boundaries and self-advocacy of others is just as important as advocating for themselves. Friendships work both ways, and understanding that other kids also have needs and limits helps your child build stronger relationships. Explain that just like they have the right to set boundaries, their friends do too — and respecting those boundaries is key to being a good friend.

You can model this by pointing out moments when someone asks for space or declines an invitation and explaining why it's important to honor that. Role-playing these scenarios helps too, giving your child a chance to practice responding when someone else advocates for their needs.

REMEMBER

By respecting the self-advocacy of others, your child learns that friendships are about listening and supporting each other. This mutual understanding helps them create more meaningful and balanced connections.

Promoting self-advocacy in children who are nonspeaking or who need additional supports

For nonspeaking children or those needing varied supports, self-advocacy is just as important, but how they express it might look a little different than some are used to. Parents and caregivers of these children play a key role in making sure they have the tools to advocate for themselves — whether that's through AAC devices, sign language, gestures, or other methods that work for them. What matters isn't how they communicate, but that their voices are recognized, respected, and understood.

Collaborate with speech and occupational therapists to create individualized strategies. As your child grows, revisit and adapt these approaches to match their evolving abilities and social needs.

TIP

Encourage your child to make choices in their social environment — such as choosing between activities or deciding which communication tool to use — so they feel a sense of control and independence. Even small choices can build their confidence and help them become more comfortable advocating for themselves in social situations.

It's also crucial to educate those around your child, like teachers, caregivers, and peers, on how to understand and support their communication methods. Make sure everyone involved is equipped to recognize and respond to your child's self-advocacy, reinforcing its importance in social settings.

Chapter **12**

Empowering Autistic Teens

aising teenagers is like riding a roller coaster: There are thrilling highs, unexpected drops, and sharp turns that leave you holding on for dear life. When it comes to raising autistic teens, the ride has unique loops and twists. These challenges are just a part of their normal development.

Autistic teens are navigating the same big milestones as their neurotypical peers — figuring out who they are, pushing for independence, and trying to make sense of the world — but they're doing it through a different lens. This chapter is all about embracing those differences and empowering your autistic teen to thrive by recognizing their strengths, supporting their growth, and celebrating who they are.

Understanding Your Teenager

The teenage years are full of surprises. Adolescence is a time of rapid growth, constant change, and plenty of challenges. With so much going on, it's natural to wonder whether the struggles you and your teen face are tied to autism or just part of being a teenager. Spoiler alert: It's often both.

Let's be real: Few parents get everything 100 percent right when it comes to raising teens. There's no perfect formula, and that's okay. The most important thing isn't nailing every challenge; it's being there for your teen that matters most.

"When I was a teenager, I needed someone to believe in me, to tell me it was okay to be different," writes autistic Australian actor Chloé Hayden in her 2022 book *Different, Not Less* (Murdoch Books, 2023). "My parents did that, and it made all the difference."

By keeping the focus on being present and supportive, you're already doing one of the most important things a parent can do.

Now, let's take a closer look at some of the typical behaviors you might see during these teenage years.

Recognizing typical teen behavior

Teenagers — whether autistic or not — are like works in progress, constantly changing as they grow. Recognizing that many of the bumps along the way are just part of growing up — not solely about autism — can help you navigate these moments with more clarity and empathy. Here are some of the most common:

>> **Mood swings:** Hormonal changes can cause moods to shift like a weather vane in a storm. One minute your teen is sunny, the next, they're all clouds and rain.

>> **Desire for independence:** Pushing back against parental control is natural for teens who are testing the limits of their freedom.

>> **Social challenges:** Figuring out friendships and social groups is hard for any teen. They often try on different social roles and behaviors, searching for what fits.

>> **Exploring identity:** You might notice your teen experimenting with new interests, styles, or attitudes, like they're trying on different versions of themselves.

Recognizing autism-related challenges

While many typical teenage behaviors are universal, autism can add unique layers of complexity. Understanding how these challenges manifest specifically in autistic teens can help you provide the right support:

>> **Sensory sensitivities:** As teens navigate new environments — like high school hallways, part-time jobs, or social gatherings — sensory overloads can hit like a ton of bricks. Loud noises, bright lights, or certain textures can become overwhelming.

>> **Communication differences:** Autistic teens often communicate in ways that are more direct or literal than their peers. As social expectations grow more complex, the nuances of teenage communication — like sarcasm, slang, or unspoken social rules — can be especially tricky. Clear and direct communication can help avoid misunderstandings and ease frustration.

>> **Routine and predictability:** Adolescence brings a demand for independence and a flood of new routines. But for autistic teens, who often rely on structure and predictability, the chaotic nature of teenage life can be stressful. Balancing the need for consistency with the inevitable changes of adolescence is key.

>> **Intense interests:** Many autistic teens have intense focus on specific topics or hobbies, which can become even more central to their identity during teen years. These interests can provide a sense of purpose and comfort amid the chaos of adolescence. These should be encouraged. However, helping your teen balance their passions with other responsibilities, like schoolwork or social obligations, may require thoughtful support.

"The teen years are a tough time for any kid, and for an autistic kid, it can be hell," writes author John Elder Robison in his 2007 memoir *Look Me in the Eye* (Crown). Robison, who is both autistic and a parent, stresses that "parents need to recognize this and do what they can to ease the transition into adulthood."

REMEMBER

While this journey can be challenging, it's also an opportunity to empower your autistic teen with the tools they need to navigate adolescence successfully. By understanding both the typical and autism-related challenges your teen faces, you'll be better equipped to guide them through these pivotal years, helping them emerge stronger, more self-assured, and ready to take on the world.

Nurturing Emotional Growth

The teenage years are an emotional journey for everyone, and for autistic teens, that path can have unique challenges. Understanding and managing emotions, building resilience, and navigating the challenges of stress, anxiety, and depression are all crucial parts of this stage. In this section, we talk about how you can support your autistic teen through this complex and essential period of their emotional development.

Understanding and managing emotions

Teens are still learning to identify and express their emotions, and for autistic teens, this can feel like uncharted territory. One of the best ways you can help is by giving them words for what they're feeling. Encourage them to explore emotions without judgment — through conversation, journaling, or creative outlets like art or music. Even if their emotions don't fully make sense to you, validating their feelings (or struggles with identifying, understanding, and expressing them) helps them feel understood and supported.

TIP

Teens learn a lot by watching how you handle emotions, so model healthy regulation. Show them how to manage stress — whether it's deep breathing, mindfulness, or taking a break. The goal isn't to avoid tough emotions but to handle them with confidence. If you slip up, own it, apologize, and talk through what you'd do differently. It's a great way to model growth and keep the conversation open.

Building resilience

Resilience is the ability to recover from setbacks, adapt to change, and keep going even when things get tough. It doesn't develop overnight; it's built over time through a mix of positive and challenging experiences.

For autistic teens, building resilience might mean learning to bounce back from setbacks, handling changes in routine, or navigating social misunderstandings. Help your teen see challenges not as failures but as opportunities for growth. Celebrate their efforts and progress, no matter how small, and remind them that it's okay to make mistakes along the way.

TIP

Encourage your teen to step out of their comfort zone when they're ready. This might mean trying something new, like a hobby, a social activity, or even a different approach to a problem. The key is to support them while also giving them the space to grow and learn from their experiences. Building resilience is all about finding that sweet spot between support and independence.

Managing stress, anxiety, and depression

Stress, anxiety, and depression are common during the teenage years, and autistic teens can be especially vulnerable to these challenges. It's crucial to recognize the signs and offer the right support when needed. Keep an open line of communication with your teen about their mental health, and make it clear that it's okay to talk about how they're feeling or thinking, no matter what those feelings or thoughts are.

Help your teen understand that stress and anxiety are natural responses to certain situations, but also teach them ways to manage these feelings. This might involve creating a sensory-friendly environment at home, establishing calming routines, or working together to develop coping strategies that work for them.

WARNING

If you notice signs of depression — such as increased withdrawal, changes in sleep or eating habits, or a loss of interest in activities they usually enjoy — take these seriously. Don't hesitate to reach out to professionals who can offer support and guidance tailored to your teen's needs.

Tips for nurturing emotional growth

What can you do to help your teen grow emotionally? Here are some ways you can get started.

TIP

>> **Name the feelings:** Help your teen put words to their emotions. Whether it's through conversation, journaling, or art, giving a name to what they're feeling can be empowering.

>> **Celebrate small wins:** Emotional growth is a journey, not a destination. Celebrate even the small steps your teen takes in managing their emotions.

>> **Create a calm environment:** When things get overwhelming, having a quiet, sensory-friendly space to retreat to can make a big difference.

>> **Encourage emotional outlets:** Whether it's music, drawing, or simply talking it out, encourage your teen to find outlets that help them process their emotions.

Fostering Social Growth

Social growth during the teenage years can be as unpredictable as a lightning storm: intense, sudden, and full of energy. For autistic teens, navigating the complex world of social interactions comes with a unique set of challenges and opportunities, but with the right support and understanding, they can build meaningful connections and develop the social skills they need to thrive.

Understanding social dynamics

Social interactions can feel like navigating a maze filled with unspoken rules and shifting dynamics. For autistic teens, this maze can be especially confusing. One of the best ways to support your teen is to break down social complexities into manageable pieces. Talk openly about social cues, body language, and context in conversations, recognizing that everyone processes these differently and may not fully grasp them now — but could over time.

REMEMBER

Social interactions can be exhausting, especially if your teen feels pressured to mask or hide their true self to fit in. Encourage them to be authentic and help them find social spaces where they're accepted for who they are. Authenticity should always take precedence over fitting in. For autistic teens, online communities can be great spaces for socializing, as long as safety is monitored.

TIP

Autistic teens naturally socialize in ways that may look different from how their neurotypical classmates do, and that's totally okay. Teaching neurotypical social skills can be helpful if the approach you take is like learning a second social language. It's a skill to be acquired, but it doesn't need to replace the way they already socialize. It's crucial that autistic teens aren't forced to change who they are (more on that in Chapter 11). Embrace their unique way of connecting with others, and make sure they have opportunities to socialize with other autistic teens. It's not just about finding friends who get them; it's about building a community where they can be themselves, feel understood, and thrive.

Building social confidence

Social confidence doesn't develop overnight, and it's perfectly okay if your teen prefers smaller social circles or one-on-one interactions. What matters most is that they feel comfortable and confident in the social spaces they choose to engage in. Start by helping your teen identify their strengths, such as being a good listener, having deep knowledge of a particular topic, or simply being kind and empathetic. These strengths can serve as the foundation for building social confidence.

TIP

Encourage your teen to get involved in activities or groups where they can connect with others who share similar interests. This might be a club at school, an online community, or a hobby group. The key is to help them find social environments that feel safe and welcoming where they can practice their social skills without the pressure to conform to typical teenage social norms.

Navigating friendships and relationships

Teenage friendships can be intense, fleeting, and sometimes downright confusing. Autistic teens may face additional challenges in understanding the nuances of friendships and relationships, but with guidance, they can build strong, meaningful connections. Talk to your teen about what healthy friendships are like, emphasizing qualities like mutual respect, trust, and communication. It's also crucial to discuss boundaries and how to set them, which can be especially challenging for teens who struggle with social cues.

When it comes to romantic relationships, the conversation can get even more complex. Be open and honest with your teen about the emotions and expectations that come with dating, and help them navigate these waters with care. It's okay if your teen doesn't show interest in dating. What's important is that they feel supported in whatever social choices they make.

Managing social anxiety

Social anxiety is a common challenge for many teenagers, but for autistic teens, it can be particularly overwhelming. If your teen feels anxious about social situations, work with them to develop coping strategies that make these experiences more manageable. This might include practicing deep breathing, creating a mental script for certain interactions, or having a trusted friend or adult nearby for support.

REMEMBER

It's crucial to respect your teen's boundaries and not push them into social situations they're not ready for. Social growth happens at different paces for everyone, and forcing interactions can do more harm than good. Instead, focus on gradual exposure to social situations, allowing your teen to build confidence at their own pace.

TIP

Remind your teen that there's no one "right" way to be social. The world is full of diverse social styles, and their way of interacting is just as valid as anyone else's. Encourage them to embrace their unique perspective and find joy in the connections they make, no matter how unconventional they may seem.

REMEMBER

Your role as a parent is to provide guidance, support, and a safe space for your teen to explore and grow socially. By fostering an environment where they feel accepted and understood, you're helping them develop the social skills they need to navigate the world with confidence and authenticity.

Tips for supporting social growth

Here are some ways you can be a catalyst for your teen's social growth:

TIP

>> **Break down social situations.** Help your teen understand social cues and context by breaking down interactions into smaller, more manageable parts.

>> **Encourage authenticity.** Remind your teen that it's okay to be themselves. Finding social spaces where they feel accepted is more important than fitting in.

>> **Start small.** Help your teen build social confidence by starting with one-on-one interactions or small groups before tackling larger social situations.

>> **Respect boundaries.** Understand that social growth happens at different paces. Don't push your teen into situations they're not ready for. Support gradual progress instead.

>> **Explore shared interests**. Encourage your teen to join clubs, groups, or online communities that align with their interests. Connecting with others is easier when you share a passion. This is especially true for autistic people, who often socialize and make friends through shared interests. (See Chapter 4 for more on this.)

>> **Teach self-advocacy.** Encourage your teen to let others know what they need in an interaction and how their traits may be misinterpreted and invite others to advocate for themselves as well.

Guiding Your Teen into Adulthood

As your autistic teen moves toward adulthood, they'll encounter many new experiences and challenges. This stage of life is about more than just gaining academic knowledge; it's about equipping them with the skills and confidence they need to thrive independently. Your role is to guide and support them as they navigate these transitions, ensuring they feel prepared and empowered to face what lies ahead.

Planning for life transitions

Life transitions are big milestones for any teen, but for autistic teens, they can feel even more overwhelming. These changes and transitions are significant — whether it's moving from middle school to high school, preparing for college, or entering the workforce. With careful planning and support, your teen can approach them with confidence.

REMEMBER

For autistic teens, transitions can be especially challenging because they often involve navigating new environments, routines, and social dynamics all at once. Autistic people tend to thrive on predictability and structure, so when the familiar changes, it can feel like the ground is shifting beneath their feet. Sensory sensitivities, communication styles, and the need for routine can make these transitions seem even more daunting.

However, with the right strategies in place, these challenges are not insurmountable. Instead, they can be opportunities for growth. By providing consistent support, clear expectations, and gradual introductions to new experiences, you can help your teen not just manage these transitions but embrace them as steps toward a future where they can flourish.

Breaking down big changes

Breaking big changes into smaller, manageable steps can make the process less intimidating. Work with your teen to map out the journey ahead, setting clear, achievable goals along the way. This might involve researching new environments, practicing new routines, or simply talking through what to expect. The more your teen knows what's coming, the more prepared they'll feel.

TIP

Start talking about transitions well in advance. Giving your teen time to mentally prepare can significantly reduce anxiety. Create a detailed plan and break each transition into smaller steps. For example, if your teen is starting a new school, visit the campus together, meet teachers, and walk through their schedule ahead of time.

Maintaining predictable routines

For many autistic teens, structure and predictability provide a sense of security. As they face new transitions, maintaining some consistent routines can help anchor them during times of change. Familiar patterns — such as keeping a regular morning routine, having set study times, or continuing favorite hobbies — can provide comfort and stability. Gradually introducing changes to their routine can also help your teen adapt more easily when big transitions come.

Exploring future possibilities

Talk openly with your teen about their hopes and dreams for the future. Whether they're thinking about college, a career, or other life paths, exploring these possibilities together is key. Help them research different options, visit campuses or job sites, and connect with mentors or professionals in fields they're interested in. Encourage them to think about what environments will help them thrive — whether that means a small college, a structured work environment, or something different.

Supporting emotional readiness

Life transitions can stir up a lot of emotions: excitement, anxiety, uncertainty to name few. It's important to acknowledge these feelings and provide your teen with the emotional support they need to process them. Encourage open conversations about their fears and hopes, and remind them that it's okay to feel a mix of emotions during these times. Work together to develop coping strategies that can help them manage stress and anxiety as they move through these transitions.

Embracing neurodiversity in every step

Remind your teen that their path doesn't have to look like anyone else's. Embracing their neurodivergence means recognizing that the way they approach life's transitions is valid and valuable. Encourage them to lean into their strengths and to seek out environments that celebrate who they are. Your role is to support and guide them as they carve out their own unique path into adulthood.

Celebrate successes and use setbacks as learning opportunities. Remember, the goal is to equip your child with the tools they need to navigate the world on their terms.

Teaching Life Skills

As your teen moves toward adulthood, helping them develop essential life skills is key. This isn't just about practical skills like cooking or managing money, although those are important, too. It's also about building the confidence to make decisions, solve problems, and advocate for themselves, as we discuss throughout this section.

Developing daily living skills

A crucial part of life skills includes daily living tasks. Teaching these to autistic teens is essential because they are the building blocks of independence and self-confidence, key components that empower teens to navigate adulthood with greater autonomy and success.

Daily living skills come at different times for everyone — some might develop them well into adulthood, and that's okay. Everyone has their own timeline, so it's important to set realistic expectations and celebrate progress along the way.

Some key daily living skills include the following:

>> **Personal hygiene:** Encourage teens to take charge of their hygiene routines like brushing teeth, bathing, and grooming.

>> **Cooking and meal preparation:** Teach basic cooking skills and safe kitchen use. Start with simple things and gradually introduce more complex recipes and tasks.

>> **Household chores:** Help teens take on chores like cleaning, laundry, and organizing their spaces independently to foster responsibility and self-reliance.

>> **Time management:** Help teens create and manage their own schedules, using planners and reminders, which is key for academic success and future employment.

>> **Money management:** Introduce budgeting, saving, and basic banking. Teens need to understand the value of money as they prepare for independent living.

>> **Health and safety:** Equip teens with the skills to manage their own health, recognize symptoms, understand medications, and respond to emergencies.

>> **Transportation skills:** Teach teens to use public transit, plan routes, and, if appropriate, drive.

Encouraging independence

Encouraging independence in your autistic teen is about helping them build the confidence and skills they need to navigate the world on their own terms. Start by giving them opportunities to make decisions, both big and small, and involve them in tasks that require responsibility.

TIP

Foster independence by gradually increasing your teen's responsibilities. Encourage them to take on tasks they can handle, offering guidance and support as needed. Provide practical support, and make sure your teen knows where to find help, whether it's from you, a counselor, or friends. Helping your teen build a network of reliable support exercises their independence and can ease the stress of new experiences.

REMEMBER

It's crucial to balance providing support with giving them the reins. Independence grows from experience. Celebrate successes and view mistakes as learning opportunities. Fostering independence isn't about fitting them into a mold; it's about empowering them to live authentically with the tools to thrive on their own terms.

Encouraging health and wellness

Taking care of both physical and mental health is essential for everyone, and for autistic teens, having a routine that supports their well-being can make a big difference. Encourage your teen to find physical activities they enjoy — whether it's walking, swimming, or dancing in their room. Nutrition is also important, but focus on balance rather than strict rules.

REMEMBER

Mental health plays a huge role in overall wellness, so help your teen develop strategies for managing stress, such as mindfulness, journaling, or simply taking time to recharge. Remember, health and wellness are about finding what works best for them rather than fitting into someone else's idea of what it should look like.

Teaching conflict resolution

Conflict resolution is crucial as your teen navigates more complex social dynamics. Autistic teens may find conflicts challenging to understand or manage, so it's important to teach strategies for handling disagreements calmly and effectively. Start by helping them recognize that conflicts are a normal part of relationships and can be resolved without negative consequences. Teach them to listen actively, express feelings clearly, and work toward solutions that respect everyone involved. See Chapter 11 for more on conflict resolution.

REMEMBER

Conflict resolution isn't about avoiding disagreements. It's about finding constructive ways to address them, strengthening relationships, and building social confidence.

Developing self-advocacy

Self-advocacy is a critical skill as your teen moves toward adulthood. It's about empowering them to understand and express their own needs, preferences, and rights. This ability to speak up for themselves and make decisions is crucial for building their independence and self-confidence, and it's a skill that will guide them through everything from school to social situations and, eventually, the workplace. (For more on self-advocacy, turn to Chapter 17.)

TIP

Nurture self-advocacy by encouraging your teen to articulate what they need. For example, they may need to ask for a sensory-friendly environment, explain their preferred communication style, or request specific accommodations. Practice these conversations in safe, supportive settings so they can build the confidence to advocate for themselves in the wider world. Your role is to encourage self-advocacy so your teen take charge of their own life, ensuring they're heard, respected, and understood.

Nurturing problem-solving skills

Teaching decision-making and problem-solving skills is key to your teen's independence and confidence. Discuss real-life scenarios and guide them through evaluating options and outcomes. Encourage critical thinking about consequences and perspectives. Let them practice decision-making in everyday situations, like choosing what to wear, planning a weekend, or making a small purchase. These experiences build confidence and sharpen their decision-making skills.

TIP

Encourage your teen to approach problems with curiosity rather than frustration. Promote the idea that they're challenges to be solved. Help your teen break down challenges into smaller steps and remind them it's okay to ask for help. Problem-solving isn't only about finding answers; it's about building the confidence to tackle challenges head-on.

REMEMBER

Give your teen space to make decisions and learn from their experiences. Trust their ability to navigate the world, even if it leads them down a path you might not have chosen. Support them when needed but also allow the freedom to grow.

4

Thriving as an Autistic Adult

Gain self-awareness, embrace self-acceptance, and strengthen self-advocacy to navigate life confidently and celebrate your autistic identity.

Navigate higher education and vocational training by choosing the right path, accessing support services, and planning for a career.

Build a successful career by landing a job, excelling in the workplace, advancing professionally, and giving back.

Develop and maintain relationships by navigating family dynamics, friendships, community, and romantic connections while resolving challenges and deepening bonds.

Chapter **13**

Empowering Yourself

Welcome to the journey of understanding, accepting, and empowering yourself. It's easy to feel like the world expects you to be someone you're not, but this chapter is all about letting go of those expectations. Here's the truth: Being autistic isn't something that needs to be "fixed" or "overcome." It's a core part of who you are, and embracing that leads to real growth.

Why is this important? Because thriving as an autistic person means living authentically, without shame. When you understand and accept your differences, you unlock new ways of connecting with others, recognizing your strengths, and navigating a world that might not always feel designed for you. The key is empowering yourself to create the life you want on your own terms.

Our intention in this chapter is to help you gain self-awareness, build self-acceptance, and strengthen self-advocacy, empowering you to embrace your autistic identity and navigate life with confidence.

Developing Self-Awareness

As humans, we have incredibly diverse ways of thinking and behaving. There's no one-size-fits-all when it comes to how our brains work, and understanding your unique traits — where you overlap with others and where you diverge — can make a huge difference in how you navigate the world.

Why does this matter? Because understanding yourself is the key to navigating a world that isn't always built with your brain and body in mind. The more you know about your traits, the better you can thrive in a society that doesn't always fit. In the next sections, we explore this self-awareness journey and what it means for you.

WARNING

Dr. Stephen Shore, an autistic professor, author, and advocate, coined a popular phrase: "When you've met one autistic person, you've met *one* autistic person." That's important to keep in mind. No two autistic people, including you, will have the exact same traits, challenges, or strengths. While there may be shared traits, your journey is uniquely yours, which is why it's so important to understand who you are.

REMEMBER

Developing your self-awareness isn't just about being autistic. In general, most people don't take the time to really know themselves. They follow routines or expectations without questioning what works for them. But when you truly understand yourself, especially as an autistic person, you can create a life that fits your strengths and needs. Self-awareness leads to better decisions, healthier boundaries, and a life more in tune with who you are. It's one of the best investments in your future.

Exploring Your Autistic Identity

Neurodiversity is the natural variation in how human brains function, think, and process information. Just as biodiversity is important for complex ecosystems to thrive, neurodiversity strengthens our society by intersecting different perspectives, problem-solving approaches, and talents, creating a richer, more adaptive, and innovative world where everyone's unique contributions matter.

REMEMBER

Autistic people are a vital part of human neurodiversity, offering unique ways of thinking, problem-solving, and perceiving the world. By understanding your own autistic identity, you're not just helping yourself; you're contributing to something bigger. The more people embrace their neurodivergent traits, the more society benefits from the full range of human thought and innovation. Your self-awareness helps build a more inclusive world that values the strengths of all minds.

TIP

Embracing your neurodivergence and autistic identity is one of the most powerful things you can do. It gives you insight into why you think, feel, and react the way you do, freeing you from the pressure to fit into a mold that wasn't made for you. Instead of struggling to conform, you can focus on your strengths, develop strategies that work for you, and handle challenges in a way that honors who you are. It's about living authentically and celebrating your unique self and everything it brings to the world.

If you've only recently come to understand yourself as autistic, it can feel like a whirlwind of emotions — both relief and confusion. Everything starts to make sense, and the validation of your experiences can be empowering. As Emma Marsh and Dr. Melanie Heyworth from *Reframing Autism* put it, "Suddenly having validation of your entire existence can feel overwhelming, and you may be left wondering what to do next."

WARNING

You might grieve the version of yourself you thought you were or worry about what this new understanding means for your future. You may even catch yourself comparing your experiences to other autistic people, wondering where you fit. But remember, everyone, autistic or not, has their own mix of strengths and challenges. No two people are exactly alike, and your journey is yours alone.

TIP

Exploring and accepting your autistic identity helps you work through this uncertainty, giving you a clearer sense of who you are and how to embrace your strengths moving forward.

Understanding how you think and learn

Cognition is how your brain takes in information, processes it, and uses it to understand the world. It's what helps you make sense of experiences, solve problems, and learn new things. Autistic brains do this differently, often focusing on details or patterns others might overlook, or processing sensory input more vividly.

Your cognition is shaped by a mix of genes, environment, and life experiences. While the core of how your brain works may not change, the way you use it can evolve as you grow and adapt.

REMEMBER

You can't change the core components of your cognition — like how you can't swap the operating system of a computer from Mac to Windows. But just as you *can* customize or update a computer with apps, shortcuts, and settings, you can adapt your environment, routines, and strategies to strengthen how your brain processes the world. This starts with understanding how your brain works best and finding tools and techniques to help you thrive — for example, by adjusting your workspace, learning new coping strategies, or building systems that play to your strengths.

Humans with autistic cognition have been a huge advantage to society's development (turn to Chapter 2 to find out how). But when you, as someone with an autistic brain, must function in a world built to support neurotypical cognition, it can come with real challenges to figure out. Figuring out how to work with your brain, not against it, makes all the difference in handling challenges and unlocking your strengths.

TIP

Understanding how you think and learn is like figuring out your unique operating system. Once you do, it's like everything starts to click, and you can move through the world more efficiently and have a ton of power over your life. When you understand how your brain processes information, you can find ways to make things work better for you as you navigate social situations, acquire new skills, or manage stress.

Understanding cognition

Let's look at some common expressions of autistic cognition. Remember, no two autistic people are exactly the same, and some traits of autistic cognition can show up in neurotypical brains too. As you go through these traits, be honest with yourself. Rate how often they resonate with you: never, sometimes, half the time, most of the time, or always. You might see yourself reflected in some of them, and who knows? You might learn something new about how your brain works.

>> **Analytical thinking and decision-making:** While others go with their gut, you think through every angle. This helps you spot things others miss, but it can slow you down if you're worried about making the "wrong" choice.

>> **Literal interpretation:** You often take language at face value, keeping promises and expecting the same from others. Sarcasm or irony? You usually get it, but a part of you still wonders if they're being serious.

>> **Learning style:** You dive deep into topics that interest you, remembering details others might miss. You're great at teaching yourself, but when applying what you've learned, you often start from scratch rather than building on past knowledge.

>> **Memory:** You remember things from long ago that others forget. Short-term memory, though, can be a challenge.

>> **Task management:** When something grabs your interest, you can focus for long stretches, refining your work repeatedly. But this makes it hard to stop or switch tasks, and interruptions or changes can throw you off.

>> **Interests:** You pour energy into the topics you love, sometimes at the expense of other things. These passions help you manage stress. You'd love a job that aligns with them.

>> **Thinking through social interactions:** You rely on logic more than intuition in social situations. Vagueness and unstated social rules can be tough to figure out.

>> **Stress response:** When stressed, you might react emotionally or withdraw — sometimes leaving a situation to avoid feeling overwhelmed.

REMEMBER

Not everything in the list will apply to you. Every person — including every autistic person — is different, after all!

Understanding executive function

An important part of human cognition is what we call "executive function" — something people use every day, even if most of us have never thought about it. Executive function refers to the mental processes that help us plan, focus, organize, manage time, and adapt to changes. Everything from writing a paper to juggling tasks to trying to get out the door on time involves your executive function, which is quietly working behind the scenes. Most people don't notice it until something goes wrong, like feeling stressed, forgetting things, or struggling to manage time.

For autistic people, understanding executive function is especially helpful because autistic brains often process and organize information differently. Knowing how your brain handles tasks or disruptions can explain why certain things may feel harder and enable you to create strategies that play to your strengths. The goal isn't to "fix" you; it's to work with your brain to make life easier and more manageable.

TIP

Here's a breakdown of some common expressions of executive functioning seen among autistic people. See which ones apply to you:

>> **Planning:** Autistic people can be incredibly detail-oriented, creating thorough plans when something sparks their interest.

>> **Organizing:** While organizing can be tricky, autistic people often develop unique systems that work well once in place.

>> **Understanding instructions:** Some may struggle with verbal instructions but excel at following written ones.

>> **Task initiation:** When motivated, autistic people dive in with focus, but unstructured or boring tasks can make starting difficult.

>> **Task management:** Breaking tasks into smaller steps is often a strength, but multitasking or switching between tasks can be harder.

>> **Time management:** Time management can be tough, but tools like clear schedules and timers can help you stay on track.

>> **Working memory:** Autistic people often have great long-term memory, but holding multiple short-term pieces of info can be more challenging.

>> **The big picture:** Some focus intensely on details, whereas others are great at seeing the big picture but may struggle with specifics.

>> **Reluctance to seek help:** Many prefer to figure things out independently, which can be great, but sometimes a quick question saves a lot of time.

>> **Impulse control and focus:** Deep focus is a strength, but stress or sensory overload can make impulse control harder.

>> **Emotional regulation:** Unexpected changes or sensory overload can disrupt emotional regulation, leading to anxiety or frustration.

REMEMBER

Understanding your strengths and challenges with different aspects of executive function helps you develop strategies to thrive in how you get things done.

Understanding how you communicate

Everyone communicates, but autistic people often do it differently than neurotypical folks. That's not bad or wrong; it's just different! The key is understanding your communication style and what makes it unique. This helps you better understand the differences in how you and others communicate so you can make communication work for you rather than forcing yourself to fit into someone else's mold.

TIP

Let's look at some ways autistic people often communicate differently. Getting to know these might help you understand yourself better:

>> **Conversation flow:** Group conversations can be tricky. Sometimes it's hard to know if you're interrupting. Other times, the topic shifts before you've had enough time to share all you want to share.

>> **Being direct:** Many autistic people prefer directness and honesty, which can be refreshing. But navigating vague situations or reading between the lines can feel confusing.

>> **Talking about interests:** Passion for a topic often leads to deep, enthusiastic conversations, but that same enthusiasm can make it tough to switch topics.

>> **Repeating things:** Repeating words or phrases can help process information — or simply be enjoyable.

>> **Tone and style:** Some people may speak in a more monotone voice, whereas others are full of energy. Some may use fewer words or speak softly.

>> **Body language:** Autistic people may use facial expressions and gestures differently from neurotypical people. You find it easier to interpret other autistics, but harder to read neurotypicals.

>> **Use of AAC devices:** Some autistic people use augmentative and alternative communication (AAC) devices to express themselves, allowing them to communicate in a way that's more comfortable than speaking.

>> **Writing:** Many autistic people express themselves well through writing, whether in detailed, formal language or quick, to-the-point communication.

Understanding how you socialize

Socializing is the act of interacting with others, exchanging ideas, and building relationships. It's crucial to humans because it fosters connection, helps us share knowledge, and creates a sense of belonging, all of which are essential for both individual well-being and the growth of society.

Socializing helps us feel accepted, understood, supported, and part of a community, which are things everyone — including autistic people — needs. Building and maintaining relationships allows us to share experiences, gain new perspectives, and develop emotional resilience, all of which contribute to a greater sense of happiness and fulfillment in life.

Autistic people socialize just like anyone else. You form connections, share experiences, and build relationships. The difference is that you might socialize in ways that don't always align with neurotypical expectations, and that's completely okay. Maybe you prefer one-on-one conversations over group settings or connect more through shared interests than small talk.

REMEMBER

These differences aren't flaws; they're just part of how your brain works. What matters is finding social interactions that feel right for you rather than forcing yourself to conform to expectations.

Here are some ways autistic people often prefer to socialize:

>> **Structure:** Predictable environments, like scheduled meetups or regular game nights, are often more comfortable than spontaneous gatherings.

>> **With other autistic people:** Autistic people naturally understand each other better and often feel more comfortable socializing together.

- >> **Sharing interests:** Talking about interests and passions can create a lot of joy, as can learning about what others are passionate about.

- >> **One on one:** Smaller, personal conversations may be more enjoyable than large group settings.

- >> **Quiet connections:** Talking face to face isn't always necessary to feel connected. Just being in the same space with a friend or loved one can be enough.

- >> **Deep connections:** When a friend has a problem, autistic people are often eager to listen and help them figure things out. But shallow small talk? Many autistic people find it fake or uninteresting.

- >> **Quality over quantity:** A smaller number of meaningful connections with others is often preferred over being widely popular.

- >> **Dependability:** Autistic people are often known to be loyal and dependable friends. If they make plans or promise to show up somewhere, they're likely to follow through.

- >> **Need for downtime:** After socializing, you may need time alone to recharge. Socializing can be fun, but it's often mentally exhausting as well.

Understanding challenges faced in socializing

When it comes to social challenges, many assume the difficulties are solely with autistic individuals. But most social norms, like making eye contact or engaging in small talk, are designed for neurotypical brains. So, when autistic people approach socializing differently, it's not because they're "bad" at it. It's simply that parts of our culture weren't built with them in mind. That's not a flaw; it's a mismatch.

REMEMBER

These differences can make socializing harder, not due to a lack of ability but because many of social norms don't play to your natural way of doing things. Understanding that is key to thriving in a largely neurotypical world.

The following list explores some common areas where autistic people might face challenges and how understanding these can help you navigate interactions more comfortably:

- >> **Eye contact:** Eye contact can cause discomfort or even physical pain for many autistic individuals. In countries like China and Japan, where prolonged eye contact can be seen as rude or disrespectful, this is less of an issue for autistic people. However, in places like the United States and Western Europe, where there's a strong social expectation to maintain eye contact, avoiding it can be more challenging.

>> **Small talk:** Many autistic people dislike small talk and prefer deeper conversations. While this works well in cultures where small talk is less valued (Germany), in many countries, the desire to avoid small talk can make social interactions more difficult.

>> **Understanding others:** Autistic people often struggle to read neurotypical body language, but they tend to understand other autistic individuals more easily.

>> **Physical discomfort:** Crowded spaces or unexpected touch can be very uncomfortable.

>> **Anxiety:** Many autistic people experience anxiety in social situations that aren't designed for how autistic people naturally prefer to socialize.

>> **Energy drain:** Socializing can be exhausting and require a lot of downtime to recharge.

>> **Making friends:** Autistic people are often seen as incredibly loyal and supportive friends. However, forming new friendships can also be tough because many relationships are built around neurotypical social norms, which can be hard to navigate.

>> **Loneliness:** Forming friendships can be tough — not from a lack of wanting friends but because neurotypical social norms don't always align with how autistic people bond.

REMEMBER

Identifying these traits in yourself can help shape your social strategies. If eye contact is uncomfortable, find other ways to show engagement. If socializing drains your energy, set boundaries like taking breaks or limiting hangout time.

Understanding how you use your senses

Autistic people often experience the world through their senses in unique ways. You might notice sounds others don't, feel textures more intensely, or be more sensitive to light. Or, you may be less sensitive to smells, touch, or pain. Sometimes, these sensory differences bring joy, like a comforting texture or noticing details in music. Other times, it can be overwhelming, like when a space is too loud or bright.

Understanding your sensory differences helps you navigate life in ways that feel right for you. When you know what brings you joy and what you find challenging, you can make choices that support your well-being. Embracing how your senses shape your experience is key to knowing yourself better.

TIP

Use the following list to map out how you process and interact with the world around you:

>> **Light:** Bright or flickering lights or bold colors or patterns can easily distract you. Alternatively, perhaps you find joy in patterns of light that others miss, like sunlight streaming through trees or the gentle glow of string lights.

>> **Sound:** Loud environments like coffee shops or public crowds can feel overwhelming. Or you may love to listen to loud music. You may struggle at times to tune out all the sounds you're able to hear. Other times, sounds like the rhythmic tapping of rain on a window can be quite soothing.

>> **Taste:** Strong flavors or certain textures can be uncomfortable. You may find comfort and joy in familiar tastes, spicy food, smooth textures, or favorite foods.

>> **Touch:** Strangers brushing against you, clothing tags, or certain fabrics can feel uncomfortable, whereas soft textures, weighted blankets, or repetitive movements like brushing your hand over smooth surfaces might bring comfort. You may crave deep pressure, strong hugs, or carrying heavy objects.

>> **Smell:** Strong smells like perfumes or cleaning products can be intense or distracting. But you may love using calming scents like fresh air, certain foods, or essential oils. You may also seek out stronger scents or even feel the need to smell things to understand them.

>> **Pain tolerance:** Your pain tolerance is either higher or lower than most people. Timely attention to injuries or illnesses may be missed due to higher pain tolerance.

>> **Temperature:** You often feel too hot or too cold in most places. You wear clothing that others find not suited for the weather.

>> **Personal space:** You're highly sensitive to others entering your personal space. Or you get very close to other people while being unaware of their personal space.

>> **Stimming:** You often fidget, tap your foot, rock back and forth, sway your body, or *love* to doodle.

>> **Body awareness:** You may feel like you're "clumsy." You may often drop things or bump into them.

REMEMBER

Understanding and accepting your sensory traits helps you navigate your environment more comfortably. If you're sensitive to noise, noise-canceling headphones can help. The same goes for stimming (see Chapter 4). Knowing your needs lets you self-soothe and regulate emotions naturally. The key is building strategies that work with your traits, not against them.

Discovering your strengths

As an autistic person, you may have unique strengths and abilities that deserve to be celebrated. Understanding and embracing these strengths is key to living fully. You might have abilities like hyperfocus, attention to detail, or a unique problem-solving approach. These traits don't make you a superhero; they just make you, you. Every person has strengths, and every person has challenges.

REMEMBER

Your strengths are more than something to be proud of; they're tools for success in everyday life. By recognizing what you're good at, you can apply your strengths in work, relationships, and personal projects.

TIP

Check out the following strengths commonly associated with autistic people to see if any resonate with you:

>> **Attention to detail:** You have a strong attention to detail and can excel at tasks that require a high level of precision and accuracy.

>> **Creativity and innovation:** You think outside the box and approach problems in unique and innovative ways, leading to creative solutions and breakthroughs.

>> **Hyperfocus:** You can hyperfocus on tasks that interest you, allowing you to accomplish a great deal in a short amount of time.

>> **Pattern recognition:** You excel at recognizing patterns and love to solve complex problems.

>> **Intense interests:** You have intense interests in specific topics or activities and hence have a deep level of expertise and knowledge in them.

>> **Strong memory:** You have strong memories and can recall details and information that others may forget.

>> **Empathy:** You have a deep understanding of the emotions of others, but express it your own unique way.

>> **Resilience:** You have a strong ability to bounce back from challenges.

REMEMBER

The strengths listed in this section are common among autistic individuals, but they vary from person to person. You may have some, all, or none — and that's okay. The key is discovering your unique strengths and building on them.

Embracing Your Total Identity

Autism is a big part of who you are, but it doesn't define you completely. Exploring your full identity means recognizing how autism intersects with other aspects of who you are: your gender, race, sexual orientation, cultural background, values, and more. Autism is one piece of the whole picture. Embrace how it shapes your strengths, like attention to detail and creativity, while acknowledging challenges like sensory sensitivities or social difficulties.

Your cultural background also influences how you see the world. How do the values you were raised with interact with your autistic identity? Does your culture embrace neurodivergence or stigmatize it? And how do your roles — like sibling, student, or professional — fit with your autistic identity?

Reflect on your values and beliefs too. What truly matters to you? How do your beliefs shape your view of the world? For some, this may also include exploring spiritual or religious identity and how it connects with being autistic.

REMEMBER

Your identity isn't static. It evolves, so stay open to growth and new experiences, and your understanding of yourself will deepen over time.

Understanding Yourself as Normal

Your way of experiencing and interacting with the world is just as valid as anyone else's. There's no single definition of *normal*. It's a spectrum that includes all kinds of human experiences, including yours.

To quote actor and television host Whoopi Goldberg, "Normal is nothing more than a cycle on a washing machine." Yes, you might think, process, or perceive things differently than others, but that doesn't make you any less "normal." It makes you uniquely you.

REMEMBER

Accepting yourself as normal means embracing your unique traits — how you process sensory information, communicate, or dive deep into your interests. You don't need to change or hide who you are to fit into society's narrow idea of "normal." Humans aren't born into boxes; we're born to be ourselves. There's no need to change or hide who you are.

Developing Self-Acceptance

In Whitney Houston's 1986 hit *The Greatest Love of All*, she famously sings that learning to love yourself "is easy to achieve." And while we're definitely big fans of Whitney, self-acceptance isn't always that simple. It actually takes a lot of work. But you know what? It's worth it!

Self-acceptance is key to thriving because it lets you live authentically and focus on what really matters. When you stop trying to meet societal expectations, you free up energy to build the life you want. It's not always easy — society pressures us to be "better" or "different" — but the work is worth it. Accepting yourself is the first step to real growth and thriving.

REMEMBER

Self-acceptance is about embracing who you are — including your flaws, strengths, and everything else — without trying to change to meet someone else's expectations. It's not about being perfect or never improving; it's about realizing you don't need to "fix" who you inherently are to be worthy of love and acceptance.

Realizing the necessity of self-acceptance

Self-acceptance is the foundation of a fulfilling life. When you truly accept yourself, you free up the energy that would otherwise be spent on conforming to outside expectations. Instead, you can focus on what truly matters to you. It's about recognizing your strengths and working on your challenges from a place of compassion rather than criticism. Without self-acceptance, it's easy to feel like you're constantly falling short or living someone else's version of your life.

For autistic individuals, self-acceptance is even more essential than for nonautistic people. It's not just about accepting your differences but celebrating them. Embracing your unique way of thinking and experiencing the world allows you to grow, form meaningful relationships, and advocate for your needs. When you accept yourself fully, you're better equipped to face life's challenges and live authentically on your terms.

Seeing the benefits of self-acceptance

There are powerful benefits to living with self-acceptance. Here, we list a few:

>> **Reduced stress and anxiety:** Trying to fit into a mold that isn't yours is exhausting. Self-acceptance removes the pressure to mask who you are.

>> **Stronger self-esteem and confidence:** When you accept yourself, you build a stronger sense of self-worth. You focus on your strengths rather than what

you think needs fixing, which can boost your confidence to pursue goals that feel true to you.

>> **Better relationships:** Self-acceptance fosters deeper, more authentic connections. It helps you attract people who appreciate you as you are and empowers you to set boundaries and communicate your needs clearly. As global icon RuPaul puts it, "If you can't love yourself, how in the hell are you gonna love somebody else?"

>> **Improved well-being:** Accepting yourself leads to greater happiness and well-being, freeing you from the struggle to be someone you're not and allowing you to focus on what truly brings you joy.

>> **Confident self-advocacy:** Self-acceptance strengthens your ability to advocate for yourself. When you embrace who you are, it's easier to speak up about your needs.

REMEMBER

Self-acceptance is about living authentically — staying true to yourself in how you express yourself, the path you choose, and how you interact with the world. Honor your unique perspective and follow a path that feels right for you.

Addressing challenges to self-acceptance

Self-acceptance doesn't happen overnight. It's a journey, and for autistic people, it can come with unique challenges. Here are a few you might encounter:

>> **Pressure to conform:** Society often expects people to behave and communicate in specific ways, leading you to mask or hide autistic traits to fit in.

>> **Stigma and misunderstanding:** Misconceptions about autism can make self-acceptance difficult, especially if you internalize negative stereotypes.

>> **Negative self-perception:** Internalized ableism may cause you to feel ashamed of your differences, impacting your self-image.

>> **Feeling "different":** Comparing yourself to neurotypical peers can make you feel inadequate or less than, which can hinder self-acceptance.

>> **Difficulty identifying strengths:** You may find it hard to recognize your strengths, especially if you've been taught to focus on your challenges.

>> **Navigating sensory and social challenges:** Sensory sensitivities and social struggles can cause frustration and self-doubt.

>> **Past negative experiences:** Bullying, exclusion, or rejection can impact your self-esteem, making self-acceptance more difficult.

>> **Fear of rejection:** You may fear rejection or misunderstanding, making it hard to embrace your true self.

>> **Difficulty setting boundaries:** Self-acceptance involves advocating for your needs and setting boundaries, which can be tough in unaccommodating environments.

>> **Complex identity:** Being part of multiple marginalized groups can make self-acceptance more complex due to additional layers of misunderstanding or discrimination.

>> **Expectation to "fix" yourself:** There's often pressure, from others or yourself, to act more neurotypical or minimize your differences.

>> **Lack of positive representation:** Finding role models who share your experience can be tough, especially if positive representation is limited.

REMEMBER

Don't let the length of this list scare you. Most people aren't aware of the challenges that stand between them and self-acceptance. Understanding your own is the first step toward working through the specific challenges in your life and embracing who you truly are.

Strategies for promoting self-acceptance

Self-acceptance is a lifelong practice. It requires patience, self-compassion, and support. As you work on self-acceptance, engage the following strategies:

TIP

>> Treat yourself with the kindness you'd offer a friend. When you struggle, remind yourself it's okay. Every step forward, no matter how small, is progress.

>> Flip negative thoughts. Instead of "I'm different, and that's bad," try "I'm different, and that's okay." Your way of being is just as valid as anyone else's.

>> Recognize that it's okay not to be able to do everything all at once.

>> Surround yourself with understanding people — friends, family, or a therapist who gets neurodiversity.

>> Practice advocating for your needs in different settings — home, work, or school.

>> Identify your strengths. Doing what you're good at or passionate about boosts confidence.

>> Find resources that present autism in a positive light. Join autistic communities, online or in-person, to share experiences and find support — you're not alone.

REMEMBER

Self-acceptance takes time, patience, and support. By learning, connecting with others, challenging negative thoughts, and embracing your strengths, you can build a stronger sense of self and live authentically. Go at your own pace. What matters is that you're moving toward valuing and accepting yourself.

Exercising Self-Advocacy

After self-awareness and self-acceptance comes self-advocacy: the crucial step of ensuring your needs are met and your voice is heard. With a clear understanding of who you are, you can begin to focus on

>> How to leverage your strengths and unique traits

>> What works best for you in different situations

>> What you truly want in life — in relationships, work, or personal growth

>> Where you need support or areas you want to improve

>> How to ensure your differences are respected and supported in environments like work, social settings, or education

These insights equip you to speak up for your needs and advocate for yourself in different areas of life. Now, let's explore how self-advocacy works in practice and how you can apply it every day.

Understanding self-advocacy

Self-advocacy is about understanding your needs, rights, and boundaries, and speaking up to make sure those needs are met — whether you live independently or need significant support. For autistic people, self-advocacy is especially empowering, allowing you to assert your boundaries and communicate what you need at home, work, school, or in social situations.

At its heart, self-advocacy means taking control of your life and ensuring your needs are respected. It's a way to live more authentically, with confidence and independence. Remember, self-advocacy is a skill that takes time to build, and every step, no matter how small, brings you closer to having your voice heard.

Practicing self-advocacy

Self-advocacy in practice means unapologetically showing up as your full self in all areas of life. In a neurotypical world, this might look like embracing your unique way of thinking and not feeling pressured to mask or hide it. For example, at work, instead of just going along with social events or expectations that make you uncomfortable, maybe you suggest alternatives or set boundaries that work for you. You can say, "Hey, I prefer not to do group lunches, but I'm happy to collaborate in a quieter setting." You want to be clear and direct about what makes you comfortable and productive.

In independent living, self-advocacy means knowing what you need to thrive and actively seeking it out. If you need accommodations, like a quieter living environment or specific organizational tools, don't hesitate to ask for them.

When it comes to relationships — with friends, romantic partners, or family — you have the right to set boundaries that protect your energy and emotional well-being. In healthcare, advocating for yourself means being clear with your providers about what you need, such as extra time to process information or requesting that they explain things in a way that works best for you.

REMEMBER

Self-advocacy isn't about making demands. It's about clearly communicating your needs and preferences to create an environment where you can be yourself and live the life you want.

Strategies for practicing self-advocacy

Let's take a look at some strategies for practicing self-advocacy:

>> **Know yourself:** Understand your needs, strengths, and challenges. Know what helps you thrive and what triggers stress or discomfort.

>> **Express your needs:** Be clear and confident when requesting accommodations or setting boundaries. You don't need to apologize for advocating for yourself.

>> **Set boundaries:** Define your limits — how much social interaction you can handle or how you prefer to communicate — and stick to them.

>> **Know your rights:** Know legal protections like the Americans with Disabilities Act (ADA) or equivalent laws elsewhere. Knowing your rights boosts your confidence.

>> **Seek support:** If you face resistance, reach out to advocacy groups, legal help, or trusted allies. Family and friends can offer great support, too.

>> **Start small:** Practice self-advocacy in low-stress situations and build up to tougher ones. It gets easier with time.

>> **At work:** Advocate for the accommodations you need: for example, quiet spaces, clear communication, or flexible hours. Show how they're a win-win for everyone.

- >> **At school:** Talk to teachers or disability services about what you need, like extra time or sensory-friendly environments.

- >> **In social settings:** Set boundaries or suggest activities that suit you. It's okay to say no to things that don't fit your needs.

- >> **Stay flexible:** Your needs will change over time, so adapt as necessary.

REMEMBER

Self-advocacy ensures your voice is heard and your needs are respected, helping you build a life that works best for you.

Nurturing Your Health and Wellness

Nurturing your health and wellness is a crucial part of understanding, accepting, and empowering yourself. After all, the most valuable resource you have is you! Taking care of yourself — body, mind, heart, and soul — builds the foundation for a fulfilling life and advocating for your needs. Prioritizing your well-being supports self-awareness, self-acceptance, and ultimately, self-empowerment.

TIP

The most valuable resource you have is yourself. You need to take good care of you! Here are some tips to nurture your whole self:

- >> **Prioritize self-care:** Make time for activities that nurture your physical, mental, and emotional health, like exercise, healthy eating, relaxation, and hobbies. Listen to your body and take breaks to avoid burnout and maintain wellness.

- >> **Monitor your health:** Pay attention to your body's signals and track any changes. Regular check-ups and self-assessments can help catch potential issues early.

- >> **Advocate for your needs:** Clearly communicate to healthcare providers your symptoms, needs, or health goals. Ask clarifying questions to ensure they understand.

- >> **Address mental health:** Practice stress management techniques like mindfulness, meditation, or exercise. Discuss mental health concerns with healthcare providers or a therapist.

Chapter **14**

Navigating Higher Education

I f you're thinking about higher education — whether it's university, community college, trade school, online learning, or a specialized program — that's a big deal. In fact, it might be one of the biggest life decisions you'll make.

There's no one right way to approach higher education. It comes in many forms, from universities and community colleges to apprenticeship programs, to culinary courses, art schools, online learning, and more. Your journey is unique, and success comes from finding a path that truly fits who you are and what you want to achieve.

This chapter is about understanding your options, choosing what works, tapping into what helps you thrive, and starting your higher education journey with future career success in mind. From exploring your choices to advocating for yourself and connecting with supportive communities, we'll make sure you're ready to navigate higher education with confidence. You have the power to shape your educational experience. It's time to dive in and consider how to make it work for you.

Understanding Your Options

Higher education is the learning that happens after high school, usually at universities, colleges, or specialized institutions, where you deepen your knowledge and skills in a specific field. When it comes to higher education, the choices are as diverse as the people who pursue them.

In a 2024 interview with *Getting Grilled with Curtis Stone*, actor and comedian Joel McHale touched on this diversity of choices while discussing his autistic son, Eddie. "We're not sure what his trajectory is," McHale said. "But he loves video games and he's good at them. So, he might just skip college. I'm like, 'Go ahead. Just start work. Learn that C++ language and start writing video games. Great.'"

REMEMBER

There are multiple paths you can take, each with its own unique benefits. Let's break down some of the most common options you may want to consider.

University and college

Universities and colleges offer a wide range of academic programs, from humanities and social sciences to STEM fields and the arts. These institutions usually provide a more traditional academic experience with a mix of lectures, seminars, and hands-on labs. Degrees typically take three to four years to complete, depending on the country and program.

This path is ideal if you're passionate about a specific subject and want to dive deep into it. Universities often come with a wealth of resources, including libraries, research opportunities, and student support services, which are valuable tools if you know how to make the most of them. In addition, many universities and colleges have specialized supports or programs tailored for autistic students. You can find more information at www.pivotdiversity.com/resources.

Community colleges (and more)

Community colleges (or "colleges" in Canada) offer a mix of academic and vocational programs, leading to an associate degree or certificate. They're typically more affordable than universities and are a great choice if you're not ready to jump straight into a full university program. In fact, about 49 percent of students who earn a four-year degree in the United States start at a community college. This pathway lets you complete your first two years of general education at a lower cost before transferring to a university to finish your bachelor's degree.

In the United Kingdom, Further Education (FE) colleges offer everything from A-levels to vocational certifications, whereas in Australia, Technical and Further Education (TAFE) institutions focus on practical, job-ready skills. No matter where you live, you can find institutions like these in many countries around the world. They all offer flexible options, such as part-time and evening courses, making them flexible and accessible.

Vocational training

If you prefer hands-on learning and want to jump straight into a specific career, vocational training (also known as trade school) could be your best bet. These schools focus on teaching skills for careers like plumbing, electrical work, automotive repair, culinary arts, hair styling, and more. Trade programs are usually shorter than university degrees, often taking one to two years, and they're very job-focused to help you hone the skills needed for your trade.

If vocational training interests you, you may also want to consider trade programs specifically designed for autistic individuals. (Visit www.pivotdiversity.com/resources.) These programs offer additional support, structured environments, and tailored teaching methods to help you thrive. A great example is Inclusion Films, founded by Joey Travolta, brother of actor John Travolta. This program trains people with developmental disabilities, including autistic individuals, in filmmaking skills like scriptwriting, directing, and editing, while also building teamwork and social skills. Programs like these open doors to fulfilling careers by focusing on your strengths and interests.

Union trade education

Many skilled trades are supported by unions that offer their own education and training programs. These programs often combine classroom instruction with on-the-job training, known as apprenticeships. Union trade education is a great option if you want to earn while you learn because apprentices typically receive a wage while gaining hands-on experience in fields like construction, electrical work, and welding. These programs also provide a clear pathway to a stable, well-paying job after completion.

Online learning and bootcamps

For those who need flexibility or prefer a self-paced learning environment, online learning is an increasingly popular option. You can find online courses and degree programs in almost any field, offered by universities, community colleges, and private institutions. In addition to traditional online degrees, there are also bootcamps — intensive, short-term programs designed to teach specific skills, often in tech-related fields like coding, data science, or digital marketing. These programs can be completed from anywhere, making them ideal if you need to balance education with other commitments or prefer learning from the comfort of your own space.

On-the-job training

On-the-job training is a powerful way to learn while actively working in your chosen field. This approach is often offered by employers who want to develop specific skills in their workforce. You might start in an entry-level position and, through direct experience and mentorship, gradually take on more complex tasks.

On-the-job training is particularly beneficial if you prefer learning by doing rather than through traditional classroom settings. In many cases, you can earn a salary while gaining valuable skills, making this an attractive option if you want to enter the workforce quickly without accumulating student debt. This path is available across various industries, from healthcare and technology to manufacturing and service sectors.

Ongoing education

Just because you've started working doesn't mean your education has to stop. In-person or online ongoing education lets you keep growing in your field or explore new ones. For example, if you're in information technology but curious about cybersecurity, online courses or certifications can open new doors. Or if you're in a corporate job but interested in graphic design, a part-time program can help you build those skills. Even learning a new language or picking up a hobby like coding through platforms like Coursera or Udemy can enrich your life. Education is a lifelong journey, and investing in it at any point is a smart move for your future.

Some ongoing education programs are specifically designed with neurodivergent learners in mind. They offer tailored support and teaching methods that align with different ways of thinking and learning. For example, the Neurodiversity Pathways program — in which our author team teaches — provides resources and courses aimed at helping neurodivergent individuals succeed in their careers by focusing on strengths and practical skills. These programs recognize that neurodiversity is an asset, and they create environments where you can thrive while continuing your education.

Choosing the Right Path

Whatever path you choose, know that your journey is valid. There's no single "right" way to pursue higher education. What matters most is what works for you. Take the time to explore your options, ask questions, and make the decision that feels right. Education is not a one-size-fits-all process. It should be a tool to help you build the life you want. It's perfectly okay if traditional college or university isn't the right fit for you. Community college, vocational training, on-the-job training, or other educational paths can be just as fulfilling and lead to successful careers.

REMEMBER

Choosing the right path is a deeply personal decision. You should find the option that aligns with your interests, strengths, and needs. And as an autistic adult, embracing your unique way of thinking and learning is key to making the best choice.

A generally helpful approach

Figure out which path works best for you, using the following framework:

TIP

» **Reflect on your interests.** What subjects or activities do you genuinely enjoy? Do you love numbers or have a fascination with technology, a passion for art, or a talent for hands-on work? Your interests can guide you toward a field that keeps you engaged and motivated. There's no "right" or "wrong" interest. What matters is what excites and inspires you.

» **Identify your strengths.** Choose a program that not only matches your academic interests but also plays to your strengths. If you're detail-oriented, analytical, or creatively inclined, find a path that lets those traits shine.

» **Consider your ideal environment.** Think about where you'll feel most comfortable and supported. Some autistic individuals prefer smaller, quieter settings, whereas others thrive in larger, more dynamic environments. Visiting campuses, talking to students, and attending open days can help you decide. Also, consider the location. Do you prefer a bustling city or a quieter, rural setting? It's crucial to find a place where you'll feel at ease both in and out of the classroom.

» **Ask for guidance.** Don't hesitate to seek help. Reach out to advisors, mentors, or professionals who understand autism and can offer tailored advice. Connecting with other autistic students who've navigated higher education can provide valuable insights. So can your family and friends.

>> **Factor in the social side.** Academics matter, but so does finding a community where you'll fit in. When considering your options, look for schools or programs with student groups or activities that align with your interests.

>> **Focus on your future.** Try to validate whether the path you're considering offers the right connections, internships, or career services to help you get where you want to go.

Considerations as an autistic student

When planning for higher education, there are specific factors to consider to ensure your experience is both successful and enjoyable:

>> **Learning environment:** Think about where you thrive. Do you prefer smaller classes with more direct interaction, or do larger lecture halls suit you? Some people find online learning better because it allows control over the environment and pace while others prefer to be in person to support their attention and other learning needs.

>> **Sensory considerations:** Consider the sensory environment on campus. Are there quiet study areas, or is it mostly busy and noisy? Knowing what helps you stay focused and comfortable can guide your choice.

>> **Support services:** Research the support services available at potential schools. Look into disability services, counseling, and programs designed for neurodivergent students. These resources can really help in navigating academic challenges.

>> **Communication styles:** Different schools have different communication cultures. If you prefer clear, direct communication, find environments where that's the norm. This might also influence your choice between in-person or online courses.

>> **Flexibility:** Flexibility in course selection, deadlines, and attendance policies can make a huge difference. Find out if the schools you're considering offer options that align with how you work best.

>> **Workload management:** Be realistic about how much you can handle at once. Many autistic students benefit from a lighter course load to balance academics with self-care.

Accessing Support

There are many support services available to you in higher education. These resources can significantly impact your experience and success, providing the accommodations and help you need to thrive.

Using educational support services

Navigating higher education can be challenging, but you don't have to do it alone. Educational support services are available to provide the accommodations and resources you need to succeed.

Start by researching the support services at the college, university, or training program you're considering. Many institutions have disability services offices that offer accommodations like extra exam time, note-taking assistance, or quiet study spaces. Reach out early, discuss your needs, and get accommodations in place ahead of time. It'll save you stress later.

For vocational training, check whether they offer supports like individualized instruction, hands-on learning, or flexible scheduling. On-the-job training programs might provide mentorship, job coaching, and personalized support. Don't hesitate to ask for these resources and ensure they're tailored to your needs.

TIP

Here are some best practices to help you secure the assistance you need when meeting with support services:

>> **Be prepared:** Before your meeting, list your needs, questions, and any accommodations you require. Clear communication helps staff understand how to assist you.

>> **Bring documentation:** Have necessary paperwork ready, like medical reports or previous accommodation plans. This ensures you get the right assistance.

>> **Communicate clearly:** Use clear, direct language when explaining the support you're seeking. The more straightforward you are, the easier it is for them to help.

>> **Ask questions:** If you're unsure about anything, ask. Understanding the available resources is key to making informed decisions.

>> **Advocate for yourself:** Be respectful but assertive in communicating your needs. If something isn't working, speak up. Engage a support person if needed. (For more on self-advocacy, check out Chapter 13.)

>> **Nurture relationships and follow-up:** Build positive relationships with support staff to foster more personalized support. After meetings, follow up with emails or additional meetings if necessary to keep your requests on track and ensure progress.

>> **Be patient:** Getting the right support can take time. Be patient but persistent.

>> **Evaluate and adjust:** Regularly review the support you're receiving and adjust your requests as needed. After all, your needs may change.

Tapping into support systems

Support isn't limited to your school. It's available all around you. Your broader network, including family, friends, and online communities, plays a big role in your journey. Lean on them for emotional support and practical advice to navigate challenges, celebrate wins, and stay grounded.

TIP

Connect with other autistic and disabled students who've been through this. They can offer valuable advice, share experiences, and provide emotional support and community. On campus, look for disability and neurodiversity groups. If none exist, check out online forums, local support groups, and social media communities. Or, learn how to start a group yourself!

Explore outside services for additional assistance. Many organizations can connect you with mentors, social groups, and advocacy services. Therapy services, like occupational or speech therapy, can provide targeted support for specific challenges. There are countless apps and tools for organization, time management, and study skills. Assistive technology, like speech-to-text software or sensory tools, can also help.

REMEMBER

It's okay to ask for help, and it's okay to need support. You don't have to do this alone. There are people and services ready to help you succeed.

Chapter **15**

Finding Work and Growing Your Career

Work is about much more than earning a living: It's about finding purpose, gaining independence, and feeling like you're contributing to something. A job can build your confidence, give you a sense of belonging, and connect you to the world in ways that matter. Everyone deserves that, and yes, that includes you.

As an autistic person, you bring unique talents and strengths that the right job will value. But let's be honest — there will be challenges, too. Finding a job that recognizes your skills while supporting your differences can be tough. And once you're hired, navigating the workplace as you adapt to new environments or communicate with coworkers comes with its own set of hurdles.

Here's the thing: Those challenges don't define you, and they don't have to hold you back. There's no one-size-fits-all solution, and there are ways to overcome obstacles and find a job that fits you. This chapter explores how you can find that job, succeed in it, and continue building your career. Your strengths are needed, and this chapter is your guide to making sure they shine. You've got this, and we're here to support you every step of the way.

Landing a Good Job

A good job isn't just about making money. It's about finding work that fits your strengths, provides support, and helps you thrive. For autistic individuals, this means looking for roles that value your unique abilities without overwhelming you with sensory stress or unclear expectations.

Knowing your strengths and needs

Understanding your strengths is one of the most empowering things you can do when job hunting — especially as an autistic person. You bring unique skills and perspectives to the workplace and recognizing those helps you find jobs that are a really good fit for you. Whether your strengths are your attention to detail, your ability to hyperfocus, your creative problem-solving, or something else, what you offer is valuable. Knowing what you excel at lets you confidently pursue roles where you can shine, contribute meaningfully, and feel fulfilled.

REMEMBER

Your skills and perspectives are valuable and recognizing them helps you find the right fit.

Starting with your strengths

Think about what sets you apart. Are you great at analyzing data, creating art, or simplifying complex tasks? Focusing on these strengths boosts your confidence and shows employers what you bring to the table. So, as you build your career strategy, here are some great questions to ask yourself:

>> **What are you good at?** Maybe it's hard skills like coding, baking, selling, or simplifying complex information. Or soft skills like communication, teamwork, or being the person who always follows through.

>> **What are you passionate about?** What makes you excited to get to work? Your intense interests and deep knowledge — creating art, analyzing data, or advocating for something you care about — guide you to roles that feel meaningful.

>> **What makes you unique?** Think about what sets you apart. Is it a different way of thinking, attention to detail, or the ability to focus when others might struggle? Is it character values like unwavering loyalty, outstanding work ethic, honesty, or integrity? Your unique strengths are what make you valuable.

>> **How can you position your strengths for jobs?** With the insights you gain about your strengths, reflect on how to approach positioning yourself for job opportunities:

- How can these strengths be valuable in the jobs you're interested in?

- Which of your core values resonate with the cultures of organizations you'd like to work for?

- How will your key educational qualifications and skills benefit potential employers?

- What experiences and accomplishments can you point to in your past that would indicate your potential for success in your desired role?

REMEMBER

Focusing on your strengths shifts attention from your challenges to what makes you capable. Your strengths tell your story.

Understanding your needs

Understanding your needs is just as important as knowing your strengths. Figuring out what kind of environment helps you do your best work will help you find a place to thrive. Do you need to have clear instructions, a quiet space, or flexible hours? When you understand your needs, you can set yourself up for success from the start by asking for the right supports and accommodations.

Accommodations at work aren't only for disabled people. Everyone uses them. For example, some people need flexible hours to pick up their kids or use apps to stay organized. Accommodations make work easier and more effective for *all people*.

REMEMBER

Knowing your strengths and needs empowers you to ask for the accommodations that will help you succeed so you can build a career that fits *you*, not the other way around. You deserve a role that values your unique contributions, and understanding what works best for you is the key to making that happen.

Advocating for your needs

Sometimes we can manage our needs on our own, but often, we need help from others. In the workplace, this means having open, honest conversations with your manager and colleagues about what you need to succeed, while also being mindful of their needs. It's a two-way street: Working together to support each other creates an environment where everyone can thrive. When you thrive, the whole team benefits.

REMEMBER

You're not the only one who benefits when you're clear about what helps you be productive. It's good for everyone you work with. When you ask for accommodations that improve your performance, you're helping the team succeed. By framing your requests in a way that shows how certain accommodations enable you to contribute more effectively, you're demonstrating that when you have what you need, everyone wins.

TIP

When thinking about the supports you need at work, take some time to reflect on your individual challenges and differences. Here are a few questions to help guide you:

>> **What sensory sensitivities do I have?** If bright lights, loud noises, or strong smells are overwhelming, would noise-canceling headphones, dimmer lighting, or a quieter space help you focus better?

>> **What communication style works best for me?** Do you prefer written instructions? Would you benefit from extra time to process and respond to requests? Is it helpful to have regular check-ins to clarify expectations?

>> **What accommodations do I need for my physical work environment?** Would a quieter room, ergonomic equipment, or sensory aids (like fidget tools) help you feel more comfortable and focused? Think back to past jobs or school experiences. What supports helped you succeed, and how could they be applied in your current or future role?

>> **Do I need flexibility in my work schedule?** Would flexible hours, remote work, or different start and end times help you manage energy levels or reduce sensory overload from commuting?

>> **What tools or technology could help me be more productive?** Are there apps, reminders, or assistive tech that could support your focus and organization? Would time management tools help you stay on track?

>> **How can I best advocate for myself?** Do you feel comfortable discussing your needs with your employer? Would having a job coach or HR representative assist you in explaining and securing accommodations?

By asking yourself these questions, you'll have a clearer understanding of what supports will help you thrive, allowing you to advocate for the accommodations that make your work experience the best it can be.

Choosing the right work environment

Finding the right work environment isn't just about landing any old job. It's about finding a place where you can thrive. It's important to seek out a workplace that values inclusion, offers flexibility, supports your personal and professional growth, and appreciates your strengths. The goal is to be in an environment where your skills are recognized, your needs are respected, and you can contribute meaningfully.

REMEMBER

The key is aligning your strengths and needs with a workplace that truly values what you bring.

TIP

Doing a little research, asking the right questions, and understanding the company's culture can go a long way in helping you find a role where you feel valued, supported, and empowered to grow. Here are some things to consider:

>> **Job types:** Think about your strengths and what kind of jobs align best with them. Consider whether you're detail-oriented, a great problem-solver, or able to focus deeply and look for roles that match your skills and allow you to use them effectively.

>> **Target industries:** Once you've identified the types of jobs that suit you, think about which industries are the best fit — for example, tech, education, or creative fields. Look for industries where your unique strengths can make an impact.

>> **Company research:** Seek out companies that actively support neurodiversity and offer accommodations like flexible hours, sensory-friendly environments, or assistive technology. Websites like Glassdoor or Indeed can give you insights into company culture and whether they're known for being inclusive.

>> **Networking opportunities:** Connect with people who work at companies you're interested in and ask them questions about the work environment. You can ask whether they feel supported, if accommodations easy to get, or if the company flexible about remote work or sensory needs. Networking can give you a real sense of whether a company's culture is right for you.

>> **Trial opportunities:** If possible, try internships, part-time roles, or volunteer opportunities to test out the work environment before committing to a full-time job. These short-term experiences can help you find out whether the company's culture aligns with your needs and strengths.

>> **Work options:** Many autistic people thrive in remote environments where they can control sensory input and structure their day in a way that works best for them. If this sounds like you, consider companies that offer remote work. Or, if you prefer a mix of office interaction and working independently, look for companies with hybrid work models that give you the flexibility to do both.

Assembling a job search toolkit

When you're job hunting, having the right tools is essential to stand out. Finding a job involves more than submitting resumes. You have to do some work to present yourself in the best possible way across various platforms. Here's how to build a strong toolkit to help you land the job that fits you:

TIP

>> **Build a great resume:** Your resume is your professional story. It's a good idea to create two versions: one that's ATS-friendly (ATS stands for Applicant Tracking Systems, which are programs employers use to scan resumes and filter out applicants) for online applications, and one that's more visually appealing for direct emails or networking. Focus on the impact you've made in previous roles by using the STAR (Situation, Task, Action, Result) method to highlight your achievements. Use an online ATS resume scanner to check how your resume scores against job listings. And don't worry about getting a perfect ATS score. 60 percent 80 percent is good enough to make it through most systems.

>> **Remember the other essentials:** Your toolkit needs more than a resume. You should also have tailored cover letters, personal pitches, and a networking strategy. Develop a personal positioning statement, which is an engaging way to explain who you are and what you stand for.

>> **Use LinkedIn or portfolios:** Keep your LinkedIn profile updated, especially the About section. If you have a portfolio or GitHub, link it! Show off your work, share your journey, and showcase your skills with photos, samples, or certifications.

>> **Refine your elevator pitch:** Create an elevator pitch: a brief, memorable summary of what makes you unique. Keep it short, clear, and reflective of what makes you great. Add a personal touch that leaves people curious and keep it conversational.

>> **Practice and improve:** Your toolkit will evolve. Keep improving your resume, LinkedIn profile, and elevator pitch as you grow professionally.

REMEMBER

Assembling these tools helps you make a strong, memorable impression.

Searching for jobs

Job hunting takes persistence, effort, and a bit of grit. Your main goal? Present yourself as the ideal candidate by showcasing your strengths, skills, and experience. Here are some effective job-seeking methods:

>> **Online job boards:** Sites like LinkedIn, Indeed, Google Jobs, and Glassdoor are great starting points. Use filters to refine your search and connect with recruiters to find roles that align with your goals.

- **Online applications:** Apply directly on company websites, and always tailor your resume and cover letter to each job. Using specific terms from the job description can boost your chances.

- **In-person applications:** For industries like retail, applying in person can make a big impact.

- **Recruiters and staffing agencies:** These professionals can match you with job opportunities in your field.

- **Networking:** Networking is crucial and often leads to job offers through referrals. Focus on quality over quantity. Build genuine connections with people who share your interests. For autistic job seekers, it's important to be yourself and let others see the value you bring.

- **Personal branding:** Your personal brand is how you present yourself to employers. Focus on what makes you unique, highlight your strengths, and communicate in a way that feels natural to you. Tell your story authentically.

- **Competitions:** In fields like coding, design, or data analysis, competitions are a great way to showcase your skills. They can open doors to job opportunities.

- **Job fairs:** These events offer a chance to connect with companies. Focus on roles that match your skills, and use referrals to help boost your credibility and stand out.

- **Career centers:** Check out your college or university for campus recruitment events by companies.

- **Autistic job clubs and professional networks:** Autistic job clubs and professional networks are powerful additions to your job search toolkit. They offer tailored support, networking opportunities, and a sense of community with others who understand your experiences. These groups can help you refine your job search strategies, build confidence, and connect with employers who value neurodiversity. Plus, professional networks can open doors to mentors, job leads, and industry insights, all while fostering a supportive environment where your strengths are recognized and celebrated.

- **Government services:** Government organizations (for example, Vocational Rehabilitation or Department of Rehabilitation), can be a huge help in your job search. They offer career counseling and job placement assistance, and they help secure accommodations in the workplace. These programs are designed to support you in finding and keeping a job that fits your strengths and needs, while also connecting you with resources like job training and educational opportunities. It's a great way to get extra support and access to tools that can make your job search more effective.

Stay authentic, keep networking, and use the tools available to land the role that matches your strengths and goals.

Interviewing with confidence

Interviews can feel intimidating, but with preparation, you can walk in feeling confident and ready to showcase why you're a great fit. Here's how to prepare and boost your confidence:

>> **Prepare mentally:** Treat the interview as a two-way conversation because you're not there only to answer questions. You're also seeing if the job fits you. Calm your nerves beforehand with deep breathing, grounding techniques, or reviewing your strengths.

>> **Understand the role:** Study the job description and focus on how your unique strengths, like attention to detail or problem-solving, align with what they need. If you're unfamiliar with something, be honest and emphasize your willingness to learn.

>> **Research the company:** Know the company's mission and values. This not only helps you stand out but also ensures the workplace aligns with your needs. Connecting with current employees can give you insight into the culture.

>> **Use the STAR method:** Structure your answers using Situation, Task, Action, Result (STAR) to keep things clear. This helps you stay focused and highlight your problem-solving and adaptability.

>> **Be authentic:** While it's important to prepare, avoid memorizing answers to the point of sounding scripted. Let your personality shine through, and keep the conversation natural.

>> **Anticipate questions:** Analyze the job description to anticipate questions related to the role. For example, expect questions about technical skills in an IT role or communication skills in a writing role.

>> **Know how to handle tough questions:** For questions like "Why do you want to work here?" use your company research to highlight values or projects that resonate with you. For areas of improvement, be honest and explain how you're addressing them.

>> **Request accommodations:** You could ask for questions in writing in advance or at the interview, dimmed lights, or breaks when the interview is long.

>> **Ask your own questions:** Don't hesitate to ask about the role's expectations, growth opportunities, or the work environment. It shows you're serious about finding the right fit.

REMEMBER

Preparation is key, but staying true to yourself is what will make you stand out. You don't need to try to be perfect. Your goal is to be confident in your strengths and show your authenticity.

Thriving in Your Job

Landing a job is a big achievement, but thriving in it requires more than just doing your tasks. You need to develop key skills that help you grow. In this section, we talk about some areas to pay attention to as you grow in your job.

Demonstrating a solid work ethic

Your work ethic is how you approach your job — being reliable, dedicated, productive, and cooperative. A job involves more than clocking hours at work. You want to work effectively and be a valuable team member.

Here are some key qualities to focus on:

>> **Reliability:** Show up on time, meet deadlines, and follow through on your commitments. Being dependable builds trust.

>> **Dedication:** Stick with tasks even when they're tough, showing that you care about doing quality work.

>> **Productivity:** Focus on working efficiently and delivering high-quality results, not just working longer hours.

>> **Cooperation:** Be a team player, which means working well with others, communicating effectively, and contributing to a positive environment.

TIP

Build a strong work ethic with these strategies:

>> **Set goals:** Clear goals keep you focused and motivated. Set daily, weekly, or long-term goals — whatever helps you stay on track.

>> **Stay organized:** Use tools like to-do lists or apps to manage your tasks.

>> **Practice time management:** Prioritize tasks, minimize distractions, and take breaks to stay productive.

>> **Seek feedback:** Regular feedback helps you improve and shows your commitment to growth.

>> **Adopt a positive attitude:** Stay resilient and motivated, even when challenges arise.

>> **Show initiative:** Take action when you see something that needs doing. Being proactive sets you apart.

By applying these strategies, you'll not only keep your job but also thrive and grow in your role.

Working well with colleagues

Working effectively with your manager and colleagues begins with clear communication and understanding your own work style. It's important to be open about what helps you thrive.

REMEMBER

Be open about what you need to do your best work, and don't be afraid to ask for accommodations that help you stay focused and productive. At the same time, take time to understand how your manager and colleagues prefer to work and communicate. By being direct, reliable, and open to collaboration, you create a stronger working relationship that benefits everyone.

Using meetings to build your success

Love them or loathe them, meetings are a part of work life. Let's look at various types of meetings you're likely to run into, plus tips on how to make each one effective:

>> **One-on-one with your manager:** This is your check-in time to discuss what's going well, what's challenging, and any goals or feedback. To make it effective, come prepared with updates, be honest about what's working and what's not, and ask for feedback on areas where you want to improve.

>> **Performance review:** A formal one-on-one where you'll discuss your overall performance, strengths, areas for improvement, and set future goals. Make it effective by reviewing your recent work ahead of time, bringing ideas for future goals, and asking for clarity on expectations if needed.

>> **Project kickoff:** The team meets to start a new project, covering goals, timelines, and responsibilities. To make this effective, make sure you fully understand your role and deadlines, and ask questions if anything is unclear. Clarify follow-up steps to ensure the project stays on track.

>> **Team meeting:** The team gathers to share updates, discuss projects, and brainstorm solutions. Make it effective by actively listening, contributing when necessary, and sharing your ideas clearly and concisely.

>> **Status update/check-in:** These are quick meetings to check on progress and next steps. Keep it effective by sticking to key updates, being clear about challenges, and staying focused on the current priorities.

>> **Client meeting:** You meet with clients to present information, gather feedback, and ensure both sides are aligned. To make this effective, come well-prepared, communicate clearly, listen to feedback, and follow up with any action items promptly.

REMEMBER

These meetings aren't limited to office jobs. They happen in all kinds of workplaces. In a restaurant, a one-on-one might cover managing tables during a busy shift. In construction, a project kickoff might be a site meeting where blueprints are discussed.

TIP

To ace any meeting, show up on time, be prepared, and stay present. If you're leading the meeting, ensure everyone's voice is heard, stick to the agenda, and wrap up on time.

Giving and receiving feedback

Giving and receiving feedback in the workplace can feel intimidating, especially if you worry about being misunderstood or criticized. But the truth is that feedback is one of the best tools for professional growth.

TIP

When giving feedback, be clear and direct, focusing on the task or behavior, not the person. When receiving feedback, adopt a growth mindset and remember it's an opportunity to improve — not a personal failure. And feedback isn't always negative! Positive feedback is a chance to recognize your strengths and contributions. If anything is unclear, ask questions to better understand how to continue doing well.

REMEMBER

Feedback, whether positive or constructive, is a tool for improvement. Take time to process it, then use it to grow and succeed in your role.

Serving your customers

Effectively serving customers starts with clear communication and understanding their needs. Take the time to listen, ask the right questions, and make sure you understand what they're asking for. If something doesn't make sense, it's perfectly okay to ask for clarification. Customers appreciate when you take the time to get it right.

Approaching customer interactions in a structured way can be helpful. Ask direct questions to keep the conversation focused, and if you need time to process or solve an issue, let the customer know you're working on it and follow through. Patience, clear communication, and careful listening will help you provide excellent service while staying within your comfort zone.

Stay calm, be polite, and show that you're there to help. The goal is to make the customer feel heard and valued through thoughtful interactions.

Exercising self-advocacy in the workplace

Very few workplaces will be perfectly suited to the way you work best, and that's okay. Most workplaces are designed with neurotypical people in mind, so some of your unique differences may present challenges or impact your performance at times. The key is understanding those challenges and advocating for what you need. Doing so can make all the difference.

You deserve to have the right supports and accommodations to help you succeed, and the first step is recognizing what those needs are. If you need more clarity in communication, adjustments to your workspace, or flexibility in your schedule, advocating for yourself is a powerful tool to get those things. (If you're looking to build more confidence in advocating for your needs, check out Chapter 13, where we dive deeper into strategies to help you grow that skill!)

Building your support network

Building your support network at work is one of the best ways to thrive in your job as an autistic person. A strong support network includes a variety of people who can help you in different ways. This may mean finding a mentor — someone with more experience who can offer guidance, share insights, and help you navigate challenges.

Peer-to-peer support is also valuable. Connecting with colleagues who understand your work environment can help you exchange advice, share strategies, and find solutions to common challenges. These relationships build trust and make it easier to reach out when you need help or want to share successes.

Employee resource groups

Connecting with other neurodivergent coworkers, or even colleagues who have neurodivergent children, can be incredibly valuable. These connections create a sense of community and understanding and give you an opportunity to share experiences, strategies, and support each other in navigating workplace challenges.

TIP

Many workplaces have employee resource groups (ERGs) focused on neurodiversity or disability, which provide a safe space for discussion, advocacy, and building awareness. Joining these groups can help you feel more connected, and they also give you the opportunity to contribute to making your workplace more inclusive for everyone.

If your workplace doesn't have an ERG, you can take the initiative to start one. Talk to HR or management about creating a formal group, or gather colleagues informally to create a supportive community. Planning meetings and sharing resources can have a big impact in fostering a more inclusive environment.

Labor, professional, and industry associations

Unions, professional organizations, and industry groups are great ways to extend your support network beyond your immediate workplace. These groups often advocate for the rights of workers and provide resources to help you succeed in your role.

TIP

Many unions and industry organizations have specific resources for disabled or neurodivergent members, such as legal assistance, job placement services, or professional development opportunities. Joining these organizations gives you access to a broader community that understands your challenges and works to create more inclusive environments across entire industries.

TIP

Professional organizations also offer opportunities for networking, mentorship, and skill development. Look for groups in your field that value neurodiversity or have specific initiatives aimed at supporting neurodivergent professionals.

These organizations can provide valuable resources, like training programs, conferences, and networking events, where you can connect with others who share similar experiences and goals. Industry-specific groups can offer insight into how others in your profession manage workplace challenges and advocate for better accommodations, while also helping you build a stronger career path.

Securing Supported Employment

If all of this feels overwhelming, that's totally understandable. For those who need more support, supported employment might be a great option. These services help individuals with disabilities, including autistic people, find and keep jobs in typical work settings alongside non-disabled coworkers while providing the necessary support to succeed. The goal is to match your unique strengths and needs with a role and workplace that can provide the right accommodations.

Take Yumi, for example. She loves organizing and quiet environments. With the help of a supported employment agency, Yumi's job coach found her a role at a library organizing books. The coach provided training, helped her communicate with coworkers, and worked with the employer to make accommodations like quieter workspaces. As Yumi gained confidence, the job coach stepped back but continued to check in. With this support, Yumi is thriving.

TIP

If supported employment sounds right for you, consider these steps:

>> **Connect with Vocational Rehabilitation Services:** These government-funded programs help people with disabilities find and keep jobs. They assess your skills, provide training, and may offer funding for job coaches or assistive technology.

>> **Work with employment support agencies:** Nonprofits and agencies specialize in helping autistic individuals find work. They offer job coaches who provide on-the-job support, helping you navigate tasks and workplace dynamics.

REMEMBER

Supported employment is about finding a role where you can thrive with the right supports. It's not about changing who you are but creating an environment that values your strengths.

Advancing Your Career

Advancing your career as an autistic adult involves leveraging your strengths, continuing to develop professionally, and learning how to communicate effectively. While it can feel overwhelming at times, taking proactive steps will help you grow in your role and open up new opportunities. Let's break down some key areas to help you move forward in your career.

Professional development is essential for career growth. This means continuously improving your skills, learning new ones, and staying current in your field. You can do this by attending workshops, taking online courses, seeking certifications, or learning from colleagues. Development involves more than technical skills; improving soft skills like communication, time management, and leadership is just as important.

TIP

Look for opportunities within your company to take on more responsibility, volunteer for new projects, or set goals that align with your career ambitions. If your company offers professional development resources, take advantage of them. Growth is a gradual process, and each step brings you closer to long-term success.

Using assertive communication

One of the most important skills for career advancement is assertive communication. This means expressing your thoughts, needs, and feelings clearly and respectfully while considering others' perspectives. Assertive communication helps you advocate for yourself, whether you're requesting accommodations, offering feedback, or asking for a raise.

TIP

To communicate assertively, be direct, clear, and respectful. Use "I" statements to express what you need, like "I need more time to complete this task" or "I'd like to discuss ways to improve team communication." This builds trust and confidence, making it easier to navigate workplace dynamics and advance your career.

Seeking promotions and pay raises

Asking for a promotion or raise can be challenging, especially if self-doubt or discomfort with self-promotion is holding you back. However, advocating for yourself is essential for career growth. Here's how to approach it confidently:

TIP

>> **Prepare your case:** Track your achievements, completed projects, and positive feedback. This gives you concrete examples to present when asking for a promotion or raise.

>> **Know your worth:** Research industry standards for your role and experience. This knowledge will help you request a fair raise.

>> **Plan the conversation:** Practice what you want to say. For example, "I've exceeded my goals this quarter and would like to discuss a promotion based on my performance."

>> **Tackle self-doubt:** If self-doubt creeps in, remind yourself that your work has value. Talk to a mentor or trusted colleague for support.

>> **Handle resistance proactively:** If your request is declined, ask for feedback on how to improve and set a timeline to revisit the conversation.

REMEMBER

Advocating for your career advancement is about knowing your worth and asserting your needs. If it feels overwhelming, start small and build your confidence over time.

Resolving conflicts with confidence

Conflict is a natural part of any workplace, but how you handle it can either help or hurt your career. Learning to resolve conflicts confidently is a valuable skill that can make you stand out as a leader and team player. The key is to approach conflict calmly and with a problem-solving mindset rather than avoiding it or responding with frustration.

TIP

When a conflict arises, take a moment to collect your thoughts and think about the outcome you want. Address the issue directly, using assertive communication to express your perspective while remaining open to the other person's point of view. Try to focus on solutions rather than assigning blame, and look for common ground where both parties can agree. By handling conflicts with confidence and empathy, you not only resolve issues more effectively but also build stronger relationships with your coworkers.

Giving back: supporting others

As you advance in your career, one of the most fulfilling ways to give back is by mentoring and supporting others. Sharing your knowledge and experience can help others navigate challenges and grow professionally. You can show support to a new colleague, someone just starting their career, or even a fellow autistic employee.

TIP

Mentorship is a two-way street. You may find that mentoring helps you develop your own leadership and communication skills as it strengthens your sense of community at work.

REMEMBER

Giving back can take other forms aside from mentoring. You might contribute to workplace culture by advocating for better accommodations, volunteering for ERGs, or simply offering your support and guidance to others who may be struggling. Being a mentor or advocate not only helps those around you but also positions you as a leader and someone who is committed to creating a positive and inclusive work environment.

Chapter **16**

Nurturing Relationships

R elationships are a big part of life. They bring joy, support, and connection, but they can also be tricky, especially as an autistic adult. The good news? There's no one "right" way to build relationships, and your natural way of connecting is valid.

Relationships aren't always easy. Miscommunication and mismatched expectations happen, but understanding your needs and staying true to yourself can help you build fulfilling connections. In this chapter, we explore different kinds of relationships: family dynamics, meaningful friendships, community, and romantic connections. We'll also talk about sexual relationships, focusing on communication, consent, and creating intimacy that feels right for you.

Key Things for Healthy Relationships

Relationships can be wonderful, but it takes some work to keep them healthy. You can use a few key tools to make things easier and more fulfilling in relationships with friends, family, or a partner. Here are some important skills to focus on:

>> **Assertive communication:** Be clear about your needs without blaming. Instead of saying, "You're always late," try, "I feel frustrated when plans start late because I like knowing what to expect." This keeps things respectful.

>> **Active listening:** Show you care by really listening. If a friend says they're having a hard day, you might say, "That sounds tough. Do you want to talk about it?" Listening helps people feel supported.

>> **Setting boundaries:** Boundaries protect your time and energy. For example, if a relative drops by unannounced, you could say, "Please let me know before you visit so I can plan." Clear boundaries reduce stress.

>> **Respect and flexibility:** Respect others' needs and be flexible when plans change. If a friend cancels because they're tired, you might say, "No problem — let me know when you're up for it." This shows you value the relationship.

>> **Repairing missteps:** Mistakes happen. If you say something hurtful, you could say, "I'm sorry I snapped earlier. I was stressed, but that's no excuse." Taking responsibility strengthens trust.

>> **Showing appreciation:** Gratitude matters. A quick, "Thanks for listening. I really needed that," or checking in with a message shows people you care. Small gestures make a big difference.

>> **Managing expectations:** No relationship is perfect. If a friend isn't great at texting but always shows up when it matters, focus on that.

>> **Consistency:** Be reliable. If you say you'll check in after something big happens, follow through. Being dependable builds trust and strengthens relationships, even if you're not perfect all the time.

TIP

In the sections ahead, we explore how these points come to life in different situations. Whether it's with family, partners, friends, or your community, these skills are practical and adaptable to all kinds of relationships. We break them down with real-life examples to show how they can help you build connections that feel supportive, respectful, and true to who you are.

Navigating Family Dynamics

Family relationships can be complicated for everyone, but as an autistic adult, you might face some unique challenges — and some great opportunities, too. Whether you're talking with your parents, building stronger bonds with your siblings, spending time with extended family, setting boundaries, or even raising kids, understanding these dynamics is important for creating meaningful connections.

Communicating with parents

Talking to parents as an autistic adult can be tough. They might still see you as the child they raised and struggle to understand how you've grown or what your experiences are like, especially if they don't know much about autism.

Conversations can also bring up emotions like guilt or frustration, which might make it harder for them to really listen. Even when they're trying to help, they might focus on "fixing" things instead of just supporting you.

Different communication styles can add to the challenge. If your parents use vague hints or emotional cues, it might feel confusing. And if you're very direct, they might think you're being blunt, even though you're just being clear.

It's frustrating when it feels like your parents aren't hearing you, but patience and clear explanations can help. Share examples of what you need or what support looks like for you. If talking face-to-face feels overwhelming, writing a letter or email can make it easier to express your thoughts comfortably.

It's important to use respectful assertive communication, which means being honest about what you need while still being kind and understanding of your parents' perspective. It's not about being pushy; it's about advocating for yourself in ways that keep talks calm and open.

TIP

This approach is especially helpful when talking with your parents, who might not always see things from your point of view. Using "I" statements like "I feel" or "I need" helps explain your experience without sounding accusatory.

If family gatherings feel overwhelming, you could talk to your parents by saying, "I want to share something that's been hard for me at get-togethers. No one's doing anything wrong. I just want to explain how I feel and what might help." Then you could add, "When there's a lot of noise and people talking at once, I feel anxious and drained. I need some quiet time to recharge." Finally, suggest a solution: "If I could take a few breaks in a quiet spot, it would make the day much easier for me." Keeping the focus on your feelings and what would help can make the conversation more productive and positive.

REMEMBER

Communication goes both ways. Listening to your parents' perspectives, even when you disagree, can create room for mutual understanding.

Building relationships with siblings

Building a relationship with your siblings can be comforting but also challenging. They often know you better than most people, which is great, but it can also make things complicated. To strengthen your bond, start with shared activities you both enjoy, like watching a show, playing a game, or going for a walk. These moments create natural opportunities to talk and connect without pressure.

REMEMBER

It's okay to acknowledge that sibling relationships aren't always easy. Maybe your sibling felt protective of you growing up, or misunderstandings caused tension. Talking openly about your experiences — and giving them space to share theirs — can help clear the air and build a stronger connection.

One technique to practice with siblings (and anyone, really) is active listening. It's key to improving your relationship. If your sibling shares a memory of feeling misunderstood, you might respond with, "I didn't realize you felt that way. Thanks for telling me. I can see how that would've been hard for you." This shows you're really hearing them and trying to understand their feelings.

REMEMBER

By listening and acknowledging their perspective, even if it's different from your own, you create space for better communication and a closer bond. Sometimes, a little understanding is all it takes to heal old misunderstandings or grow closer.

Engaging with extended family

Interacting with extended family can be tricky, especially if some relatives don't understand autism. They might make assumptions, ask uncomfortable questions, or say things that feel dismissive. This can make gatherings stressful, so it's important to set realistic expectations and set clear boundaries for yourself.

REMEMBER

You're not responsible for educating everyone or explaining your experience unless you feel comfortable doing so. Focus on connecting with supportive relatives, and don't pressure yourself to make everyone "get it." Your comfort and well-being are just as important as being polite.

TIP

Find allies in your family, like a cousin who helps you find a quiet spot or an aunt who gets you. Having someone in your corner can make events easier. You control how much you share and when, so prioritize what feels right for you.

Clear boundaries let others know what you're okay with and protect your well-being. For example, if a relative asks personal questions you don't want to answer, you might say, "I appreciate your curiosity, but I'm not comfortable talking about that right now." Or, if you're feeling overwhelmed, you could say, "Thanks for including me, but I need some quiet time. I'll join in if I feel up to it later."

REMEMBER

Being clear and direct like this helps set the tone for respectful interactions. It's okay if your family members don't fully get it right away. What matters is that you're standing up for your needs and taking care of yourself.

Raising kids of your own

Raising kids as an autistic adult comes with joys and challenges. Your unique experiences can make you an empathetic and insightful parent, which is an incredible strength. That said, balancing your needs with the demands of parenting might take some creativity. Strategies like scheduling downtime, creating routines that work for you and your children, or developing family practices that align with your sensory needs can help you find a good balance.

Talking to your kids about autism in an age-appropriate way is also a powerful tool for building understanding and empathy. When your kids learn from you firsthand, they not only get insight into your perspective but also grow up with important lessons about embracing differences and respecting others.

REMEMBER

Here's an important reminder: Don't be afraid to ask for help. Reaching out for support from parenting groups, friends, family, or a professional therapist who understand your needs is a sign of strength, not weakness. Parenting is hard for everyone, and no one has to do it alone.

Respect and flexibility are essential when parenting, especially when your needs and your kids' needs don't always align perfectly. It's about finding ways to meet in the middle without losing sight of what's important for both of you.

For example, if your child wants to play a loud, energetic game and you're feeling overstimulated, you could say, "I really want to play with you, but right now I need something quieter. How about we draw or read a book together, and we can save the loud game for later?" It's best to be precise about when "later" is so there are no disappointments. This approach shows your child that their wants are important while also modeling how to communicate your own needs respectfully.

By being flexible and respectful, you teach your kids how to navigate differences and work together. These moments not only build trust and understanding but also show them how to balance their own needs with the needs of others — a skill that will serve them well throughout their lives.

Building Friendships

Friendships can be an enriching and fulfilling part of life, but building and maintaining them can sometimes feel complicated, especially when navigating the social world as an autistic adult. The good news? Friendships come in all shapes and forms, and you don't have to follow a script to find meaningful connections. In this section, we break down how to understand social dynamics, find potential friends, develop those relationships, and keep them strong over the long term.

Understanding social dynamics

Social dynamics can feel tricky, especially because of unwritten rules and subtle cues. The good news? You don't have to change who you are to navigate them; you just need to figure out what works for you.

Take time to observe how people interact in social situations. For example, in a group setting, you might notice that people take turns speaking or use body language — like nodding or leaning in — to show interest. Picking up on patterns like these can make social interactions feel a little more predictable and less overwhelming.

REMEMBER

It's okay to ask questions or clarify social cues if you're unsure. Most people appreciate directness and openness, and it's a great way to show that you value honest communication.

Navigating neurotypical social norms

Understanding social dynamics is helpful, but it's just as important to stay true to yourself while navigating them. If you're autistic, the way you naturally socialize might be different from neurotypical norms — and that's okay. The key is to find a balance where you can notice social cues and interactions while still being yourself. If you're someone who prefers to listen more than talk or enjoys deep conversations instead of small talk, own that. Those traits are part of who you are.

REMEMBER

Learning to navigate neurotypical social norms doesn't mean you have to change who you are. It's fine to adjust in ways that feel right for you without pretending to be neurotypical.

For example, if making eye contact feels uncomfortable, try looking at someone's nose or mouth. Or, let them know that you listen better when not making eye contact. If you need a break during a conversation, saying something like, "I need a moment to recharge," can help you stay comfortable while interacting. Staying true to your way of socializing helps you build real connections based on understanding and respect.

Helping others understand your ways of socializing

Helping neurotypical friends and acquaintances understand your natural way of socializing can make friendships stronger and more comfortable. Open and honest conversations can go a long way in building that understanding.

You could say, "Sometimes I need a bit of quiet time during social gatherings to recharge, but it doesn't mean I don't want to be there," or, "I might not always respond quickly in conversations because I need time to think. It's just how I process things." These simple explanations can help people know what to expect and show them that you're being genuine.

TIP

Most people appreciate learning how they can support you better, especially if they value the friendship. By sharing what makes you comfortable and how you like to communicate, you're helping create an environment where everyone feels respected and understood.

REMEMBER

Really great friends will listen, learn, and make an effort to meet you halfway. This way, you're not only staying true to yourself but also inviting your friends to know and appreciate the real you.

Repairing missteps

Friendships sometimes hit bumps. Misunderstandings or hurt feelings happen, especially when social communication feels tricky. As an autistic adult, you might miss a neurotypical social cue or say something that comes across differently than you meant. What matters is how you handle it.

TIP

Start by acknowledging what went wrong. You might say, "I realize what I said might have upset you. I didn't mean it that way, and I'm sorry." Or, "I feel like something's wrong. Did I upset you?" Honest communication helps clear things up.

Apologize sincerely. For example, "I'm sorry for forgetting your birthday. I know it hurt your feelings, and I'll try to do better." Take responsibility without over apologizing or making excuses. If your friend needs space, respect that. Say, "I understand. I care about our friendship and hope we can talk when you're ready."

Missteps aren't always one-sided. Your friend might have said something unkind, and it's okay to speak up. You could say, "Hey, that was hurtful. Can we talk about it?" Or if they misunderstood something you said or did, offering a quick "That's not what I meant. Let me explain" can help clear things up.

REMEMBER

Repairing missteps is about honesty and effort, not perfection. Small adjustments and genuine care can strengthen your friendship.

Finding potential friends

Finding friends starts with looking for spaces where you feel comfortable and where people share your interests. This could mean joining a local club, a hobby group, or connecting with others online who share your passions. Friendships often grow from shared experiences, so starting in places that align with what you enjoy can make meeting new people feel less overwhelming.

Community events, workshops, or volunteering for causes you care about are great ways to connect with like-minded people. The goal isn't to meet as many people as possible; it's about finding people you feel good around. And it's okay if it takes time. Building meaningful connections is all about finding the right fit.

Developing and deepening friendships

Developing friendships means moving from casual interactions to more meaningful connections. This might look like inviting someone to do an activity you both enjoy or finding moments to check in and show interest in their life.

Deepening a friendship doesn't have to involve grand gestures. Often, the small things — like remembering details they've shared or following up on how they're doing — contribute most to trust and connection.

Communication is key to building friendships. If you're not sure how to express interest or start a conversation, try sharing something about yourself or asking questions about their experiences. It's also important to be yourself. Authenticity fosters stronger relationships, and finding friends who appreciate you for who you are makes the connection more meaningful.

For example, if a friend mentions they're stressed about an exam or project, you could send a quick message on the day saying, "Thinking of you — good luck today!" or follow up later with, "How did it go?" It's a simple way to show you care.

Or, if they share a new hobby, like hiking or baking, you could suggest something like, "Want to try a new hiking trail together this weekend?" or "Maybe we can bake something fun together soon!" These small gestures go a long way in showing your friend that you value them.

Appreciation is another easy and meaningful ways to strengthen a friendship. Letting your friend know you see and value them, whether through words or actions, is important.

You could simply say, "I'm so glad we're friends. You always make me laugh," or, "Thanks for being there when I needed to vent. It really means a lot." Small verbal affirmations like this help your friend feel recognized and appreciated.

Acts of appreciation can also be thoughtful gestures. If your friend loves coffee, surprising them with their favorite drink during a catch-up session shows you've been paying attention to what they like. Or, if they helped you out recently, a quick note or text saying, "Thanks for your advice the other day. It really helped," reminds them how much they matter to you.

REMEMBER

Showing appreciation doesn't have to be fancy or over the top. The point is to make sure your friend knows they're valued and that you don't take their presence in your life for granted. Showing gratitude helps to keep friendships strong.

Maintaining long-term friends

Keeping long-term friendships strong is about staying connected, even when life gets busy. You don't have to talk every day. Keeping a friendship is more about showing you care in ways that work for both of you. A quick message, a "thinking of you" text, or planning to catch up once in a while can go a long way in keeping the bond alive.

TIP

Pay attention to how your friend likes to communicate. Maybe they love phone calls, whereas you prefer texting. Finding a middle ground, like texting to set up a quick call, can help keep the relationship comfortable and easy for both of you. Check with them about how frequently they're willing to communicate and respect their wishes.

REMEMBER

Friendships change over time, and that's okay. There might be periods when one of you needs space or life pulls you in different directions. The important thing is having the patience and understanding to pick up where you left off. Long-term friendships thrive on mutual respect and the effort to stay connected, even in small ways.

Managing your expectations is also key to keeping connections healthy and fulfilling as you're building and maintaining friendships. Friendships aren't perfect, and people have different capacities for what they can give. Learning to accept that can help you avoid unnecessary frustration.

For example, if a friend doesn't text often but is always there when you need them, focus on the fact that they show up when it matters. Instead of expecting constant communication, appreciate the reliability they bring to the table. If a friend sometimes forgets social plans but makes an effort to reschedule or apologize, recognize their intention to stay connected rather than focusing on the occasional slip-up.

REMEMBER

Adjusting your expectations doesn't mean settling for less — it means understanding what each person brings to the friendship and valuing them for who they are. By being realistic and flexible, you can create stronger, more meaningful connections with your friends, built on trust and mutual respect.

Navigating Romantic Relationships

Romantic relationships can be complex but also deeply rewarding. For autistic adults, dating and partnerships come with unique challenges — and some pretty powerful insights, too. The challenges might come from things like unwritten social rules, sensory sensitivities, or communication differences. These can make dating feel overwhelming or confusing at times. But autistic people often bring honesty, depth, and a strong sense of authenticity to relationships, which can be a huge strength.

The good news? There's no single "right" way to approach romance. You don't have to fit into a traditional mold to build meaningful connections. When you focus on what works for you — your strengths, needs, and values — you can create relationships that feel right and fulfilling. Let's explore how to understand romantic interactions, find potential partners, navigate challenges, and build long-term partnerships.

Understanding romantic interactions

Romantic interactions can feel like they come with a lot of unspoken rules and expectations, and you need to approach them in a way that feels authentic to you. Understanding how people express romantic interest — through nonverbal cues like body language or by directly communicating — can help make things clearer. It's okay to ask questions or be upfront about what you need to feel comfortable.

REMEMBER

Be open about your communication preferences and boundaries. Honest, straightforward conversations about how you express affection and what you expect can help prevent misunderstandings and build deeper connections.

Searching for potential partners

Finding potential partners often starts by looking in places that match your interests and comfort level. Shared hobbies, community events, or even online dating platforms can be great options. The autistic community can also be a helpful place to meet people who might share similar values or experiences.

TIP

If traditional dating feels intimidating, join groups or activities that align with your passions. Doing what you love at a book club, gaming group, or art class can help you meet people naturally and comfortably.

Navigating challenges

All relationships come with challenges. For autistic adults, this might include addressing communication differences, sensory sensitivities, or balancing routines. The key is to approach these challenges with openness and teamwork.

If sensory issues arise, look for environments or activities that suit both of you. If misunderstandings happen, create a way to address them calmly and clearly. Taking breaks when conversations feel overwhelming is okay too. Just let your partner know you'll come back to it when you're ready.

Frustrations with flirting

Flirting can feel like decoding a secret language, and for many autistic adults, it's not just awkward; it can feel vague, unnatural, or even "false." The subtle hints, teasing, and unspoken rules often don't align with a more straightforward communication style. But good news: You don't have to flirt in the "traditional" way to show interest.

TIP

Start with direct compliments, like, "I love how passionate you are about your art," or, "You have such a kind smile." This makes your interest clear without any guesswork. You can also ask thoughtful questions, like, "What's something you've always wanted to try?" or, "What's your favorite way to spend a weekend?" Showing curiosity is a great way to connect.

If that still feels like too much, just be direct: "I'm really enjoying getting to know you." It's simple, clear, and cuts through the ambiguity.

REMEMBER

You don't have to be perfect, and making mistakes is okay. Flirting, like any communication, gets easier with practice and authenticity.

Sustaining long-term partnerships

Long-term relationships thrive on honest communication, mutual support, and flexibility. Regular check-ins, whether casual or planned, help you stay connected. Celebrate wins, share interests, and create routines that work for both of you.

REMEMBER

Differences will happen — like one partner needing structure while the other prefers spontaneity — but compromise and understanding help you adapt together. Relationships grow stronger when both people feel valued and supported.

An important factor in strong relationships is consistency, which means being reliable: following through on promises, being emotionally present, and keeping communication open. For example, if regular check-ins help your partner feel secure, making an effort to follow through builds trust. Sticking to shared activities, like watching a favorite show or taking a walk together, shows you value your time with them.

REMEMBER

Consistency isn't about perfection. It's about showing your partner they can count on you, creating trust and stability that make navigating challenges easier. Little things, like saying "I'm thinking of you" or lending a hand when they need help, build connection and reinforce the relationship over time.

Navigating Sexual Relationships

Navigating sexual relationships as an autistic adult means understanding your needs, communicating openly, and creating a connection that respects both your and your partner's boundaries and values. While this part of relationships can feel complex, it's deeply personal and can be fulfilling when approached with honesty and care. In this section, we break it down by focusing on understanding your values, practicing clear communication and consent, fostering intimacy, and addressing challenges.

Knowing your values and boundaries

Before entering a sexual relationship, it's important to know what intimacy and sex mean to you. Take time to reflect on your values, what makes you feel safe and comfortable, and what you need to feel respected. Knowing these things makes it much easier to communicate with your partner.

REMEMBER

Your boundaries are valid, whether they involve sensory preferences, emotional needs, or the pace of the relationship. Boundaries aren't just about saying "no" to what feels wrong. They're also about saying "yes" to what feels right. For example, you might feel comfortable with physical affection in private but not in public, and that's completely okay to express.

Consent and communication

Consent and communication are the foundation of any healthy sexual relationship. For autistic adults, being direct about needs, preferences, and boundaries can be a major strength. Consent isn't a one-time "yes" or "no" conversation. It's an ongoing dialogue where you and your partner check in with each other to make sure both of you are comfortable and enthusiastic at every stage.

"A" IS OK: SEXUAL INTEREST LEVELS

Sexual attraction and interest in sex vary widely, and there's no "right" way to experience it. Asexuality is a valid orientation where someone feels little to no sexual attraction, and it exists on a spectrum. Some people feel attraction in specific situations, whereas others don't at all. Romantic attraction without sexual interest is also completely normal.

For autistic adults, it can be a relief to know your level of interest in sex — whether low, high, or somewhere in between — is valid. Society pushes narrow ideas about relationships, but reality is much more diverse.

Whether you have little interest in sex or a strong interest, you deserve connection and respect. It's about understanding your needs and finding relationships that align with them. Relationships should be built on mutual respect and understanding, where everyone's boundaries are honored. Knowing yourself, being open, and embracing who you are allows you to build a life that feels true to you — on your terms.

REMEMBER

If something feels unclear, don't hesitate to ask for clarification or provide it. For example, saying, "Is this okay for you?" or, "Can we take a break?" keeps the conversation open and reduces stress. Transparency and straightforwardness help create a safe and respectful environment for both partners.

TIP

Practicing consent can be as simple as asking, "Are you comfortable if I kiss you?" while cuddling on the couch. If your partner enthusiastically agrees, that's great! If they say they'd rather just continue cuddling, respecting that and responding with something like, "Of course, that's fine," shows you value their boundaries.

REMEMBER

This kind of back-and-forth communication builds trust and mutual respect. By being open and attentive, you create a space where both of you feel safe, respected, and connected. The point isn't to make the perfect move. It's about making sure both partners are comfortable and on the same page.

Intimacy and emotional connection

Intimacy and emotional connection go beyond physical interactions; they're about building trust and closeness. This can look different for everyone. Some people need a strong emotional bond before physical intimacy, while others connect in other ways. The key is finding what works best for you and your partner.

REMEMBER

Talking about what intimacy means to you and what helps you feel emotionally connected can strengthen your relationship. This might mean sharing moments of vulnerability, doing activities that build trust, or learning each other's love languages. If verbal expressions feel challenging, showing affection through actions, shared experiences, or small gestures can be just as meaningful.

TIP

Intimacy grows through relaxed, pressure-free moments, like cooking a meal together, sharing stories, or taking a quiet walk. These shared experiences build trust and closeness naturally. Simple gestures like holding hands, cuddling, or offering a hug can deepen emotional and physical connection, while shared activities like working on a project or enjoying a hobby together strengthen your bond in meaningful ways.

REMEMBER

Intimacy is about finding ways to connect that make you both feel valued, understood, and safe.

Addressing challenges

Like all relationships, intimacy can come with challenges. Sensory sensitivities, communication differences, or anxiety about expectations may impact how comfortable you feel. The key is to approach challenges with patience and a problem-solving mindset.

If sensory sensitivities are an issue, talk with your partner about adjusting the environment to suit your needs. This might mean dimming the lights, changing textures, or finding physical positions that feel better. If communication differences create misunderstandings, try tools like writing notes or using apps to help express your thoughts more clearly.

REMEMBER

It's okay to take breaks or revisit conversations if something feels overwhelming. Challenges are part of every relationship, and navigating them with mutual respect and a willingness to adapt helps keep the connection strong. Knowing it's fine to pause, reflect, and try again later destresses the journey.

A GUIDE TO SEXUAL HEALTH

If mainstream sexual health resources have ever felt like they don't fit your experiences, *Our Sexuality, Our Health: A Disabled Advocate's Guide to Sexual Health* might be what you've been looking for. Created by Melissa Crisp-Cooper for the University of California, San Francisco, this guide addresses the gaps disabled people, including autistic individuals, often face in traditional sexual health education.

Melissa developed this guide to reflect the diversity of disabled people's experiences. It goes beyond generic advice to focus on understanding your boundaries, needs, and communication styles. Designed to be accessible and empowering, it's a resource to help you navigate sexual health with confidence and clarity.

The guide focuses on key areas like consent, communication, and self-advocacy, which are essential for navigating intimate relationships. It provides tools to help you think about what intimacy means to you, articulate your boundaries clearly, and foster mutual respect with partners. It's all delivered in a straightforward, judgment-free tone that validates your experiences and empowers you to make choices that align with your values and needs (a link to this free guide can be found on the Resources page at https://www.pivotdiversity.com/resources.).

Participating In Community Life

Being part of a community can be a powerful way to find belonging, build connections, and add meaning to your life. Community can be a group based on shared interests, a neighborhood, or even an online space.

REMEMBER

For autistic adults, finding and engaging with the right community can be transformative. It offers a sense of support and understanding that's hard to find elsewhere. Let's talk about why community matters, how to find your place, and how to engage in ways that feel comfortable and meaningful.

Communities can take many forms, like a local group for a shared hobby such as gardening or gaming, a religious congregation, a sports team, an online forum for autistic adults, a neighborhood book club, or a support group centered around a common experience. Even advocacy networks, volunteer organizations, or creative spaces like art classes become meaningful communities for many people.

The importance of community

Finding a community that gets you can make a huge difference. Being surrounded by people who understand your perspective — either online or in person — can give you a sense of belonging beyond surface-level interactions.

TIP

Connecting with other autistic people who share similar experiences can be incredibly validating. It's a reminder that you're not navigating life alone and that others truly understand you — no lengthy explanations needed.

REMEMBER

Communities can be a space for support where you can share your triumphs and challenges, exchange advice, or simply exist without judgment. Whether you find community in social groups, forums, advocacy networks, or shared-interest clubs, these connections help build confidence and reduce isolation. Engaging with a supportive community can spark new friendships, collaborations, and even partnerships.

Understanding community dynamics

Communities have their traditions, rules, and expectations. Observing how people interact within the group before diving in can help you feel more at ease. Are discussions casual, or is there a structure to how people contribute? Knowing this can make things feel more predictable.

REMEMBER

Ask questions if you're unsure how things work. Most inclusive communities welcome people who are curious and learning. Approaching with an open mind and a willingness to observe or ask can make engaging more comfortable.

Finding your community

Finding a community starts with exploring what matters to you. This could be a hobby, a cause, or a shared experience like being autistic.

REMEMBER

Community isn't one-size-fits-all. You might find your place in a local meetup, an online forum, a book club, or an advocacy group. It's okay to explore until you find a space where you feel comfortable and accepted.

Engaging with community

Getting involved doesn't have to be complicated. Start by showing up: attend a meeting, join a group chat, or just observe. Take your time. You don't have to jump into conversations right away; contribute when it feels natural.

TIP

Find ways to participate that match your strengths and interests. Volunteer if you like helping others. If smaller interactions are more your speed, consider sending a thoughtful message or sharing a comment in a group chat. Authentic participation matters more than how much or how often you engage.

REMEMBER

Connecting doesn't have to mean being the center of attention. For some, it might be joining a conversation; for others, it might be sharing creative work or contributing in quieter ways.

Finding support in community

One of the best things about being part of a community is the support it offers. In spaces where you feel understood, challenges don't have to be faced alone.

TIP

Autistic-specific communities — both local or online — can provide advice, shared experiences, and solidarity. Being able to say, "This happened to me too," and hear, "I get it," can be incredibly validating. For connections to autistic communities, visit the Resources page at https://www.pivotdiversity.com/resources.

REMEMBER

If you're feeling isolated, reaching out to a community can remind you that people have your back. Belonging to a community can help you feel grounded, connected, and less alone in whatever you're going through.

5
Empowering Autistic Individuals

Recognize universal principles for supporting autistic individuals, emphasizing respect, inclusion, and community integration.

Empower autistic clients as service providers through accessibility, effective communication, and neurodiversity-affirming care.

Support autistic students as educators by fostering inclusive classrooms, collaborating with families, and pursuing professional growth.

Create inclusive workplaces by understanding autistic strengths, providing personalized accommodations, and fostering supportive environments.

Chapter **17**

Universal Principles for Empowerment

This chapter is here to help you support and empower any person in your life who's autistic: your child, a coworker, or a neighbor. Throughout this book, we offer specific advice on how to empower autistic people in homes, schools, workplaces, and circles of friends. However, in this chapter, we focus on the universal principles and approaches that can work in any setting.

We show you how a simple shift in your perspective can make a huge impact on others, and you find out how to embrace a respectful and inclusive mindset — one that's rooted in dignity, compassion, and true understanding. Doing so allows you to include autistic people more fully in your life, develop their skills and talents, and build a better world for us all.

Shifting Our Perspective

We kick things off by acknowledging that everyone sees the world a little differently. Perspectives are shaped by each person's unique experiences, upbringing, and cultural backgrounds, guiding how we navigate everyday life. No two people have the exact same perspective, and that's not just okay: It's amazing. This diversity in how we view the world produces fresh ideas, sparks creativity, and helps us build stronger, more inclusive communities.

But having our own perspectives can also have its downsides. Sometimes, individual viewpoints can limit us, causing us to miss out on the bigger picture or overlook someone else's reality. It's totally normal and very human — something everyone experiences — but that's why it's so important to occasionally pause and consider shifting our point of view. By doing this, we open ourselves to new insights and a deeper understanding of the people around us.

As we grow, our ability to shift our perspectives with new information becomes a key marker of wisdom. This kind of growth allows us to understand others better and make choices that benefit everyone. When it comes to autism, shifting our perspective from what we think we know to a more informed understanding is crucial. It helps us move past misconceptions and assumptions, opening the door to more meaningful support and deeper connections with autistic people.

REMEMBER

We can start broadening our perspective on autism by understanding two key things: that neurodiversity is a normal part of the human experience and that society is designed to work well for lots of people *but not all*. Recognizing these truths is the first step toward creating a more inclusive world where everyone can thrive.

Recognizing the normalcy of neurodiversity

A key step in shifting our perspective — and truly empowering autistic people — is recognizing that neurodiversity and autism are normal parts of the human experience. When we talk about "neurodiversity," we're referring to the vast range of differences in how individual brains function and how people behave. And when we talk about a "normal part of the human experience," we mean that these differences in how our brains function and how we interact with the world are just as natural and real as any other human variation, like height or eye color. This concept isn't new, but our understanding and appreciation of it have evolved significantly.

In the past, if a person's brain worked differently from what was considered "typical," it was often seen as a problem that needed fixing. But now, we're realizing there's no such thing as a "normal" brain. In fact, current understanding suggests that at least 20 percent of humans are neurodivergent, meaning their brains are wired in ways that include conditions like autism, ADHD, dyslexia, and more. Each person has a unique personality, interests, and talents because our brains are wired uniquely. And that's not just okay — it's actually pretty amazing.

Imagine a world where everyone thought, spoke, and acted the same way. It would be incredibly dull, right? It's like if every song had the same melody. No matter how beautiful it is, it would get monotonous quickly. The diversity in how we think, process information, and interact with the world is what brings depth, color, and innovation to society. Our ability to grow and adapt as a species is largely due to the wide variety of ways human brains work.

WARNING

Some might wonder if emphasizing the normalcy of neurodiversity means we're downplaying the challenges that autistic people face, especially those who need lots of support. That's a really important question! But the truth is, recognizing neurodiversity as a natural part of being human is crucial to understanding that everyone deserves to be understood, accommodated, and supported — regardless of the type or level of support they need. Everyone has something to contribute.

REMEMBER

Understanding that neurodiversity is a normal and integral part of the human experience is key to shifting our perspectives. When we see neurodiversity as a natural variation, we stop obsessing about "fixing" neurodivergent brains to be more like "us" and start focusing on how to support and accommodate all the neurodivergent minds among us — autistic ones included.

As we start to recognize and embrace neurodiversity as a natural part of the human experience, it becomes clear that the way society is currently structured often doesn't account for these differences. To truly support neurodivergent individuals, we need to understand how our societal systems are designed and the impact that design has on those who don't fit the "neurotypical" mold.

Understanding how society is designed

Think about something for a second: About 90 percent of humans are right-handed, which is why so many tools and everyday items are designed with right-handed people in mind. Scissors, can openers, even shaking hands — it's all a breeze for nine out of ten people because everything's built for right-handed folks.

Then one day, you meet a lefty. They tell you about the struggles they face with everyday things, like using a computer mouse, operating a manual can opener, or writing in a spiral notebook. They even bump elbows at the dinner table or struggle with using a standard pair of scissors. If you're right-handed, you might never have thought about these challenges. Seeing the difficulties they encounter, your first instinct might be to teach them the skills and habits of right-handed people. But are their struggles really about being left-handed, or is it because the world is designed to work well for 90 percent of people but not for them?

REMEMBER

This is a lot like how society is built upon certain assumptions about how people think, learn, and behave. These assumptions work great for some but can unintentionally leave out those who don't fit the mold, like people who are neurodivergent, including those with autism, ADHD, dyslexia, and more.

"Society assumes that if we cannot express ourselves in ways that are easy for them to understand, we must not have anything important to say," says Amy Sequenzia, a nonspeaking autistic essayist and advocate in the anthology *Loud Hands: Autistic People Speaking* (Autistic Self Advocacy Network, 2012). "But this society was not designed with us in mind, and that is where the real problem lies."

In some cultures, where quiet spaces, routine, and less pressure on constant social interaction are more accepted, autistic people might find it easier to thrive. Take Finland, for example. There's less emphasis on small talk and eye contact, and the education system focuses more on individualized learning — elements that may feel more comfortable for an autistic person. Similarly, in Germany, the culture tends to value direct communication, which can align well with the straightforward communication style often preferred by autistic individuals.

But in fast-paced, high-pressure societies that prioritize extroversion and constant social engagement, autistic individuals might find daily life more challenging. In places like the United States and Japan, there's a strong emphasis on networking and socializing, and autistic people might feel overwhelmed or out of sync with societal expectations.

We're not suggesting one society is better than another but drawing attention to these differences helps us see why some environments are more supportive for neurodivergent individuals than others.

Here's the thing: Many of our societal systems — like education, employment, and even social norms — aren't really designed with neurodivergent individuals in mind. It's not that society is intentionally excluding anyone. It's just that these systems were created around the dominant, or "neurotypical," way of being, which can make it harder for those who don't fit that mold to navigate daily life.

Understanding this is a crucial step in becoming more inclusive. If someone is struggling, it's not necessarily because they're incapable or not trying hard enough. It might be that they're navigating a system that wasn't designed with their unique brain wiring in mind. This is where we can start thinking about how to make our societal systems more inclusive, accessible, accommodating, and ultimately, equitable.

TIP

But don't worry — you're not expected to redesign society on your own. Start with small, meaningful actions in your life. Think about the little things you can do to make your world more accessible to autistic people, like offering alternative communication options at work, creating quiet spaces in your home or at community events, or simply being patient and understanding with autistic family and friends.

On a slightly larger scale, you can support policies that promote inclusivity and be an ally by listening to and amplifying the voices of neurodivergent individuals. These small efforts can add up, leading to meaningful change over time. Focus on what you can do and remember that every step you take helps build a more inclusive world.

Adopting an Empowering Mindset

The right mindset can make a big difference in how you support and understand autistic individuals. It starts with treating autistic people with the same kindness, fairness, and respect you'd give anyone, while appreciating their unique perspectives. Approach every interaction with an open heart and mind, aiming to understand their experiences from their point of view. Recognize their strengths and challenges, and empower them to speak up, building their confidence and independence. In this section, we talk about ways you can do these things.

Extending dignity and respect

Extending dignity and respect means recognizing and valuing everyone's worth, no matter their background, abilities, or behavior. The objective is to treat everyone with kindness, fairness, and consideration in all interactions.

Value each person's individuality. Everyone has unique qualities that enrich our community. Honoring their right to make decisions about their own lives means listening to their preferences and considering their input when it matters. Practicing empathy and compassion is also key. Try to understand their feelings, experiences, and viewpoints. Offer support when needed in a way that respects their dignity.

Communication is crucial too. Use respectful language and listen actively without interrupting. Show that you value their opinions by responding thoughtfully.

TIP

Use respectful language, but don't stress too much about using the "right" terms. What really matters is your intent and honoring the language preferred by the person you're speaking with (for more on this, check out Chapter 1).

REMEMBER

Ensuring fair treatment is vital. Make sure everyone has access to the same opportunities and resources, without discrimination. Implement fair and transparent processes in decision-making and conflict resolution, treating everyone with fairness and justice. Creating an inclusive environment is also significant. Appreciate and celebrate the diverse backgrounds, experiences, and talents of individuals, and foster a culture that values and respects diversity. And remember to respect personal boundaries and privacy. Don't pry into personal matters unless invited, and protect confidential information shared in trust. Maintain discretion and never share sensitive information without permission.

Exercising compassionate curiosity

It's easy to fall into the habit of thinking that our way of experiencing the world is the only way — or at least the "normal" way. But that's like saying vanilla is the only flavor of ice cream. Sure, it's popular, but what about chocolate, strawberry, mint, or even unique flavors like kulfi, lavender, or rose? Just like these unique flavors, each person's brain has its own wiring, creating a diverse range of ways to experience the world.

This is where compassionate curiosity comes in, which means using an approach that combines empathy and a genuine desire to understand someone else's experience. The idea is to open your mind and heart to the idea that there's no "one size fits all" when it comes to how we think, feel, learn, or interact. It's about wanting to understand someone else's experiences and perspective — not to judge or "fix" it, but to empathize and learn from it.

TIP

Here are some practical ways to bring compassionate curiosity into your interactions with autistic people:

>> **Be aware of your expectations and judgments.** Understand that these don't foster a total understanding of someone. Recognize when you're imposing your expectations on someone else, and remind yourself that every person is unique.

>> **Don't make assumptions.** Each individual is different, and they might not fit into any stereotypes or generalizations you've heard. Approach every person as a unique individual.

>> **Suspend judgment.** When something about someone doesn't make sense, instead of jumping to conclusions, seek to understand them. Ask questions like these:

  ● "What's your experience like?"

  ● "Why did you react that way?"

  ● "How do you see this?"

>> **Listen actively.** Don't just hear the words; really focus on what the other person is saying. Ask follow-up questions to gain a deeper understanding.

- >> **Empathize.** Try to put yourself in the other person's shoes. Consider how their experiences, especially with autism, might shape their daily life.

- >> **Recognize both strengths and challenges.** Understand that every person has a mix of strengths and difficulties. Some challenges might not be immediately visible, while some talents might be easily overlooked.

- >> **Be patient.** Understanding someone else's experience, especially when it involves something as complex as autism, takes time. Be patient with both the other person and yourself as you learn and grow.

- >> **Practice self-compassion.** It's okay not to get everything right. If you make a mistake, learn from it. It's part of the process.

By practicing compassionate curiosity, we can better understand and appreciate the rich diversity of human neurodiversity. This broadens our perspective, deepens our empathy, and helps us create a more inclusive and understanding society. Who wouldn't want to be part of a world like that?

Respecting strengths and challenges

Taking the strengths and challenges of autistic individuals seriously is crucial because it's the foundation for empowering them to reach their full potential. This means truly understanding and acknowledging both the unique abilities and the specific challenges they face. For example, an autistic person might have an incredible ability to focus on complex tasks, making them exceptional at problem-solving or analytical work. However, they might also struggle with sensory overload in noisy environments.

REMEMBER

It's important not to dismiss the challenges of autistic people, nor ignore their strengths. By taking both seriously, you can provide the right support, while also creating opportunities for them to shine in areas where they excel.

Accepting differences

We teach kids from an early age that "it's our differences that make us special," but somehow, we tend to forget that lesson as we grow up. We start expecting everyone to think, act, and work the same way. That mindset can cause problems, especially when it comes to autistic people.

Being autistic means your brain works a bit differently than a neurotypical brain. This isn't a bad thing. Quite the opposite; it can lead to unique skills and perspectives. However, it does mean that autistic individuals might approach tasks differently, communicate in their own ways, or need different types of support to succeed.

When we talk about "accepting differences," we mean doing more than acknowledging that differences exist. We mean truly embracing, valuing, and understanding them.

REMEMBER

Acceptance is about embracing reality and being at peace with what is, freeing up your energy to make a real difference. This mindset helps you appreciate each person for who they truly are so that you genuinely value and embrace these differences, not just tolerate them.

TIP

Here are some specific ways you can practice acceptance with the autistic people you know:

>> **Communicate openly.** Ask about their needs, preferences, and passions, and listen to their responses.

>> **Value their perspective.** Autistic individuals often see the world differently. Appreciate this diversity of thought and the unique insights it brings.

>> **Respect boundaries.** Autistic individuals may have different comfort levels with socializing, physical touch, or sensory stimuli. Respect the boundaries they have.

>> **Foster self-advocacy.** Encourage autistic individuals to speak up for themselves. They know their strengths, needs, and boundaries best, and self-advocacy helps them secure the support and accommodations that work best for them.

>> **Practice patience.** It might take time for an autistic individual to process information, respond to changes, or communicate their thoughts and feelings.

Including for abilities

When it comes to autism, we focus on the challenges too often. Yes, the challenges that autistic people encounter are real and significant, but that's not the whole picture. It's like going to an art museum and only noticing the frames, while missing the masterpieces inside. Sure, we need to accommodate and support autistic people with the barriers they face, but we also need to recognize and celebrate the abilities, strengths, and unique talents they bring to the table.

"Including for abilities" means embracing and utilizing the unique abilities of each individual. For example, one autistic person might have an exceptional memory or incredible focus, making them fantastic at detail-oriented tasks. Others might have a knack for absorbing and retaining facts, strong visual skills, deep expertise, resilience, high integrity, attention to detail, creative problem-solving, and more. If we only focus on the challenges associated with autism, we risk overlooking these remarkable abilities. Every person contributes to our world in their own unique way, and it's essential that we recognize and value those contributions.

WARNING

As with any group of people, the range of abilities — and challenges — varies widely among autistic individuals. There's no one-size-fits-all template where you can say, "These are the strengths of autistic people, and these are their challenges." While certain strengths and challenges are often associated with autism, every autistic individual is, well, an individual. Each autistic person is unique, with their own set of abilities and challenges.

TIP

So, if there's no template, how do you get to know the strengths of an autistic person? The same way you get to know the strengths of any person: by spending time with them, listening to them, and paying attention to what they excel at and enjoy. Ask questions, observe, and be open to discovering their unique talents. It's all about building a genuine connection with a person and understanding them as the individual they are. By exercising a bit of compassionate curiosity, you will be able to develop an understanding of a person's abilities and areas of strengths more quickly.

Encouraging self-advocacy

Empowering autistic individuals to self-advocate is crucial because it directly impacts their ability to get the understanding and support they need to thrive. When people can speak up for themselves, they're more likely to access the resources and accommodations that will help them succeed. The objective is to give them the tools to effectively communicate their needs, preferences, and rights, leading to better outcomes at school, work, and in their personal lives.

"Self-advocacy" means understanding and communicating your own needs, preferences, and rights. It's about having the confidence and skills to speak up and make sure your voice is heard. Some autistic individuals might communicate differently or need support in self-advocating, but they can still advocate for themselves. It's our responsibility to provide them with the tools to do so, ensuring their voices are respected and their needs are met.

Self-advocacy builds confidence and independence. It gives autistic individuals the power to take control of their lives, make informed decisions, and feel more empowered. For example, if someone knows they need a quieter workspace to focus, clearly expressing that need can lead to the right accommodations, boosting productivity and job satisfaction. Empowering autistic individuals to self-advocate is key to helping them reach their full potential.

TIP

Self-advocacy can be taught at any age at school, home, or work. It's about helping autistic individuals understand their needs and fostering their confidence to express those needs.

TIP

Here's are some universal approaches to help you teach and foster it:

>> **Start with self-awareness.** Help them understand their strengths, needs, and preferences to build the foundation for effective self-advocacy.

>> **Encourage open communication.** Teach them how to express their needs clearly and assertively, whether it's through words, writing, or alternative communication methods.

>> **Practice in real-life situations.** Create opportunities for them to advocate for themselves in everyday settings, like asking for a quiet space or requesting specific support.

>> **Teach active listening.** Show them the importance of listening to others, so they can engage in productive conversations and negotiations.

>> **Support decision-making.** Encourage them to make decisions about their own lives, no matter how small. This builds the confidence needed to advocate for bigger needs.

>> **Celebrate successes.** Recognize and celebrate when they successfully advocate for themselves, reinforcing that their voice matters and can make a difference.

>> **Provide tools and resources.** Equip them with resources like AI chatbots, scripts, checklists, or visual aids to help them feel prepared and confident when advocating for themselves.

>> **Foster a supportive environment.** Create an environment where self-advocacy is encouraged and supported, making it a natural part of their interactions.

>> **Lead by example.** Show them what effective self-advocacy looks like by advocating for yourself and your own needs in a respectful and positive way.

A Civic and Spiritual Calling

If the approaches we've discussed so far sound familiar, it's because they echo some of the most fundamental teachings from both spiritual and civic traditions around the world.

Maybe you were taught in your house of worship to "do good to others," "love your neighbor as yourself," or to not "do to others what would cause pain if done to you." Or perhaps you learned The Golden Rule in school: "treat others the way you want to be treated," or embraced the scouting pledge to "help other people at all times."

These principles are so universal that they shape how we see ourselves as nations. In the United States, citizens pledge "liberty and justice for all," while the French motto, "Liberté, Égalité, Fraternité," emphasizes freedom, equality, and community. In Australia, the phrase "Fair go" embodies the belief in giving everyone a fair chance, highlighting the importance of fairness and equal opportunity.

At the heart of these teachings is empathy and mutual respect: Treat others with the same care and consideration you'd want for yourself. Take a moment to ask yourself, "If these principles are so deeply ingrained in our faiths, schools, and national identities, why wouldn't we apply them to our understanding of autism?"

TIP

These core values directly translate into how we should approach and support autistic individuals:

>> Recognize the inherent worth and dignity of each individual, regardless of their differences.

>> Exercise compassion and understanding toward all.

>> Emphasize the importance of community and mutual support.

>> View challenges as opportunities for growth.

>> Accommodate those who may need deeper understanding or support.

REMEMBER

Whether you call it a "spiritual perspective" or "civic values," this point of view shifts the focus from trying to change autistic individuals to be more like us to reshaping ourselves so that we may better support them to reach their full potential. It emphasizes our connectedness — to each other, our communities, and something greater than ourselves — and the need for understanding, acceptance, and empowerment. In short, it's about treating every human as, well, *human*.

Encouraging Autistic Inclusion

To fully integrate autistic individuals into our communities, we need to start by raising awareness — helping everyone better understand autism and autistic people. It also means taking steps ourselves to include autistic people within our social circles and communities and providing autistic people with the resources and space they need to grow, both as individuals and as leaders.

REMEMBER

Autistic inclusion means creating environments where autistic individuals are not just present but actively engaged, respected, and valued. Inclusion extends to workplaces that accommodate different communication styles, schools that adapt to diverse learning needs, and communities where autistic people are empowered to contribute and lead.

Encouraging social inclusion

Social inclusion means ensuring autistic individuals feel welcome and connected in all social settings. Here are some specific ways we can practice this:

>> **Be patient and open-minded.** Autistic individuals may process information differently. Allow them time to respond and interact in their own way without interrupting or rushing.

>> **Use clear and direct communication.** Avoid misunderstandings by being specific. For example, instead of saying, "Let's hang out some time," try, "Let's meet for coffee at 2:00 p.m. on Saturday at the coffee shop on Main Street."

>> **Create structured and predictable environments.** Many autistic individuals thrive on routine. Share schedules in advance to reduce stress, like saying, "Dinner at 7:00 p.m., followed by a movie at 8:30 p.m."

>> **Focus on common interests.** Autistic individuals often prefer connecting over shared interests rather than small talk. For instance, if someone loves astronomy, invite them to a stargazing event or a discussion on space exploration.

Raising herd awareness

You might be familiar with the term *herd immunity*, where a community is protected from disease because enough people are immune. *Herd awareness* brings this idea into the social realm: It means ensuring that enough people in a community understand and support the experiences of autistic individuals that an environment is created where autistic people can thrive. It's like a social immune system that helps prevent misunderstandings, stigma, and exclusion.

Why is this important? The more people understand autism, the more inclusive our society becomes. This is especially crucial in places like workplaces or schools, where policies often cater to neurotypical individuals, leaving autistic people to struggle. Raising awareness is about more than addressing challenges; it's also about highlighting the strengths and unique perspectives autistic people bring. We need to challenge narratives that frame neurodivergence as something "abnormal" or "disordered" and celebrate it as a natural form of human diversity that needs to be better understood and embraced.

TIP

Here are some specific ways you can contribute to raising herd awareness:

>> **Educate yourself.** Learn about the autistic history, autistic community, and various types and the strengths and challenges of autistic individuals.

>> **Be accepting.** Show patience, respect, and accommodate the differences of autistic people.

>> **Spread the word.** Talk to your friends, family, and colleagues about autism. Share your experiences with the autistic friends and family you know.

>> **Support organizations.** Back organizations led by autistic people that advocate for autistic people's rights and work to create more inclusive environments.

REMEMBER

Raising herd awareness about neurodiversity is a crucial step in creating a more inclusive and welcoming world for autistic people. By educating, advocating, and creating supportive environments, you can help to break down stereotypes and misconceptions about neurodiversity and improve the lives of autistic people. You have an important role to play in spreading this awareness!

Empowering autistic leaders

Supporting autistic individuals in leadership roles is essential for creating more inclusive and effective communities. Autistic leaders bring unique perspectives and innovative problem-solving skills that can drive real change. Their involvement ensures decisions about the autistic community are guided by authentic voices, leading to more empathetic and effective policies.

REMEMBER

When autistic people hold leadership positions, they become powerful role models, challenging stereotypes and raising awareness about autism. This fosters equity and social justice within organizations and society. Plus, having autistic leaders at the table means the community's needs are truly understood and addressed, creating a more diverse and well-rounded approach to problem-solving. After all, who understands autism better than someone who is autistic?

This isn't limited to autism-related roles. It's about nurturing leadership skills in autistic individuals so they can contribute across business, education, science, or the arts, bringing their unique perspectives and enriching the broader community.

Developing autistic leaders

Including autistic individuals in leadership roles requires intentional strategies to ensure their strengths are leveraged, their needs are accommodated, and they feel supported. Here's how to make that happen:

>> **Engage with advocacy networks.** Connect with autistic-led advocacy organizations to identify and recruit autistic candidates for leadership roles (for a starting point, turn to the list of resources at www.pivotdiversity. com/resources).

>> **Offer tailored leadership training.** Provide leadership training programs designed for autistic individuals, focusing on building their skills and confidence.

>> **Include autistic voices in decision-making.** Ensure autistic people are represented on the boards, staff, and committees of anything related to autism. This develops autistic leadership and enhances the quality and impact of outcomes.

>> **Involve autistic people in policy development.** Support autistic leaders in contributing to policy development and advocacy efforts on issues that impact autistic people.

>> **Recognize contributions.** Celebrate the achievements of autistic leaders through awards, recognition programs, and public acknowledgment to highlight their impact.

By implementing these strategies, we can grow the leadership skills of autistic people, benefiting from their unique perspectives and contributions.

Chapter **18**

How Service Providers Can Empower Autistic People

Think about a restaurant kitchen. There are line cooks, prep cooks, pastry chefs, and dishwashers. Each has a different job they're really good at. Line cooks are fast, they're under pressure, and they get the food on the plate quickly. Prep cooks are all about taking their time, making sure everything is chopped and prepped just right. Pastry chefs need focus and precision to make delicate desserts. And dishwashers are working constantly behind the scenes, keeping everything clean so the kitchen can keep running.

Now imagine if the manager said, "Hey, everyone has to do things the same way." Line cooks, prep cooks, pastry chefs, and dishwashers — all using the same tools, working at the same speed, in the same way. That kitchen would turn into a disaster. People would make mistakes and get frustrated, and the whole thing would fall apart. But if the manager lets each person work in the way that's best for them — giving them the right tools, pace, and environment — the kitchen flows. Everyone's doing their best work, and the food is way better because of it.

This is exactly what happens when service providers use neuroinclusive practices with their autistic clients. When they understand that different people need different kinds of support, they create environments where everyone — especially autistic people — can really thrive.

Just as in our restaurant example, a one-size-fits-all approach just won't cut it when you're supporting autistic clients. Understanding that autistic clients are individuals with their own challenges and strengths is key to providing effective service.

Most service providers genuinely want to give their autistic clients the best support possible. They care about making a positive impact and ensuring that their services are effective and accessible. Therapists, educators, healthcare professionals, and community program leaders all want those they serve to thrive.

To really make that happen, it's crucial that providers take the time to understand the unique needs and strengths of each of their clients. Providers don't need to have all the answers right away, but they do need to be open, adaptable, and willing to learn what each individual truly needs. In this chapter, we'll discuss how you can improve your effectiveness in serving your autistic clients.

Adopting Core Service Principles

To provide truly effective services for autistic individuals, it's essential to begin by understanding that no two people are the same. Each person has a unique blend of strengths, challenges, and preferences. By adapting services to meet these individual needs, you create a more supportive and empowering environment.

Recognizing that people are individuals

In the kitchen analogy in the chapter introduction, the manager needs to adapt for the line cook, the prep cook, the pastry chef, and the dishwasher. Similarly, service providers need to recognize that autistic individuals have a wide range of strengths, needs, and preferences. Some autistic people thrive in fast-paced environments, whereas others need a calm, organized space to feel comfortable. The key is figuring out what works best for each person, and that's what adopting neuroinclusive service principles is all about.

Facilitating effective services for autistic individuals means first recognizing that each person is unique. Everyone has their own mix of strengths, challenges, and preferences (for a deeper dive into these things, turn to Chapter 4). We get that service providers often want to streamline things. It makes sense to look for efficient, generalized approaches, especially when resources are stretched thin. But when you try to apply cookie-cutter solutions, you miss the mark. Instead, you need to provide the tools, environment, and respect they need to be supported.

Imagine you go in for a haircut, and the stylist doesn't even ask what you want. They just give everyone the same buzz cut because it's "efficient." How happy would you be with that service? Not too thrilled, right? You expect to be listened to and have your preferences respected. Or imagine going to the dentist, and they don't bother asking if you're comfortable before they start drilling away. Yikes! What would that feel like? You'd be out of there in a heartbeat. It's the same for autistic individuals. When services don't adapt to their unique needs, it's not just frustrating; it can feel overwhelming or even impossible to engage with.

REMEMBER

Autistic individuals aren't all the same, and what works for one person might be frustrating or even harmful for another. By listening closely and observing what helps or hinders their progress, you can shape a personalized plan that truly supports their growth. The more adaptable and responsive you are, the more your client will feel empowered and capable.

Understanding the normalcy of autism

One of the most important shifts in thinking for service providers is understanding that autism is just one of many variations of how human brains can work. Autistic individuals aren't "bizarre" or "broken." They're simply people with a different way of experiencing and interacting with the world. This shift to seeing autism as part of human diversity rather than a deficit changes everything about how you approach support. It allows you to focus on both the challenges and the strengths that come with being autistic, enabling you to ultimately provide better, more respectful services.

Accepting challenges and strengths

Yes, being autistic comes with challenges. Sensory sensitivities, communication differences, and the need for routines are real and can impact daily life. But those challenges don't define the person. Autistic individuals also bring unique strengths to the table — intense focus, creative problem-solving, attention to detail, and deep, passionate interests, to name a few. When you see both the strengths and challenges, you can offer more balanced and effective support.

This balanced perspective helps in a couple of key ways. First, it stops the damaging view that something is "wrong" with the autistic person and instead emphasizes that they have their own valid way of navigating the world. Second, it allows you, as a service provider, to tap into their strengths, helping them reach their goals and lead fulfilling lives. When the focus isn't "fixing" challenges and instead on figuring out how to work with and around them, you empower autistic clients to use their strengths to their advantage.

Understanding what this means for your autistic clients

For the autistic person you're supporting, being understood and accepted as "normal" in their own way can be life changing. When service providers view autism as a natural variation of human experience, it can help autistic clients feel more comfortable, less pressured to conform, and more confident in their abilities. They aren't forced into molds that don't fit them but instead are supported in finding ways that work for them. This acceptance helps build trust, reduces anxiety, and allows the autistic client to engage more fully in their care and personal growth.

Understanding how this leads to better services

When you see your autistic clients as individuals with their own mix of strengths and needs rather than viewing them through a deficit-focused lens, your services naturally improve. You start listening more closely, collaborating more effectively, and offering support that feels tailored to who they really are. That, in turn, creates a more positive, empowering experience for the client.

REMEMBER

By understanding that autism is a normal, natural way of being human, you not only stop seeing your clients as "difficult," "bizarre," or "broken," but you also become better equipped to meet their individual needs. You approach each person with respect for their unique way of thinking, and this leads to more effective, compassionate, and meaningful service delivery. Ultimately, that's what leads to better outcomes for your client and you.

Presuming competence

Always start by assuming that your autistic client is capable. This means believing that they can understand, learn, and succeed, even if they communicate or do things differently. Don't underestimate their abilities just because they may need support in certain areas. When you assume competence, you show respect and trust, which helps your client feel empowered and confident.

TIP

Just because someone's way of thinking or communicating is different doesn't mean they can't do something. By starting with the belief that they can, you help create a space where they can reach their potential and grow. This approach makes your support more effective and focuses on what your client can do, rather than what they can't.

Questioning what you've been taught

As a service provider working with autistic individuals, it's crucial to take a step back and question what you've been taught. A lot of what's historically been considered "best practice" in the field may not have been developed with autistic people in mind, or worse, without their input at all.

WARNING

While training and certifications are valuable, they can't always keep up with the latest understanding of autism, especially as more autistic voices are being heard. The danger with relying on outdated or inaccurate assumptions — no matter how good the intentions — can't be overstated. Well-meaning service providers have often used approaches that didn't account for the actual needs and experiences of autistic people.

REMEMBER

Methods that focus on "fixing" behaviors rather than supporting the individual have led to harm, frustration, and trauma for many autistic clients. It's a reminder that even good intentions can have negative consequences if we're not mindful enough to question and adapt our practices based on real, lived experiences. Thankfully, that's starting to change. If you're curious about how, check out Chapter 21.

TIP

To truly serve autistic clients in a meaningful way, you have to be willing to challenge old assumptions, listen to lived experiences, and stay open to new approaches. Being a service provider is more than just following a checklist; you're providing the kind of care that evolves and improves with real-world insights. Here's how to get started:

>> **Stay curious.** Don't settle for what you already know. Research new practices and listen to evolving autistic perspectives so that your approach stays relevant and effective.

>> **Challenge assumptions.** Question why certain methods are considered "best" and whether they truly help. This keeps you from unintentionally causing harm or frustration.

>> **Adapt based on feedback.** Be open to changing your methods when something isn't working. This leads to more personalized, effective support that truly respects your client's individuality.

>> **Ask autistic people.** There are lots of autistic subject matter experts out there with deep knowledge (check out the list of resources at www.pivotdiversity.com/resources for a starting point). By connecting with these experts, you're not just getting professional insights; you're getting firsthand experience about what actually works.

>> **Look for lived experience.** Prioritize training, research, and other resources developed by autistic individuals. You're learning from the real experts, which ensures better service delivery.

>> **Recognize biases.** Be mindful of internalized ideas about autism that might be outdated or harmful. This helps you provide support without misconceptions or stereotypes getting in the way.

Providing Effective Services

Supporting autistic clients effectively means making collaboration a priority and providing individualized support. Involving them in decisions from the start fosters open communication and trust. By listening carefully, adapting to their preferences, and communicating in ways that work for them, you ensure a more personalized and respectful approach. This makes the support you offer not only more relevant but also more impactful.

Collaborating with your client

Collaborating with your autistic client is crucial to providing effective and respectful support. Instead of assuming you know what's best, involve them directly in decisions about their care. This means asking questions, listening carefully to their needs, and checking in regularly to see how things are working. A helpful approach is to offer choices and be flexible — let them guide how support is provided, rather than sticking to rigid methods.

REMEMBER

Collaboration builds trust, creates more personalized support, and makes sure you're actually helping in ways that are meaningful to your clients. Plus, when clients feel heard and involved, they're more likely to thrive and advocate for themselves, leading to better outcomes for everyone.

TIP

The key to effective support is working *with* your autistic client — not making assumptions for them — to ensure the support you provide is truly individualized, respectful, and effective. Here's how to do it:

>> **Ask for their input.** Using their preferred communication method, start every conversation by asking how they prefer to be supported. What do they want to focus on? What works well for them? What doesn't?

>> **Offer choices.** Give them options for how support can be delivered. You can offer scheduling flexibility, communication options, or environment changes to let them decide what fits best.

>> **Stay flexible.** Be ready to adjust your approach if something isn't working. Regularly ask for feedback to make sure the support is still aligned with their needs.

>> **Focus on strengths.** Build a plan that emphasizes your client's strengths and goals, not just areas of difficulty. Tailor your support to help them thrive in the ways they want to.

>> **Collaborate on solutions.** If a challenge comes up, work together to find solutions. Don't assume you have all the answers. Your client knows what works for them better than anyone.

Communicating effectively

Effectively communicating with autistic clients means being clear, direct, and responsive to their individual communication styles. It's important to avoid jargon or overly complex language. Keeping things straightforward helps prevent misunderstandings.

TIP

For some clients, visual aids like pictures, charts, or written instructions can be super helpful. Others might prefer having extra time to process what's being said before responding.

REMEMBER

Make sure to check in regularly, asking if a client needs clarification or if they're comfortable with the pace of the conversation. Also, be mindful that communication isn't just about words; body language, tone, and facial expressions all play a role.

Above all, be patient and flexible, and remember that effective communication is about meeting the person where they are rather than forcing them to accept an approach. When you create an environment where they feel heard and respected, your conversations will be far more productive and meaningful.

Here are some key strategies for effective communication with autistic clients:

TIP

>> **Ask about preferences.** Find out how your client prefers to communicate: speaking, writing, with augmentative and alternative communication (AAC) devices, or visual aids.

>> **Be clear and direct.** Use simple, concrete language. Avoid idioms or abstract phrases that can be confusing.

>> **Break it down.** Divide complex information into smaller, manageable parts and explain step-by-step.

>> **Ask specific questions.** Be explicit — for example, "Tell me if you have pain in your head or stomach" — instead of asking vague questions like "Are you feeling OK?"

>> **Be patient.** Allow extra time for processing and responding without rushing or filling the silence.

>> **Check for understanding.** Regularly ask questions to make sure the client understands, or have them summarize in their own words.

>> **Set clear expectations.** Outline what will happen during your meeting or appointment so there are no surprises.

>> **Respect boundaries.** Autistic individuals may interpret social cues differently. Respect their comfort with eye contact, proximity, and topics.

>> **Encourage self-advocacy.** Support your client in expressing their needs, and help them build confidence in advocating for themselves.

>> **Adapt.** Stay flexible with your communication style, adjusting based on feedback from each individual client.

Ensuring accessible spaces

Making the physical space where services are provided accessible is just as important as how you deliver the services. For many autistic individuals, sensory sensitivities can make traditional office spaces overwhelming.

TIP

To avoid overstimulation, consider providing quiet areas with soft lighting instead of harsh fluorescent lights, reducing loud noises, and using neutral colors in the decor. Offering flexible seating options — like chairs with gentle rocking or allowing clients to stand or move around during a session — can also make a huge difference.

If you know a client has specific needs, such as needing a weighted blanket or access to noise-cancelling headphones, having those on hand can make the environment feel more welcoming and supportive.

REMEMBER

Even small changes, like ensuring there's a clear schedule or visual cue cards available, can help autistic clients feel more comfortable and in control during their time in the space. By creating environments that are calming, predictable, and responsive to sensory needs, you make it easier for clients to focus on the services rather than being consumed with discomfort or anxiety from the space around them.

Understanding trauma-informed care

Autistic individuals often face a higher risk of trauma due to sensory sensitivities, communication barriers, social stigma, and bullying. A trauma–informed approach considers these factors and offers compassionate, tailored support that promotes safety, trust, and empowerment. Here are some key tips for trauma–informed care when working with autistic clients:

TIP

>> **Recognize trauma.** Understand that behaviors like anxiety, withdrawal, or sensory overload may be trauma responses, not defiance or noncompliance.

>> **Sensory and emotional regulation.** Help clients manage sensory input and regulate emotions with tools like quiet spaces, fidget items, or calming techniques.

>> **Avoid retraumatization.** Minimize triggers like sudden changes or sensory overload and design interventions that reduce, rather than increase, stress.

>> **Honor communication preferences.** Respect your client's preferred communication method and recognize that behavior may sometimes be their primary form of expressing distress.

>> **Be willing to adjust pace.** Allow clients to proceed at their own pace, avoiding pressure or rushing. Be ready to adjust plans based on their emotional or sensory needs.

>> **Build coping skills.** Teach stress management strategies like mindfulness or provide sensory breaks and encourage strong support systems to foster resilience.

>> **Pursue continuous education.** Providers should be trained in trauma-informed care, especially in relation to autism. Regular supervision and provider self-care are also essential to maintaining a compassionate, trauma-informed approach.

REMEMBER

By showing compassion and understanding for the trauma that autistic individuals may face, you help them build resilience, strengthen coping skills, and feel more empowered to navigate the neurotypical world.

Empowering as Medical Professionals

Medical professionals can empower autistic patients by creating a healthcare environment that is inclusive, respectful, and responsive to their unique needs and preferences. Empowerment means fostering autonomy, enhancing communication, and ensuring autistic patients feel heard, understood, and actively involved in their healthcare decisions.

TIP

One key way to do this is by engaging in shared decision-making — inviting autistic patients to participate in discussions about their treatment options and procedures. This ensures they fully understand their choices and feel confident in what they are consenting to. It's important to listen with empathy, validate their concerns, and acknowledge any feelings of discomfort or anxiety.

Creating a more comfortable environment may involve adjusting sensory elements, communication methods, or offering supported decision-making, where a trusted caregiver helps the patient understand options. However, the patient's voice should always be at the center of the decision-making process.

REMEMBER

Medical professionals can best support autistic patients by being flexible, patient, and attentive to their communication and sensory preferences. By fostering trust and involving them in every step of their care, patients will feel more confident, supported, and engaged in managing their health.

Working with parents and caregivers

When working with the parents and caregivers of autistic children, medical professionals should aim for clear, compassionate communication and collaboration. Parents and caregivers know their child best, so involving them as partners in care decisions is crucial. Listen to their concerns, respect their insights, and work together to create a care plan that suits the child's unique needs. Keep explanations simple, avoid jargon, and ensure parents and caregivers understand the options available, including the potential benefits and challenges of each.

REMEMBER

Be mindful that parents and caregivers often manage many aspects of their child's care, so offering practical, flexible solutions can make a big difference. Acknowledge their role in supporting the child and encourage them to share any strategies or accommodations that work well at home or in other settings. By building a trusting, collaborative relationship with parents and caregivers, you create a stronger, more effective support system for the child's health and well-being.

Here are strategies service providers can use to collaborate with autistic patients' parents and caregivers:

TIP

>> **Keep communication open.** Maintain regular communication with parents and caregivers through face-to-face meetings, phone calls, or email. Regular updates help caregivers stay informed about the patient's progress, goals, and any concerns.

>> **Clarify roles.** Define your role and the caregivers' role clearly, ensuring everyone knows how they're contributing to the individual's support. Acknowledge caregivers' efforts and provide encouragement.

>> **Involve them in care planning.** Include parents and caregivers in creating care plans, asking for their insights on what works at home and recognizing their expertise on their loved one's routines and preferences.

>> **Offer practical strategies.** Share tools and techniques caregivers can use at home to manage behaviors, support communication, and address sensory needs.

>> **Offer caregiver training.** Provide training sessions for caregivers, demonstrating techniques and giving feedback to help them support their loved one effectively.

>> **Solicit feedback.** Create a welcoming environment where caregivers feel comfortable giving feedback and use it to improve your services and foster trust.

Effectively diagnosing autism

Diagnosing autism isn't about checking off "deficits." It's about understanding how a person thinks, communicates, and interacts with the world. Autism looks different in everyone, so a one-size-fits-all approach won't work. Traits can be overlooked when they present differently across cultures, mistaken for cultural differences, or misinterpreted as poverty-related stress, especially in individuals from low-income backgrounds. Many — especially adults, women, and those who mask — don't fit outdated stereotypes. Autistic girls, for example, may express traits in ways that don't match traditional expectations and may instinctively adapt to social norms, making their autism less apparent.

A good assessment goes beyond tests and should consider a person's full developmental history, including their strengths — not just challenges — and how they navigate social interaction, sensory processing, and emotional regulation. Communication styles vary, so flexibility is key. Open-ended questions or vague language can be difficult, so adjusting your approach helps. Input from those who know them well, along with self-reporting when possible, provides a fuller picture. A diagnosis should offer self-knowledge, support, and validation, not make someone feel like something is wrong.

REMEMBER

No two individuals experience autism the same way, so avoid stereotypes about what "typical" autism looks like. Recognizing these differences leads to more accurate and fair diagnoses.

Delivering a diagnosis effectively

When giving an autism diagnosis to parents, caregivers, or autistic adults, be clear, compassionate, and focused on empowering the person with knowledge.

Skip the technical jargon and explain things in a straightforward, easy-to-understand way. Acknowledge strengths as much as challenges, framing the diagnosis as a tool for understanding and support — not a limitation. Offer practical next steps, like referrals, counseling, or support groups, so individuals and families feel prepared to move forward and advocate for the right services.

REMEMBER

Encourage questions and acknowledge emotions so individuals or families feel heard and supported. By focusing on strengths and offering guidance, you help make the diagnosis a foundation for understanding, confidence, and meaningful support.

Empowering as Therapists

As a therapist, your job isn't to "fix" the autistic traits of your clients. It's to support their growth, autonomy, and well-being. Encourage them to develop tools that work for them without pushing neurotypical expectations. Rather than forcing conformity, focus on building confidence and skills that improve quality of life. Respect their unique perspectives and help them create coping strategies that fit their needs, leading to a more fulfilling, self-directed life. Empowerment isn't about changing who they are; it's about giving them the support to succeed as themselves.

You can empower your autistic clients using the following ways:

TIP

>> **Take a neurodiversity-affirming approach.** See autism as a natural variation that needs to be understood and supported, not something to be "fixed." Celebrate each client's unique perspective and strengths, rather than focusing only on challenges.

>> **Help clients understand themselves.** Guide clients in exploring their own thoughts, feelings, and behaviors, helping them better understand themselves, others, and how they fit into the world. This deeper self-awareness fosters acceptance, personal growth, and improved social navigation without changing who they are.

>> **Reinforce positive identity.** Help clients view autism as a natural and valuable part of them, encouraging pride in their identity rather than something to overcome.

>> **Encourage self-advocacy.** Teach clients how to express their needs, set boundaries, and advocate for themselves in everyday situations, helping them feel more confident in their interactions.

>> **Support emotional regulation.** Provide tools like sensory breaks, mindfulness techniques, or visual aids to help clients manage emotions in ways that feel natural to them.

>> **Understand behaviors.** Autistic behaviors often have deep roots and are easily misinterpreted through a neurotypical lens. What seems "unconventional" could be a coping mechanism or response to sensory overload. Instead of suppressing these behaviors, focus on understanding their triggers and meaning. Take a thoughtful, respectful approach that honors the individual's needs without imposing neurotypical expectations.

>> **Recognize past trauma.** Autistic individuals face higher risks of trauma due to multiple experiences like bullying, social stigma, sensory overload, and being misunderstood. Many have endured harmful treatment or exclusion. Use a trauma-informed approach that creates a safe, supportive environment focused on trust and healing.

>> **Create an affirming space.** Ensure that therapy sessions are free from judgment, where the client feels comfortable exploring their emotions and challenges.

>> **Collaborate on goals.** Work together to set meaningful, client-driven goals that align with their personal interests and life aspirations, rather than imposing external expectations.

>> **Be flexible.** Tailor therapy to the client's needs. Some may thrive with structure; others prefer a more flexible approach. Avoid forcing activities they're uncomfortable with, and let sessions flow according to their comfort.

>> **Review, reassess, and revise.** Regularly ask for feedback on what's working in therapy and what isn't. Encourage self-reflection to help clients understand their strengths and needs. Adapt your approach based on their preferences and progress.

Chapter **19**

How Educators Can Empower Autistic People

I n most places, students spend 6 to 8 hours a day, 5 days a week in school. That's around 1,440 hours a year in a classroom. During these hours, educators, their peers, and the school environment shape how they learn, think, and grow. For autistic students, this time isn't just about academics; it's crucial for their social, emotional, and psychological development as neurodivergent individuals in a largely neurotypical world.

As an educator, you have the power to make a lasting impact, not just in academics but by creating environments where autistic students feel accepted and included. Supporting them in learning to communicate, manage emotions, and advocate for themselves builds their confidence and lifelong self-advocacy skills.

This chapter offers strategies to help you create a classroom that supports autistic and all students. You'll learn how to involve parents and caregivers, adapt strategies for different education levels, and invest in your own growth as an educator.

Creating an Inclusive Classroom

Every student deserves a learning space where they feel safe, accepted, and valued — especially autistic students, who may face extra challenges in traditional classrooms. Autistic students need an environment that values their unique ways of thinking and learning, seeing differences as strengths. As a teacher, you shape this space, helping students build confidence, participate, and succeed. In this section, we offer practical tips for fostering an inclusive classroom that supports all learners.

Understanding barriers students face

Neurodiversity means that brains work in many different ways, each with its own strengths and challenges. These differences are a natural part of life. For autistic students, neurodiversity means they may think, learn, and communicate differently, and those differences should be understood and supported.

The differences also mean that autistic students often face challenges that make learning and participating in school difficult. Understanding these obstacles and learning how to support them effectively helps students not just navigate these challenges but thrive. Let's look at some common barriers that autistic students face, and how you can help:

TIP

» **Sensory sensitivities and needs:** Loud noises, bright lights, or certain textures can be overwhelming. Some autistic students need additional sensory input such as weighted blankets and movement breaks. Create sensory-friendly spaces with noise-canceling headphones, fidget tools, or natural lighting. Observe and adjust based on student feedback.

» **Communication differences:** Autistic students may use delayed speech, nonverbal cues, or augmentative and alternative communication (AAC) devices. Some may involuntarily repeat words or phrases others have said. Some may talk excessively while others can be very terse. Be patient and flexible. Use visual aids, allow extra time for responses, and adapt to preferred methods, like picture cards or written instructions.

» **Social interactions:** Autistic students may struggle with typical social cues or group activities. Foster an inclusive culture that values different social styles. Plan structured social activities with clear expectations and use peer mentoring or small groups to build confidence.

» **Task switching or change:** Many autistic students find routines comforting and changes stressful. Maintain consistency and give advance notice when changes are needed. Use visual schedules and explain changes clearly.

If sudden changes happen, provide reassurance and a calming space to regroup.

>> **Executive functioning:** Planning, organizing, and following multistep instructions can be difficult. Break tasks into smaller steps and give clear instructions. Use visual checklists and timelines, and provide reminders as needed.

Of course, most barriers autistic students face stem from how the world responds to them. Here are some ways to address some of these challenges:

TIP

>> **Assumptions and stereotypes:** Autistic students may face low expectations or misunderstandings. Challenge stereotypes by valuing each student's strengths and potential.

>> **Social exclusion:** Peers may not know how to engage with autistic students, leading to isolation. Create a classroom culture where differences are celebrated and students are encouraged to connect and include each other.

>> **Lack of understanding:** Teachers may lack training in supporting autistic students. Advocate for ongoing professional development to ensure educators are well-prepared.

>> **Rigid teaching methods:** Traditional teaching can be limiting. Use flexible strategies to meet varied learning styles.

>> **Inconsistent accommodations:** Inconsistent use of accommodations can hinder progress. Ensure Individualized Education Programs (IEPs) or 504 plans are consistently applied and reviewed for effectiveness.

>> **Not being taught who they are:** Autistic students often aren't taught to understand and embrace how their brains work. Foster a classroom where neurodiversity is discussed openly so students learn to celebrate who they are and see their differences as strengths.

Setting the right tone

The tone you set in your classroom affects everything: how students feel, learn, and connect. This is particularly important for autistic students, who may be more sensitive to their surroundings and how they're perceived by peers.

REMEMBER

Creating an atmosphere based on kindness, respect, and understanding isn't only about comfort. It's essential for real learning and growth. Address bullying or exclusion quickly to help make students feel safe and appreciated — qualities that are necessary for them to participate, take risks, and face challenges. When you foster a culture where differences are openly and positively discussed, everyone benefits because lessons about diversity help all students understand and value each other.

TIP

An inclusive classroom helps all students, teaching empathy, adaptability, and social awareness. They learn to value different perspectives, which deepens understanding and social skills. This fosters connections and friendships between autistic and nonautistic students, creating an environment where everyone shares strengths and learns from each other. Celebrating diversity helps build friendships rooted in respect.

Promoting student connections

Building friendships can be hard for some autistic students, so creating a supportive environment is important. Teachers can help students connect by promoting inclusion and positive interactions. These connections support social skills, boost confidence, and help students feel connected. Here are some ways to facilitate both autistic and nonautistic students to connect with each other:

TIP

>> **Create a culture of respect.** Set expectations for kindness and inclusion. Celebrate differences and address any signs of exclusion immediately.

>> **Promote understanding.** Emphasize empathy and respect as essential to friendships. Encourage discussions about individual differences to build acceptance.

>> **Provide structured activities.** Plan group activities with clear roles to help autistic students feel comfortable. Mix groups thoughtfully and consider using a buddy system.

>> **Encourage parallel activities:** Some examples of side by side socializing are coloring or drawing together, each doing their own piece; playing a video game separately but in the same room and completing puzzles or LEGO builds next to each other.

>> **Support positive interactions.** Watch social dynamics and step in as needed, suggesting ways for autistic students to join. Praise inclusive behavior to reinforce its value.

>> **Promote understanding.** Emphasize empathy and respect as key parts of friendship. Encourage discussions about individual differences in interests, backgrounds, or abilities.

>> **Teach and model social interactions.** Demonstrate simple social interactions like saying hello and taking turns. Show nonautistic students how to be inclusive by inviting their autistic classmates to join activities and discussions.

Adopting a universal approach

Imagine a classroom where every student is engaged; some are reading, others watching a video, and some drawing their ideas. This isn't just a flexible day; it's a classroom built on Universal Design for Learning (UDL). UDL is a teaching approach that makes lessons accessible for all students by planning for different learning styles from the start.

UDL offers students choices in how they engage, learn, and show what they know. Using a mix of visuals, hands-on activities, written materials, and various ways for students to share their ideas, UDL helps everyone succeed. For example, in a science lesson on the water cycle, you might show an animated video, provide a diagram, and tell a story about a water droplet's journey. Students can choose to create a poster, act out the cycle, or write a comic strip to show what they've learned. This helps students engage in the way that works best for them and builds their confidence and enthusiasm for learning.

UDL is especially beneficial for autistic students, who may excel when they can use their preferred learning styles and tools. Options like visual aids, hands-on activities, and clear instructions help autistic students participate more comfortably and confidently. UDL also allows flexibility in how students express their understanding, letting them showcase their strengths. This creates a classroom where autistic students feel seen, valued, and empowered.

UDL's true power lies in how it normalizes learning differences and accommodations. When all students are given choices and flexibility, tools like visual aids or alternative assignments become part of everyday learning. This makes accommodations feel less separate and more inclusive, helping autistic students feel more connected to their peers. It builds an environment where learning differences are seen as normal and valuable, fostering social connections and mutual respect. In this kind of classroom, autistic students can build friendships, engage fully, and thrive alongside their peers.

REMEMBER

Understanding each student takes curiosity and attention. Stay curious about how each one learns best. For example, if a student gets anxious when called on but engages in specific activities, adjust your approach to support them. There's no one-size-fits-all approach, but with these strategies and an open mindset, you can help all your students grow.

You don't have to start from scratch to incorporate UDL; you can add it to what you're already doing. Here are some simple strategies to make your classroom more UDL-friendly:

TIP

>> **Celebrate differences.** Recognize that every student, including autistic students, has strengths. Embrace neurodiversity as a normal part of life and create a classroom that supports kindness and respect.

>> **Provide learning choices.** Teach new material using videos, written content, or hands-on activities so students can choose what works best for them.

>> **Use visual supports.** Add charts or step-by-step guides to your instructions for students who learn better with visuals.

>> **Provide options for flexible assignments.** For an essay assignment, provide topic options and allow the student to pick their own topic. Allow students to choose how they show what they've learned, such as essays, videos, models, or slideshows. Be open to adjusting deadlines.

>> **Encourage group work.** While autistic students often excel at working alone, provide support for group work using methods such as scaffolding, assigned roles, and communication monitoring to encourage group work. Design group activities where students learn from each other. Rotate groups based on strengths and interests, teaching empathy, flexibility, and communication skills along the way.

>> **Offer structured routines with options.** Have a daily routine but offer choices within it, like working with a partner or independently during group work.

REMEMBER

UDL helps create a classroom where every student, including autistic students, can succeed. By using these strategies, you're building a space where all students feel valued. Start small, stay flexible, and watch your students engage and grow (for connections to UDL resources, visit www.pivotdiversity.com/resources).

Encouraging student accommodations

Teachers play a key role in making sure all students, including those with disabilities, have fair access to learning. Accommodations make learning accessible by addressing individual needs, designing effective strategies, and working with support teams and families.

REMEMBER

It's important to remember that accommodations are a normal part of life. Everyone uses accommodations in different forms: glasses to see better, alarm clocks to wake up on time, or GPS to navigate. These tools help us function more effectively, and the same concept applies to the classroom. Supporting students with accommodations allows them to learn and succeed in ways that work best for them.

TIP

IEPs or 504 plans outline specific accommodations requested by students and their families, so it's important for teachers to be familiar with these. Beyond the plans, observing students in class helps identify challenges or strengths that may not be documented. Collaborating with parents, special education teachers, counselors, or therapists creates a strong support system for each student.

You don't need to know every accommodation to make a difference. Just work with others to identify what helps each student succeed. The following sections are some common accommodations for autistic learners.

Offering predictability and structure

Autistic individuals often find comfort and security in predictability and structure, which helps them process information more efficiently and feel less overwhelmed. This stability allows their brains to focus better on learning and interacting without the added stress of unexpected changes or uncertainty.

For teachers, this means creating a classroom environment where routines are clear and consistent, which can greatly benefit autistic students. Predictability not only supports their cognitive processing but also encourages them to engage socially because they feel safer and more confident knowing what to expect.

TIP

Here are some practical things you can do as a teacher to help:

>> **Use visual schedules.** Display a daily schedule so students know what's coming next.

>> **Provide advance notice.** Give a heads-up about changes in routine or special events.

>> **Keep routines consistent.** Stick to predictable patterns in classroom activities and transitions.

>> **Create clear instructions.** Use simple, step-by-step instructions for tasks.

>> **Offer calming spaces.** Have a designated quiet area for students who need a break.

>> **Prepare for changes.** When changes are unavoidable, explain them clearly and use visual aids or narrative-based approaches to help students understand and adjust.

Using clear and direct communication

Autistic students often prefer direct communication and may struggle with processing unclear or indirect language. Simple, straightforward instructions help them understand what's expected and experience less confusion. It helps them comprehend better and participate actively, knowing they can rely on your clear guidance.

TIP

Use simple language when giving instructions. Instead of saying, "Hit the books," try, "Start your homework." Swap phrases like, "Keep an eye on this," with "Watch this closely." If you use idioms like "Break a leg," take a moment to explain it means "good luck."

Pair spoken instructions with written or visual aids. Many autistic students may need extra time to process what they hear or might miss parts if they're overwhelmed. A written or visual guide allows them to review at their own pace and feel confident about what to do. This helps them stay on track and complete tasks without anxiety.

Supporting autistic ways of communicating

Clear communication practices also involve supporting the various ways autistic students express themselves. Not every student communicates in the same way. Supporting autistic communication means recognizing that all forms of expression are valid. Your goal is to create an environment where students feel respected, understood, and empowered to communicate in the way that works best for them. (See Chapter 4 for more on autistic communication.)

REMEMBER

When you value and support different communication methods, you show students that their voices matter. This builds their confidence and encourages them to engage more in class. Supporting diverse communication isn't just about accommodation; it's about seeing each form as both valid and valuable.

TIP

Be flexible and patient with communication. Learn about and support the tools your students use, whether it's speaking, writing, or using technology. Celebrate all forms of communication and encourage students to share their thoughts in the way that's most comfortable for them.

Here are some additional tips that can empower autistic students to flourish in the ways they naturally communicate:

TIP

>> **Create a comfortable space.** Be mindful of sensory distractions. Reduce noise, dim bright lights, and minimize anything that could make communication harder.

>> **Use visual supports.** Use picture cards or written instructions to help students understand, which is especially helpful for visual learners.

>> **Allow extra time.** Give students time to process and respond without pressure.

>> **Offer alternatives to speech.** Support communication methods like AAC tools, communication boards, or gestures.

>> **Practice patience and openness.** Recognize that autistic communication might look different but is just as valuable. Approach interactions with patience.

>> **Respect boundaries.** Understand that eye contact, personal space, or social interactions may vary. Respect each student's comfort levels.

REMEMBER

It's okay to ask for help! Most teachers aren't taught to translate between autistic and neurotypical communication styles. Thankfully, there are plenty of resources available to guide you.

Highlighting strengths

Every autistic student has unique strengths. Empowering students means recognizing these strengths and using them as a base for learning.

TIP

Incorporate students' interests into your lessons. If a student loves trains, use trains examples in math or reading assignments.

REMEMBER

A strengths-based approach shifts the focus from what students find difficult to what they excel at. Autistic students often hear more about their challenges than their strengths, which can be discouraging and make them hesitant to try new things. Highlighting their strengths breaks this cycle, boosting confidence and motivation. When students see their abilities recognized, they feel more connected to their learning, gain pride, and become more willing to face challenges. This approach fosters growth, resilience, and belief in their potential.

Encouraging self-advocacy

One of the most powerful things you can do for autistic students is teach them how to advocate for themselves. This means helping them recognize their needs and giving them the confidence to express those needs.

TIP

Create opportunities for students to make choices about their learning, like selecting from different project options or choosing how they want to complete an assignment. Teach them simple signals or methods to indicate when they need a break or assistance. Reinforce that asking for help is a strength, not a weakness.

Imagine a student named Ashlee, who often feels overwhelmed during group activities. One day, she becomes tense and withdraws from participation. Instead of stepping in to ask, "What's wrong?" you've already taught Ashlee to use a visual "I need a break" card. She holds it up, and you respond with a supportive nod. Ashlee heads to the calm corner for a few minutes and comes back feeling more settled and ready to join the activity again.

Over time, Ashlee becomes more confident using her card and starts advocating for herself in other ways, like asking for noise-canceling headphones when the noise level in the room becomes too much. This empowers Ashlee and shows the whole class that self-advocacy is encouraged and respected. It creates a classroom environment where all students feel safe to express their needs and know that their voices are heard.

Teaching independence

Teaching independence is essential for helping autistic students build skills that last a lifetime. Independence isn't just about completing tasks alone; it's about feeling capable, confident, and resilient. When students learn to rely on themselves, even with supports in place, they build self-esteem and the ability to handle future challenges.

TIP

Start by breaking down tasks into smaller, manageable steps. Guide students through these steps until they become familiar, and then gradually reduce your support. For instance, if a student needs help organizing their materials, begin by creating a visual checklist together and checking it daily. Over time, encourage them to check it independently, celebrating their progress as they take charge of the routine.

Integrate opportunities for choice and responsibility. Assign roles within group projects, encourage students to manage their schedules with planners or visual timers, and give them the chance to set personal goals. These practices teach them to navigate tasks, advocate for themselves, and feel empowered to take ownership of their learning.

REMEMBER

Independence looks different for every student, so focus on what independence means for each individual. This could range from managing transitions more smoothly to completing a project with minimal reminders. Celebrate these milestones, big or small, and remind students that making mistakes is part of learning and growing.

Promoting problem-solving

Encourage students to think critically and solve problems on their own. When they face a challenge, prompt them with questions like, "What could we try next?" or "What would help you with this?" This shifts the mindset from waiting for answers to developing solutions and builds their confidence in handling difficult situations.

Fostering interdependence

Independence is great, but no one does everything alone. That's where *interdependence* comes in! Instead of your students thinking, "I have to do this all by myself," help them shift to "We all help each other in different ways." For autistic students who take things literally, this shift is especially important because independence can sometimes sound like *never* asking for help. You can teach interdependence by showing that everyone has strengths to share and areas where they need support. Maybe one student is great at math but struggles with organization, while another is a natural at keeping things tidy but needs help with fractions.

REMEMBER

By normalizing give-and-take, you create a classroom where students see themselves as both helpers and helped, building a supportive environment where everyone thrives.

Nurturing a growth mindset

Autistic students, like all students, benefit from understanding that mistakes are part of learning and that challenges help them grow. A growth mindset shows them they can learn and improve over time.

REMEMBER

The point is not to exude false positivity or pretend things are perfect. You should focus on effort, persistence, and learning from setbacks. A growth mindset emphasizes that progress matters more than perfection and that everyone moves at their own pace.

TIP

Use language that highlights effort and growth. Celebrate when students try new things or push through challenges. Remind them that everyone has different strengths and areas they're improving on.

Think of Malik, an autistic student who struggles with math and gets frustrated by mistakes. One day, he answers a problem incorrectly and starts to shut down. Instead of focusing on the mistake, you say, "Great effort, Malik! Let's see what we can learn from this." You guide him through the mistake, showing that his approach was still valuable.

Over time, Malik becomes less afraid of mistakes and takes more risks in class. This boosts his confidence, not just in math but across subjects. Soon, the class embraces this mindset, recognizing that effort and growth are worth celebrating. The classroom becomes a more supportive space where students feel safe to try, fail, and learn.

Working with Parents and Caregivers

When teachers team up with parents and caregivers, it creates strong support for autistic students. Parents know their child's strengths, challenges, and sensory needs, which helps teachers adjust classroom strategies. By working together, teachers and families can create consistent routines and expectations between home and school, giving students a solid sense of security and support.

Regular communication is key. Frequent check-ins keep everyone informed about progress and allow quick adjustments when needed. A collaborative approach ensures that IEPs and 504 plans are not just followed but adapted as the student grows. Supporting autistic students works best when educators and families work as a team.

Building trust and communication

Building trust with parents starts with open, honest communication, empathy, and a commitment to the student's success. Keep conversations consistent and two-way.

Share updates on progress, challenges, and wins. This shows parents that you're invested in their child's growth. Make space for parents to share their own insights.

Empathy goes a long way. Parents know their child best, so listen to them. Show understanding and acknowledge the challenges they face. Commitment to each student's needs builds trust. Follow through on your promises.

Include parents in problem-solving and decision-making, and be open about challenges. Respect their role as advocates and collaborate for the best educational outcome for the student.

Planning with parents and caregivers

Including parents in planning is crucial. Regular meetings to discuss IEPs or 504 plans help set clear goals and track progress. Frequent informal check-ins keep parents updated on academic and social development and give them a chance to share what they're seeing at home.

Keep parents informed through emails, calls, or digital tools so they know about successes and areas for growth. If possible, invite parents to observe class activities so they can see strategies in action and use them at home. This helps maintain consistent support between home and school.

Providing resources and support

Parents of autistic children often feel isolated. Connecting them to neurodiversity-affirming resources and communities makes a big difference. Share reliable articles, websites, or organizations that help parents better understand their child's experiences.

Recommend support groups or local and online communities where parents can share stories and get advice. Having accurate information and a support network helps parents feel more confident in advocating for their child and collaborating with you.

TIP

Point parents to resources and workshops that clearly explain the IEP process and how to navigate the school system. These can teach parents their rights, how to advocate effectively, and how to work confidently with educators.

REMEMBER

Empower parents by listening to their concerns, sharing classroom strategies, connecting them with resources, and keeping communication consistent.

Using Strategies by Educational Level

Creating a neuroinclusive classroom benefits all students and ensures that neurodivergent learners receive the support they need. Here's how you can implement inclusive strategies at different educational levels.

Elementary school (grades K – 5)

Elementary school is where the journey begins with the focus on routines, sensory support, and social development:

>> **Predictability and structure:** Use visual schedules and consistent daily routines. Provide advance notice of transitions and changes in routine.

» **Multisensory learning:** Incorporate hands-on, movement-based activities. Offer fidget tools, wobble cushions, or standing desks for sensory regulation.

» **Flexible communication:** Accept alternative communication methods (AAC, drawing, writing). Encourage "side-by-side" socializing rather than forcing eye contact.

» **Play-based and strength-based learning:** Use students' interests to engage them in learning (for example, dinosaurs, space, trains). Allow for parallel play and cooperative, structured playtime.

» **Social and emotional support:** Teach self-regulation strategies with visuals, breathing exercises, and quiet corners. Normalize asking for help and model interdependence.

Middle school (grades 6 – 8)

Middle school is a period of significant changes requiring focus on executive functioning, social flexibility, and self–advocacy:

» **Clear instructions and expectations:** Provide step-by-step guidance for assignments and projects. Use written and visual instructions to reinforce verbal directions.

» **Flexible participation and expression:** Offer options for group work versus independent work. Allow alternative ways to demonstrate understanding (videos, posters, typed reports).

» **Executive functioning support:** Teach organizational skills (planners, checklists, digital tools). Give reminders for deadlines and chunk assignments into smaller steps.

» **Social and emotional growth:** Use structured peer interactions, like guided discussions or partner activities. Encourage interest-based clubs or mentoring opportunities.

» **Sensory and movement breaks:** Allow for quiet breaks, movement options, or classroom "reset" spaces. Normalize self-regulation strategies like noise-canceling headphones or doodling. Encourage self-advocacy for sensory regulation.

High school (grades 9 – 12)

High school is the preparation ground for adulthood with greater focus on interdependence, self–advocacy, and flexible learning.

>> **Choice and flexibility in learning:** Allow multiple ways to show mastery (essays, presentations, projects). Offer alternative seating and work environments (quiet spaces, standing desks).

>> **Executive functioning and time management:** Provide structured supports like digital reminders, assignment planners, and organizational apps. Encourage self-monitoring skills (e.g., estimating time needed for assignments).

>> **Social and emotional support:** Teach interdependence: "We all have strengths and areas where we need support." Offer peer mentorship or study groups based on interests rather than forced socializing.

>> **Sensory considerations:** Allow for sensory regulation tools (fidget items, earplugs, breaks). Be mindful of classroom lighting, sound levels, and overwhelming environments.

>> **Self-advocacy and accommodations:** Normalize the use of IEP/504 accommodations without stigma. Teach students how to communicate their needs to teachers and peers.

College and university

College and university as a young adult requires focus on autonomy, advocacy, and accessible learning:

>> **Flexible learning and assessment:** Provide lecture slides, transcripts, and recorded lectures. Offer multiple assessment formats (oral exams, projects, open-book tests).

>> **Executive functioning support:** Use digital tools for organization (calendar apps, task managers). Allow flexible deadlines or extensions when needed.

>> **Inclusive classroom and social supports:** Normalize different communication styles (text-based, quiet participation, scripted interactions). Provide small-group or online discussion options instead of large-class participation.

>> **Sensory-friendly environment:** Offer quiet study spaces and allow for movement breaks. Let students use noise-canceling headphones, sunglasses, or stim-friendly tools.

>> **Self-advocacy and support networks:** Educate students on disability services, accommodations, and self-advocacy. Connect students with mentors, neurodivergent peer groups, and campus accessibility resources.

REMEMBER

Neuroinclusive strategies aren't just for autistic students. They create a more accessible, flexible, and supportive learning environment for everyone! By implementing these approaches at each educational level, you help all students thrive in ways that work best for them.

Becoming a Better Educator

To help your students thrive, start with yourself. Check in regularly. What's working; what isn't? Seek feedback from students, parents, and colleagues for fresh insights. Being the best teacher means staying curious, flexible, and connected. Keep learning, try new strategies, and recognize each student's unique needs. Stay open to feedback, reflect on what works, and adapt as needed. It's how you grow and meet your classroom's needs.

Overcoming your own barriers

Teaching comes with constant challenges, and supporting autistic students can bring unique ones. Recognizing these barriers can help you find better ways to navigate them.

TIP

Here's a look at common barriers with tips on how to tackle them:

>> **Lack of training:** Most teacher training programs don't adequately focus on understanding or supporting neurodivergent students. Even when there is initial training, ongoing support is often missing, leaving teachers feeling unsure about strategies to use. Advocate for more neurodiversity-affirming and autism-specific training in your school or seek out workshops and webinars independently. Even one course can increase your confidence and understanding.

>> **Limited resources or staff support:** Resources can be scarce. You might have a crowded classroom with limited support staff or lack access to sensory tools and other accommodations, making it hard to give each student the attention they need. Focus on small, low-cost adjustments. Create a quiet space or use simple visual aids. Set up flexible, predictable routines. Sharing resources and ideas with other teachers can also help. Partner with parents for insights or supplies that can benefit their child.

>> **Strict curriculum requirements:** Standardized testing and strict curriculum requirements often push teachers to follow a rigid plan, limiting the ability to tailor lessons for learning differences. While you may not control the content, you do control your approach. Use differentiated instruction to provide

various ways for students to engage with material and show their learning. This could include breaking tasks into smaller parts or offering visual projects or oral presentations as alternatives. See prior section on UDL for more.

>> **Your own biases and assumptions:** We all carry biases that can show up in the classroom. That's human. You might find yourself making quick judgments about what a student can or can't do or what "appropriate" behavior looks like, shaping your teaching without realizing it. Commit to regular self-reflection. Notice moments when you might make assumptions and be open to learning from autistic perspectives through books, articles, and social media. This can help shift your mindset from seeing neurodivergence as a challenge to understanding it as part of natural human diversity with strengths and needs that deserve support.

>> **Time constraints:** With lesson planning, grading, meetings, and other responsibilities, time is always tight. Adding new strategies or learning more about autism can feel like another item on an already full to-do list. Start small. Choose one or two strategies to try, like adding a visual schedule or starting the day with a check-in. Small changes can make a big difference and lay the groundwork for building more inclusive practices over time.

REMEMBER

Being a great teacher for your autistic students is about growth, not perfection. Recognize the barriers you face, take them one step at a time, and remind yourself that each small action counts. By adapting and learning, you create a classroom where autistic students feel seen, supported, and included. And in doing so, you become the teacher who helps all your students thrive.

Investing in your own development

The best teachers are always learning. To support your autistic students, investing in your own growth is essential. Expanding your knowledge and skills helps you meet their unique needs and guide them to success.

Workshops and training on neurodiversity and autism offer practical strategies for communication, accommodations, and sensory support. Special education courses or certifications can deepen your expertise even more. Collaborating with special education professionals like speech or occupational therapists provides hands-on experience. Joining teacher groups focused on autism lets you share ideas and learn from others. Stay curious: Read articles by autistic authors, watch webinars, and take online courses. Reflect on your teaching approach and seek feedback from neurodivergent voices, peers, or parents to keep improving.

Chapter **20**

How the Workplace Can Empower Autistic Individuals

Imagine someone at your workplace — we'll call her Camila — who might seem withdrawn, hesitant to join conversations, or take some time to respond. Maybe she avoids eye contact or skips group outings. And then there is Ramon, who is loud, energetic, and always ready to jump into a conversation. He speaks his mind without hesitation, sometimes interrupting or coming across as intense. At first glance, these behaviors might be confusing or frustrating, but before making assumptions, it's important to approach the situation with compassionate curiosity.

This chapter explores how workplaces can support and empower individuals like Camila and Ramon. We offer practical strategies to recognize strengths, address challenges, and create a workplace where everyone can thrive. The goal is to foster a work environment that prepares for the future — a future where diversity and adaptability are essential for success.

Understanding Autistic Employees

Autistic employees, like all employees, bring unique strengths, experiences, and perspectives to the workplace. Their goals — to contribute meaningfully, grow in their careers, and feel valued — are no different from their neurotypical peers. While their communication or processing styles might differ, their potential is the same, and they may have strengths that make them invaluable to a team.

Appreciating workplace strengths

Autistic individuals have always been part of the workforce, contributing at all levels, from entry-level positions to leadership roles. Yet, many workplaces haven't fully supported their needs and consequently have missed out on the full potential these employees can offer. Imagine the benefits if businesses created environments that accommodated and celebrated their strengths.

REMEMBER

By fostering inclusion, companies not only empower autistic employees to thrive but also unlock innovation, efficiency, and creativity. Supporting autistic employees is about more than doing the right thing — it's about building a more effective workplace for everyone.

While every person — including every autistic person — is different, there are strengths commonly associated with autistic people. Understanding these strengths and how they might manifest in the workplace can help you more deeply appreciate and support autistic colleagues. Here are some strengths autistic employees may bring to the workplace:

>> **Attention to detail:** Autistic people often excel in roles requiring attention to detail, whether it's quality control on a manufacturing line, welding, car washing, or proofreading in a publishing role. Their ability to spot small errors ensures high standards are met.

>> **Strong focus and concentration:** In graphic design or woodworking, autistic individuals can focus for long periods, producing intricate, detailed work. In research or coding, their ability to stay focused on complex problems leads to innovative solutions.

>> **Exceptional memory:** In fields like plumbing or automotive repair, a strong memory helps recall specific techniques and past solutions. In data analysis or legal work, the ability to remember complex details and patterns aids in efficient problem-solving.

>> **Logical and analytical thinking:** Autistic individuals thrive in roles like HVAC repair, automotive diagnostics, or software development, where logical thinking is crucial for diagnosing issues or writing efficient code.

>> **Honesty and integrity:** In construction, an autistic person's commitment to transparency builds trust with clients. In compliance or finance, their dedication to honesty ensures ethical practices and adherence to regulations.

>> **Unique perspectives and creativity:** In mural painting, tattoo artistry, writing, or marketing, autistic individuals bring fresh, creative ideas that stand out. In engineering or product design, their outside-the-box thinking leads to innovative approaches.

>> **Reliability and consistency:** In blue-collar roles such as machine operation or assembly line work, consistency and reliability are key to success. In administrative positions, this same reliability ensures deadlines are met and operations run smoothly.

>> **Advanced technical skills:** Autistic individuals often excel in technical fields like data science, electronic circuit design, or cybersecurity, where their ability to troubleshoot and solve complex technical issues is highly valuable.

>> **Precision and accuracy:** In custom cabinetry, metalworking, or scientific research, an autistic person's precision can ensure work is of the highest quality, whether they are crafting a piece of furniture or conducting a lab experiment.

>> **Strong adherence to rules and procedures:** In food or manufacturing industries, safety protocols and procedures are to be followed to the letter. In finance and accounting, adherence to regulations guarantees accurate financial reporting. Autistic people may perform exceptionally in these roles.

>> **Ability to recognize patterns:** In fields like textile design or photography, pattern recognition leads to visually compelling work. In data science or machine learning, autistic individuals excel at identifying trends that drive business decisions.

>> **High degree of integrity:** In roles like culinary arts, artisan baking, customer service, or legal work, autistic individuals' strong sense of integrity ensures quality, transparency, and adherence to ethical standards.

>> **Deep knowledge and expertise:** In specialized trades like blacksmithing or electrical work, an autistic person's deep knowledge drives innovation. In fields like medical research, law, or engineering, their passion for in-depth learning can make them valuable teachers and mentors and contribute to cutting-edge advancements.

By recognizing and leveraging these strengths, employers can create a more inclusive, effective workplace that benefits from the diverse talents autistic individuals bring.

REMEMBER

Autistic strengths may not always be immediately visible, often because of differences in communication or cognition. A thoughtful, supportive approach is needed to uncover and celebrate these strengths.

WARNING

It's important to remember that while these strengths are often associated with autistic traits, they don't apply to everyone. Autistic people, like anyone else, have their own unique personalities, abilities, and challenges. Assuming that every autistic person has the same set of traits can be limiting and, honestly, unfair. Just because someone is autistic doesn't mean they'll automatically have an exceptional memory or a laser focus. Some autistic people might not excel in detail-oriented work, whereas others thrive in it.

REMEMBER

The objective is to see each person as an individual. Listen to their needs, recognize their unique talents, and avoid falling into the trap of stereotyping. The best way to support anyone — autistic or not — is by appreciating their personal strengths and helping them grow in a way that works best for them.

Understanding workplace challenges

Autistic individuals may have workplace-relevant differences that can pose challenges for themselves and their colleagues. Here are a few examples and how they can affect the work environment:

>> **Communication style:** Autistic employees may communicate directly or struggle with small talk or sarcasm. Colleagues might misinterpret this as rudeness or lack of engagement. For example, blunt feedback in a meeting could cause tension with others who are not used to such directness.

>> **Social interaction:** Some autistic individuals find social interactions difficult, including reading neurotypical social cues or engaging in casual office activities. This can lead to feelings of isolation or misunderstandings. For example, avoiding office gatherings might be seen as disinterest, even if that's not the case.

>> **Sensory sensitivities:** Many autistic individuals are sensitive to noise, light, or other sensory inputs. Open-plan offices with loud sounds or bright lighting can lead to sensory overload, making it hard to concentrate.

>> **Preference for routine:** Autistic employees often thrive on routines and may find sudden changes stressful. Last-minute shifts in schedules or project tasks can disrupt their workflow and cause anxiety.

>> **Focus and attention:** Autistic individuals may exhibit intense focus on specific tasks, sometimes to the detriment of other responsibilities. For example, hyperfocusing on one aspect of a project might delay other critical tasks, which can frustrate colleagues.

>> **Nonverbal communication:** Differences in nonverbal cues, such as fewer gestures or facial expressions, can lead to misunderstandings. Colleagues might misread this as disinterest or lack of engagement.

>> **Processing time:** Some autistic individuals need more time to process information and respond. In fast-paced meetings, this may be mistaken for hesitation or a lack of preparation.

>> **Sensitivity to feedback:** Autistic employees often prefer clear, specific feedback. Vague or indirect comments can cause confusion, leading to stress or performance issues.

>> **Heightened emotional response:** Some may exhibit during times of anxiety or stress what appears to be a "heightened" response.

REMEMBER

Challenges are unique to each individual and may fluctuate based on other life stressors. Understanding and accommodating these differences helps create a more supportive and effective workplace for everyone.

Practicing effective communication

Effective communication is key to understanding an autistic individual's strengths and navigating workplace challenges. The first step is to approach conversations with compassionate curiosity, putting aside assumptions and focusing on clear, respectful dialogue.

Starting with communication basics

People have different communication preferences spoken or written, for example. Some autistic individuals may use augmentative and alternative communication (AAC) devices, and exchanges using AAC might be slower than you're used to. Here's how to adapt:

TIP

>> Ask the person what their preferred mode of communication is — oral, email, text, and so on — and align with that mode as much as possible.

>> Be patient with slower exchanges when an AAC device is involved.

Turn-taking in conversations can also be a challenge. For some, it may be difficult to know when to jump in during a discussion. Conversely, others may struggle with knowing when to pause and give others a chance to speak.

It's worth noting that turn-taking challenges aren't exclusive to neurodivergent individuals. Societal contexts can create similar situations. For example, being the only woman, person of color, or immigrant in a group can generate pressures that cause self-doubt and hesitance to voice one's thoughts.

For example, picture a gathering or a meeting where everyone is participating except for one person: Paul. He's just sitting quietly. If you're leading the meeting or you have any influence over the exchange of information, you could directly address him, "Paul, we'd love to hear your thoughts on this matter." By doing this, you're giving Paul the opportunity to join the conversation without feeling pressured or rushed.

Keep the following things in mind:

>> Ask direct questions to encourage participation.

>> Allow multiple modes of communication to expand participation.

>> Encourage input from all of your team members, especially the ones who don't proactively jump into a discussion.

>> Make sure everyone has a chance to participate by gently balancing the discussion if some people tend to speak more than others.

>> Avoid rapid-fire exchanges among a few vocal individuals that can leave others out who take a bit longer to form answers.

Bear in mind that some neurodiverse individuals may experience auditory delays, which can cause a delay between thought and verbal expression. For example, you ask a question in a meeting, and someone remains quiet for a long while. You might feel a bit awkward or confused, wondering if you've been heard. Remember that everyone has their own way of processing information, and they may need more time to think before responding.

You could talk to them privately, mentioning what you observed and expressing your desire to understand them better. "I noticed that you often need some time before you respond. Can you help me understand why that is?" This way, you open the door for them to share their experiences. They might explain that they need time to sort out their thoughts before speaking.

In situations like job interviews, auditory delays might be detrimental to the individual if the interviewer isn't familiar with this characteristic. Try to avoid filling the silence and let the person respond.

All these differences underline the importance of understanding and accommodating diverse communication styles, thereby fostering an inclusive environment where everyone feels heard and valued.

Strengthening effectiveness with reflection

When a conversation with an autistic colleague doesn't go as planned, don't chalk it up as a failure. Instead, use it as a chance to grow. Reflexive communication helps you do that by being mindful, empathetic, and intentional in how you engage with others. By focusing on these principles, you can create stronger connections and more meaningful interactions.

Start by embracing a "not knowing" stance. This means coming into the conversation without assumptions and being open to learning something new. Follow that up with curiosity and compassion. Truly listen before jumping in with your own thoughts. And lastly, aim for collaboration. By merging your perspectives with those of your colleague, you can create solutions that are stronger and more inclusive.

Being reflexive also means paying attention to your own biases. Reflect on how your background shapes your views, and consider how the other person might see things differently. Stay alert to signs of confusion or frustration, and be ready to adjust your communication style if needed.

Teams that prioritize this approach ensure that everyone's voice is valued, fostering an inclusive and supportive environment. Managers who practice reflexive communication also tend to give feedback that's more constructive and empathetic because they're mindful of their own biases and the other person's experience.

Ultimately, reflexive communication isn't just about exchanging words. It's about building trust and understanding. It makes every conversation more productive and meaningful, helping you grow as a communicator and a team player.

TIP

Here are some ideas for practicing reflexive communication to improve interactions with an autistic colleague (or anyone, really):

>> **Be introspective.** Stay aware of your own preconceptions and biases during the conversation. Try to see and hear yourself from the other person's perspective.

>> **Be observant.** Look for signs that the other person might be overwhelmed, stressed, or confused. Do they seem lost in thought or visibly uncomfortable?

>> **Engage in active inquiry.** Ask open questions like, "How are you feeling?" or "What questions do you have?" Dive deeper by asking, "Did this help or hinder your understanding?" or "What are your takeaways?"

>> **Be flexible.** If the conversation isn't flowing smoothly, adjust your communication style or explanation. Flexibility shows your commitment to mutual understanding.

Here are examples of using reflexive communication in the workplace:

>> **Teams:** Reflect on communication during meetings to ensure everyone's voice is heard. This improves team dynamics and encourages inclusive dialogue.

>> **Managers:** Use reflexive communication when providing feedback, considering your own biases and the employee's performance context to give more constructive, empathetic responses.

REMEMBER

Reflexive communication emphasizes self-awareness, mutual understanding, and adaptability. By practicing it, you'll build stronger relationships and foster more productive interactions in any setting.

Understanding Accommodations

Accommodations don't have to be daunting or costly. They're often simple adjustments that make a significant difference for autistic employees. Small tweaks like noise-canceling headphones, dimmable lights, or flexible work arrangements help employees perform at their best. Accommodations like these create a work environment that supports everyone's success.

Take Brian, for example. He's a great programmer, but open-plan offices were too noisy for him. After speaking with his manager, he got noise-canceling headphones and access to a quiet room. Now, his productivity has shot up, and he's much happier. Simple adjustment, huge payoff.

Or Emily, who was juggling multiple projects and struggling to stay organized. Human resources set her up with project management software, and now she's on top of her tasks and feels way more in control. One small tool made a world of difference.

Then there's Priya, who's autistic and deals with sensory overload. Her office added dimmable lights and moved her to a quieter space. These small changes made a big impact on her focus and productivity.

REMEMBER

Accommodations like these aren't scary or expensive. They're practical solutions that help employees thrive. It's a win-win. Employees feel supported, and organizations see better performance and well-being.

Defining reasonable accommodations

Reasonable accommodations might sound like a formal and stuffy term, but it just refers to practical tweaks that help employees thrive without flipping the whole workplace upside down. These accommodations are all about making sure people can contribute their best without causing an undue burden on the employer. The idea is to give everyone the tools they need to succeed, not special treatment.

Reasonable accommodations is the legal term used in the United States for adjustments that allow employees with disabilities to do their jobs effectively. Many other countries also have similar laws and concepts. Here are a few:

>> **United States:** The Americans with Disabilities Act (ADA) has been around since 1990, so many companies, especially larger ones and public sector employers, are used to providing accommodations like flexible schedules, special equipment, or modified workspaces.

>> **Europe:** The European Union requires all member countries to provide reasonable accommodations. In places like Germany and the Netherlands, accommodations often include adjusted work hours, specialized equipment, and job modifications.

>> **United Kingdom:** Under the Equality Act 2010, employers must make reasonable accommodations, like adjusting work hours or providing accessible equipment.

>> **Canada:** With laws like the Accessible Canada Act and provincial regulations, common accommodations include modified workstations, flexible work, and accessible environments.

>> **Mexico:** The Federal Labor Law requires employers to provide necessary accommodations, such as flexible work hours or accessible workspaces, especially in larger cities and in international companies that are more aware of these needs.

>> **Brazil:** The Brazilian Law of Inclusion mandates that companies provide accommodations, like assistive technologies and accessible workspaces. Companies with more than 100 employees are required to meet a hiring quota for people with disabilities.

>> **India:** The Rights of Persons with Disabilities Act (2016) mandates accommodations like physical workplace adjustments and assistive devices. While implementation is still a challenge in many areas, awareness is growing, particularly in larger companies.

>> **Australia:** The Disability Discrimination Act requires accommodations such as ergonomic equipment, adjusted job duties, and flexible schedules.

>> **Japan:** Progress is growing under the Act on the Elimination of Disability Discrimination, with more companies offering assistive technologies and adjustments to workspaces, though traditional attitudes can be a hurdle.

>> **Other countries:** Globally, it's a mixed bag. Some countries have limited resources and awareness, offering accommodations mainly due to international companies or nongovernmental organizations. The UN Convention on the Rights of Persons with Disabilities (CRPD) has prompted positive changes in many countries, but implementation varies due to awareness, training, funding, and cultural attitudes.

REMEMBER

While accommodations are becoming more common worldwide, progress is stronger in countries with well-established legal frameworks. Thanks to global efforts, though, the future of inclusive workplaces is looking brighter everywhere!

Shifting your mindset

While noise-canceling headphones or adjusted lighting are helpful, the most important accommodation is a shift in mindset. A workplace culture that recognizes individual differences, focuses on abilities, and embraces diversity is what truly empowers autistic employees.

Managers and organizations must be open to learning, experimenting, and refining approaches that work for each employee. This shift in perspective benefits everyone, fostering an environment where all employees feel valued and capable of reaching their full potential.

A shift to a modern mindset includes:

>> **Recognizing uniqueness:** See each employee as a unique individual who deserves to be known and respected.

>> **Focusing on abilities:** Value employees for their skills and what they bring to the table.

>> **Accepting differences:** Embrace diversity and let go of outdated ideas about what "normal" looks like.

>> **Understanding and learning:** Take time to learn about each person's strengths and differences.

>> **Offering collaborative solutions:** Work with employees to find the right accommodations, both material and behavioral.

>> **Practicing experimentation and refinement:** Be open to trying new strategies and tweaking them to help employees succeed.

TIP

If you're serious about embracing neurodiversity, it's important to reflect on whether you're ready to adjust your current mindset. You likely already have autistic employees who may not be getting the support they need.

REMEMBER

Shifting your mindset to be more inclusive helps everyone — not only autistic or neurodivergent employees. Changing the way you think and act at work can be challenging, but it's absolutely worth it. As you take on this journey, be ready to confront and adjust your expectations and biases. Trust us, the effort will pay off in ways you didn't expect.

Creating an Inclusive Workplace

The modern workplace still has a long way to go when it comes to fully supporting autistic employees. Many workplaces operate on outdated norms and structures that overlook the needs of not only autistic workers but all people with neurodivergence — ADHD, dyslexia, or other differences.

There's plenty of room for improvement in how we create environments where everyone can thrive because the modern workplace wasn't designed with neurodivergent individuals in mind. Traditional 9-to-5 schedules, open-plan offices, and constant collaboration aren't ideal for everyone. However, as awareness grows and workplaces evolve, we're seeing positive shifts toward more flexible, inclusive environments.

By embracing neurodiversity and adapting to the needs of all employees, companies can create workspaces that unlock creativity, productivity, and innovation — ensuring the future of work is truly inclusive.

Understanding how we got here

No workplace starts out thinking, "Let's make things harder for autistic employees!" It's just that a lot of workplace norms have been shaped by neuro-typical perspectives, like a feedback loop that's been going on for generations.

Take the standard 9-to-5 schedule. It's rigid and assumes everyone's at their best during those hours. For many people, energy levels can fluctuate throughout the day, and that schedule just doesn't fit.

Then there's the physical office setup, often designed to maximize space and encourage social interactions. While some people thrive in that setting, for some autistic individuals, it can be overstimulating and distracting. The same goes for communication. Most workplaces emphasize constant collaboration and group decision-making, which doesn't always suit different communication styles, like those preferred by autistic employees (or introverts).

REMEMBER

Again, workplaces haven't been actively trying to make things difficult. These norms have just become so ingrained that we often don't realize they might not work for everyone.

As awareness of neurodiversity grows, a shift is occurring. Trends toward more flexible and remote work and a focus on mental health are slowly creating more inclusive environments where autistic employees can thrive. There's still a long way to go, but progress is happening as we move toward more diverse and supportive work cultures.

Seeing where we can go

The first big step toward creating an inclusive workplace is raising awareness about the normalcy of neurodiversity. When everyone accepts that autism is just one of many ways the brain can function, you can create an environment where autistic employees can truly thrive. This kind of acceptance helps people feel comfortable being themselves, which boosts both confidence and productivity.

To raise this awareness, start with education. Offer training sessions and work-shops that explain what autism is and why neurodiverse perspectives are such a huge asset to the workplace. Invite autistic individuals to share their own experiences. Firsthand stories are powerful tools for breaking down stereotypes and building empathy. You can also create a resource library with articles, videos, and books on autism for employees to explore.

GREEN FLAGS IN TRAINING PROVIDERS

When you're picking a training provider for autism awareness in the workplace, there are a few key things to look for. First, ensure the trainers are qualified and have real experience in autism and neurodiversity. It's even better if they include autistic individuals in their training team because firsthand insights are invaluable.

The training should be practical and engaging, offering actionable strategies that you can use right away. Look for sessions that involve Q&A sessions, discussions, and hands-on activities to keep everyone engaged. It's important that the content is up to date with the latest research and best practices and uses language that focuses on strengths and is respectful.

Finally, check for positive feedback from other organizations that have used the trainers' services. Providers who offer follow-up resources and support show they're committed to continuous improvement. Focus on these essentials, and you'll find a provider who can help create a more inclusive and supportive workplace.

Another great step is to celebrate autism through events and initiatives. Recognize Autism Acceptance Month with special activities or feature the stories and successes of autistic employees in company newsletters or meetings. By encouraging open conversations about autism, you foster a culture of understanding and acceptance.

Adopting inclusive recruiting practices

Recruiting is the process of identifying and attracting potential candidates to your organization. The goal? To build a large and diverse pool of qualified individuals who can contribute to your team. Setting a tone of intentional inclusivity starts with how you approach recruiting.

By focusing on inclusive recruiting practices, you not only widen your pool of candidates, but you also show that your organization values diversity, making it clear from the start that everyone has a place at the table.

Following are some ways to make your recruiting practices inclusive:

TIP

>> Build an inclusive culture where everyone — no matter their differences — can succeed. Make it a priority to include autistic people, not just as employees, but as leaders.

>> Show your commitment to inclusion in your branding, both inside and outside the company. Internally, raising awareness about neurodiversity helps create a more understanding and supportive workplace.

>> Make your job postings accessible and straightforward. Create listings that clearly state qualifications and skills while highlighting the strengths that help people thrive. Including LinkedIn profiles of current employees can give candidates a realistic, relatable view.

>> Host info sessions for potential candidates, similar to a university open house. Use them to highlight your company's mission, culture, job openings, and your commitment to disability inclusion.

>> Be upfront about the accommodations you offer. This is huge. Make sure accommodations are baked into every step of the recruiting and hiring process. Using platforms like Inclusively can help keep this initiative strong.

REMEMBER

Cultivate an inclusive culture, provide clear opportunities, and make sure the right accommodations are in place. That's the recipe for an inclusive recruiting process.

Implementing inclusive hiring practices

Hiring is the process that kicks in after recruiting, where you select the best candidate from your talent pool. It involves interviews, skills assessments, reference checks, salary negotiations, and, ultimately, making a job offer. To make your hiring process more inclusive for autistic candidates, here are some ideas to consider:

TIP

>> **Job descriptions:** You've seen those listings asking for people to walk on water and juggle while coding, right? A lot of autistic candidates will see those and immediately think they're not qualified. So, keep it clear and structured. Write a solid overall description, list the key duties, and — importantly — separate the "required" skills from the "nice-to-have" ones. Also, highlight any accommodations you can provide right there in the job posting.

>> **Applicant feedback:** Wherever possible, provide feedback — even if it's automated through an Applicant Tracking System (ATS). That feedback helps candidates see what worked and what didn't, and it helps you stand out as an inclusive employer. No one likes the "black hole" experience of never hearing back, especially autistic candidates, who might find the uncertainty extra stressful. Feedback creates clarity, reduces anxiety, and makes the whole process feel more thoughtful.

>> **Interviews:** Focus on whether the candidate can do the job, not on their perceived social skills or "culture fit." Give them specifics upfront, like where the interview will happen, how long it'll take, and who will be asking

the questions. Share the types of questions they can expect and walk them through how they'll be evaluated. This helps reduce stress.

» **Environment:** Whether it's in-person or online, create a calm, distraction-free setting. For virtual interviews, minimize background noise, make sure there's a solid connection, and ensure both sides are ready to roll. Whenever possible, send the questions in advance or provide them in writing at the time of the interview. And keep in mind that eye contact, handshakes, or stimming are not indicators of someone's ability to crush it at work. Focus on their skills and how they'll fit into the team.

» **Interview style:** Avoid vague or open-ended questions. Be clear and direct. Ask about their past experiences or interests. If they get stuck on a question, be patient and help steer the conversation in a way that works for them.

» **Alternatives:** Not everyone shines in a traditional interview, so consider alternatives like asking for a portfolio, an essay, or a technical test. Offering a "homework assignment" gives candidates time to think and show their best work.

Making the workplace more supportive

Every workplace has certain physical characteristics and policies — like work areas, meeting spaces, and what's expected of employees. For autistic employees, these norms can present challenges if their work styles or workspace needs differ from the typical setup. Here are some ways you make these environments more accessible and accommodating for different work styles:

TIP

» **Physical workspace adaptations:** Not all thrive in a noisy, open-plan office. For instance, someone with ADHD might benefit from a standing desk or quieter workspace. Others might need specific lighting or sound conditions. Policies should allow for modifications that help employees work more comfortably and effectively.

» **Flexible work arrangements:** Offering flexible hours or remote work options can be a game-changer. Some employees might need to start later due to medication or work better in shorter bursts with frequent breaks. Adopting flexible policies helps everyone work in ways that suit them best.

» **Training and development:** Offer training materials in different formats — video, audio, text — to accommodate various learning styles. Allow enough time for training, and educate managers on how to best support autistic employees.

>> **Workplace policies:** Ensure neurodivergence is explicitly included in your nondiscrimination policies, giving autistic employees the same rights and protections as everyone else. If issues arise, there should be a clear, safe reporting process.

Now, in addition to workplace environments, let's dive into some specifics on how to update workplace processes to better support autistic employees:

TIP

>> **Communications:** Encourage clear, straightforward communication. Ditch the jargon and provide information in different formats. Sending out meeting agendas ahead of time or including visual aids during presentations can help those who process information differently.

>> **Task management:** Not everyone excels at juggling multiple tasks. Some thrive when focusing on one task at a time, with scheduled breaks. Promote a culture of monotasking or let employees manage their tasks in ways that suit them best.

>> **Teamwork and collaboration:** Brainstorming and team projects are valuable, but some employees may need more time to process information or prefer working independently. Follow-up emails after meetings allow extra time for those who need to think through their ideas.

>> **Feedback and performance evaluation:** Offer feedback that's clear, constructive, and aligned with the individual's communication style. Performance evaluations should recognize the diverse ways employees can excel, not just traditional success metrics.

>> **Check-ins:** Hold regular forums where employees can share their needs or concerns, ensuring the workplace evolves to meet everyone's requirements.

REMEMBER

Updating processes to support autistic employees doesn't require a complete overhaul to your organization. Rather, it's about flexibility, understanding, and putting people first. Creating a workplace where everyone can thrive sounds like a win-win to us!

Championing Employee Resource Groups

Building connections between neurodivergent employees — whether they're autistic or have ADHD, dyslexia, or other differences — creates a strong sense of community and mutual support. Additionally, fostering connections between autistic employees and colleagues who parent neurodivergent children brings valuable insights that benefit both parties.

Employee resource groups (ERGs) focused on neurodiversity provide a platform for advocacy, peer support, and awareness-raising initiatives. For organizations, these groups drive engagement, retention, and inclusivity, benefiting the workplace as a whole.

If your organization doesn't have a neurodiversity ERG, empowering autistic employees to create one is a powerful step. With the right support from leadership — like meeting spaces, funding, and visibility — these groups can make a significant impact, creating an inclusive culture that champions every employee.

6

Building an Autism-Inclusive Future

Build a better world for autistic individuals through effective communication, shared goals, and bridging diverse perspectives.

Advocate for inclusion and representation by shaping policy, empowering autistic voices, promoting accurate media narratives, and supporting ethical, community-driven research.

Celebrate diverse autistic voices and experiences, showcasing personal stories from individuals across the spectrum and their unique achievements.

Chapter **21**

Working Together for a Better Future

I f there's one thing we can all agree on, it's that we all want a world that is supportive and inclusive of autistic people. But getting there can be complex. It involves different perspectives, sometimes conflicting ideas, and balancing many needs. Progress doesn't happen in isolation. Whether you're an autistic or a nonautistic individual and an adult, a parent, a family member, a service provider, or a researcher — working together is what will drive real change.

This chapter is a call to action — a guide for unity and teamwork that respects different experiences, encourages open conversations, and builds strong connections. We look at how to work together effectively, even when we don't always agree. We start with why unity matters and how seeing different perspectives can turn challenges into opportunities. Then we go over practical ways to collaborate, communicate openly, and move past misunderstandings. Finally, we explore how to create lasting connections that use everyone's strengths. The path isn't always easy, but it's worth it. Let's dive in and see how we can make real change — together.

Moving Forward Together in Unity

Whether you're autistic, a parent, family member, service provider, or researcher, you're part of a bigger story. It's a story full of challenges and potential, and to move forward, we need each other.

The past has had plenty of division: arguments over approaches, language, and perspectives. But if we focus on what unites us, we can do so much more. It's time to set aside differences and come together for one vision: a world where autistic people are accepted, supported, and empowered to live full lives.

An inclusive and supportive world

Imagine a world where autistic people and their families don't have to fight for understanding or basic accommodations because those things are built into the fabric of society. A world where schools are not just places of academic learning but spaces that celebrate every way a child's brain works — where autistic students are supported with tools and teaching styles that make them feel empowered, not sidelined. Picture workplaces that recognize the unique strengths autistic adults bring, offering flexible structures that encourage their best work and true inclusion. This world doesn't just accept differences; it thrives because of them.

In this world, families don't feel isolated or overwhelmed trying to navigate a system that wasn't built with them in mind. They find community, resources, and support at every stage — from early diagnosis to adulthood — without having to piece everything together themselves. It's a place where healthcare, social services, and education are coordinated, and professionals listen to autistic voices and their families, ensuring their perspectives shape policies and programs.

REMEMBER

This isn't a far-off dream; it's an achievable vision that starts with all of us working together, sharing knowledge, and pushing for meaningful change. Let's make it happen. Because when we build a world that supports autistic people and their families, we create a better, richer, and more compassionate society for everyone.

Centering autistic voices and families

Centering autistic people in conversations about autism leads to better, more effective outcomes. When autistic people are empowered to lead, and autistic perspectives are allowed to shape programs and resources, they become more practical, targeted, and aligned with real needs. This ensures that the work being done is grounded in lived experience, making it more meaningful and impactful for everyone involved.

For parents and caregivers, this shift can ease frustrations with navigating a system that often feels like trial and error. Instead, they gain access to tools and strategies that work in real-life situations, bringing relief and confidence. It also fosters a partnership where families feel supported, not isolated, as they help their loved ones thrive.

WARNING

To be truly effective, every autism organization must include autistic people in its leadership. This isn't just about representation; it's about making sure the people the work is meant to serve are guiding it. Without the input of autistic leaders, organizations risk creating programs and policies that miss the mark for the very community they aim to help.

TIP

Organizations without autistic leadership can take practical steps to fix this. Start by forming advisory boards made up of autistic individuals who can directly shape decision-making. Recruit autistic professionals for leadership roles, ensuring they have the authority to drive change. Offer mentorship opportunities to develop autistic talent and create a pipeline for future leaders. These aren't token efforts. They're essential for making sure advocacy, programs, and policies are truly effective and impactful for the people they're designed to support.

At the same time, autistic adults have a responsibility to include the needs and voices of parents and caregivers. Their experiences with managing daily challenges and advocating for services offer invaluable insights. When both groups listen and learn from one another, they create trust and shared purpose, building systems that truly work for autistic people and the families who support them.

Moving forward means leaning into collaboration. Families bring firsthand knowledge of daily realities, autistic individuals share their lived expertise, and professionals like service providers and researchers offer tools and systems to make ideas actionable. Each perspective strengthens the others, and working together creates solutions that are more comprehensive and impactful than any single viewpoint could achieve.

REMEMBER

Collaboration isn't about agreeing on everything. It's about agreeing on what matters most. It's about showing up with open minds and a commitment to action. Working together, we can create a future where autism isn't just "managed" but embraced as a valued part of human diversity.

Bridging Perspectives and Experiences

Bringing different experiences and perspectives together isn't always easy, but it's one of the most powerful ways to make progress. People won't always see things the same way but finding common ground leads to stronger and more effective solutions. Bringing together different perspectives and experiences improves problem-solving and drives real progress.

TIP

Bridging perspectives starts with open dialogue. Everyone should feel comfortable sharing their ideas and experiences without fear of judgment. Autistic voices should lead the conversation, but all perspectives matter. Parents and families bring firsthand experiences that can shape support systems, while researchers and service providers offer expertise to help put those ideas into action.

We also need to focus on shared goals. It's easy to get caught up in disagreements, but stepping back and finding common ground can move conversations forward. Remembering that we all want a better world for autistic people helps keep us united.

Collaboration also means using empathy and curiosity. Don't assume a different perspective is wrong. Instead, ask questions: Why do they think that way? What can we learn from their experience? Curiosity turns conflict into understanding and builds lasting connections.

Finally, respect is key. Even when we disagree, seeing the value in someone else's experience can turn tension into a productive conversation. The more we respect and learn from each other, the better we can create solutions that meet the range of needs across autistic individuals and their families.

Ensuring broad representation

To truly bridge perspectives, we have to include the voices of autistic adults who are nonspeaking or minimally speaking or who may need additional supports. These individuals have valuable insights that are often overlooked, and they're essential for accurately understanding autistic experiences. Including these voices means making communication accessible by using augmentative and alternative communication (AAC) tools, providing interpreters, and creating spaces where people can contribute at their own pace and in their own way.

REMEMBER

When we actively involve autistic people who are nonspeaking, minimally speaking, or need additional supports to participate in discussions and decisions, we ensure true representation. That's important because it helps us create solutions that serve the whole community, not just a small part of it.

Understanding the need to collaborate

Working together is essential. When we unite, we see real results: more inclusive policies, better support systems, and a stronger, more understanding society.

These changes benefit autistic people, their families, educators, service providers, and beyond. But this only happens when we choose to collaborate and act as a team.

When we work together, real change happens. Programs shaped with input from autistic individuals offer meaningful support instead of one-size-fits-all solutions. Research becomes more impactful when guided by those it's meant to help. These successes show that when autistic people, parents, families, professionals, and researchers contribute, the outcomes are more effective.

The cost of not working together is high. Division leads to bad policies, ineffective services, and research that misses the mark. It reinforces harmful stereotypes and leaves people unheard. Worse, it wastes time and resources while failing those who need support. We don't have time to wait. The world keeps moving, and the longer we delay, the longer it takes to build a future that works for everyone. By combining our knowledge, experience, and resources, we can push forward with real impact.

REMEMBER

We all want a world where autistic people are not just accepted but included and supported to thrive and celebrated. To make that world a reality, we need to come together, respect each other's perspectives, and focus on what matters most. The time for unity is now, and our future depends on moving forward as one.

Building empathy and understanding

Working together requires building empathy and understanding, especially when we don't agree. Empathy turns potential conflict into productive conversations. It helps us see different perspectives and still move toward shared goals. Lasting change comes when we look beyond our own views and take the time to understand why others think and feel the way they do. This is what makes collaboration work.

REMEMBER

Empathy doesn't mean agreeing with everything. It's about being open to seeing things from someone else's perspective, even if their experiences and views are different from yours.

Parents and families often have concerns shaped by their day-to-day caregiving. Service providers may face challenges adapting programs to meet different needs. Researchers might focus on data and evidence, missing the real-life context. Autistic individuals often advocate for self-determination and respect, sometimes feeling overlooked by systems meant to support them. Each perspective comes from wanting better outcomes, even if the approaches differ.

To build understanding, listen actively, which means not just waiting for your turn to speak but really hearing what others are saying. Ask questions to learn, not to challenge. What experiences shape their views? Why do they feel strongly about certain approaches? This builds empathy and reduces the friction that blocks progress.

Without empathy, collaboration breaks down. Misunderstandings turn into resentment, making common ground harder to find. But with empathy, we don't just work together; we learn from and respect each other, making space for every voice. Empathy is what allows people to come together to create something bigger than the sum of its parts.

EMPATHY IN ACTION

Imagine an autistic adult named Alex and a parent of an autistic child named Jamie. They're both at a community event about improving local support programs for autistic people. Initially, they're on different pages. Alex is passionate about self-advocacy and wants to see more programs that empower autistic voices directly, while Jamie is focused on practical daily support and worries these programs won't meet the specific challenges she faces every day.

During a break, Jamie shares a story about her child's struggle with transitions at school and the frustration of trying to find effective strategies. Instead of jumping in with their own opinions, Alex listens and asks questions to really understand what Jamie is going through. Alex begins to see how these daily, intense challenges shape Jamie's priorities. Meanwhile, Jamie, seeing Alex's genuine interest, asks about Alex's experiences with school as a child and how they navigated similar struggles.

Alex shares their experience of feeling overlooked and how self-advocacy programs had changed everything for them — teaching them to speak up and ask for the accommodations they needed. Jamie realizes that these programs don't just benefit older autistic people but could teach children like hers how to build confidence and self-awareness at an early age. Alex, on the other hand, gains insight into how advocacy-focused programs could include more practical tools for children, helping parents like Jamie feel more supported.

By exercising empathy, Alex and Jamie leave the event not only with a deeper understanding of each other's perspectives but also with ideas for new programs that blend empowerment with hands-on support. Their conversation inspires a proposal for a new workshop that offers advocacy training for both autistic individuals and parents, creating a more holistic approach. Empathy didn't erase their differences, but it helped them find common ground and a better solution that benefits both perspectives.

Collaborating Effectively

Collaboration isn't just about getting people into a room or onto a video call; it's about fostering an environment where real progress can happen. To collaborate well, we need to go beyond surface-level interactions and use practices that build trust and make everyone more productive. This means valuing dialogue, keeping communication open, overcoming misunderstandings, and recognizing differences while staying focused on shared goals. Here's how we can do that.

Valuing the importance of dialogue

Dialogue is more than just talking; it's the backbone of understanding. When we value true dialogue, we make space for every voice, which strengthens our efforts.

For example, having meetings where autistic individuals, parents, educators, and researchers all contribute equally ensures that different perspectives shape the conversation. This kind of dialogue makes decisions more well-rounded and benefits the whole community.

You can do this in your own community by holding regular forums, meetings, or discussion panels where everyone is encouraged to share their experiences and insights. Make it a priority to listen actively and respond thoughtfully.

Encouraging open communication

Open communication is essential for collaboration. It means creating an environment where people feel safe to share their thoughts, ask questions, and voice concerns without fear of judgment. When people feel truly heard, they're more likely to engage and contribute meaningfully.

One effective way to encourage open communication is by setting clear guidelines that promote respect and openness from the beginning. For example, a team working on an autism support initiative could establish ground rules: Everyone listens without interrupting, feedback stays constructive, and assumptions are questioned with curiosity, not criticism.

Overcoming misunderstandings

Misunderstandings are normal when people with different backgrounds and experiences come together. What matters is how we handle them.

EFFECTIVE COMMUNICATION IN ACTION

Imagine a team working on a project to create an autism-friendly public library program. The group includes autistic teens, librarians, educators, and local community organizers. At first, they hit a roadblock. The librarians focus on the practical side: scheduling events and managing the space. The educators want programs that align with educational goals, like teaching social skills. Meanwhile, the autistic teens feel like their preferences aren't being fully considered, and they hesitate to speak up.

One of the organizers notices the disconnect and suggests focusing on open communication. The group pauses and sets ground rules: Everyone gets a turn to share, ideas are respected, and questions are used to clarify, not criticize.

This simple shift changes the tone of the conversation. The teens begin sharing their needs, which include quiet spaces, sensory-friendly adjustments, and activities that don't force group participation. The librarians realize these changes are manageable and start brainstorming ideas like noise-reducing materials and flexible seating. Educators suggest optional workshops, like creative writing or storytelling, that balance social interaction with personal expression.

By the end, the group creates a program that includes quiet zones, sensory-friendly adjustments, and engaging, optional workshops. Everyone leaves feeling heard, and the teens are excited about returning to a library designed with them in mind. Open communication didn't just solve a challenge; it built trust for future collaboration.

Overcoming misunderstandings takes patience and the willingness to clarify when needed. For example, a parent might see a policy change as vital for their child's support, whereas an autistic person might worry that it overlooks autonomy. Instead of letting this become a conflict, both sides can ask questions to understand each other's concerns and find common ground.

REMEMBER

We can overcome misunderstandings by pausing to restate what we've heard and asking others if our understanding is correct. This helps prevent assumptions from building walls and instead fosters bridges that lead to solutions. The point isn't to win an argument; it's to make sure everyone is on the same page.

Building on differences with shared goals

Recognizing our differences is important, but staying focused on shared goals keeps collaboration effective. We're not always going to agree on everything, and that's okay. Autistic individuals may emphasize self-advocacy and independence, parents may focus on daily support, researchers may prioritize data-driven methods, and service providers may look at systemic solutions. Additionally, the perspectives of autistic and nonautistic parents, researchers, and service providers may also differ, adding another layer to the discussion. These perspectives might seem at odds, but the shared goal of building a supportive, inclusive world stays the same.

REMEMBER

Focusing on shared goals means revisiting what all parties want to achieve and remembering why they're working together. For example, a group working to improve educational resources should frame discussions around the ultimate aim: creating better, more inclusive learning environments for autistic students. Grounding conversations in this shared purpose turns differences into strengths that contribute to complete solutions rather than obstacles.

Turning differences into positive outcomes

Working with someone who has a different perspective can be challenging, but it's one of the most productive things you can do because it broadens your understanding, encourages creative solutions, and leads to better outcomes. When you combine diverse viewpoints, you create more well-rounded, inclusive approaches that benefit everyone involved.

Picture a group of autistic adults and a team of service providers discussing how community programs should be designed. The autistic adults emphasize the importance of flexibility and participant-led activities that allow individuals to engage on their own terms. The service providers, experienced in managing large-scale programs, may prioritize structured schedules and consistent routines, concerned that too much flexibility could create logistical issues or overwhelm participants.

At first, these perspectives might seem at odds, and conversations can become tense. But when both sides refocus on their shared goal, it changes the tone of the discussion. Recognizing this common ground allows them to approach the topic with empathy and openness. Together, they can brainstorm solutions like offering core structured activities while also providing breakout sessions where participants have the freedom to explore at their own pace. This balance ensures that programs are both organized and responsive to individual needs.

Effectively resolving conflicts

Conflicts are bound to happen when people with different ideas and goals come together, but conflict doesn't have to be negative. It often signals that people care about the outcome. The key is to handle it in a way that moves everyone forward instead of creating barriers.

Start by staying calm and listening, which may sound simple, but in the moment, it's easy to get defensive. Take a breath and really hear what the other person is saying. Ask questions to ensure you understand their point of view before responding. The goal isn't to "win" but to understand and find a way to meet in the middle.

Next, focus on common ground. Even if you don't agree on every detail, you're likely aiming for similar outcomes, like better support for autistic students or more inclusive programs. Keeping that shared goal in mind can turn tense moments into opportunities. Work together to brainstorm solutions that acknowledge everyone's concerns. It's okay if this takes time; lasting solutions aren't built overnight.

TIP

If things get too heated, don't be afraid to step back and take a break. Coming back with a fresh perspective can make significant difference. Remember, resolving conflicts effectively strengthens relationships and helps everyone move forward as a team.

Building Alliances

Creating meaningful change around autism requires strong alliances — partnerships that can tackle challenges and drive lasting progress. Forming alliances involves reaching out to communities, organizations, and allies beyond the autism space. This section looks at how you can make that happen.

Identifying key stakeholders

The first step is knowing who should be involved. The world connected to autism includes many groups: autistic individuals, parents, families, educators, service providers, advocates, and researchers. Each group brings unique perspectives and expertise. Identifying these key stakeholders helps you capture the whole picture and hear every side.

But don't stop there: Building alliances means looking outside the typical circles, too. Think about potential allies in fields like mental health, employment services, community organizations, and policymakers. Their support and collaboration can expand resources and solutions that benefit everyone.

Establishing common goals

Once you know who's at the table, set common goals. This step is crucial for building strong alliances. Shared objectives are what people rally around, even when their perspectives differ. Start with honest conversations about what everyone wants to achieve. What are the nonnegotiables? What shared values guide the work?

For instance, whereas an autistic adult might push for educational programs that emphasize independence, a parent might focus on strong support systems to ensure success. The groups probably share a common goal, though: creating learning environments where autistic students thrive. Zeroing in on shared goals helps keep everyone focused and moving forward.

Effectively communicating

Good communication is key for any alliance. People need to feel safe sharing their thoughts and be confident that they'll be heard. This means making space for questions, keeping disagreements respectful, and encouraging everyone to contribute openly.

TIP

Use clear, simple language, and remember that everyone has their preferred way of communicating. Some might prefer structured meetings, whereas others might be more comfortable with informal discussions or written feedback. Address misunderstandings directly: Clarify, restate, and ask for feedback to make sure everyone is on the same page.

Chapter **22**

Turning Vision into Reality

n Chapter 21, we discuss the vision for a more autism-inclusive future. Now, we want to focus on turning that vision into action! There's a lot we all can do to create a world that works better for autistic individuals and their families. This chapter covers five key areas: shaping public policy, ensuring accurate news reporting, telling authentic autistic stories in media, modernizing autism research, and improving accommodations.

The good news is that you have the power to make a difference. By getting involved in these areas, you can help drive real change. Whether advocating for better laws, reporting on autism more accurately, telling well-rounded stories, or advancing autism research, every step counts.

Shaping Public Policy

Shaping effective public policy around autism requires a thoughtful, inclusive approach that listens to the needs of autistic individuals and their families. Policies must go beyond basic accommodations and actively work to create environments that are accessible, supportive, and empowering across areas like education, healthcare, employment, and housing. And public policy should ensure that autistic people have the opportunities and resources to thrive, while also addressing the barriers they may face.

Effectively serving autistic constituents

As a policymaker, you manage budgets, priorities, and the pressure to make informed decisions. With many voices and agendas to consider, it's vital to rely on accurate information. The best way to shape autism policy is simple: listen to autistic people and their families. Too often, policies are influenced by outdated ideas or assumptions from nonautistic people rather than focusing on those who are directly affected by the policies.

REMEMBER

When autistic people and families come to you with concerns, take them seriously. Their insights are vital for creating effective, impactful solutions.

TIP

At the same time, when organizations lobby you on autism-related issues, check who's driving the conversation. Are autistic people included within the group's leadership, and how have they helped shape the policy requests being brought to you? Some groups claim to advocate for autistic people but don't significantly include them in decision-making or pushing outdated ideas and priorities that don't reflect what autistic people actually want or need.

Support at every stage of life

Autistic people's needs extend beyond childhood. Policymakers must create policies that support individuals across their lifespan and across all areas — education, work, healthcare, and housing. Without policies that address needs at all ages, autistic people may struggle to access resources and support as adults. By addressing autism across the lifespan, lawmakers can empower autistic individuals to lead fulfilling lives.

Improving existing services

"It's important to remember that very few of the services autistic people use come with the word 'autism' on them," says Ari Ne'eman, assistant professor of Health Policy and Management at Harvard University's T.H. Chan School of Public Health.

Ne'eman, who is autistic, highlights the need to focus on improving current systems like education, healthcare, employment, and housing rather than creating separate autism-only programs. Here are some areas of focus that policymakers can address:

>> **Simplify access to services:** Ensure autistic people and families can easily find and use available resources. This includes improving coordination between agencies, streamlining processes to reduce delays, and reducing red tape — like complex applications, long wait times, and inconsistent eligibility rules — while training staff on how to better assist autistic constituents.

>> **Update employment policies:** Revise policies to support the long-term success of autistic workers. This can mean expanding hiring and retention incentives for businesses, offering employers clear guidance and practical support for workplace accommodations, and ensuring government employment services have staff trained in neurodiversity.

>> **Strengthen education policies:** Ensure teachers have the training and resources to support autistic students in both general and specialized classrooms. This can be done by integrating neurodiversity training into teacher certification, funding ongoing staff development, and providing more resources. Policymakers can also streamline accommodations by reducing paperwork, setting clear standards, and providing schools with the support to implement them quickly.

>> **Improve healthcare access:** Update the healthcare system so autistic people of all ages can get the diagnoses, care, and support they need. Lawmakers can improve coordination between general practitioners, specialists, and mental health services; set accessibility standards for sensory-friendly care, and reduce wait times by increasing provider availability. They can also ensure essential services are funded, simplify paperwork and eligibility rules, and expand telehealth by improving coverage, investing in technology, and increasing provider participation.

>> **Expand housing options:** Support policies that promote stable, flexible living arrangements, such as independent living, family housing, or supportive housing. These policies should prioritize community integration, offering social connections, independence, and access to services. For autistic individuals with more support needs, lawmakers can ensure funding for personal assistants and aides, facilitate access to supported living resources, and fund home modifications for accessibility needs.

Supporting community integration

"We shouldn't be creating special autism classrooms or schools — we should be supporting autistic students in general education classrooms," says Ne'eman. "Similarly, we don't need special autism housing — we need inclusive homes and community-based services."

Making these changes may feel like a big shift from how things have been done in the past. For a long time, the focus has been on creating segregated environments for autistic people, like special classrooms or programs.

But just like stepping stones lead to broader steps, moving toward integration is a necessary part of improving how services work. Instead of continuing to isolate autistic individuals, we need to strengthen the systems that help them be a part of their communities.

Effectively working with policymakers

If you're autistic or a family member, your voice holds power. Lawmakers rely on the real-life experiences of the people they serve to shape their decisions. By sharing your perspective with policymakers, you help ensure policies meet the needs of those they aim to support.

Share your experience with policy makers

Autistic people and families have the power to shape better policies. Lawmakers make decisions that affect daily life, but they rely on the people they serve to tell them what's needed. Speaking at public meetings, filling out surveys, or writing to elected officials turns lived experiences into action.

Even a single story can make a difference, especially when it comes to improving education, healthcare, jobs, and public services. The more voices that speak up, the harder they are to ignore — and that's how real change happens.

Jessica Benham, an autistic lawmaker and a member of the Pennsylvania house of representatives, notes, "Building relationships with lawmakers is an essential part of being involved in the legislative process. If autistic people and their families share their experiences with their elected officials, it truly impacts how legislation is crafted and voted on."

TIP

Benham notes that while phone calls and emails to lawmakers can be helpful, meeting with elected officials in person is one of the most effective ways to make a lasting impression.

Work with advocacy groups

Advocacy organizations amplify the voices of autistic individuals and families. By joining one, you connect with others already making a difference. These groups run campaigns, train people to talk to lawmakers, and help shape public policy.

THE POWER OF ADVOCACY: ASAN

Picture a room where decisions about autism policy are made. For too long, the people most impacted by these decisions weren't in that room, or their voices weren't leading the conversation. The Autistic Self Advocacy Network (ASAN) has helped to change that. Run by and for autistic individuals, ASAN believes autistic people should lead conversations about the policies that shape their lives.

ASAN advocates for policies on issues like education, healthcare, antidiscrimination laws, and employment rights. They conduct research, develop resources, and ensure that lawmakers hear from autistic people on the issues that directly impact them. ASAN also equips autistic people and their families with the tools and knowledge to advocate for themselves. This community-driven approach ensures policies are based on real experiences, not assumptions or outdated stereotypes.

By making sure that autistic voices are part of the decision-making process, ASAN helps lawmakers shape policies that improve the lives of autistic people in practical ways. This approach also benefits parents and families of autistic children by ensuring policies provide the support and resources they need to help their children thrive. ASAN shows that when those most impacted by policy decisions are involved in making them, policy becomes more effective and better equipped to meet needs.

Getting involved can be as simple as signing a petition, attending a meeting, or sharing your experiences. When people come together, their voices are louder and their impact stronger. Policies improve when autistic individuals and their families push for them, and advocacy organizations make that push even more powerful.

Take part in policy discussions

When crafting public policy, many government bodies hold public meetings on education, healthcare, and job policies, where people can share their input. For example, if a school district is deciding how to fund special education, autistic individuals and families can advocate for better teacher training and classroom support.

You can also get involved in town council meetings where local policies are discussed or participate in public comment periods when agencies are making rules about things like healthcare access or disability services. Speaking up in these settings helps ensure that policymakers consider the needs of autistic individuals.

Hold policymakers accountable

Good policies only work if they're put into practice. Tracking how policies are working ensures lawmakers follow through on their commitments. Asking for updates and pushing for independent reviews — where an outside group checks if the policy is effective — helps ensure policies achieve their goals.

For example, if a city creates sensory-friendly public spaces, you can follow up to see if they truly benefit autistic people or if more changes are needed to ensure the policy isn't just a promise. When you build positive relationships with lawmakers and follow up on their commitments, you also hold them accountable. This can take many forms, like sending a follow-up email or inviting lawmakers to community events to see firsthand how policies are impacting people.

"This can't be a one-time interaction," says Benham, emphasizing that consistency with lawmakers is the key to success. "Creating these relationships requires consistent engagement with elected officials over the course of years. But once built, those relationships provide the foundation for educating legislators about the issues folks with disabilities face and help push forward laws that benefit our community."

Ensuring Accurate News Reporting

Autism is a complex topic, and its complexity gives journalists the power to shape public understanding through accurate, thoughtful reporting. Because misinformation is common, even well-intentioned coverage can overlook key perspectives or reinforce outdated ideas. Thoughtful reporting requires careful research, reliable sources, and the right questions — not just to avoid mistakes but to provide a fuller, more accurate understanding of autistic experiences.

Common frustrations with autism reporting

Many autistic people and their families are frustrated by how autism is covered in the media. Too often, stories frame autism as a tragedy, an extraordinary difference, or something to be "fixed" rather than recognizing autistic people as individuals with full, complex lives.

Sensational headlines, misleading research claims, and outdated stereotypes fuel misunderstanding. Many studies are reported without context, making it seem like autism is a problem to be solved rather than a fundamental part of how an autistic person thinks, communicates, and experiences the world.

Best practices for reporting on autism

REMEMBER

Good journalism requires getting the story right — not just repeating the loudest voices. Thoughtful, well-researched reporting on autism requires accuracy, context, and a commitment to representing autistic people in an accurate way. Here are key principles for getting it right:

» **Center autistic voices.** Journalists should prioritize autistic individuals as primary sources in autism stories to ensure accuracy and avoid bias. Parents, researchers, and others can provide useful perspectives, but reporting without autistic voices is incomplete and unethical. Strengthen reporting by seeking out and building relationships with autistic sources and autistic-led organizations, as with any other community.

» **Be aware of power imbalances.** Not all voices have equal access to media platforms. Many well-funded organizations and individuals claim to speak for autistic people, but their perspectives may not reflect those of the people they claim to represent. While these groups have the resources to put out press releases, field media interviews, and shape public narratives, autistic individuals often struggle to be heard.

» **Include a range of perspectives.** Autism is not one experience, and covering it well means hearing from autistic people and families with different backgrounds and experiences. Many stories focus on those who can easily participate in interviews, but this often leaves out nonspeaking autistic people, those who need multiple supports for daily living, and autistic individuals from different cultural backgrounds.

» **Go beyond "color commentary."** In your reporting, do not limit autistic voices to personal stories ("color commentary"). Strive to include autistic subject matter experts such as researchers and advocates who bring both lived experience and expertise.

» **Use accurate, modern language.** Most autistic people prefer identity-first language (for example, "autistic person"), but always ask individuals what they prefer. Avoid terms like "suffers from autism" or "high-functioning," which reinforce outdated ideas. Steer clear of labels like "profound" and "severe," which focus on nonautistic interpretation of autistic traits rather than an autistic person's full lived experience.

» **Watch for sensationalism.** Press releases for autism research often use dramatic language to attract attention, but they may not fully reflect a study's findings. Before reporting, read beyond the press release, and avoid falling into any sensationalism meant to bait or persuade your coverage.

>> **Stick to credible sources.** Misinformation about autism is everywhere, from outdated theories to pseudoscientific "cures." Be cautious of sources that push autism as a tragedy, a disease to be fixed, or something caused by vaccines or environmental factors.

>> **Make interviews accessible.** Autistic people communicate in different ways, so flexibility is key. Offer email or text-based options, allow extra processing time, share topics in advance, and avoid rushing or interrupting. Use concrete questions instead of open-ended ones, and be patient with pauses or alternative communication methods like typing or augmentative and alternative communication (AAC) devices. Be mindful of tone — avoid a slow, exaggerated, or overly upbeat voice, which can sound patronizing.

>> **Tell a complete story.** When covering autistic people, focus on what makes the story meaningful beyond their diagnosis. Autistic people live full, complex lives, and good reporting highlights these experiences. Avoid framing everyday activities as "inspiring" just because an autistic person is doing them.

TIP

Eric Garcia, an autistic journalist whose work has appeared in *The Washington Post*, *The Hill*, *The Independent*, and more, emphasizes that autistic people should not be framed as inherently unusual or newsworthy simply because they are autistic. "Consider whether you would write about a nonautistic person in the same way," says Garcia. "If a story only seems newsworthy or inspirational' because someone is autistic, ask yourself why." He stresses the importance of applying the same journalistic standards used for any other subject, including avoiding sensationalism and stereotypes.

Supplemental style guide for reporting on autism

This glossary is designed to help you report on autism clearly, accurately, and respectfully. It includes terms that reflect current scientific understanding and how autistic people prefer to be described, giving you a more precise way to discuss autism and related experiences.

By using these terms, you'll avoid outdated language and better reflect the real experiences of autistic individuals. Whether you're covering research, personal stories, or social issues, this guide will help ensure your reporting is up to date, inclusive, and impactful.

>> **Autism:** Use *autism* as the standard term. Avoid *autism spectrum disorder* unless discussing the diagnosis. Do not use *Asperger's* as it is now classified under autism.

>> **Autistic:** Use *autistic* as the default term for an autistic person. Respect individual preferences; some may prefer *person with autism*, but most prefer identity-first language.

» **Autistic community:** This refers to autistic individuals and their shared experiences. Use this instead of *autism community*.

» **Autistic traits:** Use *autistic traits* rather than *symptoms*, which implies a medical condition requiring a cure. *Traits* is neutral.

» **Cognitive/communication/developmental/processing/sensory differences:** Use *differences* instead of inaccurate terms like *difficulties* or *challenges*.

» **Co-occurring conditions:** Use this to refer to additional conditions that may exist alongside autism, such as ADHD or anxiety, rather than terms like *comorbidities*, which imply a secondary or less important condition.

» **Disability:** *Disability* refers to societal barriers that impact individuals. Use terms like *disabled* respectfully, focusing on inclusion (for example, "Accessible design ensures disabled individuals can participate fully").

» **Intense interests:** Use this to describe specific, intense areas of interest that are common among autistic individuals, avoiding terms like *obsessions* or *fixations*, which can carry negative connotations.

» **Meltdown:** Use this term to describe an intense physiological reaction to feeling overwhelmed, often involving crying, anger, or frustration, rather than framing it as a *tantrum*, which implies misbehavior.

» **Neurodevelopmental differences:** Autism is a neurodevelopmental difference, not a disorder. Frame it as a natural variation in how the brain develops.

» **Neurodiverse:** *Neurodiverse* describes a group of people with different neurological experiences. Do not describe an individual as *neurodiverse*.

» **Neurodivergent:** *Neurodivergent* refers to individuals whose neurological functioning differs from the norm.

» **Neurodiversity:** *Neurodiversity* recognizes neurological differences as natural human variation. It highlights both strengths and challenges.

» **Neurotype:** Use this to describe an individual's neurological makeup, whether neurotypical or neurodivergent, as a neutral term that emphasizes variation without implying any hierarchy. Examples of different neurotypes include ADHD, dyslexia, and autism.

» **Neurotypical:** *Neurotypical* describes individuals whose neurological development aligns with societal norms.

» **Self-advocacy:** Self-advocacy is when autistic individuals speak up for their needs, rights, and perspectives.

>> **Self-advocate:** A self-advocate is an autistic person who advocates for their own needs. Only use it if someone identifies themselves as a self-advocate.

>> **Shutdown:** Use this term to describe when an autistic person becomes less responsive or withdraws due to an overwhelming body or brain response, rather than framing it as a "lack of cooperation," which inaccurately implies choice.

>> **Speaking and nonspeaking:** Use *speaking* and *nonspeaking* to describe common ways that autistic people communicate. Use these terms instead of older terms like *verbal* and *nonverbal*.

>> **Stimming:** Use this to describe soothing movements or behaviors that help individuals regulate sensory input or manage emotions, rather than terms like *repetitive behavior*, which can carry a negative connotation.

>> **Support needs:** Avoid inaccurate labels like high-functioning, low-functioning, profound, and severe. Instead, describe the specific needs of the individual (for example, "requires support with communication" or "benefits from sensory accommodations") and use "support needs" for a clearer, respectful description of their requirements.

Portraying Autism in Creative Media

Storytelling shapes how people see the world. Whether you're writing a novel, producing a film, or directing a play, how you portray autism matters. Representation isn't just about getting details right. It influences public understanding, challenges stereotypes, and helps autistic audiences see themselves in meaningful ways.

A 2023 study from Australian Catholic University found that "the way autism is represented in fictional media can impact people's views of autistic people." This influence can be harmful or helpful, depending on how autistic characters are portrayed. "For example, representations may contribute to negative views of autistic people as being unusual or dangerous, or they may challenge stereotypes and instead highlight the strengths of autistic people."

REMEMBER

For those in creative media, remember that how you portray autism has a real-world impact. Thoughtful, well-rounded storytelling shapes how audiences understand autistic people and can influence perceptions for better or worse.

Telling authentic stories

To portray autism in a way that is respectful and accurate, it's important to focus on telling complete stories. Autistic characters shouldn't just be defined by their autism; they should have depth, personality, and experiences beyond it. Here's how you can approach this:

» **Collaborate with autistic people:** One of the most effective ways to create a well-rounded portrayal is to involve autistic people in the process. This can include consulting with autistic writers, actors, or advisors to ensure authenticity.

» **Portray diverse experiences:** Every autistic person is unique. Avoid one-size-fits-all portrayals. Include characters with a range of traits, needs, and abilities, reflecting the diversity of experiences within the autistic community.

» **Tell full stories:** Don't reduce autistic characters to a single trait or a "special skill." Like all characters, they should have desires, motivations, and personal growth throughout the story. Their autism might shape how they interact with the world, but it should not be the only thing that defines them.

» **Focus on strengths, not just challenges:** Highlight the strengths and talents that autistic characters bring to the table. Whether it's creativity, problem-solving, attention to detail, or unique ways of thinking, showing these qualities can help audiences see autistic characters as multidimensional.

» **Avoid harmful tropes:** Be mindful of harmful tropes like portraying autistic characters as "geniuses" or "socially awkward" without deeper context. These clichés limit how autistic people are perceived. Instead, focus on their full humanity, showing them as complex and nuanced individuals.

REMEMBER

Telling authentic, meaningful stories shapes a more accurate view of autism. Your portrayal influences how people see autistic individuals in real life.

Going deeper than stereotypes

One common challenge is moving past stereotypes. A study from 2018 by Anders Nordahl-Hansen and colleagues found that nearly half of autistic characters in TV and film were shown with extraordinary abilities, like being a "savant." In reality, only about 10 percent of autistic people have these abilities. This creates a misleading idea that autism is only interesting when tied to rare talents, which doesn't reflect the full range of real autistic experiences.

To make characters feel more authentic, go beyond just surface traits. Take time to consult with autistic people, listen to their experiences, and build characters with depth. They should have emotions, goals, and relationships, just like any other character. This helps create a fuller, more realistic portrayal that feels true to life.

The importance of nuanced narratives

As creators, it's crucial to recognize that the portrayal of autism goes beyond just breaking stereotypes. It's about creating nuanced, thoughtful characters who live within rich, meaningful narratives. These characters should interact with their environment, face challenges, and have their own personal growth arcs — just like any other well-developed character.

Think about how autistic characters experience the world. Instead of merely focusing on what makes them different, show how those differences shape their unique perspectives. For instance, a character might have challenges with certain social interaction but connect deeply with others in other meaningful ways. Or they might love certain sensory experiences, like bright colors or loud music, that others don't understand right away. These details make the character feel real.

REMEMBER

Accurate portrayals show the full range of real-life traits. It's important to high-light autistic people's strengths and talents but also acknowledge their challenges in a true-to-life way. Balance presents them as authentic individuals rather than either burdensome or unrealistically perfect.

Modernizing Autism Research

Scientific research pushes knowledge forward — questioning assumptions, challenging outdated ideas, and developing solutions that improve lives.

While many fields have advanced by integrating new perspectives and prioritizing real-world impact, autism research has been slow to adapt. Priorities often reflect outdated theories and donor whims, not the needs of autistic people and their families. As a result, other crucial areas of study remain underfunded and underexplored.

The goal of autism research should be clear: to improve understanding, support, and quality of life for autistic individuals. This means asking the right questions, exploring real-world solutions, and ensuring autistic voices guide research that directly affects them.

While autism research has made progress, it often still focuses on medicalizing autism or treating it as a problem rather than recognizing it as a human variation to be understood. Funding structures reinforce these outdated approaches, leaving essential topics — like communication supports, inclusive education, and adult services — overlooked. Modernizing autism research means shifting focus to studies that create meaningful, real-world change.

Aligning research with community needs

Autistic individuals and their families have expressed a need for research that addresses the practical challenges they face in everyday life. However, much autism research still doesn't align with these needs.

"The majority of funding for autism research is currently spent on biological studies and on the search for treatments and a cure," writes Dr. Monique Botha in a 2024 study on autistic research priorities for the University of Stirling. This study, the largest on autistic research priorities, also found that "autistic people want applied research into diagnosis, mental health, and topics which can enable a good quality of life." Families of autistic individuals also consistently voice these same priorities, highlighting the importance of practical solutions and support.

Let's explore the key areas that autistic people and their families consistently ask for from autism research:

>> **Expanding research beyond childhood:** Most autism research focuses on children, yet at least 75 percent of autistic people are adults. In the United States, only 3 percent of research addresses adult experiences, leaving key autistic experiences poorly understood. This also reinforces the public misconception that autism is a childhood condition, which makes it harder for autistic adults to get the support they need.

>> **Studying autism across the lifespan:** The experiences and needs of autistic people change over time, influenced by factors like support systems, employment, and co-occurring conditions. A child thriving in a supportive school may struggle as an adult without proper transition resources. Researching autism as a lifelong experience can dramatically impact millions of autistic lives.

>> **Improving autism diagnosis:** Getting diagnosed is often difficult, frustrating, and full of barriers. Delayed or missed diagnoses mean people go without support for years. Research is needed into what can make diagnosis more accessible, accurate, and inclusive, especially for often overlooked groups.

>> **Examining co-occurring conditions:** Anxiety, depression, epilepsy, dyspraxia, and gastrointestinal issues (among others) are common in autistic people but often ignored in research. These conditions and others affect daily life, making it harder to access education, stay employed, or build relationships. More research in this area could lead to and improve the quality of life for many autistic people.

>> **Researching practical supports:** Autistic people and families continue to ask for research that leads to real-world solutions, such as better communication tools, sensory accommodations, and inclusive education.

>> **Studying mental health:** Autistic people experience high rates of anxiety, depression, and burnout due to stress, trauma, lack of support, and inaccessible systems. Despite this, it remains an understudied area. Prioritizing research into the mental health experiences of autistic people can lead to better stress management tools and therapy approaches, and better training for mental health professionals.

Conducting effective autism research

Autism research should expand knowledge and drive real-world improvements. Strong studies deepen understanding, explore practical solutions, include autistic voices, and move beyond outdated deficit-based framing. Here are key approaches to make autism research more effective:

>> **Ditch the deficit model:** Too much research treats autism as a problem to fix rather than a way of being to understand. Effective studies explore why traits exist and how to create environments where they thrive. This doesn't mean ignoring challenges; it means studying them in a way that respects autism as human variation rather than pathology.

>> **Focus on impact:** Research should address solutions for autistic people's needs, like sensory sensitivities, communication, and support access. Even abstract areas, like genetics, can reframe studies in ways that demonstrate how they might improve daily life.

>> **Include autistic voices from the start:** To make your research meaningful, involve autistic people as collaborators, not just subjects. Their insights help shape better questions, challenge assumptions, and ensure studies meet real needs. Work with autistic-led organizations, fairly compensate contributors, and codesign studies with the people they impact.

>> **Challenge bias:** Bias creeps into research at every level — cultural, institutional, and personal. Funding structures often prioritize early childhood over adult supports, and researchers unconsciously focus on participants who are easiest to study. Acknowledging bias makes research stronger.

>> **Be transparent:** Participants deserve to know what your study is about, how findings will be used, and what impact it might have. Be clear, avoid jargon, and give space for questions. Also, manage expectations. Overhyping research creates false hope, especially for parents. Be honest about limitations while showing how their contributions drive long-term progress.

>> **Look beyond averages:** Researchers often use averages to identify trends, but this can hide important insights. For example, if a study finds that "most autistic people" develop speech by age four, it may overlook nonspeaking individuals or those who speak later. Including outlying data — such as from those that need multiple supports for daily living — can deepen understanding.

>> **Remove barriers to participation:** Research should be accessible, offering virtual options, sensory-friendly spaces, and plain-language instructions.

Addressing participation selection bias

Many autism studies focus on individuals who are easier to communicate with because they are easier to research. This skews data, reinforces stereotypes, and overlooks the experiences of autistic people who are nonspeaking, minimally speaking, have an intellectual disability, or need extra supports (for example, a personal aid for behavior or communication support). The result is incomplete research with negative, real-world consequences.

"If I have not fully understood my own disability, it is, in part, because there has been little research to help autistics like me understand the full scope of it," wrote neuroscientist Hari Srinivasan in *Time* in 2023. Srinivasan, who is autistic and minimally speaking, described how a speech therapist assumed he was a literal thinker based on existing research. "How did this line up with my love of philosophy, for instance, which is very much abstract and heavily nuanced? Or of all the autistics who are poets and painters, for surely art involves a lot of imagination and abstraction?"

Autism research must do better. Exclusion distorts scientific understanding, while broadening participation improves accuracy.

THE PARTICIPATORY AUTISM RESEARCH COLLECTIVE

If you're an autism researcher, the Participatory Autism Research Collective (PARC) can improve how you conduct your studies. Founded in 2015 by Dr. Damian Milton, PARC is a global network of autistic individuals, researchers, and allies focused on making autism research more relevant and impactful. The collective addresses a major problem: Much of the existing autism research is done on autistic people rather than with them. This often results in research that is inaccurate, reinforces harmful stereotypes, or fails to lead to meaningful change in the lives of autistic people.

PARC shifts this dynamic by encouraging researchers to treat autistic people as active partners and coresearchers, not just subjects of study. By involving autistic voices at every step — from developing research questions to interpreting data — PARC ensures that studies are grounded in real-life experiences and address the most pressing issues faced by the autistic community. This leads to research that is not only more accurate and respectful but also directly applicable to improving the lives of autistic people.

For researchers, PARC provides concrete support. It connects you with autistic collaborators who can offer firsthand insights, guides you on adopting inclusive and ethical research practices, and helps you move beyond outdated assumptions that limit the potential of your work. Working with PARC isn't just about improving your research methodology; it's about creating outcomes that directly benefit autistic people in real-world settings. (To connect with PARC, visit https://participatory autismresearch.wordpress.com.)

Understanding funding pressures

If you're an autism researcher, you know that what gets studied isn't always what's most needed. It's what gets funded. Universities push for grants that boost institutional prestige, funders prioritize research that fits their existing agendas, and researchers often have to reshape proposals in response to these pressures.

"The funding climate has typically prioritized research into the causes of autism or potentially successful drug interventions," says Dr. Deb Karhson, a neuroscientist and autism researcher.

Autism research funding is often shaped by personal, institutional, and market-driven priorities. Private donors frequently fund research into potential "cures" and behavior-focused studies, while research that improves autistic people's quality of life remains underfunded.

These pressures shape university research, often pushing scholars toward studies that attract large grants, high-profile publications, revenue-generating patents, donor maintenance, and institutional prestige.

As a result, funding favors genetics, early intervention, and pharmaceuticals — areas already well-funded — while research on accessibility, communication, and autistic adulthood is neglected. When funding dictates research priorities, critical needs are overlooked, leaving many autistic people without research that could improve their lives.

Navigating funding pressures

Researchers focused on real-world solutions must carefully navigate funding constraints without compromising their mission. However, working within the system doesn't mean researchers need to sell out their values or scientific focus.

Many are finding ways to align proposals with funders' priorities while keeping autistic needs central. As Dr. Karhson notes, success often comes from understanding the "hidden curriculum" of autism funding — knowing how to navigate the expectations that shape funding decisions.

A key tool is the Notice of Funding Opportunity (NOFO), which outlines funders' priorities, methods, and desired outcomes. Researchers who tailor the language of their proposals to meet NOFO criteria — while still staying true to their focus — have a better chance of securing funding.

TIP

For those conducting autism research, here are some additional tips on how to navigate funding pressures without losing sight of your mission:

>> **Align with the right funders.** Matching your approach to funders with similar values increases your chances of success. Advocacy groups and public foundations are often a strong fit. As Dr. Karhson puts it, "If you're conducting human research, applying to a funder who has historically funded animal models likely isn't going to work out for you."

>> **Speak their language.** Funders' priorities may differ, but you can align your research without compromising your values. For example, if a funder focuses on "problem behaviors," frame a study on autistic strengths as addressing "stressors" or "creating supportive environments." This connects your goals with theirs while staying true to your mission.

>> **Collaborate with the community.** Partnering with autistic individuals or organizations strengthens your proposals and demonstrates direct community benefit.

>> **Start small.** Pilot studies help build a foundation for larger funding opportunities. Even niche projects can gain traction once they have supporting data.

>> **Diversify your funding.** Relying on one source can be risky. Tapping into public, private, and nonprofit funding streams gives you more flexibility and freedom.

REMEMBER

"Most of all, don't give up after one rejection," says Dr. Karhson. "Be willing to reframe your question — not your core values — until your rationale is so clear and well-aligned with the NOFO that they have no choice but to fund you."

TIP

The key isn't changing your work; it's framing it in a way that resonates with funders. With persistence, you can navigate the funding landscape and secure support for research that truly benefits the autistic community.

Modernizing research institutions

Autism research institutions — such as universities, funding organizations, and advocacy groups — hold significant influence over what gets studied. However, they often prioritize genetics, early intervention, and behavior-based approaches, driven by outdated models and donor priorities, while neglecting research that could improve autistic people's daily lives.

Areas like communication, accessibility, healthcare, mental health, employment, housing, and lifelong support — especially for autistic adults — remain underfunded and understudied. Meanwhile, weak ethical and oversight practices mean research often lacks accountability, respect for autistic people and families, and reduced real-world impact.

WARNING

There are over 1,800 autism research institutions worldwide, yet few have autistic people in leadership. Without autistic perspectives shaping study design, funding, and ethics, research fails to address many of the most pressing needs of autistic people. Research without autistic expertise isn't just incomplete; it's often ineffective and unethical, leading to misdirected priorities and missed opportunities.

To effectively modernize their practices, research bodies must be ethical, impactful, and aligned with autistic needs. Here are ways they can do so:

>> **Require autistic leadership.** Autism research is most effective when autistic experts help shape its priorities. Institutions should ensure autistic voices are represented in organizational leadership.

>> **Update ethical standards.** Autism research should respect autistic experiences, not reinforce deficit-based assumptions. Ethical review boards must include autistic voices and assess studies for real-world impact. "Autistic people deserve research that adheres to quality standards," said Dr. Kristen Bottema-Beutel in a 2020 interview with *The Thinking Person's Guide to Autism*. "We shouldn't have a separate set of lower standards that we only apply to autism research."

>> **Enforce conflict of interest (COI) policies.** Many autism studies are unduly influenced by funding sources with narrow or biased agendas. Stronger COI policies are essential for research integrity. "Having a conflict of interest does not automatically mean that your research is biased," explains Dr. Bottema-Beutel, "but properly disclosing a COI invites additional scrutiny of your methods and interpretations, which is a good thing."

>> **Ensure accountability and transparency.** Research institutions should disclose funding, decision-making, and institutional priorities in accessible formats and plain language. Stronger public engagement helps keep research relevant, ethical, and focused on real needs.

>> **Accurately measure research success.** Journal citations don't reflect real-world impact. Research should also be judged on how it improves policies, expands supports, and enhances quality of life.

>> **Fund research that leads to real-world outcomes.** More attention should be placed on long overlooked areas of study like aging, communication tools, workplace accessibility, inclusive education, and healthcare.

>> **Invest in lifespan research.** Too much funding is concentrated on early childhood and genetics, while issues like aging, independent living, and long-term accessibility remain underfunded.

>> **Ensure autism research reflects real-life experiences.** Studies should consider factors like cultural background, gender, support needs, and communication differences to better understand the full range of autistic experiences.

>> **Build robust, interdisciplinary research teams.** Including autistic professionals alongside relevant specialists in adjacent areas of education, public health, sociology, and technology ensures research tackles challenges from multiple angles and leads to practical, impactful solutions

REMEMBER

Autism research can significantly increase its impact by prioritizing autistic people's needs, ensuring accountability, centering autistic voices, upholding ethical standards, and adjusting funding priorities.

AUTISTIC RESEARCHERS COMMITTEE (INSAR)

Autism research is evolving, and a new generation of autism researchers who happen to be autistic themselves are helping to drive that transformation. Their combination of scientific expertise and lived experience is challenging outdated assumptions, sparking fresh insights, and ensuring studies and areas of focus reflect autistic realities.

Historically, autistic researchers have faced barriers that limited their participation and voice in the larger research community — barriers such as inaccessible conferences, exclusion from leadership roles, and pressure to mask their autistic identities. Recognizing this, in 2020, the International Society for Autism Research (INSAR) established the Autistic Researchers Committee (ARC) to support the growing number of autistic researchers and ensure their representation across INSAR programs.

This mirrors similar shifts in adjacent fields, such as healthcare, where in 2019 Autistic Doctors International (ADI) was founded to support autistic medical professionals. Now a network of over 1000 autistic doctors and medical students, ADI has grown its focus to include research on the experiences of autistic doctors and patients, along with advocacy and education, to improve healthcare and promote a neurodiversity-affirming approach in medicine.

Like ADI, the Autistic Researchers Committee (ARC) not only supports its members but strengthens its field as a whole. By increasing autistic representation in research, ARC helps ensure studies ask the right questions, use better methods, and produce findings that actually reflect autistic experiences. This leads to more accurate, useful, and innovative research.

Building Effective Accommodations

Technology designed for autistic people works best when autistic people are involved from the start. Too often, tools and apps meant to "help" autistic individuals are built by nonautistic developers who focus on fixing perceived deficits instead of addressing real needs.

The result is products that might look promising on paper but don't actually work in real life. Whether it's a communication device, a sensory-friendly app, or an accessibility tool, autistic voices should guide the process to ensure the technology is practical, respectful, and useful.

The best tech is designed *with* autistic people, not just *for* them. It should simplify life, boost communication, and support independence by removing barriers, not adding them. This requires direct input from autistic users, not just assuming their needs

Involve autistic people at every stage of development, from users to subject matter experts to designers and developers. Their insights help identify what works, what doesn't, and what needs improvement.

It's also important to recognize that consulting is real work and should be compensated. If an autistic person is sharing their expertise, whether as a subject matter expert or a beta tester, they deserve fair pay.

Chapter **23**

Voices from the Spectrum

This book highlights autistic voices because their experiences and insights are essential to understanding autism. In this chapter, we go further, sharing additional stories, perspectives, and practical wisdom from autistic people, families, and allies on issues they believe need more attention.

When we listen and learn from each other, we all grow — and that's what this chapter, and this book, is all about.

Centering Autistic Voices

When it comes to autism, one rule stands out: Listen to autistic people.

"It's important that people learn about autism directly from autistic people," writes Casey "Remrov" Vorner in *Connecting with the Autism Spectrum*. That's because autistic individuals offer firsthand knowledge filled with real-world expertise and nuances often missed by others.

Centering autistic voices replaces secondhand assumptions with firsthand insights, resulting in better policies, tools, and support systems. Ignoring autistic input creates gaps in understanding, leading to inadequate support.

Everything about us, with us

"Parenting neurodivergent children can feel really isolating," says Dr. KD Harris, a mom of two autistic kids and founder of Let's Talk Learning Differences. "But so can being a neurodivergent kid. So, we created a space where parents can share, support each other, and connect — and where students can meet other kids who truly understand them."

From the start, the group has included autistic voices in its programming and leadership, transforming it from a support network into a collaborative community. Working together, families, educators, and service providers gain valuable insights directly from autistic people, learning what approaches truly help students thrive.

Harris's model embodies "Nothing about us, without us" — the motto ensuring autistic people are included in decisions about their lives. For autistic individuals, this means being heard, respected, and empowered. But remember that centering autistic voices isn't just good for autistic individuals; it leads to better outcomes for everyone involved.

By working with autistic people, those supporting autistic people don't have to guess at what works. Instead, they can create real solutions based on direct input, by building everything about autistic people, with autistic people. Families, educators, and caregivers gain valuable insights that strengthen relationships and make support more effective. It's not just guessing at what might work but finding real solutions by building everything about autistic people with autistic people.

Empowering autistic people to lead

In Australia, Andrew Eddy has taken a similar approach as the cofounder of Untapped Talent and the creator of Neurodiversity Hub. These initiatives focus on creating job opportunities for autistic individuals and connecting neurodivergent students with universities and employers.

What sets Eddy's work apart is his commitment, as an ally, to empowering neurodivergent professionals to shape and lead these efforts. Rather than taking charge himself, Eddy focuses on cultivating neurodivergent leaders who design and guide programs, ensuring they are relevant and effective.

The result is stronger collaboration between autistic individuals, schools, and workplaces, as well as more targeted solutions and services that genuinely meet the needs of those they are designed to support.

Advancing real outcomes

Eddy's leadership philosophy extends to his work with La Trobe University in Australia, which takes the same approach — partnering with neurodivergent experts to codesign projects and programs. This collaboration has put neurodivergent leadership at the center of the university's approach to neurodiversity.

Dr. Beth Radulski told *The Age* in 2023, "I found the effort required to mask at work and in the classroom exhausting, and I would burn out and I wouldn't be able to continue with my studies." For Radulski, the constant pressure to conform left her struggling to keep up with studies, caught in cycles of burnout and fatigue.

After disclosing she was autistic as a student, Radulski — now a scientific researcher — began working with La Trobe and Eddy to help create a campus where autistic students and staff feel supported without the pressure to mask or conform. This has led to a university where autistic individuals can connect, advocate for themselves, and fully participate, while students studying autism learn directly from autistic scientists, educators, and professionals.

This approach not only makes the campus more inclusive but also strengthens La Trobe's scientific research. By working directly with autistic people, La Trobe has established itself as a global leader in autism research and innovation.

The mission statement of the university's Olga Tennison Autism Research Centre states, "Our work is informed by autistic people. . . . Where possible, research projects are co-designed or co-produced with autistic partners." The center aims to improve the lives of autistic individuals and their families rather than "fixing" them.

Dispelling autism stereotypes

Centering autistic voices challenges stereotypes by highlighting the wide range of autistic experiences. It helps others better understand autism while allowing autistic people and their families to feel more understood and supported.

The idea that autistic people are rigid and lack flexible thinking is one such misconception. "Sometimes the way you solve something isn't the way that another person would solve something," says principal program manager Bear Grant, in a video Pacific Gas and Electric Company (PG&E) published in celebration of its neurodivergent workers. "And that's what I can bring to the table."

This is why it's so important to hear directly from autistic people. While the preceding quote addresses one misconception, there are still many stereotypes to break down. Centering autistic voices moves us closer to that.

Respecting Complex Needs

Respecting autistic individuals with complex support needs means recognizing their humanity. This means valuing their strengths, understanding their challenges without judgment, and treating them just as you would anyone else.

Challenging negative narratives

"Despite the work of so many self-advocates, parent advocates, and allies, the dominant message in our society is still that autism is horrible, and that autism, intellectual disability, and other significant cognitive disabilities mean that you aren't really a person," write Julia Bascomb and David M. Perry in *The Nation*.

These harmful narratives dehumanize individuals and instill fear in parents. These stereotypes also silence autistic people with complex support needs by assuming they are "less than" and unable to contribute their perspectives.

"We are tired of people speaking over us," writes the moderator of the High Needs Autistic Advocates (HNAA) group in a 2023 post on the *Wrong Planet* website. Rather than being spoken over, individuals with complex support needs deserve to have their voices heard just as much as anyone else.

Recognizing and rejecting these stereotypes is the first step toward meaningful change. For autistic individuals, this means embracing their own worth. For parents, it means reflecting on fears and challenging outdated beliefs.

"Which is where the allies come in," continues the HNAA moderator. "It's your job to help advocate for our ideas and help get them out there. This does not mean speaking for us, but amplifying our voices, and helping us advocate for ourselves when we don't have the energy to."

REMEMBER

Every autistic person, including those with complex support needs, is whole and valuable. This means seeing their strengths, challenges, and unique self.

Ensuring respect and dignity

Everyone deserves respect and dignity, including autistic people with complex support needs. This extends to how we include them in our communities, support their needs, and ensure they have a voice in decisions about their lives.

"He still needs a lot of support, and always will," says Matt Carey, in a 2024 interview with *KQED*, discussing his autistic son. "When my father was growing up, people like my son would be institutionalized. When I was growing up, people with disabilities were hidden. Now that my son is growing up, he lives in a time and a community in which people are aware that he needs support. They respect him and know he deserves respect."

REMEMBER

Respect and dignity mean valuing autistic people with complex support needs like anyone else — listening, accommodating, and involving them in decisions.

Embracing individuality

"I wish I had never learned to speak," writes the author of the *Autistic AAC Underground* blog in a 2019 post. While learning to speak brought some benefits, it pulled her away from her first "language" of sensory-based thinking and forced her into a form of communication that became exhausting and left many of her thoughts lost in translation.

What works for one person may not work for another, and that's okay. Supporting autistic people with complex support needs means understanding their differences, offering tailored support, and respecting their individual preferences.

"Over the last few months, we have been trying to do a thing where I am only verbal at home and use AAC apps out in public," says the author. "This enables me to better manage my environment, navigate social situations and helps reduce the amount of overload I experience."

Modeling inclusive attitudes

One afternoon, Shannon Des Roches Rosa took her teenage autistic son Leo for a walk around a shopping center. Public strolls aren't always possible for him, but that day, he was up for it. After wandering several shops, they eventually found themselves at a hardware store, a favorite spot for exploring things to fidget with.

Her son finds joy in everyday objects, which is part of what makes his autism unique. So does his party-like enthusiasm. As they wound through racks of specialized cooking tools, Shannon began to worry that her son's energy might not be welcomed. Then, a cashier happily called out, "Hey guys, how are you doing?"

The cashier's friendly attitude sent a clear message: They were welcome. At checkout, he spoke directly and cheerfully to her son without expecting a response, making them feel respected and comfortable.

"That cashier's attitude?" continues Rosa. "It is what I want most from society, for my son: Other people accepting my son on his terms, and letting him know he's considered part of the community."

Listening to Nonspeaking Voices

We all have a voice. Some use spoken words, while others rely on devices, gestures, or sounds. No matter how it's expressed, every human voice deserves to be heard.

"God gave you a voice — use it!" said Elizabeth Bonker, encouraging her classmates during her valedictorian speech at the 2022 Rollins College commencement. "And no, the irony of a nonspeaking autistic encouraging you to use your voice is not lost on me. Because if you can see the worth in me, then you can see the worth in anyone you meet."

Realizing voices speak in many ways

Communication doesn't look the same for everyone. For Bonker, it meant typing her speech with one finger while a communication partner held her keyboard, so it could be played later for the audience to hear.

"I communicate via an application on my iPad by typing letter-by-letter, which then generates words and speaks aloud when I'm ready," said Jordyn Zimmerman in the 2022 documentary *See Us, Hear Us*, produced by filmmaker Dan Habib. "It's difficult to explain the intense emotions of what it was like before I had effective communication. I was really unhappy."

Zimmerman faced daily restraints in school and had no way to share what was happening. "I repeatedly went home with bruises and other injuries but was unable to share about the trauma I was enduring."

Despite doubts from professionals, Zimmerman credits her mother's persistence in prioritizing her communication needs over addressing atypical behaviors. This determination transformed her life and allowed her to express her voice.

"When I learned to communicate with the letter board, my life changed dramatically," writes Mateo Musso in *The Art of Autism*. Mateo began using the tool at age 11. "It was as if duct tape had finally been ripped off my mouth."

"Presuming that a nonspeaking child has nothing to say is like presuming that an adult without a car has nowhere to go," writes Ellen Notbohm in *Ten Things Every Child with Autism Wishes You Knew*.

"We use our eyes, body language, and sometimes, even noises that are hard to understand," says writer Amy Sequenzia in a 2012 interview with *Thinking Person's Guide to Autism*, highlighting that communication extends far beyond spoken words. "People should not only pay attention to these forms of communication but also support them."

Figuring out what works

Nicole Gottesman tried all sorts of approaches to help her son Gabe communicate. When they found that spelling with a letterboard worked best for him, the family started paying for private lessons out of pocket because his school didn't teach it.

"Do us a fine party united and fun," typed Gabe during a spelling session over the holidays. Understanding that her son wanted a Christmas party where he could socialize and dance, Nicole quickly made it happen.

"All he wanted for Christmas was to have a party and dance!" shares Nicole, posting a video of Gabe dancing, stimming, and smiling to holiday music. Watching him spin repeatedly to *Wham!*'s "Last Christmas," no words were needed to understand the happiness and excitement Gabe was clearly communicating. Nicole noted that Gabe certainly "broke a record in how many spins he can do" during the song.

REMEMBER

Communication goes beyond spoken words. iPads, letter boards, and picture cards can be transformative, while gestures, movements, and sounds also convey powerful emotions and ideas.

James, a text-based communicator writing for Communication for Education, shares this advice: "Help your kids by giving their body easy commands while speaking to them the same way you speak to anyone their age. Simplify movement instruction and also provide us with rich listening experiences."

TIP

Talk to nonspeaking individuals as you would anyone their age and include them in decisions about communication. This shows respect, builds confidence, and strengthens communication in any form.

Amplifying Voices of Color

Autism is one part of a person's identity. Being both autistic and part of a racial minority brings unique challenges often overlooked by professionals, service providers, and media. This section highlights the experiences of autistic people of color and their families as they navigate barriers, find strength, and embrace joy.

Navigating additional barriers

Many challenges that autistic people face are because of how others react to their differences (see Chapter 1). Misunderstanding, exclusion, and a lack of support often create barriers.

"I was bullied as a kid, and I thought it was because I was autistic," writes Kayla Rodriguez in a blog post for *Rewriting the Narrative*. "But in reality, I was bullied because of people's reaction to me being autistic. It wasn't my autism's fault, it was society's fault because of how they see and treat autistic and disabled people."

For autistic people of color, bias and unfair treatment add extra barriers, leading to delayed diagnoses, limited access to services, and cultural stereotypes that leave their needs misunderstood and unmet.

"They sweep this under the rug and don't mention it to anyone," Anna Wang told *Smithsonian Folklife* magazine in 2024, recalling the pressure from other families to hide her son Lawrence's autistic traits. Rather than staying silent, Wang took action by founding Friends of Children with Special Needs, a nonprofit supporting neurodivergent Asian Americans and their families. As Wang put it, "living in hiding was no way of having a future."

"I believe that my experiences as an autistic person has definitely been affected by my gender and race," Dr. Morénike Giwa Onaiwu told *Quartz* in 2018. "Many characteristics that I possess that are clearly autistic were instead attributed to my race or gender," she continued. "As a result, not only was I deprived of supports that would have been helpful, I was misunderstood and — at times — mistreated."

REMEMBER

The additional hurdles autistic people of color face don't come from their autism, cultural background, or race. They stem instead from misunderstanding, bias, and exclusion. While unfair, many find that having to navigate these obstacles also builds unique perspectives and strengths.

"Being Black and autistic means navigating a world that often misunderstands both," said Finn Gardiner on a 2023 episode of the *Noncompliant* podcast. While it can be tough to face these misunderstandings, Gardiner notes they also create resilience and a distinctive way of seeing the world. "It's a double-edged sword, but it's also a source of strength."

Ensuring accurate media coverage

A lack of accurate media representation worsens barriers for autistic people of color. Media portrayals often focus on white, male individuals, excluding much of the autistic population and reinforcing harmful ideas.

"People often say to me, 'You don't look autistic!'" says Rian Phin. "But that's because your perception of what you think autism looks like is wrong."

Phin, a Black creative who has been featured in *Interview* magazine and *Vogue*, highlights how narrow portrayals of autism can mislead people and make it harder for undiagnosed autistic individuals to recognize themselves. "Think about it. How many autistic people who look like me have you seen in the media?"

Media should reflect the diversity of autistic experiences, which is why autistic novelist Helen Hoang decided to include an autistic, Vietnamese American heroine in her book *The Kiss Quotient*. Seeing yourself represented in media can be powerful, especially for those who feel pushed to hide their autistic traits. "Women are under more social pressure to conform so even if we're on the spectrum, we're pushed to the max to fit in," Hoang told *NBC News* in 2018.

"I wouldn't have known I was autistic. Being a Black, African, refugee settled in Adelaide, topics like autism and ADHD aren't even spoken about," human rights activist Khadija Gbla told *The Advertiser*, an Australian newspaper. "I was diagnosed with autism at 34, but looking back, the signs were there in my childhood — the struggles, the brilliance, and the loneliness."

Because so many individuals and families feel unseen, some have started creating their own materials to make sure their experiences are understood.

"I didn't see that many resources or information that looked like me or my child," Dr. Rachel Francis told *Reckon* in 2022. "I wanted other African American people to see us and our journey, so they know that we are not alone."

Inspired by her nonspeaking son and the needs of others, Francis created *See Me Through My ABCs*, a picture book offering culturally relatable, easy-to-understand information for children and families.

Improving representation starts with simple, meaningful actions: reporting diverse autistic experiences in the news, bringing autistic voices into writers' rooms, and casting autistic actors authentically (see Chapter 22). This expands the understanding of autism and empowers autistic creators to tell their own stories.

"I was safe to be myself," actor Sue Anne Pien said in a 2024 *Variety* roundtable, reflecting on her experience on *As We See It*. The show's supportive environment featuring autistic actors, writers, and directors allowed her to feel professionally accepted as an autistic actor. "I'm not weird or out of place or I don't belong in this world — I fit right in here."

Finding joy in identity and yourself

For many, embracing both autism and cultural identity instills both joy and pride. It helps them feel like their true, complete selves in ways that aren't always seen.

Jen White-Johnson, an Afro-Latina artist and advocate, coined the term *autistic joy* after seeing her son Knox celebrate his unique traits with pure happiness.

"I started to recognize how uncomfortable I was with the way that Black and Brown disabled folks and neurodivergent folks are viewed in the media, in visual culture, in the school system," White-Johnson told the *Disability & Philanthropy Forum* in 2023. "I started to get really uncomfortable with how much joy was left out of the conversation."

Inspired by Knox, White-Johnson used her design skills to create stickers, posters, and media celebrating autistic and disabled joy. Her work quickly resonated with autistic adults and parents alike, sparking a growing movement of positivity through the hashtag #AutisticJoy.

Parenting Autistic Kids

Parenting an autistic child is a journey filled with challenges, surprises, and growth — both for you and your child. It begins with believing in their potential and trusting your instincts as a parent.

Presuming competence in your child

Supporting an autistic child can feel like uncharted territory, but it doesn't have to be overwhelming. The most important thing you can do is start with a mindset of belief — in your child's abilities, potential, and your capacity as a parent.

"We don't normally define people by what they are not," writes autistic teacher Evaleen Whelton on LinkedIn. "We usually define people by who they are."

Presuming competence means recognizing that autistic children are just as capable of learning, thinking, and feeling as anyone else. It's about setting high expectations, providing meaningful support, and creating an environment where they can grow.

Assume that kids are capable

While some might think presuming competence applies only to those with fewer support needs, it's "most important for the kids who really do have intellectual disabilities, who really can't read or use full sentences and who really do need extensive support," writes Julia Bascomb in her 2019 essay *Dangerous Assumptions*.

Assuming a child is capable, even if they need significant support, encourages their growth and gives them opportunities to showcase their abilities in their own way. Without this mindset, their ability to show what they can do is often overlooked.

"Challenge my mind," writes Patrick Saunders, a nonspeaking autistic individual, in his blog *The Story Speller.* "Challenge my body. Challenge yourself, your opinions, your preconceptions of me. Challenge me."

Believe in yourself, too

Presuming competence doesn't stop with children — it also applies to parents. "Also presume competence in yourself," writes Whelton. "I see sometimes how quickly parents become disempowered after the child receives a diagnosis. They get advice from so many different people that it's easy to lose faith in your own abilities. Trust your own instincts too, have faith in your own parenting abilities."

Building connections

"It can get overwhelming," Caroline Ndebu told *NPR* in 2024. "Some days are tough, and others are easy." As a mother of two autistic kids, Ndebu found support and reassurance by connecting with other families through a WhatsApp group.

Building connections with others who understand your experiences can boost your confidence as a caregiver and help you see strengths in yourself and your child.

"We encourage each other, especially if one of us has had an overwhelming day," said Ndebu. The online support she received from other families inspired her to create Gifted Gems, a group dedicated to providing caregivers across Kenya with vital resources, meaningful connections, and valuable information.

Planning for possibilities

When raising an autistic child, it's natural to feel overwhelmed by the unknown. But focusing on what's in front of you can better prepare you for days ahead.

"No one expects one person to change the entire world," writes autistic advocate Lei Wiley-Mydske in *Sincerely, Your Autistic Child*. "What you can do is change your world. You can give your child the tools to be a strong self-advocate. You can give your child an example of a true ally by changing the conversation about autism and disability in your own lives and homes."

Learning from your kids

Parents often find they learn as much from their children as their children learn from them. For parents of autistic kids, this can mean discovering how to interpret subtle forms of communication, finding creative ways to support their child's interests, and learning to be flexible in daily routines and unexpected situations.

For William Butchart, understanding his autistic children's communication styles helped him recognize his own autistic traits. "I realized I had autism when my children were diagnosed," the church minister told *BBC Scotland* in 2025.

Noticing the differences in autistic traits between his nonspeaking son and his speaking daughter showed him how autism can look different for everyone — including himself. "Once I started to learn what autism actually was, it began to chime more and more with me."

This led to Butchart's own diagnosis and participation in a program run by the autistic-led Scottish group Autistic Knowledge Development. There, he gained a deeper understanding of his traits and practical strategies for daily life — insights he might never have found without the lessons first learned from his autistic kids.

Helping your child accept who they are

It's natural to worry about your child's feelings about their diagnosis. But helping them understand their autism can be one of the most empowering things you do.

"Children should know about their diagnosis so they can develop a sense of identity," writes Jenna Gensic on the website *Learn from Autistics*. "All children deserve to know who they are, and understanding autism is essential to that discovery."

When autistic children understand their diagnosis, they can better make sense of their experiences and feel less alone. This understanding can boost their confidence and help them embrace who they are.

"I wish more people understood that autism diagnoses literally save lives," writes Trevor Carroll on Instagram. "Before I knew I was on the spectrum, I felt so much shame and confusion. There were points in my life where I didn't want to exist anymore."

Knowing their diagnosis can help children accept themselves and understand the world around them. "Now I have a better understanding of how my brain works," writes Carroll. "I can accommodate myself better. And most importantly, I can practice accepting and loving even the most difficult parts of myself."

Living as an Autistic Adult

As with any human experience, living as an autistic adult comes with its own challenges, discoveries, and rewards. Navigating a world that often misunderstands your needs can be tough, but it's also a chance for growth. It's about figuring out what works for you and finding your place.

Understanding your autistic traits

Discovering and accepting your autistic traits can be transformative. Recognizing your unique characteristics — whether in childhood or later in life — can bring clarity and empower you to navigate challenges while embracing your strengths.

"My autism was missed in childhood," wrote Amelie Geiss in a 2025 piece for the *Australian Broadcasting Corporation*, explaining how her meltdowns from sensory overload were dismissed by teachers as tantrums. Things began to change, however, when she was diagnosed with autism at age 18.

"Once I understood why I was so sensitive to sound in my environment, I could start to accommodate myself," says Geiss. "I began wearing noise-cancelling headphones and high-fidelity earplugs in public spaces that were previously too loud for me to comfortably navigate."

Learning from other autistic people

Autistic people often discover practical strategies — like Geiss's noise-cancelling headphones — by learning from each other and sharing experiences and tips.

"A lot of people think routines need to be rigid in order for them to work, but that's not true," says Tyla Grant in a 2025 YouTube video. She encourages tailoring routines to your energy levels instead of sticking to rigid schedules. "If in the morning you're actually full of energy, maybe that's not the time you want to meditate," she explains, suggesting activities like exercise might better suit high-energy periods.

Grant also suggests other ways to make routines more flexible, like tidying during a lunch break instead of after a tiring day or adjusting social plans for recharge time. (Read more on "alone time" in Chapter 4.) "The easiest way to build a routine that works for you is to focus on flexibility," she concludes.

While these tips may seem straightforward, they reflect how much autistic people aren't taught about the autistic experience — as kids or as adults. To bridge this knowledge gap, autistic individuals share personal strategies, trading insights to support each other. This makes connecting with other autistic people an essential life skill. (See Chapter 1 for more.)

Connecting with others

Navigating relationships as an autistic adult can be rewarding but not always easy. Understanding your needs and boundaries helps. Relationships don't have to look the same for everyone. Find connections that work for you and bring joy.

Understanding challenges

People often misunderstand how autistic individuals connect — like bonding over shared interests or deep conversations instead of small talk. These differences can be mistaken for rudeness, disinterest, or being "odd," leading to exclusion.

"I feel that we autistic people actually often fall into a kind of 'uncanny valley' as far as neurotypical people are concerned," writes Pete Wharmby in a 2025 Facebook post. "We behave in a slightly different way, our expressions are a bit different, our tone a little 'off' — as a result non-autistic people respond to us with fear and confusion: we are not what they expect, we don't act like they're used to, and they react in this extreme way."

Despite misunderstandings, autistic people do form meaningful connections with neurotypical people, often through shared passions and mutual respect. This can lead to deeply rewarding relationships.

However, even when connections form, autistic people may face the challenge of being accidentally cast by neurotypical acquaintances as a "magical" friend — praised for their authenticity, talents, unique insights, or blunt honesty and advice. While these traits may be deeply appreciated, autistic individuals are often unconsciously treated as highly valued exceptions in social circles rather than as ordinary equals among friends.

Another challenge many autistic adults face is being left out of group texts or activities — even by close friends.

"I often feel like a dog at a garden party," says one autistic adult, who asked not to be named. "If I unexpectedly show up at a social gathering, people are excited to see me, glad that I'm there, and I can tell they love having me around. But as much as you might enjoy the surprise of having a dog at a party, you never think to text the dog to see how it's doing. You don't call up a dog and ask it to hang out."

This happens when neurotypical friends assume autistic people aren't interested or prefer to be alone. Fast-paced conversations and unspoken cues can also make socializing harder. Even if unintentional, exclusion is hurtful and deepens isolation.

Addressing social isolation and loneliness

Famed Japanese writer Osamu Dazai opens his 1948 semi-autobiographical novel *A Failed Human* (often translated as *No Longer Human*) by detailing two things: the excitement he felt as a child upon seeing his first train and the lifetime of loneliness that followed due to a struggle to connect with others.

"Mine has been a life of much shame," writes Dazai in the first paragraph. "I can't even guess what it must be to live the life of a human being."

Although we can't retroactively diagnose people from the past, scholars often note the autistic traits displayed by historical figures (Chapter 2). Among them is Dazai, whose stories feature characters whose neurodivergent traits and social isolation closely reflected his own.

REMEMBER

Like Dazai, many autistic people today face isolation — not due to who they are, but how society responds.

"Many of us are lonely people, and that loneliness affects our lives and the ways we experience the world," says Chris Williams, diagnosed as autistic at 36 after his nonspeaking daughter's diagnosis. "Being diagnosed helped me recognize the patterns of disconnection and isolation in my life — and how many other neuro-divergent people face the same struggles."

Respecting yourself

Loneliness isn't an inherent part of being autistic — it's shaped by misunder-standings and societal barriers, but it doesn't have to be permanent.

Focus on forming relationships with people who appreciate you for who you are. Building friendships based on mutual respect can help you feel valued and reduce feelings of isolation.

"When I meet people, I try to tell them that I'm autistic and part of an autistic family if I get the chance," says Williams. "Often, they'll share their own experi-ences in return. These conversations create shared moments and connections, and some have even led to lasting friendships."

Appreciating different types of connections

One of the best ways for autistic adults to feel understood is by connecting with other autistic people. These friendships create a sense of belonging by allowing people to be themselves without pressure to mask or conform.

"The first time I was in a room full of autistic adults, I was overwhelmed with both longing and joy," says Williams. "Being around people who embraced their autistic identity and weren't trying to hide it felt like finding a long-lost family I didn't know I had."

Connecting with neurotypical people can also lead to meaningful friendships. Bridging communication or social differences can take effort, but being upfront about your needs and finding shared interests can help.

TIP

If you're neurotypical and want to connect with an autistic person, try reaching out regularly and directly — it makes a big difference.

"Friendship is about understanding," writes artist Chloé Hayden on Instagram. "Being autistic means I've learned to treasure those who take the time to truly know me."

REMEMBER

While our social styles may vary, our differences should never make us feel, as Dazai did, like "a failed human."

Being yourself

You don't have to represent all autistic people. Your experiences are uniquely yours. Sharing your perspective helps others understand, but no one speaks for everyone, and that's okay.

"All we can ever do is speak for ourselves," says Saudi-born autistic novelist Natasha Burge in a 2025 interview with the Arab News. "Individual authors can't speak on behalf of every single person in an entire culture or place," she says, adding that autistic people shouldn't be expected to represent the entire autistic community either.

7

The Part of Tens

Discover ten key concepts to deepen your understanding, acceptance, and support for autistic individuals.

Explore ten practical strategies to help autistic people thrive and foster inclusive, empowering relationships.

Chapter **24**

Ten Key Concepts About Autism

Understanding autism is about more than just knowing the basics. It's about embracing the many ways autistic people think, learn, and connect with the world. This chapter breaks down ten key concepts that can help you better understand, accept, and support the autistic individuals in your life.

Autism Is a Natural Part of Life

Autism isn't an illness or something that needs to be "fixed" or "cured." It's a natural variation in the way people think, learn, and interact with the world. Autistic children grow up to be autistic adults, and their autistic traits continue to shape who they are throughout life. Autistic people bring unique perspectives and strengths that can be powerful sources of creativity, insight, and problem-solving. Recognizing autism as part of the rich diversity of human experience helps shift the conversation from being focused on "fixing" differences to accepting and supporting them.

That said, acknowledging autism as a natural part of who someone is doesn't mean ignoring the challenges or barriers autistic individuals may face with sensory processing, communication, or navigating social situations. Acceptance isn't about pretending these difficulties don't exist. It's about recognizing them as part of the whole picture and working together to find the best ways to support the autistic person's growth and well-being.

When we view autism as part of human diversity, it helps create a world where differences are valued, not just tolerated. This approach shifts our focus from trying to change an autistic person to fit into a narrow definition of "normal" to finding ways to adapt environments and support systems so they can thrive as they are. It's about empowering them to use their strengths, find their voice, and build confidence without feeling pressured to be someone they're not.

Understanding that autism is a natural and normal variation enriches families, schools, and communities. It encourages an attitude of support and acceptance, where challenges are addressed with empathy and creativity and strengths are celebrated. This perspective helps build a more inclusive world, where autistic people feel respected, supported, and ready to share their unique gifts.

Every Autistic Person Is Unique

The saying goes, "If you've met one autistic person, you've met one autistic person." This reminds us that while there may be some common characteristics, every autistic individual is unique. Some may love routines and find comfort in predictability, whereas others are more flexible. Some might talk a lot, and others may not speak using words but communicate in other ways. Understanding that each person has their own strengths, challenges, and preferences is key to creating supportive and personalized environments.

REMEMBER

An autistic person may present with many obvious autistic traits while another person's autistic traits might be less noticeable to you. Regardless, autistic people often share many of the same challenges, strengths, and life experiences. Recognizing this shared thread helps build understanding and respect.

WARNING

All autistic people, regardless of whether they are speaking, nonspeaking, minimally speaking, need minimal support or varied and extensive supports deserve to be valued, included, and treated as normal human beings — because they are. Their needs may be different, but their worth is the same. They should have access to accommodations and support that allow them to live full, meaningful lives. This means communication tools like augmentative and alternative communication (AAC) devices, tailored education programs, accessible housing, and healthcare designed with their needs in mind.

When we acknowledge the individuality of each autistic person — their strengths, challenges, and experiences — it helps us connect and respect one another as equals. Whether we communicate differently, move differently, or experience the world in unique ways, seeing each other as individuals builds a more inclusive and supportive world for everyone.

Acceptance Is Better Than "Fitting In"

One of the most important things to understand about supporting an autistic person is that acceptance matters far more than trying to make an autistic person fit into a mold. True acceptance means seeing and valuing someone for who they really are, not trying to change them so they match what society considers "normal." When we focus on helping autistic people be themselves, rather than asking them to mask or hide parts of who they are to blend in, we create an environment where they feel safe and valued.

Masking, or pretending to be someone they're not just to fit in, can be exhausting and even harmful for autistic people. It can lead to stress, anxiety, and feeling disconnected from their true selves. By embracing their natural ways of communicating, playing, learning, or interacting, we allow them to grow with confidence and authenticity. This doesn't just benefit autistic individuals. It also enriches families, schools, and communities by bringing in diverse ways of thinking and problem-solving.

Parents, teachers, and communities play a huge role in creating spaces where acceptance is the norm. This means understanding that different isn't less; it's just different. It's about creating a world where autistic children and adults don't feel pressured to act a certain way to be liked or included but are welcomed for who they truly are. This support can make all the difference in how they see themselves and their place in the world.

When we value people for their unique traits and support them in expressing those traits freely, it opens the door for them to contribute their unique perspectives. Authentic voices bring fresh ideas and approaches to everything from school projects to friendships to careers. That benefits everyone. Acceptance leads to stronger, more inclusive communities where everyone has the chance to be seen, heard, and appreciated for who they are.

REMEMBER

In the end, acceptance isn't a gift to only the autistic person; it's a gift to everyone. It teaches empathy, flexibility, and a deeper understanding of what it means to be human. Supporting someone in being their true self creates a world where differences are not just tolerated but truly celebrated and where everyone can find their place without needing to change who they are.

Communication Can Happen Through Various Means

Many autistic people use spoken language to communicate, but not everyone does, and that's perfectly okay. Communication includes more than spoken words. It's about connecting and understanding one another. Some autistic individuals use sign language, picture boards, or communication devices to express themselves. Others may communicate by speaking but in ways that look different from what most people expect.

Additionally, some autistic people might use unique speech patterns, like speaking very softly or very loudly, using various intonations including a monotone voice, scripting (repeating phrases or lines from movies), speaking in a highly detailed or literal way, or taking more time to find the right words. All of this is valid and part of how they share their thoughts and feelings.

REMEMBER

The most important thing is finding and supporting the communication methods that work best for each individual. When you embrace their method — whether it's spoken words, gestures, or technology — you're showing them that their voice matters, even if it doesn't sound the way we might expect.

When we adapt how we communicate to connect better with an autistic person, we're creating a space where they feel understood and respected. This can mean using a communication app, offering extra time to respond, or using direct language to make conversations clearer. Supporting how someone prefers to communicate can make everyday life and interactions more comfortable and fulfilling.

This approach builds trust and reduces frustration, making connections stronger. It helps autistic individuals express themselves confidently, knowing their way of communicating is appreciated and respected. By recognizing and supporting these different forms of communication, you can create a more inclusive and understanding world.

Socialization May Look Different

Autistic people socialize, but they may do so in ways that are different than you're used to. These ways might not fit the usual expectations of social interaction, but they're just as valid. Understanding how autistic individuals connect with others helps create environments where they can thrive and form genuine friendships.

Socialization in autistic children

For many autistic children, socializing can mean parallel play — playing next to another child rather than directly with them. This type of interaction isn't a sign of disinterest; it's simply how they feel comfortable engaging. Some kids might enjoy activities where they can focus on a shared interest, like building with connecting blocks or talking about dinosaurs. Structured activities that align with their passions can be a great way for autistic children to connect with peers in a way that feels natural.

REMEMBER

It's also common for autistic children to have a need to take breaks from social situations to recharge. Large groups or extended social interactions can be overwhelming, so allowing space for quiet time or individual activities can help them manage their energy and enjoy being part of a group on their own terms. Supporting their way of socializing encourages confidence and helps them feel accepted for who they are.

Socialization in autistic adults

For autistic adults, social interactions might mean connecting through deep, focused conversations about shared interests or spending time together in quiet, low-pressure settings. They may prefer small gatherings over large social events and may need time to process social experiences after they happen. Some adults may choose to engage in online communities where they can communicate in a controlled environment that feels comfortable to them.

REMEMBER

These preferences don't mean autistic adults don't value friendship or connection; they simply seek it in ways that align with how they experience the world. Respecting these preferences and being flexible in how social interactions are structured can lead to strong, meaningful relationships that are built on mutual understanding and shared interests.

The benefits of autistic friendship

Friendships between autistic and neurotypical individuals can be rewarding for both sides. Neurotypical children and adults who befriend autistic peers learn to appreciate different perspectives and develop empathy and flexibility. Autistic friends often bring fresh insights, unique problem-solving skills, and deep loyalty to their relationships. Their passion for specific topics can be contagious, sparking curiosity and shared enthusiasm.

Encouraging social connections

Encouraging friendships for autistic individuals starts with asking them how they prefer to connect and respecting their choices. You can try organizing small, interest-based groups for children or creating opportunities for adults to meet in low-stimulation settings. Helping autistic people socialize in ways that work for them leads to real, meaningful connections. Respecting breaks, adapting conversations, and valuing shared activities can make social interactions more enjoyable for everyone involved. Ultimately, understanding that socialization looks different for autistic people — and that it's just as meaningful — helps create a world where they feel valued and included.

Autistic People Think in Unique Ways

Autistic people often think and process information in ways that are different from what most people expect, and that's not a bad thing. These differences can be powerful strengths that contribute fresh ideas and new perspectives. For example, some autistic individuals are excellent at noticing details that others might miss, finding patterns, or thinking outside the box when it comes to problem-solving. Their minds may work in a more visual or logical way, leading to creative solutions or deep expertise in specific areas of interest.

However, these differences can sometimes mean that learning and communication might not follow the typical path. An autistic child may take longer to answer questions because they're thinking deeply or processing language in a different way. They might jump from one idea to another, make connections that seem unrelated at first, or approach a problem from an unexpected angle. While this may be misunderstood as being off-topic or distracted, it's often a sign of how uniquely their mind works to see the bigger picture or details others don't notice.

These cognitive differences can be challenging, too. Switching between tasks or adapting to new routines can be difficult because autistic people often thrive on familiarity and focus. But with understanding and support, these challenges can be managed, so the strengths shine through.

REMEMBER

When we recognize and embrace these differences, we create space for autistic people to bring their whole selves to the table. This understanding encourages not just acceptance but true appreciation for the unique ways autistic individuals think, learn, and contribute. It's a reminder that there's no one right way to process the world, and that diversity in thinking is something to celebrate.

Sensory Experiences Can Be Vivid

Autistic people often have unique sensory experiences that make the world feel more vivid or intense. Sounds might seem louder, lights brighter, or certain textures more noticeable. While these sensory differences can be challenging at times, they can also be sources of joy and fascination. For example, an autistic person might feel deep satisfaction in the softness of a blanket, the rhythm of music, or the patterns of light and color.

REMEMBER

Sensory needs can shift based on the situation or even from day to day. A bustling park might be an exciting adventure one day and too much to handle the next.

Understanding these experiences helps create supportive environments where autistic people feel comfortable. Simple changes — like noise-canceling headphones, dimmed lights, or quiet spaces — can make a big difference. Fidget toys or weighted blankets can help those who seek sensory input feel more centered. Supporting these needs isn't just about reducing discomfort; it's about embracing the positive, allowing autistic individuals to engage with the world in their own way and find moments of wonder and connection.

Intense Interests Are Strengths

Many autistic people have deep, focused interests in specific topics, sometimes called "special interests." These interests can be powerful tools for learning, building skills, and finding joy. They might range from trains to coding to art, and supporting these passions can lead to significant growth. Embracing these interests shows that what excites them is valuable and worth exploring. Plus, these interests can create opportunities for social interaction, community, and career.

Stimming Is Normal and Important

Stimming refers to self-stimulatory behaviors like hand-flapping, rocking, or repeating certain phrases. While it might look unusual to those who don't understand it, stimming is often a way for autistic people to regulate their emotions, manage sensory input, or simply express happiness. It's important to allow stimming when it's safe and not overly disruptive to others. Recognizing that stimming is a natural and helpful behavior can make environments more accepting and comfortable for autistic individuals.

Routine and Predictability Are Comforting

For many autistic people, routine is more than just a preference; it's a source of stability and security. Knowing what to expect can make navigating the day easier and reduce anxiety. Find ways to engage autistic children and adults in creating their own routines. Sudden changes or unpredictable events can be stressful. Giving advance notice, providing additional support for creating and following a new routine or creating visual schedules can help make transitions smoother. Supporting routines isn't about being rigid; it's about understanding what makes an individual feel safe and comfortable.

as normal

» **Practicing compassionate curiosity and providing clear support**

» **Including autistic people**

Chapter **25**

Ten Ways to Help Autistic People Thrive

Helping autistic people thrive isn't about changing who they are; it's about creating an environment where they feel supported and understood. Autistic people bring unique strengths and perspectives, and with the right support, they can flourish as their true selves. In this chapter, we explore ten practical ways to help autistic people thrive, empowering them while building stronger, more inclusive relationships. Let's get started!

Embrace Neurodiversity

Neurodiversity recognizes that differences like autism, ADHD, and dyslexia are natural variations of the human brain. They aren't deficits. Embracing neurodiversity means valuing these differences and creating environments where everyone can thrive.

REMEMBER

You don't need to know everything about someone's neurotype to help. Start by accepting them as they are, including them in activities, and asking how to support them. A little understanding and openness can build trust and show you care.

Learning about neurodivergent conditions fosters more inclusive classrooms, workplaces, and communities. By being informed and supportive, you can help autistic people and their families feel respected, valued, and empowered.

Understand Autistic People as Normal

Autistic people are a natural part of human diversity. Autism isn't something to "fix," and autistic people aren't deficient versions of others — they're fully themselves. Autism is one of many ways humans experience and interact with the world. Recognizing autistic people as normal means understanding that they, like everyone else, have unique strengths and challenges.

WARNING

This doesn't mean ignoring the real difficulties of being autistic. Challenges like sensory sensitivities, communication differences, or specific routines are real, but all humans face challenges of some sort. Autism is simply another way of being.

REMEMBER

By recognizing autistic people as normal, we move away from trying to "fix" them and begin to see autistic people for who they are. It shifts our focus toward creating environments that embrace, accommodate, and support autistic people.

Center Autistic Voices

To help autistic people thrive, the most important thing you can do is listen to them. Autistic voices provide the clearest insight into what works, what doesn't, and what support looks like from their perspective. Centering these voices benefits not only autistic individuals but also parents and caregivers, offering valuable guidance for more effective and compassionate support.

Why it matters

Every autistic person's experience is unique. Listening to a diversity of voices helps us see that autism isn't a single uniform experience. Including a range of perspectives ensures we're not overlooking anyone, especially those who face the greatest barriers to being heard.

Centering autistic voices moves the focus away from outdated ideas of what they "should" be and toward understanding who they actually are. Their insights reveal real challenges and practical solutions, not assumptions.

How it helps parents and caregivers

For parents and caregivers, listening to autistic voices can be transformative. Hearing directly from autistic people — especially those with similar experiences to their loved one — offers new perspectives, practical advice, and validation.

For instance, a parent of a nonspeaking autistic child might learn from an adult AAC user about the importance of communication opportunities. A caregiver of someone who needs additional supports might gain insights into advocating for routines or sensory-friendly spaces. These lessons empower caregivers to provide deeper support.

Practice Compassionate Curiosity

Compassionate curiosity is a powerful way to support autistic people. When you demonstrate compassionate curiosity, you ask thoughtful questions and listen with empathy, aiming to understand others' experiences and challenges without judgment.

REMEMBER

Compassionate curiosity combines two essential elements:

>> **Compassion:** Showing kindness and empathy by respecting someone's experiences and emotions without dismissing or invalidating them.

>> **Curiosity:** Being open to learning by asking questions and listening with genuine interest instead of making assumptions.

Together, compassion and curiosity create powerful tools for building trust, reducing misunderstandings, and strengthening relationships.

Provide Clear and Consistent Support

Clear and consistent support helps autistic people feel secure and empowered. Predictability reduces stress and makes navigating the world easier. Being reliable and clear makes a big difference whether you're interacting with a child or an adult.

Supporting autistic children

Children thrive when they know what to expect. Consistency and clarity in routines helps them feel safe and confident. Here are some examples:

- **Clear instructions:** Break tasks into small steps. For example, say, "First, pick up the blocks and put them in the bin. Then put the cars on the shelf."

- **Explaining changes:** If routines need to shift, give a heads-up. For instance, say "Today, we're going to Grandma's house after school instead of going home, but you'll still have time to play after dinner."

- **Visual schedules:** Use pictures to outline routines, like brushing teeth or getting dressed, to make mornings less overwhelming.

Supporting autistic adults

Clarity and consistency are just as important for adults, whether as a friend, coworker, partner, or someone you're supporting.

- **At work:** Instead of vague requests like "Can you take care of this?" give clear instructions like, "Please send me the meeting notes by noon on Friday."

- **In friendships:** Be specific about plans, such as, "Let's meet at 2:00 p.m. on Saturday at the coffee shop on Main Street."

- **In romantic relationships:** Planning regular date nights, like "Let's pick Fridays for our dates so we both know what to expect," helps build trust and reduces stress.

- **Directly supporting an autistic adult:** Break tasks into clear steps. For instance, "First, take the bread out of the bag. Next, spread peanut butter on one slice. Then add jelly."

REMEMBER

Predictability and clarity create a sense of control in a world that can feel overwhelming, as does demonstrating consistent support.

Foster Independence

Independence looks different for everyone, and that's okay. For one autistic person, it might mean living on their own. For another, it might mean expressing preferences, making small choices, or participating in routines with support.

Independence isn't about doing everything alone. It's about having a say in your own life.

For autistic children

Helping children practice independence starts with small, achievable steps:

>> **Making choices:** At mealtime, you could ask, "Would you like the blue cup or the red cup?" This simple decision helps them practice making choices in a safe, low-pressure way.

>> **Practicing daily skills:** For a child learning to dress, you might lay out two outfits and ask, "Which one do you want to wear?" Breaking the task into steps, like starting with socks, makes it manageable while boosting confidence.

>> **Taking responsibility:** Encouraging a small task, like watering plants, builds a sense of pride.

REMEMBER

Children who have difficulties with these tasks can and should be taught independence, with the presumption of competence. Give them opportunities to make choices, like using an AAC device to express what they want to eat or do. This reinforces their right to have control over their lives, even with extra support, and builds confidence along the way.

For autistic adults

For autistic adults, fostering independence means respecting their preferences and supporting them in navigating life in ways that work for them.

>> **At work:** If an autistic coworker prefers structure, you might say, "Would you like to take on Task A or Task B first? Either works for me." Giving them control over how they approach their work allows them to feel more in charge of their tasks.

>> **Managing daily life:** Building independence might involve learning to grocery shop with a visual list or practicing public transportation routes. Providing guidance while letting them take the lead helps build confidence and practical skills.

For adults who do not live on their own and need additional supports, independence might mean choosing their outfit with help, deciding what music to listen to, or expressing how they want to spend time through gestures or an AAC device. Supporting these choices respects their preferences and empowers them to feel more in control of their daily life.

Reduce Barriers That People Face

Finding reliable information and accessing support can feel like navigating an obstacle course for families of autistic children and autistic adults. Confusing systems, long waitlists, and unclear guidance add stress. Anything we do to simplify these processes can make a big difference.

For families, sharing resources, forming support groups, and hosting workshops on school accommodations or assistive tools can be a big help. And advocating for accessible services and reducing barriers like sensory-unfriendly spaces or poor communication in workplaces and healthcare helps autistic adults thrive and eases stress for caregivers

By advocating for better services, promoting inclusion, and simplifying access to resources, we can remove unnecessary hurdles and help autistic individuals and families focus on what truly matters: thriving.

Include Autistic People in Activities

Including autistic people in activities is about being intentional. It's not just about inviting them; it's about making sure they can participate and feel part of the group.

Make participation comfortable by offering clear instructions instead of vague ones. For example, say, "Here's what you do, and we'll take turns," rather than, "Just follow along." Be flexible by offering alternatives if the activity feels overwhelming, like helping to organize or taking a quieter role. Let them know it's okay to take a break and rejoin when they're ready, so they feel included on their own terms.

Including someone intentionally means paying attention to their needs and making adjustments so they can participate in ways that feel right for them.

Respect Boundaries

Boundaries are essential for everyone's well-being, especially for autistic people. If they say "no" to something overwhelming or unsafe — like a loud event or a difficult topic — it's important to listen and respect that. Honoring boundaries builds trust.

For example, if a coworker declines a crowded lunch outing, respecting their choice without pressure shows you care. Or if a friend needs a quiet moment during a conversation, giving them that space helps them feel safe and understood.

REMEMBER

Helping autistic people establish and maintain boundaries protects their well-being, but it also empowers them to navigate the world on their own terms.

Provide Tools for Self-Advocacy

Self-advocacy helps autistic people express their needs and take charge of their lives. The goal is to build their confidence and independence to help them manage things like asking for support at school, requesting workplace accommodations, or setting boundaries in relationships. Clear communication is crucial. Teach simple phrases like, "I need a break," or help them practice using AAC or gestures to express discomfort or needs. It's also important they understand their rights, like requesting accommodations.

REMEMBER

By providing tools for self-advocacy, you empower autistic people to be heard, respected, and included, helping them thrive and build stronger relationships.

Index

C

calming spaces, 291

career. *See* work and career growth

career centers, 227

caregivers, 14

  and centering autistic voices, 386–387

  connecting with autistic adults, 131

  connecting with other, 131

  early diagnosis and role of, 46–47

  finding respite care and support, 129–131

  routines, 131

  self-care for, 129–131

  working with educators, 296–297

  working with medical professionals, 280–281

Carey, Matt, 361

Carroll, Trevor, 369

centering autistic voices, 324–325, 357–359, 386–387

Centers for Independent Living (CILs), 133–134

cerebellum, 24

Chabria, Khushboo (author/neurodiversity specialist), 16

CHD8 gene, 18

check-ins, 230, 318

childhood disintegrative disorder (CDD), 27

children, autistic. *See also* autistic people

  actively listening to, 89–90

  adapting sensory needs of, 92

  building trust and rapport with, 90–91

  communicating clearly with, 91

  communicating sensory needs, 104

  communicating with, 81–82

  fostering independence in, 389

  helping child to communicate, 88–89

  overview, 81

  providing consistency and reliability to, 90

  recognizing early signs of differences in, 83–84

  seeking professional support for, 93–94

  sensory strengths, 102, 103–104

  socialization in, 380

  supporting, 388

  teaching sensory regulation skills to, 102–103

children with complex needs. *See also* autistic people with complex needs

  achievements and progress of, 122

  celebrating strengths of, 121–122

  choosing right educational settings for, 126–127

  compassion in care of, 120

  developing daily living skills of, 122–124

  health and medical care of, 127–129

  individualized education programs for, 125–126

  planning for future of, 132–136

  raising, 119–137

Chinese Classification of Mental Disorders (CCMD), 44

civic calling, 266–267

classic autism, 30–31

classroom accommodations, 125. *See also* accommodations; inclusive classrooms

classroom aides, 157

client meetings, 230

cognition, 197–199

cognitive flexibility, 64

cognitive skills

  creative and abstract thinking, 147–149

  executive functioning, 143–146

  flexible thinking, 147

  learning styles and, 142–144

  overview, 141–142

  problem-solving skills, 146–147

collaboration

  conflict resolution in, 331–332

  dialogue and, 329

  effective, 329–332

  in inclusive workspaces, 318

  open and effective communication in, 329

  overcoming misunderstandings in, 329–330

  with service providers, 276–277

  shared/common goals in, 330–332

  in special education services, 160

  turning differences into positive outcomes, 331

  understanding need for, 326–327

colleges, 214–215, 299

color commentaries, 341

communication

  alternative methods, 70

  assertive, 235, 237

  in autistic adults, 200–201

  body language, 71

  in collaboration, 329

About the Authors

John Marble, Khushboo Chabria, and **Ranga Jayaraman** are co-authors of the book *Neurodiversity for Dummies*.

John Marble is the founder of Pivot Neurodiversity, an organization empowering companies to modernize recruitment, hiring, and culture to better support neurodivergent employees. He is also a classroom instructor and training partner with Neurodiversity Pathways. A writer and speaker on innovation, workplace culture, and neurodiversity, he has served as an advisor to various policymakers and as an aide to two U.S. presidents. In 2009, he was appointed by President Obama to serve in the United States Office of Personnel Management, where he became the first openly autistic presidential staff member in American history.

Multiply neurodivergent, John credits his ADHD, autism, and dyscalculia as gifting him with a curiosity and passion to understand the world around him. This has led him to build a career centered on understanding and valuing the diverse perspectives and experiences of others. His ability to see various viewpoints proved particularly beneficial in the often-divided world of politics, allowing him to develop solutions that were inclusive and effective for everyone. John brings this same approach to his work as a teacher, consultant, public speaker, and visual artist. He is committed to promoting neurodiversity in a way that fosters mutual understanding among everyone involved, ensuring that neurodivergent people, parents, and allies are heard, empowered, and understood.

Khushboo Chabria is a neurodiversity specialist and transformational leader on a mission to advocate for and help improve access to high-quality support services for neurodivergent individuals. Khushboo is a program manager, career coach, and speaker focused on educating and supporting neurodivergent individuals to help launch their career and supporting organizations to integrate neurodivergent employees into the workplace through belonging and empowerment at the Neurodiversity Pathways program of Goodwill of Silicon Valley. Its tagline is "Inclusion for Abilities and Acceptance of Differences," and the program's mission is to inspire and improve the intentional inclusion of neurodistinct individuals in the workplace.

Khushboo also sits on the board of Peaces of Me Foundation and is involved in consulting, writing, and professionally speaking on the topics of neurodiversity, DEIB, leadership, psychological safety, mental health, and coaching. With varied experiences in supporting neurodivergent individuals of all ages and their family members, working as a therapist and clinician, studying organizational leadership, and discovering her own ADHD, Khushboo brings an interesting mix of skills and experiences to this field of work. Khushboo aims to make a meaningful impact in the world through education, empowerment, authentic engagement, and unbridled compassion.

Ranga Jayaraman is the director of the Neurodiversity Pathways program of Goodwill of Silicon Valley in San Jose, California. He is a neurotypical father of a neurodivergent son. Ranga's current passion is to empower neurodivergent individuals with the desire and ability to contribute to find meaningful, rewarding, and sustained employment and to help organizations in their journey to embrace neurodiversity inclusion in their workplaces.

Previously, Ranga was an accomplished senior executive of digital transformation, contributing innovative solutions and services to enable and support business strategy and growth in information technology and higher education organizations. His real-life experience, executive leadership, and business background helps shape the classroom curriculum and learning experience Ranga provides to neurodivergent individuals and organizations. Ranga is driven by the core beliefs that everyone is a unique creation of the universe, fully equipped to fulfill the purpose for which they are here and that his life's purpose is to *Love All, Serve All, Help Ever, and Hurt Never.*

Dedication

This book is dedicated to all the wonderful neurodivergent people in our lives — family members, friends, colleagues, and students. We have learned so much from them. We are better humans and our lives are immeasurably richer because of them. Thank you!

John Marble: To the future generations of autistic people who will think this book outdated because they understand much more than we do now; to my mom, Shannon Des Roches Rosa, and all parents and families of autistic children navigating this journey with love; and to Dave Noble and Steve Silberman, representing our allies who listen, learn, and stand with us.

Ranga Jayaraman: To my constant guide and guru, Bhagavan Sri Sathya Sai Baba.

Khushboo Chabria: To my guides, my mentors, my loved ones, and my community for empowering me and helping me become who I am today.

Authors' Acknowledgements

We want to acknowledge and thank four groups of people:

Our friends and families, for standing by us, cheering us on, and giving us the dedicated time for focusing on this important work.

Goodwill of Silicon Valley leadership, Trish Dorsey, Michael Fox, and Chris Baker, for supporting our work in the Neurodiversity Pathways program and affording us the time to work on this book. Many of the principles we have covered in this book evolved through our work in Neurodiversity Pathways.

Our students in the Neurodiversity Pathways program, for opening our heads and hearts to many insights and perspectives into the beauty and power of neurodivergent minds. We have learned more from you than we may have taught you!

Our team at Wiley: our acquisitions editor, Elizabeth Stillwell, for encouraging and convincing us to undertake the writing of this book; our project editor, Charlotte Kughen, for keeping us focused on every deadline and cheering us on when we felt overwhelmed; and our technical editor, Sara Sanders Gardner, for ensuring our content and tone is empowering, inclusive, and aligned with the modern understanding of autism.

John would like to additionally thank Cody Arnold, Pedro Belo, Aubrey Blanche, Cindy Cramer Blanchard, Ovidio Calvo, Karen Chin, Derek Gerson, Todd Elmer, Jon Heilbron, Thomas George, Temple Grandin, Alex Kotran, Rohan Mahadevan, Cass Nelson, Dave Noble, Rachel Payne, Amitesh Parikh, Mark Perriello, Toby Quaranta, Heather Quilici, Dick Sincerbeaux, Noah Zoschke, and the entire Tzaba family for their support. He also would like to express his appreciation for the examples provided to him by Jessica Behnam, Josie Blagrave, Jen Emira, Chris Ereneta, Sharon Farmer, Bear Grant, Al Gore, Liz Miller, Jen White-Johnson, Knox and Kevin Johnson, the Brooke and Lars Olsen family, Gabor Pap, Amitesh Parikh, Anne Pinkowski, Scott Robertson, Shannon Des Roches Rosa, Leo Rosa, Callie Shell, Eric Stern, Eve Wanetick, the Tim and Gwen Walz family, Mel White, Liam Whitworth, and Betina Wildhaber. He also acknowledges the foundational research and writing of James Baldwin, Lydia X. Z. Brown, Barb Cook, Eric Garcia, Sue Fletcher-Watson, Deb Karhson, Sara Luterman, Dylan Matthews, Damian Milton, Haley Moss, Morénike Giwa Onaiwu, Yenn Purkis, Beth Radulski, Steve Silberman, Alice Wong, and others. He is also deeply appreciative of the advocacy and leadership of AASCEND, the Autistic Self Advocacy Network, Julia Bascom, Sascha Bittner, Rebecca Cokley, Lois Curtis, Carly Danesh Jones MBE, Andrew Eddy, Finn Gardner, Elizabeth Grigsby, KD Harris, Frank Kameny, Judy Heumann, Margaux Joffe, Steve Lieberman, Sheraden Nicholau, Ross Pollard, Ed Roberts, Kayla Smith, Hari Srinivasan, Chris Williams, Elaine Wilson, Bob Witeck, and Stella Young. John thanks Ari Ne'eman for telling him to write something practical because the world didn't need to read another autistic memoir.

Khushboo would like to express heartfelt gratitude for the unwavering patience, understanding, and support extended by her parents, Vijaya and Anup Chabria; her brother, Manish Chabria; and her loyal companion, Emily, during the writing of this book. Special thanks are also extended to friends and supporters: Patricia Clariza, Dr. Thelmisha Vincent, Warfred Cabanes, Akanksha Aurora, Tseten

Dolkar, Mahathee Chetlapalli, Dr. Marylou Ryder, Dr. Tim McCarthy, Daniel Hodges, Brian Hilliard, Linda Fisk, Farrow Communications, and the leadership teams at Wiley, Goodwill of Silicon Valley, Peaces of Me Foundation, and the Ed.D. Organizational Leadership Program at UMass Global for their unwavering encouragement and support. Lastly, sincere appreciation is extended to every neurodivergent person whom Khushboo has had the pleasure to meet, connect with, support, and empower in this lifetime. It is an honor to serve this community. Of course, this journey could not have been undertaken without the invaluable contributions of Khushboo's neuroinclusive author team, who have not only empowered her as a neurodivergent individual but have also significantly shaped and expanded her understanding of neurodiversity in both profound and subtle ways.

Ranga would like to express his deep gratitude to his wife, Shamala Jayaraman, for all her unwavering faith in him and unflinching support that have been his bedrock and backbone through many ups and downs through the last 40 years; loving appreciation to his children, Aparna and Prashant, for all the joy and love they have given him and for all the learning opportunities they have provided him; and special thanks to Jose Velasco and Thorkil Sonne for opening his eyes to autism and all that can and needs to be done to make life better for neurodivergent people like his son. Lastly, Ranga's heartfelt appreciation to his coauthors, Khushboo and John, whose deep collaboration made this book a reality.

Publisher's Acknowledgments

Acquisitions Editor: Elizabeth Stillwell

Project Editor: Charlotte Kughen

Technical Editor: Sara Sanders Gardner

Production Editor: Saikarthick Kumarasamy

Cover Image: © Vitalii Vodolazskyi/Shutterstock